COLLEGE TEACHING TODAY

COLLEGE TEACHING TODAY
A Handbook for Postsecondary Instruction

KENNETH H. HOOVER

ARIZONA STATE UNIVERSITY

ALLYN AND BACON, INC.

BOSTON   LONDON   SYDNEY

Portions of this book first appeared in *The Professional Teacher's Handbook: A Guide for Improving Instruction in Today's Middle and Secondary Schools*, Second Edition, by Kenneth H. Hoover, copyright © 1976 by Allyn and Bacon, Inc., and *Learning and Teaching in the Secondary School*, Third Edition, by Kenneth H. Hoover, copyright © 1972 by Allyn and Bacon, Inc.

Library of Congress Cataloging in Publication Data
Hoover, Kenneth H
    College teaching today.
    "Outgrowth of a similar work prepared for secondary teachers entitled The professional teachers handbook."
    Includes index.
    1. College teaching—Handbooks, manuals, etc.
I. Title.
LB2331.H63   378.1'2   79-12932
ISBN 0-205-06662-3

Manufacturing Buyer: Linda Card

Printed in the United States of America

To my teenage daughter, **Shelly-Belle**
Whose quest for learning will take her far

CONTENTS

UNIT III   METHODS AND TECHNIQUES: FOCUS ON THE LARGE GROUP

PREFACE

In a sense, this book is about the future—a future that is largely unpredictable. In coping with tomorrow's problems, today's learner will face issues never experienced by mankind—overpopulation, inadequate food supplies, energy shortages, a polluted environment, and interplanetary space travel, for example. The one aspect of future society that *is clearly defined is change itself.* Tomorrow's citizen must be prepared to re-examine existing competencies and values and to alter them to meet the demands of accelerated change. Thus the educated person in the future must be flexible, a self-directed learner who is a skillful decision maker.

Today's extended lecture, whether it be employed in the college classroom or in a private business enterprise, will be outmoded tomorrow. Although there will be a place for an occasional lecture-forum (lecturette), "... it will be overshadowed if not dwarfed by a battery of teaching techniques ranging from role-playing and gaming to . . . the immersion of students in what we might call 'contrived experiences.' "* The emphasis will be on decision making or problem solving. Although methods applications will continue to be as diverse as the professors who use them, the structural properties of all methods will be strikingly similar since all will be extrapolated from the processes or decision making.

This book is based on the premise that the processes of learning are more important than the products of learning. It presumes that data are less important than the processes of finding and selecting data, that proposing alternatives is less important than the processes of evaluating and choosing alternatives, and that a final decision is less important than the tentativeness with which it is held and an individual's willingness to rethink or alter it constantly. The *products* (concepts) of learning are also important, however, since they provide much of the data entering into future learning. Thus processes and products are allied; one is not complete without the other.

The materials and techniques described in this book are treated from a conceptual framework of problem solving (that is, decision making, or reflective thinking). *Representative* of existing and emerging methods, they all have common structural properties. Each method, however does not include all the steps of the problem-solving process; in fact, some emphasize only a small portion of the total process (for example the lecturette or brainstorming) and thus must be supplemented with complementary techniques. Similarly, those methods that do focus on the entire problem solving process also employ other complementary methods and techniques (for example, the lecture-forum and discussion techniques).

---

*Alvin Toffler, *Future Shock* (New York: Random House, 1970), p. 361.

Today's college instructor faces a dilemma in teaching individuals to deal with the complexities of tomorrow's world since most have been prepared for the task under the outmoded belief that knowledge of subject matter automatically establishes one's qualifications for teaching. Little educational emphasis has been placed on instructional methods, especially on those required for teaching students to make intelligent decisions in the future. Where can one turn for much needed assistance? This book, for the first time, provides college teachers with a much needed tool for rethinking and restructuring their instructional methods. Although it may not yet be as indispensable as the medical doctor's "little black kit," it should at least provide one essential instrument.

Each chapter is divided into four parts. The first part provides a theoretical framework and rationale for the technique offered so that the reader can determine what basic learning outcomes can be expected from using it. The second section provides a step-by-step description of the technique, that delineates its structional properties. The third section is a brief summary of the major values associated with the technique and the problems that may be encountered in using it. This section should help assist the instructor decide whether to employ the technique under prevailing conditions. The final section provides the teacher with sample applications in his or her own field of specialization.

This book is an outgrowth of a similar work prepared for secondary teachers entitled *The Professional Teacher's Handbook* (Allyn and Bacon, Inc., 1973; 1976). It represents a specific demand from college professors all over the country, some of which purchased copies of the original handbook. As a "first" in the field, some important areas may have been omitted. Reader feedback is encouraged so that the book can be kept current and thus meet the needs of a changing student population.

Kenneth H. Hoover

OVERVIEW FOR THE USER

Today's extremely complex society is creating pressures on our educational system not even imagined a decade or so ago, resulting in the emergence of three stark realities. First, it is becoming increasingly apparent to all private and public business enterprises that the young college graduate is *not* ready to assume his or her place in the working world. A college education, at best, can only prepare an individual for other specialized work-related instructional programs. In many businesses, these educational programs can extend from a few weeks to several months. Even the young college professor whose competence traditionally has been assumed is being encouraged (or required) to enroll in a well-planned faculty development program. Indeed, almost all major universities have developed programs for their faculty and staff.

Second, specialized educational programs that merely provide information are usually inadequate. Professors are often ill-prepared for teaching students to become self-directed learners. Although professors may be experts in their field, they have probably received little or no education in instructional technology.

Finally, accelerated change makes it imperative for all private and public professional employees to keep abreast of new instructional methods. Like business technology, educational techniques and methods are constantly changing and becoming increasingly sophisticated, since they are designed to deal with the complexities of modern society. The emerging methodologies range from decision-making techniques to humanizing experiences.

This book provides a first-time reference of instructional techniques and methodologies. It should be useful to any college, university, junior college, or private business enterprise concerned with maintaining a high quality of instruction for its clientele. Instructors of specialized work-related programs and workshops should find it particularly useful.

Perhaps the most important use of this book may come from professionals in a variety of fields who desire to improve their work-related instructional techniques and procedures. The specialized body of theoretical and complex knowledge that characterizes a profession, in effect, frees the individual from control over management. Although management can control the resources connected with work and even the terms and conditions of work, the professional controls the work itself and that work is the key to production. Thus he or she alone often must assume full responsibility for maintaining competence in instructional-related techniques.

All the techniques in this book embody a common conceptual framework based on the best-known methods of inquiry. By applying this framework, the reader should also be able to employ other less popular techniques not described in this book. The framework, which relates closely to the processes operating at the time of actual learning, provides college instructors with a systematic, flexible means of teaching students to learn. It should be emphasized that the flexibility is in the applicability of the technique to various instructional settings and not in the manipulation of the framework itself.

This basic conceptual framework consists of the following:

1. Recognition of a specific problem of policy worded in an open-ended manner so that an unlimited number of possible solutions can be considered. To illustrate: What steps should be taken to curb inflation?

2. Analysis of the problem. Prior to consideration of the alternatives, suggested by the problem, all the available facts, opinions, and controversies in the area must be offered and evaluated. This step often is the most time-consuming aspect of any method (lesson).

3. Development of acceptable hypotheses or possible solutions to the problem. These may be solutions that have been tried previously in a limited way or often creative outcomes prompted from a serious analysis of the problem.

4. Derivation of generalizations. Although the logical outcome of weighing possible alternatives is a definitive solution, often the problem is far too complex to resolve completely. Some problems may be considered, which have baffled the experts for years. The problem of inflation, for example, is baffling but, nevertheless, must be understood as much as possible. Thus all that is necessary, from one lesson, is the development of a few basic ideas on the problem. Generalizations should be derived by the learners themselves.

As indicated elsewhere, not all methods incorporate each of the four structural properties, simply because these steps are commonly (or may be) used in conjunction with other methods. The total instructional experience, however, must encompass all the elements of the structural properties described.

Preinstructional Activities

Effective teaching represents the culmination of a series of preparatory activities. Long hours of careful preparation often go into one class period. In setting the stage for effective instruction, the teacher must be a skillful predictor of events. Knowledge of students and a thorough knowledge of the subject field are necessary prerequisites to instructional excellence. Yet, of themselves, they are inadequate. The professional competence of a teacher ultimately rests on his or her ability to anticipate student needs and behaviors in advance of the actual experience. Instructional preparation, then, involves imaginative planning of the classroom experience—the topic of Unit I.

Instructional methods and techniques are designed to facilitate the teaching of content, whether the course be algebra, U. S. history, biology, or a foreign language. What facts in these courses should be emphasized? If, as believed, most facts are quickly forgotten, should they be taught at all? Chapter 1 discusses how facts can be organized to promote the attainment of concepts. Since concepts transfer readily from one situation to another, they become the foundation of all instruction.

Once basic concepts have been identified, instructional aims, or purposes, can be developed. The teacher, in establishing educational direction, focuses on unit and lesson aims or goals. Once purpose has been determined, the instructional process begins to take shape. The key to effective planning and teaching is the formulation of goals in behavioral terms. Attention also must be given to a variety of goal types, or objectives, and levels. Objectives have been grouped into three basic taxonomies: cognitive, affective, and psychomotor. These categories are discussed in Chapter 2.

Long- and short-range planning, discussed in Chapter 3, remains a controversial instructional issue. The issue is not whether one should or should not plan; rather, it is the nature and extent of planning necessary. There are effective teachers who prefer an unstructured classroom experience just as there are those who insist on a highly structured classroom experience. Some teachers need the psychological security of thoroughly developed lesson plans; others feel limited or boxed in by them. Both extremes can be beneficial in certain situations, depending on the particular objectives involved. When lesson planning is viewed as a problem-solving experience, the dilemma becomes much less ambiguous. Each person must resolve problems in an individual manner.

To provide a basis for the varying needs associated with lesson planning, detailed long- and short-range planning techniques are offered. Every teacher needs some experience in detailed unit and lesson planning. Just as a beginning lawyer relies heavily on his or her debate brief, so a beginning teacher needs the benefit of elaborate planning. As the lawyer gains experience, the need for extensive planning diminishes. The same holds for experienced teachers. The precise amount of written planning necessary must be decided by each teacher in each teaching situation. In the final analysis, the essential function of planning is to set the stage for learning. In a sense, it is a dress rehearsal for the real thing. Even the best laid plans go awry. Nevertheless, the mere act of planning can prepare one for the unexpected!

chapter 1

GAINING THE CONCEPT

Key Concepts

1. Unit concepts, as defined in this chapter, are analogous to broad generalizations, principles, laws, or axioms.
2. Concepts exist at different levels.
3. Factual materials provide background information essential to the derivation of concepts.
4. Concepts are retained indefinitely; facts not used repeatedly are not retained.
5. Students learn concepts from their school experiences.
6. Instructional goals and class activities are evolved from unit concepts.
7. Unit and lesson concepts are most useful when phrased as simple declarative statements.

New Terms

1. Unit Titles   Derived from broad course concepts, unit titles are the titles of the various instructional units. The term "theme" "focus," or "thrust" refers to the planned emphasis of the unit.
2. Unit Concepts   Basic structural properties (ideas) on which a unit is based. Each unit concept embodies a real-life application.
3. Lesson Generalizations   The culminating products (ideas) of a specific lesson. Collectively, they embody the unit concept on which a lesson is based.
4. Classificational Concepts   Concepts used to clarify essential properties, processes, or events. Usually derived from facts, they provide the learner with a much needed organizational pattern for isolated bits of information.
5. Correlational Concepts   Concepts used to relate specific events, observations, or variables to other concepts. Such concepts embody an if . . . then dimension.
6. Theoretical Concepts   Concepts used to advance ideas from the known to the unknown. These concepts are based on existing facts, but go beyond them.

7. Concept Attainment   The product of reflective thinking or problem solving. Each instructional method is based on this basic process of cognition.
8. Intuitive Thought   Thought that, although it is apparently based on processes of reflection, does not seem to follow any logical order. Frequently, it is characterized by a sudden flash of insight.

Questions to Guide Your Study

1. Unit concepts, identified by the teacher in preinstructional activities, should be presented to students prior to the instructional experience. Defend or refute.
2. What is the relationship between concepts and instructional activities?
3. Why must a teacher avoid strict adherence to the steps of the cognitive, or reflective, process?
4. Using concepts as an instructional foundation is more appropriate in some subject fields than in others. Defend or refute.

There are two basic dimensions to teaching and learning: processes and outcomes. While this book basically is concerned with the former, the outcomes or products sought have an important bearing on the processes employed. Indeed, evidence suggests that the effectiveness of any instructional approach is dependent on the desired outcome.

The ultimate objective of the learning experience is its application to future experiences. The outcomes of learning may be applied or *transferred* to future experience in two ways. One is through *specific* applicability to tasks highly similar to original ones. This phenomenon is referred to by psychologists as *specific transfer of training*. In essence, it is an extension of habits and associations and seems to be limited to the learning of basic mental and motor skills. The other is through the transfer of principles or attitudes, often referred to as *nonspecific transfer*. One initially learns not a skill but a general idea that can be used as a basis for solving subsequent problems. This type of transfer, according to Bruner, ". . . is at the heart of the educational process. . . . The more fundamental or basic is the idea . . . the greater will be its breadth of applicability to new problems."[1] Principles, attitudes, and generalizations are often called *concepts*. They are treated in the first section of this chapter.

---

[1] Jerome S. Bruner, *The Process of Education* (Cambridge, Mass.: Harvard University Press, 1961), pp. 17-18.

The *processes* involved in concept formation are discussed in the second section of this chapter. When an individual thinks, a definite process is involved. First, the person encounters something that raises a doubt which must be resolved before he or she can continue with normal activities. Second, the individual makes sure what the difficulty is and develops an idea to correct the situation. Third, the individual checks the idea against the available facts. Fourth, the person draws conclusions that seem to be supported by inquiry. Finally, the individual implements the ideas to see if they work. The steps of thinking do not always follow an ordered sequence, however. Sometimes, for example, the problem is stated last, and within any act of thinking, the differing steps may be repeated many times. Moreover, the unitary nature of each testing step must be emphasized. Verification (through testing) must be done at each step of the process.

This thought process is a *basic* one, given various labels, some of which are problem solving, cognitive processes, reflective or analytical thinking, and scientific method. The teacher conducts classes so that students will learn to take these steps as the normal way of learning. Although many of the teaching methods and techniques described throughout this book are based on such an approach, it should not be inferred that all worthwhile learning involves problem solving or reflective thought. Indeed, some of the most useful learning comes in a "flash of insight." According to Bruner,[2] *intuitive thinking* does not follow a pattern. In addition, man, like lower animals, also learns through the process of conditioning.

Fundamental Properties

A teacher must be able not only to teach but also to understand clearly the *ends* of instruction. Problem solving is not the center of learning; concept formation is. Problem solving is a means of attaining concepts. *A concept is a reduction of related experiences or events into a basic idea or pattern.* As a concept gains meaning from subsequent experiences, it is usually accompanied by feelings. Concepts help us classify or analyze and associate or combine. They thus make up the *fundamental structure* of school subjects and exist at many different levels of abstraction. Although concepts represent the end results of instruction, they must not be treated as fixed entities. As Kean suggests, "Most concepts are like guesses which we accept at the moment. They are subject to instant dismissal if new experiences or ideas make them obsolete. . . . We are nonetheless left with the necessity to interpret the world as we now find it. . . ."[3]

---

[2] Ibid., p. 13.

[3] John M. Kean, "Concept Learning in the Communication Art Curriculum," in *Concept Learning: Designs for Instruction*, by Peter H. Mortorella (Scranton, Pa.: Intext Educational Publishers, 1972), p. 135.

What Basic Instructional Strategies Are Associated with Concept Teaching?

The term "concept teaching" is misleading since it implies a particular kind of instruction. *Since all instruction essentially involves concept teaching*, both processes and products of teaching are conceptual in nature. This is merely a way of saying that ideas represent the basic structure of knowledge.

As emphasized throughout this book, the basic purpose of all instructional activities is *concept attainment.* Concept attainment is linked very closely with reflective thinking processes, which involve categorizing, organizing, and relating observations into an overall pattern and making inferences and eventually verifying data. Concept attainment originates with the problem to be solved and culminates with conferring meaning on previously meaningless facts and events.[4] Thus in this chapter and throughout this book, the terms "concept attainment," "reflective thinking," or "critical thinking," "problem solving," and "cognitive process(es)" are used interchangeably.

In order to teach students to learn concepts, sometimes all that is needed is *concept demonstration.* The teacher's strategy consists of explaining the concept to students, providing examples (and nonexamples) through various means, and eventually engaging them in practice experiences with the concept. Once the concept is learned, the instructional objective is that of *concept augmentation.* This involves deepening and expanding understanding of the concept by teaching students to make more associations to it.

Considerable evidence suggests that college professors tend to employ concept demonstration or concept augmentation approaches when they should be employing a concept attainment approach. The lecture or demonstration, for example, so widely used by college teachers, is ideal for demonstrating or augmenting a concept but generally a poor method for teaching concept attainment. Misuse of these methods tends to result in the students' memorization of concepts and facts, but *not* in their understanding of them. In order to minimize memorization, teachers should consider concept demonstration and concept augmentation necessary prerequisites to concept attainment. Under such conditions, a lecture, for example, would be viewed as merely one phase of the problem-solving process. This not only would circumscribe use of the lecture method but also would alert the learner to expected concept application.

What Are Some Basic Types of Concepts?

Learning involves both process and product concepts. *Process concepts* include procedures and techniques for gathering, formulating, and evaluating knowledge, while

---

[4] For a thorough description of the link between reflective thinking and concept formation, the reader is referred to Peter H. Mortorella, *Concept Learning: Designs for Instruction*, pp. 11-12.

product concepts evolve from process activities. They are the major outcomes of learning and vary from axioms and propositions in mathematics to hypotheses and conclusions in science. Traditionally, emphasis has been placed on product concepts. Recently, however, attention has also turned to process concepts since understanding product concepts without also understanding the accompanying process concepts may result in rote learning. One is unable to make the connection between the concepts that are developed and the manner in which they are used.[5] Although their specific nature depends on the nature of the subject area being explored, product concepts can be categorized into those groups, which are discussed in the following sections.

Classificational. This kind of concept is the most common one in classroom instruction. It defines, describes, or clarifies essential properties of phenomena, processes, or events. It is often developed from the classification of facts into organized schemes or patterns. In the field of science, an example of a classification concept is "An insect is an animal with six legs and three body cavities." The student is provided with a series of experiences for learning this principle. For example, he or she might be asked to inspect a number of specimens, noting their characteristics. The learner would then classify those sharing the same characteristics in one group. In this case, the group would be called insects.

Correlational or relational. This type of concept is derived from *relating* specific events or observations; it involves a prediction. According to Pella,[6] it consists of the formulation of general principles. In the field of science, an example of a correlational concept is "When voltage is constant, the electrical current varies with the resistance." A correlational concept consists of an if . . . then dimension. Involved is a relationship between two variables. The concept evolves from directly observable events.

Theoretical. A theoretical concept facilitates the explanation of data or events into organized systems because it involves the process of advancing from the known to the unknown. Examples include "Unemployment leads to social unrest"; "indiscriminate bombing tends to strengthen enemy resistance"; and "an atom is composed of electrons, protons, and other particles." A theoretical concept goes beyond the facts, but must be consistent with the known facts.

The list of concepts that follows has been derived from different instructional units in various content fields. The reader is urged to classify each according to concept type. Some concept types are more prevalent within a given field than other types. In the social science area, for example, theoretical concepts usually predominate.

---

[5] Alan Voelker, "Concept Learning in the Science Curriculum " in *Concept Learning: Designs for Instruction*, p. 161.

[6] Milton O. Pella, "Concept Learning in Science," *The Science Teacher* 33, no. 9 (December 1976): 31-34.

1. Ill-advised public expression may adversely affect statesmanship.
2. As population increases, pollution problems are increased.
3. The world's population is increasing at a geometric rate.
4. The conditions of the times influence the nature of literary contributions.
5. Definitions, assumptions, and previously established principles become the basis for developing proof.
6. Equations resemble a scale; both sides must be equally balanced.

As one proceeds to the theoretical, there is less concern for actual things and events and increased concern for the "why" of the object, process, and event. Thus objectivity gradually gives way to increased subjectivity. Although the thinking process normally proceeds from lower to higher levels of cognition, it also may follow the reverse order.

How Do Concepts Differ with Respect to Level?

The recent expansion of knowledge has focused attention on the importance of analysis, generalization, and application of knowledge. Rather than emphasize specific content materials as ends in themselves, teachers have attempted to help students reduce content learnings to basic ideas that, in turn, can be expanded or generalized to a wide variety of problems and situations. In order to do this, it is necessary to divide concepts into three levels:

Unit titles. Unit titles represent the most abstract conceptual level of instructional planning. The first step in planning for teaching is to identify which broad content areas will be emphasized. Perhaps this task is best accomplished by examining several current textbooks in the subject field. The teacher is likely to find that most textbook writers emphasize many of the same broad content areas. (Final selection, however, usually is left to the individual teacher; it is *not* dictated by textbook writers.)

Once the broad areas have been identified, they are divided into appropriate unit titles. A unit (treated fully in Chapter 3) consists of a group of related concepts. Each unit title calls attention to the content area *and also to the major thrust, or focus, for the unit.* The thrust, or focus, is a constant reminder to the teacher of the reason for teaching a given unit and thus should suggest a real-life application. In deciding on the major thrust, the teacher must ask the question, "Why should this unit be taught?" Only after the teacher provides some practical, real-life application, *immediate to the lives of students*, is she or he ready to proceed further with planning activities. Popham and Baker refer to this activity as the principle of "perceived purpose."[7]

Each subject area has its own specific requirements. In literature, for example, the

---

[7]W. James Popham and Eva L. Baker, *Systematic Instruction* (Englewood Cliffs, N.J.: Prentice-Hall, Inc., 1970), pp. 80-82.

content area involving the study of Julius Caesar might be focused on the unit theme of *ambition*. Thus the unit title might be Julius Caesar: Unbridled Ambition. Such a unit would begin with a study of contemporary issues of vital concern to the learner. Emphasis would be placed on developing the concepts of ambition and the characteristics that compose it. Julius Caesar would provide the basic content reference to the study of ambition. Other *thematic* units might include frustration, loneliness, and death. In the study of the English language, the unit title might be Sentence Structure: Exploring Language. The title is a reminder that the unit will focus on the practical conveying of one's thoughts in writing. Unit titles in several different subject areas will suggest a variety of unit functions:

History. The Roosevelt Era: A Socialistic Trend
Home Economics. Clothing: Improve Your Personal Appearance
Art. Sketching: A Gateway to Good Design
Physical Education. Team Sports: Cooperative Relationships
Chemistry. Carbon: The Chemistry of Life
Mathematics. Set Theory: Understanding Relationships
Business. Economic Losses: Protection through Insurance
Humanities. The Arts in Ancient Greece: Idealism as a Guide to Behavior
Biology. Body Systems: Interdependency Functions
Foreign Language. The Spanish Alphabet: English Parallels

Unit concepts. Each unit is broken into six or eight unit concepts. Based on content, they provide the basic threads of a unit. Stating them specifically, *in advance of the instructional experience*, provides direction to the unit and ensures that none of the important threads will be omitted. It is usually best to state each concept in a simple declarative statement. Again, an application to real-life experiences is essential. In many subject areas, this is not an easy task. In history, for example, a two-step process seems necessary. First, one must identify the major ideas of the unit and then expand them into generalizations that are viable today. Without the second step, history teaching is likely to remain a dry and generally useless process of memorizing names, dates, and places (see Illustrated Planning section of Chapter 3).

In some subject fields, the task of concept identification is complicated by textbook organization. In literature, for example, textbooks may be organized around literary genres, historical themes, and the like. An historical theme on colonial America, for example, offers the reader numerous selections, each with its own story theme. The teacher's task, again, is twofold in nature. First, it is necessary to identify major unit themes and then to choose the particular selections that can be used in teaching each given concept. (This process is fully illustrated in Chapter 3.)

The following are some unit concepts in various subject fields:

Industrial Arts. Accuracy in measuring influences the work of those who must interpret meaning from a drawing.
Home Economics. Fabric content determines what can be made from a selected fabric.

Physical Education. One must be physically active to achieve a high level of physical fitness.

Chemistry. Sugars and starches are products of natural organic chemical processes.

Humanities. Idealism can result if a society believes that there is a rational order to the universe.

Health. Many aspects of health are personal; others are community problems.

Business. A personal budget helps one see exactly how his or her money is spent.

Mathematics. Sets can unite, intersect, or differ greatly.

Art. Inspiration for design can be found in almost everything in our environment.

Of course, unit concepts will vary, depending on the individual teacher's frame of reference. This, in part, accounts for observed instructional differences between teachers of the same subject. By jointly developing unit concepts, teachers of the same subject field can maximize the parallel nature of their classes. Even so, differences must be expected since concept attainment rests with students.

Lesson generalizations. Each lesson is based on a unit concept previously identified by the teacher and culminates in the students' derivation of a number of important generalizations (specific concepts). Lesson generalizations embody the unit concept of the lesson, although they are more specific than the unit concept. To illustrate from a lesson on health:

Concept: Use of drugs may permanently damage an individual's health and well-being.

Lesson generalizations

1. LSD users may incur permanent brain damage.
2. While under the influence of LSD, a person loses his or her ability to distinguish between reality and fantasy.
3. Use of LSD may render an individual emotionally dependent on the drug.

Although generalizations can be derived by students in a number of ways, some authorities insist that they be written out. In this manner, the teacher can help those who are experiencing difficulty. In many situations, however, teachers find it convenient to let students evolve generalizations from a culminating class discussion. Usually a few students will quickly formulate key lesson generalizations. When generalizations are placed on the chalkboard, students having difficulty can write them in their notes and then later memorize them for a test. Understanding may be partially or totally lacking. As a safeguard, considerable probing is necessary since experiences cannot be rushed.

Figure 1-1 illustrates the development of the concept abstraction process from broad concepts, derived by the teacher, to specific lesson generalizations, derived by

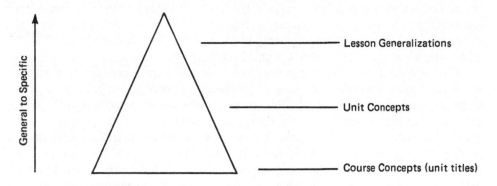

FIGURE 1-1 *Concept Abstraction Process*

students. Students can also develop unit concepts from lesson generalizations. Review methods are especially appropriate for this purpose (see Chapter 9). Unit concepts essentially represent the end results of learning that, in turn, are transferred to future learning experiences.

What Is the Role of Concepts in Subsequent Learning?

As implied in the preceding discussion, one unit concept (rarely two or three) becomes the basis for lesson planning. Each unit concept is used to derive a suitable problem for reflective thinking experiences. Thus the heart of the instructional process is to engage students in reflection, leading to their development of viable concepts. These concepts, in turn, become an important source of data in subsequent learning.

The teacher sets the stage for the student's use of prior knowledge by providing an introductory framework for each instructional experience. This may be in the form of an overview, or in the form of an *advance organizer*. Generally an *overview* is designed to introduce new material and to familiarize students with the central argument. As Hartly and Davies point out,[8] an overview may emphasize key concepts, principles, and technical terms as well as prepare students for the basic structure of the material to be studied. Thus a learning set is established. An overview is at the same level of abstraction, generality, and inclusiveness as the lesson. Its effect is largely due to the repetition and simplification provided.

An *advance organizer* is especially useful when the lesson is designed to focus on factual materials as does the lecture method. Its function (like the overview) is to provide a link with what the student already knows. Unlike the overview, however, the

---

[8] James Hartley and Ivor K. Davies, "Preinstructional Strategies: The Role of Pretests, Behavioral Objectives, Overviews and Advance Organizers," in *Review of Educational Research* 46, ed. Samuel Messick (Spring 1976): 244.

advance organizer is also designed to help the learner discriminate between new ideas and existing concepts. It is more complex than the overview, having a higher level of abstraction, generality, and inclusiveness. (For a more complete description of advance organizers, the reader is referred to Chapter 10.)

Although conceptualization processes have been investigated extensively, there are as yet no definite ways of making use of previously acquired concepts in subsequent learning. Klausmeier and others,[9] after examining the available research in the area, speculate that procedures which help the learner remember stimulus information and *also past hypotheses* should facilitate learning. They warn, however, that attempts to teach too many concepts at once are likely to strain memory and lead to trial-and-error performance. Thus pacing becomes an important consideration. It would seem that prompting or cueing students to remember relevant information also should facilitate learning.

Strategies for Teaching Concepts

This book emphasizes those methods and techniques that professors use to facilitate learning. Learning, as defined by Gagne,[10] is evidenced by a change in human disposition (for example, a change in attitude, value, or interest) or capacity (for example, increased capacity for some type of performance that persists over a period of time). This "added capacity" is retained by the learner in the form of concepts or ideas to be recalled when needed. Thus this chapter is foundational since it provides the essential tools for learning, regardless of the instructional method used.

As indicated earlier, instructional strategies deal with concept demonstration, concept augmentation, and concept attainment. Although each strategy may have a different instructional emphasis, many (indeed most) concern the three goals of concept demonstration, augmentation, and attainment.

What General Instructional Strategy May Facilitate Concept Demonstration and Augmentation?

Based on considerable research, a pattern is beginning to emerge relative to instructional essentials at these basic levels.[11] These levels are clearly defined and described by Merrill and Tennyson.[12]

---

[9] Herbert J. Klausmeier et al., *Conceptual Learning and Development: A Cognitive View* (New York: Academic Press, Inc., 1974), p. 104.

[10] Robert M. Gagne, *The Conditions of Learning*, 3rd ed. (New York: Holt, Rinehart and Winston, 1977), p. 3.

[11] For an excellent summary of this research, the reader is referred to Klausmeier, *Conceptual Learning and Development: A Cognitive View*.

[12] M. David Merrill and Robert D. Tennyson, *Teaching Concepts: An Instructional Design Guide* (Englewood Cliffs, N.J.: Educational Technology Publications, 1977).

First, a definition is presented. This must include each critical attribute and how they are combined. It is desirable to provide the learner with a near synonym so that his or her existing repertoire of concepts may be brought to bear on the situation. It is not essential that the individual learn the rule *statement* (the definition); the definition merely represents the classifying rule to be applied.

Next, an expansion of the definition is provided in which both examples and nonexamples are offered. Each attribute is provided with a "matched example/nonexample pair." This, in turn, is followed with examples that are as different or divergent as possible to illustrate the attribute under consideration. As Merrill and Tennyson point out,[13] use of all easy examples will produce *undergeneralization*, while use of similar examples will produce *misconception*. Failure to match examples with nonexamples will produce *overgeneralization*.

Third, the learner's attention must be directed to potentially confusing attributes of a variable nature. By using specific examples and nonexamples, the presence or absence of the critical attribute under consideration must be emphasized. Merrill and Tennyson refer to this as *attribute isolation*. The following is a self-instructional activity for identifying potentially confusing aspects of unit concepts.

From the list of concepts, place a check by those that meet the criteria (attributes) of a properly stated *unit* concept.

1. A man who admits his mistake and places himself at the mercy of the court is a courageous individual.
2. Courage is displayed in many ways.
3. Courage is essentially a willingness to take a stand in the face of adversity.
4. Definitions of courage change from culture to culture.
5. Young men who refused to fight in the Vietnam conflict had to exercise considerable courage.[14]

Items two and three provide central ideas linked with the present. Thus they are properly stated unit concepts. Items one and five are too specific since they describe courage based on particular situations. Item three is a definition, not an attribute.

Fourth, the learner must practice selecting unit concepts by engaging in exercises like the preceding one. The list of unit concepts and nonunit concepts must be rather extensive, and feedback must be provided to facilitate comparison of responses. The previous sample, for example, was taken from a list of twenty items, nine of which were unit concepts. The answer list provided a justification for each correct and incorrect response.

---

[13] Ibid., p. 4.

[14] Kenneth H. Hoover, *Secondary/ Middle School Teaching: A Handbook for Beginning Teachers and Teacher Self-Renewal* (Boston: Allyn and Bacon, Inc., 1977), p. 8.

Finally, the learner should be given a test to provide additional practice and to encourage learning transfer. Again, feedback must be given.

What Instructional Strategy May Facilitate Concept Attainment?

Concept attainment, basically involves processes of problem solving or reflective thinking. According to Gagne,[15] problem solving is a process by which the learner discovers a combination of previously learned rules that can be applied to achieve a solution for a new situation. As indicated earlier, certain cognitive processes seem to be employed when an individual thinks. The following describes each step of the analytical thought process. Although all the steps will not always be employed or follow the same sequence, the instructor should become familiar with them in order to prepare for classroom experiences.

How is the problem stated and clarified?   A problem arises when the concepts do not fit the observed events. This may produce a vague feeling of dissatisfaction with things as they are—from unhappiness, to confusion, to mere curiosity. Whatever the feelings, the problem should be stated as precisely as possible.

Frequently, the instructor formulates a realistic problem from the unit concept that has been previously identified. For example, from the concept in general business "Customer satisfaction is the most important product of sales promotion and advertising," the teacher may formulate the problem "How might a customer feel when he or she is pressured into buying a product?" The teacher then determines an instructional method for guiding students in solving the problem.

In doing this, the teacher is involved in at least two separate creative acts: (1) the identification of important ideas (concepts) that will become the end result of teaching and (2) the designing of appropriate learning situations in which the concepts may be derived. One logically follows the other. If the concept is poorly formulated, it will become evident when one attempts to plan specific learning experiences. To illustrate, "Each family functions differently" is a poor unit concept. In order to provide an appropriate learning experience, one must focus on a particular area of family relationships. An appropriate problem might be "What policy should govern the financial aspect of family living?" Again, various methods and techniques are employed for dealing with such an issue. The concept might have been more appropriately stated as "The management of family finances is dependent on the personalities of the family members." Thus the teacher works constantly back and forth from concept to method as he or she engages in preinstructional activities.

How are facts sorted and analyzed?   The terms of a problem must be clarified, cause and effect relationships must be examined, and the importance of the issue must

---

[15] Gagne, *The Conditions of Learning*, p. 155.

be established. This involves identifying and evaluating all the important facts and relationships associated with the problem. Students are prone to confuse personal opinion with facts and to confuse their opinion about facts with the facts. They also tend to jump to conclusions on the basis of limited evidence, and to seek facts that will support a given point of view. Data on all sides of a question must be perused in the interest of intellectual honesty.

One of the most crucial tasks of the instructional process is guiding students in their selection and analysis of facts. Too often, students rely on teachers and textbooks as the final authorities. It must be remembered that concept seeking is a searching, an inquiring process. Therefore the teacher must encourage students to seek widely for facts or data; he or she must guide students into uncovering facts that will contribute to widely differing points of view. In discussing facts, students need to listen, to actively pursue contrasting hypotheses, and to follow their ideas to conclusions (if . . . then). As indicated in later chapters, buzz groups contribute to such analysis. Students must be assisted in keeping to the problem and supporting their contentions with evidence. Whenever possible, students should compare conclusions based on personal experience with those drawn from the evidence.

How are hypotheses developed? Once the problem has been stated and clarified, the individual has already moved into the next step in the analytical thought process. At this point, one develops some hypotheses—bold guesses or hunches with respect to the problem. The untrained individual tends to accept the first guess (hypothesis) as correct. Thus further thinking is blocked. The trained individual delays closure and deliberately "casts about" for several possible solutions. *It is important to remember that hypotheses are necessary guides in the acquisition and sorting of facts.* They are based on the facts in the original situation from which the problem developed. Hypotheses cannot be guaranteed or controlled; they just appear. There are techniques, however, for minimizing ordinary inhibitions built up from past experience. One of these, brainstorming, for example, is discussed in Chapter 13.

What is the role of inference in analytical thought? From an analysis of facts, the individual formulates tentative conclusions or inferences. *Conclusions* are possible explanations for a chain of events or suggested courses of action. *Inferences* are leaps from the known to the unknown. This *movement* from present facts to possible facts represents the heart of the thinking process. Each individual is continually making inferences as he or she deals with large and small difficulties of daily existence. Since the process is so commonplace, there is a tendency to jump to unwarranted conclusions. It is the function of the instructional process to guide students into making *tested* inferences.

Both deductive and inductive reasoning processes are normally used in problem-solving experiences. Involved in the process of making inferences are *assumptions.* An assumption is anything taken for granted—anything assumed to be self-evident. A teacher may offer considerable assistance by requesting students to state their implicit assumptions, thus making them aware of them.

How are conclusions tested?   Conclusions are tested by evaluating their effectiveness in solving a problem. The complexity of many instructional problems may render an immediate evaluation impossible, however (see Chapter 8). The student does not do the actual testing but is encouraged to evolve pertinent generalizations (concepts) from the experience. These will not be identical to the major concept that gave rise to the problem. Rather, they will be supporting concepts that collectively encompass the major concept.

Lesson generalizations derived by students are more meaningful when written out and illustrated. Provision also must be made for their application to new situations, with emphasis on exploration of relationships, comparisons, and prediction of consequences.

What Is the Role of Intuitive Thinking in Concept Formation?

Any treatment of the processes of concept formation would not be complete without attention to those thought processes that do not seem to follow the five-step scheme outlined on the preceding pages. It has long been recognized that many of the really great contributions to human knowledge have come in sudden flashes of insight. Frequently, after an individual has labored over a problem for hours, days, or even weeks, the idea suddenly emerges. This very often occurs after the problem has been put aside. It was Archimedes who supposedly jumped from the bathtub and ran down the street shouting "Eureka" at his sudden discovery. The fact that he neglected to put on his clothes was completely overshadowed by his sudden flash of insight. Jerome Bruner describes this process as *intuitive thinking.*[16]

No one knows whether intuitive thinking follows a definite pattern. Most writers suggest that too much emphasis on the formal structure of analytical thinking processes is detrimental to intuitive thought. Bruner, however, stresses the complementary nature of the two when he says:

> Through intuitive thinking the individual may often arrive at solutions to problems which he would not achieve at all, or at best more slowly, through analytic thinking. Once achieved by intuitive methods, they should if possible be checked by analytic methods, while at the same time being respected as worthy hypotheses for such checking. Indeed, the intuitive thinker may even invent or discover problems that the analyst would not. But it may be the analyst who gives these problems the proper formalism.[17]

From individuals who have engaged in intuitive thinking, a few characteristics of these processes have emerged:

---

[16] Jerome S. Bruner, *The Process of Education* p. 58.

[17] Ibid.

1. The ideas come as a sudden flash—a "Eureka."
2. The ideas emerge after a problem has been put aside, often when least expected. Thus an incubation period is necessary.
3. The ideas do not seem to follow any logical sequence.
4. The ideas seem to be based on a broad understanding of the field of knowledge involved.
5. Individuals engaged in these processes seem to indulge in bold guessing. They seem to have the ability to cut through the conventional, the mundane, the expected.
6. They seem to be willing to abandon false hypotheses no matter how well liked.

How Do Teaching Methods Relate to Analytical and Intuitive Thought Processes?

The preceding analysis of how we think is not intended as a formal outline to be followed during the instructional process. A general, flexible scheme is not only possible but necessary. Teachers should conduct their classes so that students learn to take the steps involved in analytical thinking as a normal way of learning. In an atmosphere that is reflective in quality, thinking may be expected to break out at any moment. The mind, contrary to widespread belief, has natural tendencies to generalize, to draw inferences, to be critical, and to accept and reject conclusions on the basis of evidence. The student learns to think by thinking and needs guidance in perfecting the ability to select and clarify problems, to hypothesize, to secure and analyze facts, to make inferences from data, and to reach valid conclusions. It is the teacher's responsibility to provide students with ample opportunities for doing this.

A final word of caution is in order, however. Teachers should not constantly emphasize analytical thinking. As indicated throughout this book, there is a valid place for drill, lecture, and even recitation. These and other methods are useful in concept demonstration and in concept augmentation.

In the development of the various instructional approaches in this book, reflective processes have been used as a guiding theory for teaching. To suggest that such a theory is complete, however, would amount to gross oversimplification. They are viewed always as avenues that follow the normal processes of inquiry. The patterns are flexible and offer ample opportunity for each instructor to bring his or her own personal creativity into focus. Still, their validity rests on this unifying structure of how we think.

The Value of Learning Concepts

Emphasis on concept learning enhances transfer to related areas. Often referred to as *nonspecific transfer,* general ideas (concepts) transfer widely. The higher level concepts transfer more readily than lower level concepts.

Concepts provide a basic structure for course, unit, and lesson planning. Essentially, it is the conceptual framework of a course that gives order to related experiences.

Evaluation, in terms of basic concepts, encourages retention of learning.

Concepts tell the learner what *facts* to look for and the meaning to assign to these facts. They are easily stored and rearranged for the derivation of new concepts.

Limitations of, and Problems with, Concepts

Inadequately developed concepts result in distortions, biases, and prejudices and are often difficult to correct since they are accompanied by feelings.

A teacher cannot "give" students concepts since they must be learned through direct pupil involvement. Sometimes a mental image (concept) is so clear to the teacher that he or she is tempted to eliminate some steps in the learning process. This temptation is especially great when one is running short on time.

The different levels of concept formation necessitate selection of an appropriate level(s) of learning experiences.

Teachers who emphasize lesson "topics" risk covering too much material in a given lesson. Concept formation cannot be crowded or pushed.

It is extremely difficult to determine the degree of concept attainment. Since concepts gain meaning through experience, the teacher can never be certain of the optimum number of experiences essential to the adequate transfer of learning.

Illustrated Concepts

To repeat, instructional concepts exist at three different levels: course (unit titles), unit, and lesson. Lesson concepts (generalizations) are derived *by students* as the culminating lesson experience. They essentially embody one basic unit concept (formulated by the teacher in preplanning activities). The concepts of a unit, in turn, collectively embody one course concept (frequently called a unit or unit theme). The following provides examples of course and unit concepts. Lesson generalizations are illustrated in the chapters dealing with different instructional methods.

Course concepts (unit titles or themes)

   I. Useful in earth science classes
     A. Our Dynamic Earth and Its Materials
     B. Master Cycle Rules and Earth's Events
     C. The Evolution of the Earth's Mountains
     D. Mother Earth and Her Autobiography
     E. Planet Earth and Its Environment in Space
     F. The Potential and Kinetic Climates of Our Planet Earth
  II. Useful in home economics classes
     A. Understanding Ourselves and Others
     B. The Family
     C. Boy-Girl Interests
     D. Marriage

E. Marital Problems
F. Parenthood
G. Family Finance
III. Useful in algebra classes
    A. Symbols: A New Way to Represent Numbers
    B. Set Theory: Understanding Relationships
    C. Solving Problems by Equations
    D. Formulas: How Mathematics Saves Time
    E. Polynomials: Expressions with More Than One Term
    F. Graphs: Visual Representations
IV. Useful in American literature classes
    A. The Beginnings of the American Tradition
    B. Democracy
    C. Internationalism
    D. Conflict
    E. Comic Spirit
    F. Dissent
    G. Power Structures
V. Useful in American history classes
    A. Birth of Democracy
    B. Reconstruction Period in the South
    C. Influence of Industrialization on the Economy
    D. Problems and Growth of the Worker
    E. City Growth and Its Problems
    F. Immigrants and Their Contributions to the United States
    G. Isolationism and Its Effects on the United States
VI. Useful in physical education classes
    A. Instilling Self-Confidence
    B. Developing a Will to Win
    C. Teamwork in Sports and Society
    D. Discovering Recreational Values
    E. Extending the Body's Capabilities
    F. Making the Learner Socially at Ease
VII. Useful in chemistry classes
    A. Matter and Energy: Building Blocks of the World Around Us
    B. Oxygen and Hydrogen: Common Chemical Reactions
    C. Solutions and Equilibrium: The States of Matter That Affect Us
    D. Carbon: The Chemistry of Life
    E. Nuclear Chemistry: A New Source of Energy
VIII. Useful in art classes
    A. Developing Sensitivity and Awareness
    B. Relating the Five Elements of Design
    C. Exploring New Art Media
    D. Perspective, Structure, and Composition
    E. Art Appreciation and Vocabulary: An Introduction
    F. The Three-Dimensional Experience

Unit concepts

I.   Useful in earth science classes

  Unit: Our Dynamic Earth and Its Materials

  Concepts

  1. Observations and measurements of the earth's surface contribute   to knowledge about the earth's hidden interior.
  2. The face of the earth is constantly changing.
  3. The sequential order of events enables us to reconstruct the earth's history.
  4. Minerals are the earth's building blocks.
  5. Rocks on and in the earth's crust are continually changing in response to fluctuating environmental conditions.
  6. A basic frame of reference is necessary to express motion.

II. Useful in home economics classes

  Unit: The Family

  Concepts

  1. Some form of family life is universal.
  2. Each family functions differently.
  3. Understanding the family is essential to modern-day living.
  4. Traditions, customs, and rituals play a major part in family development.
  5. Families can be loving, noble, dictatorial, and vindictive.
  6. Families of today differ substantially from those of earlier times.
  7. Each person, to some degree, is a product of his or her family.
  8. The family stages offer new and varied experiences.

III. Useful in algebra classes

  Unit: Formulas: How Mathematics Saves Time

  Concepts

  1. The world is full of unknowns that can be represented by use of formulas.
  2. Formulas allow one to express rules in a concise form.
  3. The principles and facts that make a formula possible are more important than memorizing the formula itself.

IV. Useful in American literature classes

  Unit: The Beginning of the American Tradition

Concepts

1. Political writers influence the development of American ideals.
2. Conflicts of interest (as in the American colonies) inspire political writers to reflect the revolutionary spirit.
3. Talented political leaders (scientists) are responsible for some of our most valuable documents (for example, the Constitution of the United States).
4. American tradition is rooted in the colonial period.
5. The individuals who created the literature of colonial America (like modern writers) were, by and large, not professional writers.

V. Useful in U.S. history classes

Unit: Birth of Democracy

Concepts

1. Communication between people is essential.
2. Responsibility is the partner of freedom.
3. The Constitution is a series of compromises.
4. The President's office is one of the most powerful offices in the world.
5. The check and balance system is an integral part of all forms of democratic life.

VI. Useful in physical education classes

Unit: Teamwork in Sports and Society

Concepts

1. We are on teams all our lives.
2. Each player has a responsibility to the team.
3. It is as important to bring others into team participation as it is to make an individual contribution to the team.
4. Principles of teamwork in sports are readily transferred to teamwork in society.
5. All people must be able team workers to function effectively in society.

VIII. Useful in art classes

Unit: Developing Sensitivity and Awareness

Concepts

1. Originality in art stems from awareness and sensitivity.
2. An artist must continually search for new stimuli from various backgrounds and details.
3. Eagerness and an open mind are necessary ingredients for the growth of awareness and sensitivity in art.

4. The "odd ball" approach encourages the artist's search for new ideas and ways of using art media.
5. The fully developed awareness of Van Gogh, Michelangelo, Arnason, and Frank Lloyd Wright set these artists apart from their peers.
6. The importance of individual awareness becomes evident when one observes its absence.

ESTABLISHING INSTRUCTIONAL OBJECTIVES

Key Concepts

1. Objectives are derived from the basic concepts of the unit.
2. Instructional objectives are divided into three somewhat overlapping domains: cognitive, affective, and psychomotor; each essentially embodies the problem-solving process.
3. Attainment of outcomes in one domain does not necessarily imply attainment in the others.
4. Instructional objectives range from simple to complex. Higher order outcomes incorporate lower order outcomes.
5. The end result of instructional objectives is projected pupil behavior outcomes.
6. Degree of outcome specificity will vary, depending on whether the outcome is a minimum-essentials or a developmental type.
7. Instructional objectives and their behavioral outcomes provide a sound basis for subsequent planning of instructional and evaluational experiences.

New Terms

1. Cognitive Objectives A domain of objectives, ranging from simple to complex, that involves basic reasoning (problem-solving) processes.
2. Affective Objectives A domain of objectives, ranging from mere attention to internalization of the value or value system. Attitudes and emotions are involved.
3. Psychomotor Objectives A domain of objectives that incorporates the necessary steps in the acquisition of mental and motor skills.
4. Behavioral Outcomes Actual pupil behaviors that may be anticipated at the culmination of a given learning experience or sequence.
5. Minimum-Essentials Outcomes Most appropriate in the mental and motor

skills area, these outcomes constitute the *specific conditions* and *minimum level* of performance anticipated.

6. Developmental Outcomes   Primarily concerned with the academic areas, this group of outcomes suggests a class or group of anticipated behaviors. Since *maximum* achievement is sought, anticipated conditions and minimum performance-level criteria are not needed.

7. Entry Behaviors   Behaviors indicating competencies that are assumed prerequisite to a given learning experience. Some type of preassessment, such as a pretest, is essential.

8. En Route Behaviors   Intermediate behavioral outcomes deemed prerequisite to attainment of final (terminal) outcomes.

9. Terminal Behaviors   Behaviors indicative of ultimate goal achievement.

Questions to Guide Your Study

1. How do behavioral outcomes (stated as a preinstructional activity) set the stage for learning and evaluational experiences?

2. Since the three instructional objectives overlap, why should they be treated separately?

3. The higher, more complex levels of educational objectives also include the lower, less complex objectives. The reverse, however, does not necessarily apply. Explain the implications of this structure on teaching.

4. Developmental outcomes (in the cognitive domain) that specify the conditions and minimum level of performance expected are classified as the "recall variety." Defend or refute.

The most fundamental aspect of teaching is the formulation of worthwhile aims, or goals.[1] Just as a list of educational purposes helps determine the nature of the curriculum, course and unit goals guide the teacher and student in selecting, organizing, and evaluating learning experiences. Goals, or purposes, are the center around which all other instructional activities revolve.

Unless goals are stated in specific terms, they serve no worthwhile purpose. Although most teachers acknowledge their importance, relatively few actually use goals effectively to guide their selection of appropriate learning and evaluational activities. The inevitable consequence is an unimaginative, rote-learning experience

---

[1] In this chapter, the words "aims," "goals," "objectives," and "purposes" are used interchangeably.

that emphasizes textbook facts as ends in themselves. Accordingly, relatively little transfer or application to related real-life problems can be expected.

Once the teacher has identified major unit concepts, he or she can develop unit objectives. Each major concept must be analyzed in order to determine the precise nature of the objective (purpose or goal) sought. It may be that an understanding or comprehension is desired; sometimes an attitude or value must be developed or altered; frequently a mental or motor skill will be emphasized. This basic decision will determine the nature of the instructional experiences.

Fundamental Properties

The ends of instruction (goal attainment) become basic ideas (concepts) in one's repertoire of learning experiences. Ideas are internalized, however, in different ways. One idea, for example, may represent basic understanding, while another may be accompanied by strong emotion. Still another may be associated with mental or motor dexterity. All three components are usually associated, in some measure, with each idea or concept. Nevertheless, the instructional experience will vary considerably with the nature of the outcome sought. Attainment of one outcome does not guarantee attainment of another.

What Are the Properties of Cognitive Goals?

Traditionally, the most common educational objective has been the acquisition of knowledge or information. Thus successful completion of a course, a unit of work, or a lesson has been judged by how well certain facts are remembered. In many cases, acquisition of knowledge has been the primary, if not the only objective sought. Recognizing the discrepancy between knowing and doing, some teachers have attempted to develop realistic situations also demanding *application of knowledge.* Cognitive objectives vary, then, from simple recall of facts to highly original and creative ways of combining and synthesizing new ideas and materials.

For many years, teachers have used the terms "to know," "to understand," and "to comprehend" to denote cognitive or intellectual goals of learning. Such terms, however, do not make sharp enough distinctions between cognitive levels. The term "to know," for example, can imply memorization, comprehension, application, analysis, synthesis, or evaluation. Because teachers and students have difficulty determining which level is intended, poor quality teaching and learning often result, consisting essentially of the recall (memorization) of facts and principles. Fortunately, a useful taxonomy of cognitive objectives has been developed in *Taxonomy of Educational Objectives, Handbook I: Cognitive Domain,* edited by Benjamin S. Bloom (New York: David McKay, Inc., 1956). The elements in the taxonomy range from the simple to the more complex behaviors and from the concrete or tangible to the abstract or intangible. The six cognitive levels follow:[2]

1. Knowledge. This is the lowest level of learning and includes recall and memory. At this level, the learner is expected to recall specific facts such as dates, events, persons, places, and basic principles and generalizations.

2. Comprehension. This is the lowest level of understanding. The individual is expected to use facts or ideas without relating them to each other (for example, paraphrasing or even interpreting something gained from reading or listening). At the highest level of this category, the learner may be able to extend thinking beyond the data by making simple inferences. For example, in science class, the student may draw conclusions from a simple demonstration or experiment. The speech student may predict the consequences of action urged in a persuasive speech.

3. Application. This intellectual skill entails the use of information in specific situations. The information may be in the form of general ideas, concepts, principles, or theories that must be remembered and applied. The science student, for example, who draws conclusions from a particular experiment at the comprehension level is now able to apply the basic principle(s) to related experiments or scientific phenomena. The social studies student can relate concepts or principles concerning the separation of powers to current problems.

4. Analysis. This skill involves taking apart information and making relationships in order to discover hidden meaning and the basic structure of an idea or fact. The student is able to read between the lines, to distinguish between fact and opinion, and to assess degree of consistency or inconsistency. Thus the science student is able to distinguish between relevant and extraneous materials or events. Similarly, the social science student is able to detect unstated assumptions that can be inferred only by analyzing statements within a document.

5. Synthesis. At this level, the learner is able to reassemble the component parts of an idea in order to develop new or creative ideas. While a certain amount of combining is involved at the lower levels, at this level, the process is more complete. The learner draws on elements from many sources in addition to those of the particular problem under consideration. The science student, for instance, may propose a unique plan for testing a hypothesis. The mathematics student may make a discovery or generalization not evident from the given communication.

---

[2] Summarized from David R. Krathwohl, "Stating Objectives Appropriately for Program, for Curriculum, and for Instructional Materials Development," *Journal of Teacher Education* 16, no. 1 (March 1965): 83-92. Used by permission of the publisher.

6. Evaluation. This highest level of cognition involves making judgments on the materials, information, or method. It represents the end process of cognition, involving distinct criteria as a basis for such decisions. When conceived in relation to the problem-solving or cognitive process, it involves selecting one of the proposed alternatives over all the rest.

What Are the Properties of Affective Goals?

In addition to the attainment of intellectual or cognitive objectives, teachers should emphasize the attainment of emotional or affective goals, defined as interests, attitudes, or appreciations. As Krathwohl, Bloom, and Masia point out, "We need to provide a range of emotion from neutrality through mild to strong emotion, probably of a positive, but possibly also of a negative kind."[3] They have developed a taxonomy for affective goals which, like that for cognitive objectives, ranges from simple to complex emotions. The relative degrees of these emotions are described in terms of *internationalization.*[4] By internationalization, Krathwohl means a process through which a desired emotion is first tentatively adopted in the early stages of learning and then completely adopted in the later stages of learning. The five levels of the affective domain follow:

1. Receiving (attending).   At this first level, the learner becomes aware of an idea, process, or thing and is willing to listen to a given communication. From a purely passive role of captive receiver, the individual may advance to one of directing attention to the communication, despite competing or distracting stimuli. For example, the student listens for rhythm in poetry or prose read aloud.

2. Responding.   This level involves displaying an interest in the subject. At this low level of commitment, the student does not yet "hold the value"; that is, to use a common expression of teachers, "He or she displays an interest in the phenomenon." From obedient participation, the student may advance to making a voluntary response and finally to having a pleasurable feeling about, or sense of satisfaction with, the subject matter. This feeling may be expressed by the goal "Reads poetry for personal pleasure."

3. Valuing.   As the term implies, at this level, the learner values a thing, phenomenon, or behavior. Thus it might be said that the individual "holds the value." At this level, the individual is motivated by his or her commitment to the behavior. At

---

[3] David R. Krathwohl, Benjamin S. Bloom, and Bertram S. Masia, *Taxonomy of Educational Objectives, Handbook II: Affective Domain* (New York: David McKay Co., Inc., 1964), p. 26.

[4] David R. Krathwohl, "Stating Objectives Appropriately for Program, for Curriculum, and for Instructional Materials Development," pp. 83-92.

the lower end of the continuum, the learner might be said to hold the belief somewhat tentatively; at the other end, his or her value becomes one of conviction—certainty "beyond the shadow of a doubt." Indeed at the upper end of the continuum, the learner is likely to persuade others to his or her way of thinking.

4. Organization.   At this level, the individual has established a conscious basis for making choices by organizing values into a system—a set of criteria for guiding behavior. Thus the individual will be able to defend his or her choices because a rationale for making them has been established.

5. Characterization.   At this level, the internalization process is complete. Values *are integrated* into some kind of consistent system. Thus the person is described as having certain controlling tendencies and a recognized philosophy of life.

Prior to the development of the affective taxonomy, teachers had considerable difficulty developing adequate evaluational experiences in the affective domain and thus tended to neglect the emotional aspects of learning. The affective taxonomy is an extremely useful technique for clarifying this problem.

Complex affective goals are not as easily achieved as complex cognitive goals. Indeed, the levels of organization and characterization are not reached in any one course. They represent a culmination of many years of educational experience.

What Are the Properties of Psychomotor Goals?

A third major instructional domain is the development of mental and motor skills. For example, as a result of certain instructional activities, students should acquire motor skills such as those needed in playing tennis or basketball; they should also develop certain mental skills such as those required in writing and talking. Emphasis in this domain is on the development of the skill, which also requires the attainment of certain affective goals (or emotions) and of the cognitive level of basic understanding.

Goals in this realm traditionally have been labeled "skills," although those responsible for developing taxonomies in the cognitive and affective domains recommend the term "psychomotor behaviors" since they believe the term "skills" does not define the entire range of behaviors required. Several models for classifying psychomotor behaviors have been developed recently. Two of these are taxonomic in nature (that is, ranging from the simple to the complex).[5] The Simpson model has seven levels,[6] while the Harrow model has six.[7] The Simpson model closely parallels the one

---

[5] Elizabeth J. Simpson, *The Classification of Educational Objectives: Psychomotor Domain*, University of Illinois Research Project, no. OE5, 1966, p. 85-104; and Anita J. Harrow, *A Taxonomy of the Psychomotor Domain* (New York: David McKay Co., Inc., 1962).

[6] Perception, set, guided response, mechanism, complex overt response, adaption, and organization.

[7] Reflex movements, basic-fundamental movements, perceptual abilities, physical abilities, skilled movements, and nondiscursive communication.

the author has developed. The Harrow model seems unnecessarily complex for most practitioners. For these reasons, the author has chosen to discuss his own, which was extrapolated from established methods, sometimes called drill techniques.

This model has four levels:

1. Observing. At this level, the learner observes a more experienced person performing the activity. The learner is usually asked to observe sequences and relationships and to pay particular attention to the finished product. Sometimes reading directions substitutes for observation, although often reading supplements direct observation. For example, the beginning tennis student may read a manual and then watch the instructor demonstrate certain techniques.

2. Imitating. By the time the learner has advanced to this level, he or she has acquired the rudiments of the desired behavior. The individual follows directions and sequences under close supervision, making a deliberate effort to imitate the model. The total act is not important; neither is timing nor coordination. The tennis player, for example, may practice a prescribed stance or stroke.

3. Practicing. The entire sequence of steps is performed repeatedly at this level. Conscious effort is no longer necessary once the performance becomes more or less habitual in nature. At this level, we might reasonably say that the person as acquired the skill.

4. Adapting. The terminal level is often referred to as "perfection of the skill." Although some individuals develop much greater skill than others in certain areas, there is always room for greater perfection. The process involves adapting minor details that, in turn, influence the total performance. These modifications may be initiated by the learner or by the teacher. This is the process engaged in, for example, when a good basketball player becomes a better player.

Like the cognitive and affective domains, the psychomotor domain involves a graded sequence of levels from simple to complex, and evaluational techniques vary considerably with the different levels. By deciding on the degree of skill development needed, the instructor is able to plan instructional activities most efficiently.

What Are the Essential Differences in Formulating Minimum-Essentials and Developmental Outcomes?

Reaching instructional goals with specific behavioral outcomes is a relatively simple task. There is considerable controversy and confusion, however, over how the outcomes should be stated. Many leaders in the field suggest that in addition to specific behaviors, the teacher should also specify the *conditions* under which the behavior is exhibited and the *minimum level of performance* expected. The following is an example of an outcome specifying both the conditions and the minimum level of performance. "Given 20 sentences containing a variety of mistakes in capitalization, the student is able, with at least 90 percent accuracy, to identify and rewrite correctly each word that has a mistake in capitalization."[8] This outcome, according to Gronlund,[9] might be considered one of several expected of all students. Minimum-essentials outcomes are quite easily achieved and serve as prerequisites to further learning. Although minimum-level standards are easily established, an acceptable basis for such standards is much more difficult to defend. In the preceding example, one might just as logically establish a minimum standard of 89 percent or 92 percent accuracy. Defensible minimum levels may be adjusted on the basis of instructional experience. Certain standards have evolved over a period of time. For example, in typing, a maximum of two mistakes is acceptable.

Developmental outcomes, according to Gronlund,[10] normally account for a major portion of preplanned instructional outcomes, especially in academic courses. These outcomes are more general than those at the mastery level since emphasis is on encouraging each student to progress as far as possible toward predetermined goals. At the developmental level, *maximum achievement* is sought, rendering levels of performance practically impossible to define. For example, the developmental outcome "Ability to identify fallacies in arguments" does not call for a minimum standard of performance since its definement will depend on each student's interpretation.

Both minimum-essentials and developmental outcomes are useful in most classes. In skill areas (for example, typing, shorthand, physical education, and shop courses), more emphasis is placed on the minimum-essentials type of outcome than in academic areas (for example, English, biology, history, and general business courses) where the developmental type of outcome dominates. Generally, outcomes should be stated as simply and concisely as possible by using such action words as "identify," "name," "construct," "describe," and "order."

What Are the Differences among Entry, En Route, and Terminal Behaviors?[11]

Basic to all instruction is this question, What learnings must the student possess if he or she is to reach the intended goal? To answer this question, a systematic program of *preassessment* is recommended. According to Popham and Baker,[12] a pretest

---

[8] Thorwald Esbensen, "Writing Instructional Objectives," *Phi Delta Kappan* 48 (January 1967): 246-47.

[9] Norman E. Gronlund, *Stating Objectives for Classroom Instruction* (New York: The Macmillan Co., 1970), pp. 33-36.

[10] Ibid.

[11] The reader should refer to learning outcomes illustrated in sample lesson plans and attempt to classify them relative to domain, level, and type.

[12] W. James Popham and Eva L. Baker, *Systematic Instruction* (Englewood Cliffs, N.J.: Prentice-Hall, Inc., 1970), pp. 72-74.

includes terminal behaviors as well as essential entry and en route behaviors. They contend that the number of hours wasted each year on teaching skills learners already possess is staggering to the imagination. Literally thousands of students suffer through the teaching of facts they already know simply because instructors do not pretest student knowledge. Similarly, those students who do not possess the skills necessary for success in a course are doomed to failure unless appropriate corrective action is taken.

A *terminal* behavior is the end result of the learning experience, the ultimate goal achievement. For example, in English class, a terminal behavior might be writing a paragraph with a well-constructed topic sentence. *Entry* behaviors are those competencies assumed prerequisite to a learning experience. For example, entry behaviors for writing a paragraph would include the ability to write sentences and to spell and punctuate correctly. Those students deficient in entry behaviors are likely to experience difficulty in subsequent learning experiences unless remedial instruction is provided.

En route or intermediate behaviors are those deemed necessary to lead the learner to the terminal behavior. A logical question to ask is, What must the learner do before he or she can successfully perform the terminal behavior?

Instructional outcomes (at the unit level) will generally focus on those terminal behaviors anticipated from the learning experiences, although they may also emphasize en route behaviors. Frequently, they will suggest a terminal behavior that will be identical to one or more en route behaviors. The case method, for example, may be used during the instructional sequence (en route) and also at the end of the activity. Similarly, students may do a written exercise during the course of instruction and at the end of it. *Lesson* outcomes will always emphasize en route behaviors within the total unit context.

What Ethical Limits, If Any, Should Be Imposed in the Affective Realm?

What attitudes and values should be taught? This is a basic question faced by every teacher. It is an especially critical concern in the social studies area, although it certainly needs to be answered in all subject areas.

In the cognitive and psychomotor domains, achievement and productivity are considered the school's responsibility, but one's beliefs, attitudes, values, and personality characteristics are more likely to be viewed as private matters. An individual's attitude toward religion, politics, and family, for example, are usually respected as private, personal affairs. "Every man's home is his castle" is a cliche indicating the strength of this position.

On the other hand, schools and colleges have long been charged with the responsibility for teaching values. Acts of delinquency and other deviant behaviors are often linked with criticism of the schools. Some religious leaders literally make the school a whipping post for not teaching moral and spiritual values. These contrasting views have left the teacher confused, and basic affective goals have been neglected as a result of this uncertainty. There is a definite need for clarification on this issue.

For purposes of analysis, values can be considered in three broad categories: behavioral, procedural, and substantive.[13] The first of these concerns classroom procedures. Certain standards of behavior are expected and enforced. Teachers cannot tolerate unnecessary interruption when they are talking, for example. Neither can they tolerate other disruptive behavior. Such behaviors are classified under the heading of class control. Compliance is expected. Without it, there can be no effective teaching!

The second broad value category, according to Fenton, is procedural in nature. In describing this value he says, "Critical thinking is better than uncritical thinking; this canon underlies the entire scholarly world. If a student insists that his prejudices should not be challenged and defends them with an emotional appeal, he should be forced to subject them to the test of evidence and to defend them in the face of the full array of scholarly argument."[14] Thus critical thinking itself is seen as a value—one that the teacher has the right to emphasize. Without this right, Fenton argues, teachers cannot teach their subject areas.

The third category consists of a broad range of substantive values, representing the "goods" and "bads," the "rights" and "wrongs" of our society, and gives rise to some of society's greatest controversies. Some of these values have been codified into law; others are commonly accepted as moral law. This domain of substantive values, according to Fenton, is what cements and unifies our society. Thus they must be discussed in class and left for the learner to decide whether to accept them. The following are examples of substantive values: Religion is a good thing; therefore, young people should attend church. The family is the basis of society; so divorce should be discouraged. Young people ought to follow the crowd rather than pursue an independent course.

Although values provoking controversy should not be taught, according to Fenton, the teacher does have the right and responsibility to teach about such values. By this, he means raising questions for discussion and analysis. In short, Fenton supports treating such issues through the avenues of procedural values, that is, through critical-thinking processes. In such situations, however, the teacher must not make decisions for students. To illustrate, "Should we teach students to conform or to be leaders or to contribute to charity? I do not want teachers to make such statements to my children, even if I agree with them. On the other hand, I do want teachers to raise these issues for discussion, always keeping the discussion under the control of evidence within a framework of critical thinking."[15]

---

[13] This analysis is based on Edwin Fenton's "Teaching about Values in the Public Schools," in *Teaching the New Social Studies in Secondary Schools: An Inductive Approach* (New York: Holt, Rinehart and Winston, Inc. 1966), p. 40-45.

[14] Ibid.

[15] Ibid.

Ordering educational objectives into taxonomies has called attention to areas neglected in teaching, pinpointed a need for more specific goal formulation, and raised a number of questions concerning important goal relationships. Before the practitioner can effectively implement instructional developments, he or she must perceive how they can be integrated into the total instructional framework. Accordingly, this section discusses relationships among the three goal taxonomies, between goals and instructional procedures, between broad and specific goals, and between goals and concepts. Each is treated as a separate problem.

How Are Cognitive, Affective, and Psychomotor Goals Related?

In both the cognitive and psychomotor domains, the major concern is increased learner proficiency. In the affective domain, however, the concern relates to what the individual does with this knowledge or skill. Although *evaluation* of goal achievement has emphasized the *can do* dimension, it is the *does do* dimension that every teacher seeks. Thus an individual who has internalized a specific value *voluntarily* behaves in a manner indicating he or she holds that value. The difficulties of setting up an evaluational system for observing voluntary behavior are complicated by the fact that social pressure often dictates behavior that may contradict one's values.

It has been generally assumed that achievement of cognitive goals automatically insures achievement of affective goals. It must be recognized that the three domains are not mutually exclusive. Emotion is an essential aspect of intellectual processes, and motor and mental skills have an affective dimension. Some behaviors are more intellectual than emotional, whereas others are more emotional than intellectual. Still other action requires more mental and physical dexterity than anything else.

Negative as well as positive emotions may accompany intellectual learnings. A literature teacher, for example, may instill a knowledge of good literature in students while producing an aversion to, or at least a reduced interest in, the subject. Although the objective "Reads good poetry with pleasure" is seldom stated, it is nevertheless implied. After reviewing the evidence, Krathwohl, Bloom, and Masia conclude, "The evidence suggests that affective behaviors develop when appropriate learning experiences are provided for students much the same as cognitive behaviors develop from appropriate learning experiences."[16] Thus instructional goals and procedures must be consistent with the major domain involved. *At the same time, one must be cognizant of the influence of the other domains that are always present.*

Many goals in a given domain are reached through another domain. For example, every good teacher attempts to develop interest (affective goal) in an area so the student will learn it (cognitive goal). At other times, instruction is given in order to

---

[16] David R. Krathwohl, Benjamin S. Bloom, and Bertram S. Masia, *Taxonomy of Educational Objectives*, p. 20.

change attitude. The really outstanding teacher has probably achieved this status because of his or her intuitive ability to reach cognitive goals through the affective domain. The most liked and respected teachers, for example, are often described by students as those who take a deep interest in them, who challenge them, who understand their anxieties, who respect their opinions and do not embarrass them, who maintain high interest, and who instill a love of the subject.[17] Each of these attributes are affective in nature.

What Is the Relationship between Goals and Instructional Procedures?

Formulating an instructional goal, or purpose, is the very first step in instruction. Once this task has been completed, the teacher selects the learning experiences that seem most appropriate for reaching the destination (goal). Finally, evaluational techniques are developed for determining how well the goal has been reached.

In the *cognitive domain,* the lowest level (knowledge objectives) can be reached by a variety of learning experiences. The basic requirements are an attentive and well-motivated learner and the presentation of accurate information. For the more complex and higher categories of this domain, however, more involved learning experiences are required. Much more *activity* and *student participation* are essential for the learner to gain insight into his or her own thinking processes. As one advances through the sequence of critical thinking (which characterizes the hierarchial structure of the cognitive domain), group processes take on added significance. The lower levels of cognition are reached *in the process of achieveing the higher levels.* The reverse, however, does not follow. Achievement of knowledge objectives does *not* insure achievement of the higher levels of cognition. If the higher levels of cognition are the objectives of a given course, the more complex learning experiences should become the basic instructional theme. These include various techniques of discussion, debate, and simulation; project work of all kinds; and lectures.

Similar principles apply to the affective domain. At the lowest level, the student merely listens to an effective presentation in an atmosphere free from distractions. As one moves into the next level (responding), however, far more complex instructional arrangements are essential. Krathwohl, Bloom, and Masia believe that if the higher affective objectives are to be reached, considerable time and effort must be expended.[18] Some objectives may take several years to attain. Coordinated curriculum planning is essential.

Research evidence indicates that the more complex affective goals are not easily achieved by mere exhortations. What is needed, it seems, is for learners to examine

---

[17] Ardelle Llewellyn and David Cahoon, "Teaching for Affective Learning," *Educational Leadership* 22 (April 1965): 469-72.

[18] David R. Karthwohl, Benjamin S. Bloom, and Bertram S. Masia, *Taxonomy of Educational Objectives*, p. 19.

their feelings together so that they can compare them and move from an intellectual awareness of value to an actual commitment to it.

The young adult, however, tends to identify readily with his or her *peer group*. Thus the professor may rely heavily on group processes such as sociodrama and case techniques for changing attitudes. (These methods are discussed in Chapters 11 and 12). Sociodrama and case techniques have been especially effective in identifying the peer values of students. A realistic problem is essential, however, if this identification is to be achieved.

Psychomotor learning seems to parallel cognitive and affective learnings. At the lowest level (observing), the learner may profit from several techniques designed to provide basic information. As one moves to the higher, more complex levels, however, active involvement is essential. Much of this involvement must be individualistic in nature. Even in teaching motor skills associated with team sports, much individual practice is necessary prior to, and along with, the final phases of skill development. In particular, drill techniques used in group practice of mental skills have been criticized as unsound pedagogy because they promote learning by memorization.

How Are Broad and Specific Goals Related?

Instructional aims and objectives vary considerably in degrees of abstraction. As said before, higher level goals are more complex and abstract than lower level goals, and course goals are more abstract than unit goals, which, in turn, are more abstract than lesson goals.

Teachers sometimes wonder if achievement of lower level goals, in a more or less piecemeal manner, will lead indirectly to acquisition of the more complex ones. Will the attainment of the cognition levels of knowledge, comprehension, and application, for example, eventually increase the learner's capacity to utilize the whole cognitive process? It is quite likely that this does occur to a limited degree. It is extremely important, nevertheless, that the learner experience all levels of the cognitive process in an integrated sequence as often as possible (as implied from studies in field psychology). Thus the learner must develop a mental picture or pattern for most efficient learning. For this reason, learning is emphasized throughout this book as a process of problem solving. The concept is also supported through unit-teaching procedures.

In the affective domain, the problem is even more complex. Observations indicate that interests, attitudes, and other personality characteristics develop slowly, sometimes over a period of several months or years. If this is so, are affective objectives the responsibility of any one teacher in any one particular course? The answer seems to be no. Although while some interests, attitudes, and values may evolve over a long period of time, there is mounting evidence that they can be altered rather suddenly. The impact of some dramatic or traumatic experience, for example, is well known. It seems quite likely that some objectives in the affective domain and some objectives in the cognitive domain may be attained quickly, while others in both domains may be developed only over a long period of time. Similar principles probably apply to the psychomotor domain.

Implied in the preceding discussion is the need to plan educational objectives. Lesson and unit goals contribute to the attainment of course goals, and course goals contribute to the attainment of broad subject-area goals. Consequently, instructors must work together if related course goals are to be sufficiently integrated to attain certain long-range objectives. The recent developments in team teaching provide a definite advantage here.

What Is the Relationship between Goals and Concepts?

As indicated in Chapter 1, concepts are the outcomes, or products of learning. Many cognitive goals, when achieved, can be stated as generalizations or concepts. A cognitive goal at the analysis level, for example, might be stated as "Pupil possesses ability to detect fallacies in arguments." As an attained concept, the idea may be stated as "Arguments often contain fallacies."

Goals in the affective and psychomotor domains, however, can be translated into concepts only in the cognitive sense. An affective goal at the valuing level, for example, may be stated as "The learner possesses a love of good literature." As an end product, the new concept may be stated as "Good literature consists of plot, style, and movement." The affective goal when stated as a concept loses its affective dimension.

Once the teacher has identified major unit concepts, he or she can develop unit objectives. Each major concept must be analyzed in order to determine the precise nature of the objective (purpose or goal) sought. For example, it may be that understanding or comprehension is desired; sometimes an attitude or value must be developed and altered; frequently a mental or motor skill will be emphasized. This basic decision will determine the nature of the unit experience. Generally, each unit concept will provide the basis for the development of at least one unit goal.

Goal Formulation

For many years, goals have been stated too vaguely to be meaningful. The result has been overemphasis on textbook teaching and relatively little application to related life problems. The procedure recommended below represents one way of correcting the difficulty.

How Are Goals Constructed?

A great deal of confusion exists over the relationship among concept, goal, and behavioral outcomes. Some authorities advocate omitting the general goal or objective entirely. Instead, the instructor would proceed directly from the concept to specific behaviors students are to display at the culmination of instruction.[19] This practice does have some drawbacks, however. For example, the specific behavior "Define selected technical terms according to definitions given in textbook" is most useful in programmed instruction and at the training level of performance. For conventional class instruction, however, it tends to suggest that the identified behaviors are ends in themselves. Thus the student's degree of achievement would logically be assessed in terms of ability to recall mere facts.

Another approach and the one recommended by the author has been clarified by Gronlund.[20] It involves stating the general instructional objectives (derived from a given unit concept) and then listing samples of specific behaviors that are acceptable evidence of goal attainment) for example, "Understands the meaning of selected technical terms by defining the terms in his own words." Thus the goal is now one of understanding. Specific outcomes of defining, using, identifying, or relating are merely samples of behaviors suggestive of goal attainment and thus open the door to many types of learning experiences. Degree of goal achievement is now assessed in terms of understanding, not in terms of what has been taught and recalled.

When achieved, an instructional goal is internalized as an idea or concept. The nature of ideas, however, varies according to the three broad domains previously described. Either stated or implied in a worthy goal is a real-life application. To focus attention on the student, each instructional goal should begin with the introductory clause "After this unit (or lesson), the student should . . . ."

The next step is identification of the domain to be emphasized. The words "understanding," "attitudes" and "appreciations," and "skills" are commonly employed to denote the cognitive, affective, and psychomotor domains, respectively. For example, "After this lesson, the student should have furthered his or her understanding of . . . ." Each goal should be restricted to a given domain and to a single idea.

How Are Pupil Behaviors Incorporated into Instructional Goals?

Although learning is internalized as ideas or concepts, there are many outward manifestations of that which is learned, the most obvious being the student's behavior referred to as a behavioral outcome. For each instructional goal, there will be a number of pupil outcomes suggestive of goal achievement or means to achievement. Accordingly, for each goal, the teacher should select those specific behavioral outcomes most likely to reflect progress toward goal achievement or final goal achievement. The teacher should identify as many outcomes as possible and then select those that seem most practical for guiding instructional activities.

Behavioral outcomes are usually incorporated within the goal framework. For example, "After this unit in American Literature, the student should further ap-

---

[19] R.F. Mager, *Preparing Instructional Objectives* (Palo Alto, Calif.: Fearon Publishers, 1962).

[20] Norman E. Gronlund, *Stating Objectives*, pp. 4-6.

preciate the social inequalities resulting from a social class structure, as evidenced by his or her (1) realistic responses in a class discussion on U.S. policy toward migrant workers, (2) willingness to examine reactions resulting from a sociodrama designed to portray feelings in a specified social situation, and (3) greater cooperation with underprivileged students in class and society." Outcome one relates to the second level of the affective domain (responding), while outcomes two and three suggest different aspects of the third level of this domain (valuing). By becoming thoroughly familiar with the various levels of each instructional domain, the teacher can select those outcomes most appropriate for any given set of circumstances.

Unit outcomes provide definite clues to desirable class activities. In the previous example, outcomes one and two are *intermediate* behaviors that are possible avenues to goal achievement. Outcome three is a *terminal* behavior impossible to measure under normal school conditions. It primarily serves to remind the teacher of the ultimate behavior being sought.

In *evaluating goal achievement,* the teacher must direct attention to *terminal* behaviors. In the previous example, outcome one can be rendered sufficient for evaluational purposes by identifying various processes essential in a problem-solving class discussion. These might include one's ability (1) to identify the central issue, (2) to recognize assumptions, (3) to evaluate evidence, and (4) to draw warranted conclusions.

In considering techniques that may be used to judge goal achievement, one should focus on actual overt *behavior* or the *products* of learning obtained from tests. All too often, emphasis has been placed on test scores. Although performance on tests and various other written assignments is indeed a valid indicator of achievement, *overt* behavior is an equally valid and sometimes superior indicator of goal achievement. For example, a speech student's making an effective impromptu speech at the culmination of a unit may be the best possible indication of goal attainment. This assumes, of course, that records of preliminary experiences have been kept so that progress can be effectively measured.

The Value of Formulating Goals

Appropriate formulation of goals provides the basis for development of consistent learning and evaluation experiences.

The process of formulating goals, in terms of behavioral outcomes, emphasizes the transfer of learnings to related areas.

Preliminary formulation of lesson goals and their appropriate behavioral outcomes expand one's perception of the many avenues available for reaching these ends. Thus a variety of instructional techniques may be employed.

Appropriate goal formulation relegates the selected textbook to its proper use as only one of many instructional resources.

Goals, or aims, when inappropriately formulated, are a waste of time. Thus many teachers consider them the *least* important rather than the most important aspect of the instructional process.

Many worthy instructional outcomes cannot be observed or evaluated within the context of a given course. As a consequence, certain important learning experiences may be minimized, simply because they cannot be evaluated effectively. One solution to the problem involves the formulation of long-range goals, evaluated by several teachers over an extended period of time.

Many worthwhile goals can be derived for each instructional unit. There is a tendency to emphasize the cognitive over the affective domain. Again, this practice is apparently related to the ease of evaluating cognitive, as opposed to affective, learning. With the development of a taxonomy of educational objectives in the affective domain, this imbalance can be corrected.

There is considerable confusion over those behaviors sought *during* the learning experience and those sought *at the end* of the experience. The teacher's first concern must be to designate those behaviors likely to contribute to achievement of terminal goals. Eventually, however, the teacher must state the desired terminal behaviors in more specific terms than those used to explain how the goals will be reached.

Illustrated Goals

Additional examples of unit goals are provided in Appendix A. Lesson goals are illustrated in the sample lesson plans provided in each methods chapter.

chapter 3

PLANNING FOR TEACHING

Overview

Key Concepts

1. The unit concept is fundamental to instructional planning.
2. A functional unit concept is broader in scope than the specific material on which it is based and embodies a real-life application.
3. Unit concepts are not given to students; rather students develop them as the culminating experience of each lesson.
4. Lesson plans are generally based on a single unit concept.
5. Behavioral unit outcomes suggest instructional methods and techniques.
6. A lesson plan is a proposed analytical development of a selected problem.
7. Since the resolution of a given problem may extend well beyond a single class period, the *daily* lesson plan is a misnomer.

New Terms

1. The Yearly Plan The overall course plan, consisting of unit titles (evolved from general course concepts).
2. The Teaching Unit A group of related concepts from which a given set of instructional and evaluational experiences is derived. Units normally cover three to six weeks of material.
3. The Lesson Plan Those specific learning activities that evolve from a given unit concept. Each lesson plan is structured around a problem specifically designed to guide the processes of reflective thinking.

Questions to Guide Your Study

1. Why do textbook units often make rather poor teaching units?
2. Unit planning is more appropriate for academic courses than for skills development. Defend or refute.

3. In what ways has the unit approach to instruction affected lesson planning?
4. What are the basic differences between the content outline and a list of major unit concepts?
5. It has been observed that experienced teachers are more likely to omit lesson goals than any other aspect of their planning activities. Yet, experts consider a statement of goals among the most basic components of planning. Evaluate this apparent discrepancy between theory and practice.

Planning, like map making, enables one to predict the course of events. In essence, a plan is a blueprint—a plan of action. As any traveler knows, the best-laid plans sometimes go awry. Sometimes unforeseen circumstances even prevent one from beginning a well-planned journey; other times, conditions on the trip may cause one to alter plans drastically. More often, however, a well-planned journey is altered in *minor* ways for those unpredictable "side trips" that may seem desirable from close range.

Similarly, teachers must plan classroom experiences. They must plan the scope and sequence of courses, the content within courses, the units to be taught, the activities to be employed, and the tests to be given. While few teachers would deny the necessity of planning, there is some controversy over the scope and nature of planning. Indeed, methods specialists themselves differ about the scope of planning needed. Some feel that unit planning renders lesson planning almost unnecessary. Others stress the importance of lesson plans and minimize the value of unit plans. Although the planning needs of teachers vary markedly, there is considerable justification for *both* unit and lesson planning.

The Yearly Plan

The process of planning begins when a teacher determines what major ideas or dimensions will be emphasized during the year. All available textbooks, cirriculum guides, and course-of-study aids should be examined for this purpose. Although each professor often prepares his or her own yearly plan, increased emphasis is being given to joint preparation by all members of a department. Joint preparation promotes appropriate integration of related courses and a common method of teaching the same course. At the same time it leaves each instructor free to develop various aspects of the course in his or her own way.

Unfortunately, some teachers rely on only one selected textbook in their yearly planning. Such a practice makes both teachers and students slaves to a single frame of reference. Textbook units and topics are studied on a chapter-by-chapter basis. A textbook, at its best, merely provides all learners with one comprehensive source of information. Since textbooks are designed to fulfill the needs of as many people as possible, they usually contain some materials of marginal value to individual instructors. Since each textbook writer tends to emphasize certain aspects over others, the teacher should survey as many sources as possible in order to ascertain what aspects he or she will emphasize.

How Are Major Course Concepts Identified?

As indicated in Chapter 1, concepts exist at different levels. For instructional purposes, the most abstract level is identification of several broad ideas or concepts (often totaling as many as twelve) that should be developed during the course and stated as declarative sentences. For example, from a course in general business, the course concepts could be:

1. Production standards in the United States make this nation the distribution center of the world.
2. Retail markets in the United States are consumer oriented.
3. Selling is a joint process of communication between buyer and seller.

After several tentative course concepts have been stated, they are revised and reworked until six or eight basic ideas remain. (Some teachers prefer to incorporate course concepts into course objectives. This step is not essential, however.)

Frequently, two or more units may evolve from a single major concept and thus create the need for more specific concepts. Eventually there will be a unit for each major concept. Appropriate unit titles, based on the concepts given previously for a general business course, follow:

1. The United States: Distribution Center of the World
2. The Consumer Determines the Market
3. Sales Promotion and Advertising

After major unit titles have been tentatively established, an approximate time schedule reflecting the degrees of emphasis to be given to each unit is established. Time limitations may necessitate basic changes. For example, sometimes certain units must be omitted. (It usually takes three to six weeks to complete a unit.)

How Are Major Course Purposes Developed with Students?

After major units have been selected, the teacher provides students with an overview of the major course aspects in order to give them an opportunity for developing expectations about the course. Students ask questions and offer suggestions. Such an experience creates initial interest in the activities that follow.

This introduction may take the form of a lecture-discussion. With a little added imagination, however, an atmosphere of eager anticipation can be established. Almost any instructional method or technique can be useful in attracting students to the particular course of study. There is an abundance of instructional media available for such purposes.

At least one class period should be devoted to this introduction. An example of a course introduction can be found in the unit plan in Appendix A.

The Teaching Unit

The teaching unit centers the work of the class around meaningful patterns and focuses the work of different days on a central theme until some degree of unified learning is attained. *The basic elements of a teaching unit consist of a number of related concepts, grouped together for instructional purposes.* The process is essentially one of combining related ideas into some intellectual pattern. It provides opportunities for critical thinking and for generalization and application of ideas to many situations.

Unit titles, as illustrated in the yearly plan, do not usually correspond to textbook units. In order to make instruction most effective, a teaching unit should focus on a central practical idea, or theme. Although some English teachers might structure a unit around Julius Caesar, for example, students would likely find a unit dealing with ambition more meaningful. Such a unit, of course, would focus on Julius Caesar as an means of realizing the major objectives.[1] Instead of studying evolution, a science teacher might construct a unit around the concept of change. The idea of evolution would become one dimension of a much more comprehensive theme. Such a unit concept approaches what Jerome Bruner terms the basic structure of knowledge.[2]

Implicit in unit planning are three different phases: initiating activities, developing activities, and culminating activities. The first phase of unit planning is similar to the steps in yearly planning. Unit planning is necessarily more restricted and specific than yearly planning. In all cases, however, the process must be consistent with, and fit into, the overall framework established in the yearly plan.

What Purpose Does the Content Outline Serve?

To aid in developing a series of cohesive experiences, a content outline of each unit should be developed. Various aspects of the unit can be readily developed if basic content is clearly delineated by topic. Basic textbooks serve a useful purpose in this phase of unit planning.

The content outline must be detailed enough to indicate points of emphasis, yet brief enough to be useful in the derivation of major unit concepts. The content outline

---

[1] John B. Chase, Jr., and James L. Howard, "Changing Concepts of unit Teaching," *The High School Journal 47,* no. 4 (February 1964): 180-87.

[2] Jerome Bruner, *The Process of Education* (Cambridge, Mass.: Harvard University Press, 1961), pp. 17-18.

that appears in Appendix A is rather brief. For a subject such as history or political science, a more detailed outline would be needed.

How Are Major Unit Concepts Identified?

Using the unit outline as a broad frame of reference, the teacher develops from six to ten unit concepts. They are most appropriately expressed as complete thoughts and become the structural foundations of the unit. As indicated in Chapter 1, if properly developed, concepts have high retention and transfer value and *are most appropriately phrased as generalizations suggesting real-life applications.*

The major unit concepts that follow are based on a unit in general business entitled "Sales Promotion and Advertising":

1. Customer satisfaction is the most important product.
2. Customer needs are the prompters for purchasing decisions.
3. Advertising can be an effective means of preselling products.[3]

In many subject areas, it is relatively easy to meet the criterion of a real-life application. In a few subject areas, however, this is a rather complicated but essential task. First, one must identify the major ideas of the unit and then expand them into generalizations that are viable today. Without the second step, history teaching is likely to remain a dry and generally useless process of memorizing names, dates, and places.

The following unit idea and unit concept were developed from a unit entitled "World War I: To Make the World Safe for Democracy."

1. *Major unit idea.* Wilson's mistake of advocating for a peace treaty caused his unpopularity at home.
2. *Major unit concept.* Ill-advised public expression (for example, riots against Wilson) can adversely affect statesmanship.[4]

As the preceding examples illustrate, each major unit concept is derived from an idea specific to a given time in history. Since many concepts occur again and again throughout other history units, the student becomes aware of the repetitive nature of history. New concepts, of course, also will be emphasized in each subsequent unit.

How Are Instructional Goals and Behavioral Outcomes Derived from Unit Concepts?

Unit goals and their accompanying outcomes are developed from unit concepts. Unit goals provide a necessary transition from what the teacher views as the ends of

---

[3] See Appendix A for a complete list of concepts for this unit.

[4] This process of developing unit concepts is further illustrated in the last section of this chapter.

instruction to what is expected of the student in order to achieve the desired learning. Frequently, each unit goal will embody a different unit concept, but sometimes two or more *may be* embodied within a single goal. Indeed, there are usually more concepts than goals.

As stated in Chapter 2, instructional outcomes may refer to *minimum-essentials objectives* or to *developmental objectives.* If they are the minimum-essentials variety, the particular conditions and expected level of performance must be specified. If, however, outcomes are developmental in nature, as in academic courses, this degree of specificity is not appropriate. The example that follows is developmental in nature.

Concept: Customer needs are the prompters for purchasing decisions.

Instructional goal and accompanying behavioral outcomes

After studying this unit the student should have furthered his or her understanding of the role of basic human motives and wants in selling, as evidenced by:

1. The application of appropriate psychological principles in simulation games.
2. The interpretation of sales resistance evident in a sociodrama.

The behavioral outcomes are complex, calling for a whole group of responses, and suggest specific methods and techniques for attaining goal achievement. Lesson outcomes are much more specific than unit outcomes.

How Are Learning Experiences Evolved from Anticipated Behavioral Outcomes

As indicated in the previous examples, each behavioral outcome suggests one or more methods that will contribute to goal achievement. Both a simulation game and a sociodrama could be used to attain the instructional goal and behavioral outcomes in the preceding examples. At this point, the teacher identifies the specific methods and issues to be developed. To illustrate:

1. *Simulation game:* "People, U.S.A."
2. *Sociodrama*
   Problem: How does a customer feel when he or she is pressured into buying a product?

   Broad situation: Mary wants to buy a gift for her husband's birthday. Jim is a salesman in a department store.

The teacher's preplanning of some activities does not mean that he or she must assume the role of taskmaster. Students may actively participate in planning class activities *suggested* by the teacher. Because different pupils often will be involved in different activities, provisions for individual differences should be included in the unit plan. Beginning teachers should make a special note of this.

How Is Goal Achievement Assessed?

Although unit evaluation is not a preinstructional activity, it is predicted during preinstructional planning. Indeed, a unit plan may become ineffective if students anticipate being asked to recall specific facts while the teacher focuses planning on specific unit concepts. Measurement and evaluation must be consistent with unit goals and anticipated behavioral outcomes. As indicated in Chapter 2, behaviors appropriate as learning activities are usually not adequate for evaluating learning. They do provide sound bases, however, for the development of needed evaluational experiences. For example, the case analysis activity (cited as one of the learning activities) should help students identify pertinent facts, feelings, and relationships associated with selling. Thus any case dealing with these factors, whether or not it directly addresses the situation of a salesperson pressuring a customer, could be used to test student understanding.

Essentially, unit activities provide *practice* essential to the achievement of identified behavioral outcomes. This practice will tend to be *identical* to terminal assessment experiences when minimum-essentials objectives are involved (for example, a minimum level of typing). When developmental objectives are involved, the unit experiences usually will be similar, but not identical. A case analysis, for example, will not necessarily be followed by another case analysis as a terminal assessment activity. Since the case method is designed to portray human emotion in a conflict situation, any test item that deals with this topic would be appropriate.

How Are Major Unit Purposes Developed with Students?

To assist students in gaining an overall perspective of the unit, teachers should discuss with them the major objectives and some of the anticipated activities. This not only makes students ready to learn but also provides teachers with valuable feedback. A teaching unit is *not* preplanned for the purpose of prescribing all aspects of the learning experience; rather it is designed as a basis for further planning with students. Modifications must be expected.

The unit introduction involves setting realistic expectations with students and impressing on them the nature of the concept approach to teaching and learning. (After a unit or two has been completed, this introductory activity may not be needed.) It is not appropriate, however, at this time to identify specific unit concepts. By following this approach, students should begin to see the need for various unit activities and assignments.

A lesson plan is an expanded portion of a unit plan, providing a detailed analysis of a particular *activity* described in the unit plan. For example, one of the unit activities is called *class discussion*. While the problem title was stated in the unit plan, no indication was given concerning *how* the problem would be developed. In discussing a *problem of policy*, as described in Chapter 8, careful planning is essential. The lesson plan serves such a purpose.

The essentials of a lesson plan are somewhat similar to those of a unit plan. Although forms and styles differ markedly from one teacher's plan to another, a lesson plan usually contains a goal statement, lesson introduction (approach), lesson development, and lesson generalizations. Depending on the nature of the lesson, it also may include a list of materials needed, provisions for individual differences, and an assignment.

The common elements of lesson planning erroneously suggest a more or less standard routine. While it is true that most plans will be structured around the common elements described, significant differences may be found within this framework. Different teaching methods are designed for different instructional purposes; they involve different sequences. Thus lesson plans must be modified accordingly. *Sample lesson plans, prepared for the purposes of illustrating each of the major teaching methods, appear in the respective methods chapters.* A comparison of some of these plans is recommended. The particular style of lesson planning illustrated in this book is suggestive only.

What Is the Role of the Unit Concept in Lesson Planning?

Each lesson plan is based on a *unit* outcome (stated in the lesson plan), essential for the achievement of the *unit* concept. Thus behind every lesson plan is a concept. Two or more lessons may be essential for ensuring the attainment of a single concept. Although some authorities feel that in certain contexts the teacher should state the concept to help the student understand it, most apparently feel that students should be guided inductively toward concept achievement. Restating the unit concept in each lesson plan simplifies further planning and helps the teacher focus on one and only one major idea during the lesson.

How Are Lesson Goals and Outcomes Evolved from the Unit Concept?

From each unit concept, the teacher must decide what major goal domain must be emphasized (that is, cognitive, affective, or psychomotor). It may be that two or even all three goal domains should receive emphasis. Usually, there will be a different lesson for each major goal domain emphasized. Sometimes, however, more than one domain may be stressed in a single lesson. This applies especially to certain inquiry methods that involve several unified lessons.

For illustrative purposes, unit concept III from Appendix A is reproduced below along with unit goals 1 and 2.

Unit concept: Advertising can be an effective means of preselling products.

Unit goal: After studying this unit, the student should have furthered his or her understanding of the relationship between impulse buying and advertising, as evidenced by:

1. The ability to test hypotheses of impulse buying in a class discussion.
2. The ability to apply appropriate advertising principles in role-playing situations.

Unit outcome 1 suggests class discussion and the cognitive domain (although the affective domain can be stressed in certain types of discussion). Using the unit concept as a guide, the teacher can then derive a lesson goal with appropriate lesson outcomes. To illustrate: "After this lesson, the student should have furthered his or her understanding of the importance of impulse buying as evidenced by (1) the questions asked during the discussion, (2) the ability to offer and evaluate hypotheses posed during the discussion, and (3) the ability to derive generalizations from the discussion." The specific learning outcomes represent behaviors that can be expected during a problem-solving discussion experience.

How Is the Lesson Problem Developed?

Every major instructional method is based on a problem. With the exception of the lecture method, instructional methods often incorporate some form of policy problem (see Chapter 8 on discussion methods). For example, "What can we as marketers do to stimulate buying?"

Since the processes of reflection demand a constant referral back to the basic problem, it should be placed on the chalkboard. In this way, the problem helps to guide the learning experience. An inappropriately worded problem usually results in an ineffective lesson.

What Is the Function of the Approach to the Lesson?

Every lesson must be designed to capture student interest at the outset. Techniques may range from two or three introductory questions in a class discussion to a five- or ten-minute demonstration in a science class. Whatever technique is employed, the purpose is to prepare the learner for subsequent class activities.

The approach to the lesson is comparable to the course and unit introductions except that it applies to a specific lesson. The teacher should not prolong this activity since it merely sets the stage for learning.

What Are the Essentials of Lesson Development?

Major activities of the lesson are incorporated in this phase of a lesson plan. Subdivisions of lesson development will vary with the particular method used. The teacher must first identify the different aspects of the reflective process germane to the particular method involved and then prepare points, questions, and comments essential to the instructional process. For class discussion, for example, preparation may consist of only two or three key questions in each area to be explored. (At this point, the reader should study the illustrated lesson plans provided in the methods chapters.)

Asking key questions (or planning events) in the proper sequence is extremely important in achieving lesson objectives. Essentially, questions serve a dual role since they focus on the content being discussed and on the cognitive processes. Instructional processes that foster critical thinking must also be introduced in the proper sequence. The first questions concern assessment of the problem and are followed by those pertaining to the higher levels of cognition, analysis, and synthesis of hypotheses or proposed solutions. Finally, some attention is given to the highest level of cognition (evaluation).

How Is the Lesson Concluded?

The culminating portion of a lesson is often neglected or rushed. This is particularly unfortunate since it is at this point that students are expected to derive concepts or generalizations. The culmination of almost every lesson should involve students in the derivation of generalizations, based on the lesson experiences. The lesson generalizations are collectively equal to the basic unit concept on which the lesson is based. Some authorities insist that students write out lesson generalizations. In many instances, students verbally derive lesson generalizations that are then written on the chalkboard for students to record in their notebooks.

Basic unit concepts, as opposed to lesson concepts or generalizations, are derived by teachers as they plan for instruction. Concepts, at the unit level, are sometimes inductively derived by students as a *culminating* unit review activity. The instructor usually writes one or two anticipated lesson generalizations in the lesson plan to be used as instructional guides only. The following are examples of lesson generalizations derived from the unit on selling:

1. Buying is associated with personal status.
2. Quality products sell themselves through satisfied customers.

The Value of Unit Planning

Unit planning provides a basic course structure around which specific class activities can be organized.

Through careful unit planning, the teacher is able to integrate the basic course concepts and those of related areas into various teaching experiences.

Unit planning enables the teacher to maintain a balance between various dimensions of a course. By taking a long-range look, one is able to develop priorities in advance of actual classroom experiences.

The unit plan is the best technique developed to date for enabling teachers to break away from traditional textbook teaching.

Emphasis on behavioral outcomes in both unit and lesson planning results in a more meaningful series of learning experiences.

Limitations of, and Problems with, Unit Planning

A teacher may become a slave to his or her plans. This is a special hazard for those who prefer detailed lesson plans.

Excessive planning may promote an authoritarian class situation. This factor becomes apparent when the changing needs of students are largely disregarded.

Unless caution is exercised, lesson plans may become a mere outline of textbook materials. If practical lesson goals, along with specific behavioral outcomes, are developed *as a basis for* class activities, this situation will not exist.

Thorough planning takes time—more time, in fact, than is available to some new professors. Furthermore, it is usually impractical to construct lesson plans more than three or four days in advance of the experience. (By making substantial use of marginal notes, a teacher may use effective plans as a basis for subsequent planning.)

Illustrated Planning

I. A unit plan is given in Appendix A. Lesson plans are provided in each of the chapters dealing with instructional methods.

II. Useful in history classes

The following example depicts the two-step process of changing unit concepts of historical events into concepts with viable real-life applications. Instructional goals are derived from the latter. The example is based on a unit in U.S. history entitled "World War I: To Make the World Safe for Democracy."

Content ideas (specific to a given unit)	*Major unit concepts* (generalized understandings)
1. The assassination of Franz Ferdinand of Austria was the "kick off point" that led to war.	1. Insignificant events often lead to unforgettable disaster.
2. Wilson's personal belief that dem-	2. The misleading idea that "Democracy

ocracy could save all mankind, greatly affected the United States' involvement in World War I.

3. America's entrance into World War I was related to her isolationist policy.
4. Wilson's idea of peace without victory was impractical.
5. Germany's submarine warfare influenced our decision to enter the war on the side of the Allies.
6. The United States was solidly united due to the war effort.
7. Bitter feelings of the Allies toward the Central Powers made peace terms very demanding.
8. The Big Four's acceptance of the League of Nations necessitated compromise that led to the organization's ultimate demise.
9. Wilson's stance on the peace treaty led to his unpopularity at home.
10. High reparations and other demands assessed against the defeated countries contributed to the depression of 1929.

can save all mankind" originated with Woodrow Wilson.

3. Isolation and lack of communication, whether between nations or individuals, lead to inevitable conflicts.
4. Peace without victory may set the stage for later conflict.
5. Aggression (for example, submarine warfare during World War I) tends to widen gaps between peoples.
6. A common cause (for example, World War I) tends to unite peoples.
7. Bitter feelings between individuals and nations (for example, the Allies' attitude toward the Central Powers following World War I) make peaceful relationships difficult to establish and maintain.
8. Unwanted compromise tends to lessen the effectiveness of peace-keeping organizations (for example, the League of Nations) and treaties.
9. Ill-advised public expression (for example, riots, etc., against Wilson) can adversely affect statesmanship.
10. Misuse of power by the victor (for example, reparation demands of the Central Powers following World War I) may adversely affect intergroup relations for many generations.

Each of these major concepts is derived from an idea specific to a given time in history. Many of the concepts will occur again and again as the student studies other history units. In this way, the learner can become aware of the repetition of history. New concepts, of course, also will be emphasized in each subsequent unit.

III. Useful in literature classes

Illustrated below is the two-step process of identifying major unit ideas (concepts) and then organizing content selections that develop each idea. The illustrated unit in American literature is entitled "Colonial America: Birth of a New Culture."

Concept: The conditions of the time influence the nature of literary contributions.

Illustrated by: *Of Plymouth Plantation*
The Prologue
The Author to Her Book
The Preface
Upon a Spider Catching a Fly

Sinners in the Hands of an Angry God
Diary of Samuel Sewall
The History of the Dividing Line
From the Journal of John Woolman
Letters from an American Farmer

Concept: Puritan ideals still have an influence on our social system.

Illustrated by: *The Prologue*
The Author to Her Book
The Preface
Upon a Spider Catching a Fly
Sinners in the Hands of an Angry God
Diary of Samuel Sewall

Concept: Reaching worthwhile goals involves hardships and struggles.

Illustrated by: *Of Plymouth Plantation*
The History of the Dividing Line
From the Journal of John Woolman
Letters from an American Farmer

Concept: Freedom involves responsibility and man's interdependence.

Illustrated by: *Of Plymouth Plantation*
Sinners in the Hands of an Angry God
The History of the Dividing Line
From the Journal of John Woolman
Letters from an American Farmer

Concept: Realities of life are not always consistent with ideals.

Illustrated by: *Sinners in the Hands of an Angry God*
Diary of Samuel Sewall
The History of the Dividing Line
From the Journal of John Woolman
Letters from an American Farmer

Concept: One's perception of reality must change if ideals are to be achieved.

Illustrated by: *Of Plymouth Plantation*
Sinners in the Hands of an Angry God
Diary of Samuel Sewall
The History of the Dividing Line
From the Journal of John Woolman
Letters from an American Farmer

Methods and Techniques:
Focus on the Individual
and the Small Group

Learner independence is not only a goal but a necessity at the college and university levels. From these institutions will emerge our future local, state, and national leaders who must be prepared to deal with the complexities of the modern world. Traditionally, methods (involving varying degrees of teacher domination) for dealing with large groups have been emphasized, almost to the exclusion of other techniques. Currently, however, there is a decided trend toward greater individualization of instruction. For example, the Keller Plan for personalizing instruction (a development of the 1970s) has been described as the most revolutionary approach to college teaching in the past fifty years. As Robin points out,[1] since its introduction barely ten years ago, personalized systems of instruction (all closely related in nature) have become accepted instructional technology and have attained national recognition.

Chapter 4 offers an approach to personalized self-instruction that is based on individual competency and that incorporates a variety of methods patterned after earlier programmed learning techniques. The specific technique described in this chapter was first developed by the author for beginning public school teachers and contains many parallels with the Keller Plan.[2] Essentially, the technique follows a four-step process: preliminary cognition of the task, modeling experiences, application under close supervision, and observation in actual settings.

Chapter 5 discusses a variety of related small-group techniques that have been used by college professors for many years. Small-group techniques have taken on a new focus since the emergence of various individualized instructional approaches. In the early 1960s, the inadequacy of small-group instruction became apparent to the

---

[1] Arthur L. Robin, "Behavioral Instruction in the College Classroom," *Review of Educational Research* 46 (Summer 1976): 313-54.

[2] Kenneth H. Hoover, *Secondary/Middle School Teaching: A Handbook for Beginning Teachers and Teacher Self-Renewal* (Boston: Allyn and Bacon, Inc., 1977).

authors of the Trump Plan as evidenced by their comment, "In countless classrooms, we have observed that teachers and students tended to act in much the same manner they customarily did in classes of 25 or 35."[3] Many college professors too have experienced difficulty with these techniques.

Chapter 6 is devoted to the seminar method. Although this approach is almost as old as the lecture itself, it is widely misunderstood by college and university teachers. For many years, the seminar has been a major instructional tool for graduate students, representing a compromise between teaching the ideal small group of five to seven students and the large group of more than twenty students. Since this method has been used in so many different contexts, it is little wonder that most college professors are confused about its application.

---

[3] J. Lloyd Trump and Dorsey Baynham, *Guide to Better Schools* (Chicago: Rand McNally and Co., 1961), p. 25.

chapter 4

BEHAVIORAL INSTRUCTIONAL PROCEDURES

Overview

Key Concepts

1. Behavioral instruction enables the learner to progress at his or her own pace.
2. Mastery learning is desirable for all students.
3. Behavioral approaches to learning are based on the premise that all students can achieve mastery if given enough time.
4. Behavioral learning packages are structured to lead the learner from the lower to the higher levels of cognition.
5. Behavioral instruction emphasizes performance through frequent testing, review, and practice.
6. The small group is the primary vehicle for social interaction.

New Terms

1. Mastery Learning Learning well all (80 to 90 percent) that is assigned with no concern about depth of understanding.
2. Learning Activity Package (LAP) Instructional materials and resources (including various assessment items) needed for a given learning sequence.
3. Preassessment Experiences Experiences that determine existing levels of knowledge and provide a basic framework for the learner.
4. Self-Assessment Items Test questions administered at different check points, enabling the learner to evaluate his or her own progress.
5. Postassessment Experiences Experiences that determine whether or not mastery has been achieved and that diagnose areas of deficiency.
6. Teaching Assistants Individuals responsible for providing feedback and tutorial assistance. These people can be either outstanding students in the class or individuals who have already completed the course.

Questions to Guide Your Study

1. A conventional class setting inhibits the application of an individualized instructional program. Defend or refute.
2. There are trends toward both an increased ratio of pupils per teacher and more personalized instructional programs. How does one explain these apparent contradictions?
3. What steps might a regular classroom teacher take to encourage greater individualization of instruction?
4. Individualized instructional programs are needed more in some content areas than in others. Defend or refute.

Professor Jones is very concerned about his first few years of college teaching. Although he has employed many different instructional procedures and techniques, he detects complacency, boredom, and half-hearted interest among his students. Some students miss class frequently; others are hostile in class. Each semester a few students earn A's, while the majority merely "pass." Several students seem convinced that they too could make "top" grades if the course could be extended for a few days or weeks.

Professor Jones's observations are no different from those of thousands of college and university professors throughout this country. Is such a state of affairs inherent in college teaching? In view of our country's advanced state of technology, it hardly seems likely. Because college is a tremendous investment in both time and money, most students are *potentially* interested in their classes. They realize the importance of thoroughness in learning, want to earn high marks, and expect to assume leadership roles in society.

Fortunately, considerable advances in college teaching have been made during the past decade, the most important of which are individualized approaches to learning similar to the widely publicized Keller Plan.[1]

This chapter is designed especially for instructors who are willing to break away from traditional instructional practices. Rather than ask them to give up tried and tested instructional techniques, the new approaches provide teachers with increased precision in teaching and a reference point for organizing and arranging various techniques for maximum effectiveness. The innovations are consistent with all known psychological principles of learning and have been investigated rather thoroughly even at this early date. Like other instructional methods, they view problem solving as the key to effective teaching.

---

[1] Fred S. Keller and J. Gilmour Sherman, *The Keller Plan Handbook* (Menlo Park, Calif.: W.A. Benjamin, Inc., 1974).

Before applying an individualized approach to learning, one must consider several crucial concepts. The following are crucial concerns in individualized instruction, although they are also important in general instruction.

What Is the Basic Purpose of Individualized Approaches?

The basic aim of most instructional innovations is mastery learning (an A grade). For too many years, few students have achieved the mastery level of learning; most have earned B, C, and D grades. A number of leading educators, notably Bloom and his associates,[2] believe this process can be reversed and that 85 to 90 percent (or even more) or any given college class can achieve mastery.

Those who believe in mastery learning accept the premise that any student *if given enough time* can meet all the necessary requirements, although they acknowledge that in a few classes the amount of time needed to do this may be prohibitive. There are instructional strategies, however, for reducing the amount of time needed by slower students. These two assumptions thus provide the basis for the different individualized instructional innovations emerging in all parts of the country.

How Are the Higher Levels of Cognition Reached?

As learning programs developed in the 1960s demonstrate, it is relatively easy to devise performance-based experiences for the lower levels of cognition. Developing experiences for the higher levels of cognition is not easy, however. (See Chapter 2 for a thorough explanation of these levels.)

The first phase of most behavioral instructional programs emphasizes the learning of basic concepts, principles, and theories; often involves reading and writing activities; and takes the learner through the first two levels of cognition (knowledge and comprehension).

The second phase helps students derive meaning and attach significance to the basic knowledge acquired in phase one. Small-group work and practice are emphasized as students observe and inspect models and try out what they have learned in phase one. Students may also engage in simulation exercises, listen to lectures, or view films, for example. All the higher levels of cognition are involved, namely, application, analysis, synthesis, and evaluation.

The third phase takes the student into the realm of individualized performance activities. Utilizing the basic learning developed in phase two, the student puts his or her newly acquired concepts into practice. The pupil may also observe more experienced individuals making real-life applications. At all times, however, discrepancies between instructional and applied applications are noted and evaluated. Again, the

---

[2] Benjamin S. Bloom, *Learning for Mastery* (Los Angeles: University of California Press, 1968).

higher levels of cognition are involved.[3] Note that the activities of each level are dependent on the successful completion of each preceding level.

What Is the Role of Student Teaching Assistants?

The influence of an individual college professor on a student's academic progress has been recognized for many years. Although the same has not been true for student teaching assistants, they have been used for many years to supplement the role of the teacher in providing instruction and tutorial assistance.

Many individualized instructional programs, such as the Keller Plan, make use of teaching assistants, students who have mastered a given unit of work before other members of the class. Also structured into such programs are extensive small-group experiences. For many purposes, teaching assistants are just as capable and sometimes more capable than the instructor in explaining difficult points. Often they are able to relate better to their peers than someone from the "outside," such as the college professor or selected business leader. This is especially evident when the threat of grade competition is removed.

Why Is Self-Pacing Important?

Each student possesses a unique style of learning. For various reasons, some proceed at a faster pace than others. Whereas traditional teaching provides a single tract system for all students, behavioral instructional plans allow for individual differences in learning.

In the first place, content is usually broken into fairly small segments, or modules, and a hierarchial structure of modules is developed. The learner is expected to master one level before progressing to the next one. At no time is a student held back until the rest of the class "catches up."

A student may finish a course by demonstrating mastery in each module of work. In a sixteen-week semester class, for example, an individual may be permitted to finish well ahead of the rest of the class. Slower students, on the other hand, may take more than the allotted sixteen weeks. Thus a grade of "incomplete" is used frequently. Structured into the program are alternative activities for meeting individual needs. These may take the form of additional instruction and practice for those students who do not master the course the first time they attempt it.

---

[3] For an excellent treatment of individualized instruction as applied to the levels of cognition, the reader should consult John F. Feldhusen and others, "Using Instructional Theory and Educational Technology in Designing College Courses," in *Improving College and University Teaching Yearbook*, ed. Delmer M. Goode, (Corvallis, Oregon: Oregon State University Press, 1975), pp. 64-69.

To What Extent Are Behavioral Approaches to
Learning Self-Instructional?

When programmed learning became popular in the early 1960s, many people (especially some educational psychologists) predicted the demise of the college professor as a facilitator of instruction since they believed that individualized programs would enable most students to teach themselves. This did not happen, however.

Behavioral instructional innovations of today, nevertheless, do emphasize self-instructional learning. For example, students decide when they are ready for post-assessment exercises and often correct the exercises themselves. If problems develop, a teaching assistant (or class instructor) may be consulted. A final mastery test is often provided as a culminating experience. In addition to individualized and small-group work, a variety of other instructional methods is usually employed to supplement these learning experiences. These supplements include the lecture or demonstration method, films and recordings, and simulation exercises, for example.

What Is the Role of Reinforcement?

Reinforcement is one of the most widely accepted learning concepts. First popularized by B. F. Skinner through his experiments with animal behavior, the concept suggests that behavior positively reinforced or rewarded is likely to occur again. Skinner, through his work with teaching machines and learning programs, has been instrumental in bringing principles of reinforcement to the attention of teachers everywhere.[4]

The small units, or modules of work, in behavioral instruction are often sub-divided into separate self-contained learning packages. (Seldom does a learning package extend beyond two weeks of class time.) Each module (and package) builds on the previous one. Each must be mastered before the learner can progress to the next one.

Each package is structured to provide maximum reinforcement to the learner. First, objectives described in special behavioral terms are provided; then preassessment tests are offered to help the learner determine his or her knowledge in the area. Following each learning activity are self-assessment questions often accompanied by answers and supporting explanations. If not, they are given by teaching assistants. There is no grade or "punishment" for not reaching established performance criteria.

The learner may take as much time as necessary to reach mastery. Performance is assessed against established criteria and the number of learning activity packages (LAPs) completed rather than against the progress of one's classmates. (This sets the stage for a cooperative learning environment rather than a competitive one.) In

---

[4] Two books by Skinner highly recommended for background reading in this area are *Science and Human Behavior* (New York: The Macmillan Co., Inc., 1953) and *The Technology of Teaching* (New York: Appleton Century-Crofts, Inc., 1968).

addition, most learning segments or packages include statements designed to encourage the learner at every step. When the expected performance level is not acheived, the learner is provided with an alternative activity. All tests are assessed immediately, and the results are shared with the learner.[5]

Behavioral Instructional Procedures

Behavioral instructional procedures (BIPs) are closely related approaches to college instruction that employ principles of contingency management (SR) and reinforcement theory, as Robin suggests.[6] The following describes all essential steps of program development and points out differences (and sometimes conflicting interpretations) among the approaches now being employed.

For convenience to the reader, the components of a typical learning activity package are depicted in Figure 4-1.

How Is the Learner Prepared for the Learning Activity Package (LAP)?

As the term "learning activity package" suggests, all behavioral instruction programs include one or more study guides. Each begins with a brief rationale for the LAP, consisting of introductory comments linking the new material with existing concepts (comparable to an advance organizer) and reasons supporting the importance of the LAP. This section is usually short, consisting of two or three paragraphs.

How Are Instructional Objectives and Behavioral Outcomes Developed?

Instructional objectives and behavioral outcomes pinpoint what is expected of the learner. Objectives correspond to the major activities to be developed in the LAP.

As the examples in Appendix B illustrate, behavioral outcomes are the minimum-essentials type in which both the *specific conditions* and *minimum level of performance* are clearly described. Most programs establish a minimum acceptability level of 80 to 90 percent. Although theoretically a level of 100 percent would be expected for mastery, some allowance for human error must be made. Even so, the minimum acceptability level is more or less arbitrarily determined.

The development of behavioral outcomes is probably the most crucial aspect of the program as it sets the stage for the entire LAP. It is usually desirable to engage students in reading and writing activities since performance cannot be assessed without product results.

---

[5] For an illustration of this technique, the reader should consult Appendix B and also the author's book *Secondary/Middle School Teaching* (Boston: Allyn and Bacon, Inc., 1977).

[6] Arthur L. Robin, "Behavioral Instruction in the College Classroom," *Review of Educational Research* 46(Summer 1976): 313-54.

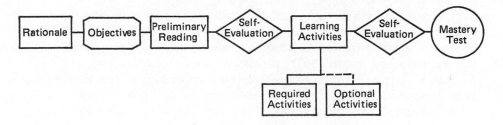

FIGURE 4-1   *Components of a Learning Activity Package*

What Is the Purpose of a Preliminary Reading Section?

The common aim of behavioral instruction programs is to make learning self-instructional and thus to teach college students to assume increased responsibility for their education. As in conventional classes, part of this responsibility involves requiring learners to do some reading before engaging in specific class activities. Preliminary reading provides students with the basic concepts essential for further study and investigation. It may not be necessary for all students, although if done, the selections must be brief and to the point and provide necessary background for the preassessment experiences that follow.

How Are Preassessment Experiences Developed?

Preassessment experiences are the most difficult aspects of the LAP to construct. They help determine the student's present level of understanding and the kind of LAP experiences that should follow. Meeting the minimum level of acceptability on the preassessment measure should entitle the learner to bypass the entire LAP experience. Because students may object to the preassessment experience as just another "test," they must be convinced that such a test will help them fully comprehend subsequent activities.

Since each LAP usually emphasizes all levels of cognition, the preassessment test must also deal with each of these levels. Thus one set of test items will concern recall of acts and principles, along with minimum understanding; another with application of ideas (see the examples provided in Appendix B); and others with analysis, synthesis, and evaluation. Thus the learner may be asked to construct or develop something related to the area under investigation. (Note that the preassessment section of the illustrated LAP in Appendix B concludes with a request for the student to construct an objective.)

How Are Learning Activities Developed?

As might be expected, there is probably greater diversity among the behavioral instructional approaches used to develop learning activities than among those applied to other aspects of the package. Generally, emphasis is placed on learning foundational concepts; thus there is often considerable reading of basic textbook materials followed by some writing activity. Self-assessment tests and instructor assistance are provided to help learners achieve mastery before they begin the more complex activities.

The next level of activity usually involves application of principles through a small-group effort. The class members may be divided into groups of three to six for study and analysis. They inspect models and then attempt to emulate them. This may involve production of samples, simulations, and the like as the situation demands. If students are having difficulties, the instructor may bring the class together for a lecture or discussion.[7] When clarification is complete, work in small groups continues until mastery is achieved. A discussion of application problems follows. This activity, in turn, is followed by self-assessment written or oral tests.

The third level of activity usually involves some form of *individualized project*. Students are expected to complete an assignment outside the classroom environment. In an academic subject, the project may be to demonstrate the skill in a realistic setting. The prospective teacher, for example, teaches an actual class; the prospective lawyer argues an actual case in a mock courtroom environment. Finally, the learner may be asked to observe others in actual situations. Discrepancies between earlier developed models and actual observed practices or products are noted and discussed, often in a small-group setting. Again, self-assessment experiences are employed.

How Are Alternative Activities Employed?

A primary advantage of behavioral instruction is its ability to provide alternative learning activities for meeting the differing needs and interests of learners. These exercises are usually first employed in the second phase of the learning activities. For example, small-group work that enables students to see a variety of applications definitely expands perceptual learning.

Optional applications are especially appropriate in the third phase of the learning activities. For example, an elaborate simulation may be developed for those situations where actual on-the-job experience and observation are impractical. Thus at the higher levels of cognition, broader options are often provided. Finally, optional activities may be devised for those who fail to achieve mastery of the LAP the first time. These are not always necessary if some form of tutorial assistance is available.

What Is the Function of the Postassessment Experience?

The postassessment experience is very similar to the preassessment experience. It is usually a written exercise (sometimes oral) for determining whether mastery of the LAP has been achieved. As in the case of the preassessment experience, all levels of

---

[7] Note that in the Keller Plan, the lecture is used for motivational purposes only.

cognition are tested. Items range from recall to recognition of principles in applied situations to responses involving direct application.

In some programs, the postassessment test is administered and corrected by the teacher who then evaluates the student's achievement and informs him or her whether additional instruction or tutoring is required. The postassessment experience is repeated until mastery is achieved; usually optional experiences are offered those students deficient in certain areas.

In other programs, the postassessment experience is a structured part of the LAP. Answers and justifications for them may be provided in the LAP. In such cases, a supplementary midterm and final exam are usually given. Although similar to the various postassessment tests, the final exam includes different test situations and applications.

How Is Achievement Measured?

Achievement ideally is based on the number of units, modules, or LAPs completed. The time needed to complete the learning experiences is not a factor. In other words, no grade difference would be made between a student who reached mastery the first time through a given LAP and a student who reached mastery only after a fourth effort.

There has been considerable controversy about this marking system since it departs radically from traditional grading practices. In a mastery grading system, for example, any student regardless of ability can theoretically achieve an A grade, while under conventional systems, only those who complete the course the first time around and hold a certain rank or position within the class can receive an A. A mastery grading system, however, makes it difficult for administrators of graduate schools, professional schools, and commercial enterprises to judge the applicant's capabilities.

To make them more compatible with traditional marking systems, behavioral programs often employ grades based on rank. Supplementary final and midterm exams, for example, are administered, and may constitute up to 25 percent of a class mark. Sometimes the final individualized result or application associated with each LAP experience is evaluated on a point system, above the minimal level of mastery. Thus some distribution of grades is possible, although usually grades tend to fall at the *A* or *F* (fail) levels. Incomplete grades are also common. There is some evidence suggesting students prefer a multilevel marking system.[8]

The Value of Behavioral Instruction

Behavioral instruction enables the learner to progress at his or her own pace. The approach tends to be self-motivating, since learning is broken into small units and continuous self-assessment of progress is emphasized.

---

[8] Arthur L. Robin, "Behavioral Instruction in the College Classroom," pp. 339-41.

As the term implies, behavioral self-instruction represents a systematic effort to apply the most basic principles of learning, that is, reinforcement, feedback, behavior shaping, frequent review, and practice.

These learning programs emphasize progressive levels of learner independence. The teacher is relegated to a diagnostician and facilitator of learning.

Group cooperation replaces group competition for grades. A student's mastery is based on achievement of a predetermined level of performance and not on comparison with the performances of other class members.

Behavioral instruction seems superior to conventional methods in both initial learning and retention of concepts.[9]

Limitations of, and Problems with, Behavioral Instruction

Behavioral instruction demands careful, extensive preparation of materials to meet the various learning needs of students.

The programs limit teacher flexibility. Once a learning alternative has been selected, the activities are prescribed and outlined for the learner with few opportunities for adjustment.

Behavioral instructional programs demand a restructuring of existing facilities and personnel relationships.

The approach is not appropriate when the objective is familiarization or orientation to a broad field of study.

Behavioral instruction will probably not be effective for the professor who views his or her role as a provider of information.

When mastery learning is emphasized, less content coverage is possible. This, of course, is a reflection of mastery learning levels established.

Drop-out rates in behavioral instruction classes are high. Apparently, the procrastinator and the anxiety-ridden student have difficulty coping with the specific requirements involved.

---

[9] Ibid., pp. 320-21.

chapter
5

SMALL-GROUP TECHNIQUES

Key Concepts

1. The optimum small-group size is usually about five students. (Effective small-group work, however, may be accomplished in groups of as many as twelve students.)
2. The small group may be used as a testing ground for effective group inter-action.
3. Small-group experience is an ideal means of increasing student participation.
4. Small-group experiences may be short or long lived, depending on the nature of the activity involved.
5. Small-group techniques are frequently used in connection with other in-structional methods.

New Terms

1. Short-and Long-lived Groups A short-lived group may function ten or fifteen minutes for a class period or two. Long-lived groups (sometimes called committees), on the other hand, may function for a week or more.
2. Learning Styles The ways learners process information. Some students, for example, seem to learn more effectively through verbal discourse; others tend to learn more effectively by listening to others.
3. Group Therapy Use of the group as a means of altering personality. This technique is inappropriate when not under the control of a specialist.
4. Task (Committee) Groups Usually long-lived groups that carry a task to its conclusion. The entire reflective process is involved.
5. Buzz Groups Usually short-lived groups that often focus on only one aspect of a problem.
6. Fishbowl Technique A training technique whereby group roles are assigned, played, and reflected on in a controlled setting. Designed to develop group cohesion and awareness of the influence of various individual roles.

Questions to Guide Your Study

1. What are the relative merits of short-and long-lived groups?
2. The creation of small groups tends to minimize teacher-domination. Defend or refute.
3. Why should group therapy (including sensitivity training) be carefully avoided by the regular classroom teacher?
4. What implications do different learning styles have on the formation of small groups?

In addition to the properties of a group, described more fully in other chapters, a *small* group is characterized by face-to-face communication between individuals. Each person in a small group must have a distinct impression of the other members, thus enabling him or her to react to them as individuals. A group of twenty members is usually considered small by sociologists. For effective total group interaction, much smaller groups are preferred, however. The optimum small-group size is usually about five people. Essentially, a small group must be large enough to develop unity but small enough to discourage factions.

Fundamental Properties

The small-group is a microcosm of a larger group. As such, it is characterized by all the group forces necessary for group dynamics, which are discussed more completely in Chapter 8. The properties treated in the following sections have a special bearing on the success of small-group processes.

How Does Group Size Influence Interaction Patterns?

Freedom from restraint and cohesiveness tend to diminish and eventually disappear as group size increases. A minimum number of three people may constitute an effective small group. The group should be large enough for adequate input and small enough for total group interaction. In groups of five or less, all members generally speak to each other. In groups of seven or more, the more inhibited students tend to restrict their comments to the one or two verbose individuals who "carry" the conversation. As the group becomes even larger, talk centers more and more around a few individuals. The rest of the group merely watches and listens. If a group is long lived, small cliques are likely to emerge. A skillful group leader is essential for maintaining total interaction and cohesiveness as the group increases substantially from the optimum size of five to seven members. Groups in which there is an odd number of people tend to be more effective in discouraging group factions than those in which there is an even number of people.

Long-lived groups tend to specialize in various task roles, as further described in Chapter 8. With specialization comes a hierarchy within the group. It has been observed, for example, that high-status members tend to lead the discussion, while low-status members are usually content to reflect on the points mentioned. If a low-status member does introduce an idea, it may be summarily rejected unless a high-status member takes up the cause.

What Constitutes a Cohesive Group?

Cohesiveness exists when all members of a group work together as an effective team and do not fear disagreement and conflict. In fact, one mark of cohesiveness is healthy conflict. Necessary controversial issues are raised in the interest of the group's task and its productivity. In such a group, for example, an individual feels free to say "I disagree" and expects to have the opportunity to express his or her point of view. In a noncohesive group, little disagreement is expressed. At the most, such expressions as "I'm confused" may be heard.

The group first goes through a warming-up phase of polite social conversation. Then, as the group begins to concentrate on the task, conflict may arise. Most groups release tension through occasional joking. Humor is a temporary flight into "safe" areas and should be encouraged to a certain degree.

Frequently, one individual may threaten the cohesiveness of the group by being argumentative or sarcastic. The group tends to go through a series of steps to bring this member back into harmony. First, after listening to the person for a protracted period of time, the group may try to joke about the comments made in an attempt to inform the individual of his or her nonconformity and to release tension. If the sarcasm continues, more serious persuasive techniques may be employed. If they fail, the individual will be rejected and isolated from the group. At this point, the group has decided that the disruptive person cannot be changed.

In the case of long-lived groups, a skillful observer (teacher) can sometimes expedite group progress by working individually with disruptive members. Sometimes, a word of caution or suggested technique may help individuals alter their behavior patterns or personality traits. Often, individuals are unaware of their ineptness in group participation and thus unable to change without some expert direction.

How Does the Small Group Contribute to Testing of Ideas?

When an individual is grouped with other students in an intellectual encounter, he or she feels increased responsibility to participate. The usual inhibitions that characterize conventional-sized classes are missing. A teacher cannot lecture to a group of this size; neither can one or two members readily "carry" the discussion. Active participation generates feelings of independence and responsibility as individuals assess the immediate impact of their contribution on others.

The intimacy of a small group provides a testing ground for ideas. Like the family, a small group has a "private" audience for determining how well a "brilliant" idea can stand up under the full force of intellectual logic. Because of the nature of the group, criticism tends to be sincere and constructive. No longer is one motivated to talk merely for the purpose of impressing others. In fact, the atmosphere almost compels an individual to listen as well as to contribute. This is a unique experience for some people.

What Are the Relative Merits of Long- and Short-lived Groups?

Small-group experiences can be short or long lived, depending on the purpose(s) to be served. In conventional classes, the well-known committee assignment may extend over several days. At other times, the group assignment may not extend beyond a single class period. When associated with flexible scheduling, small groups are usually short lived, serving as a transition between large-group instruction and independent study.

Short-lived groups demand much less structure than long-lived groups. Although the same group structure exists, each session must be treated as a separate unit. Group cohesion tends to develop slowly over a period of a week or more. Group cohesion in short-lived groups is desirable but may not be attained unless some preliminary instruction and training are provided. Evidence suggests that most teachers and students are inadequately prepared for short-lived small-group instruction.

In response to this need, some schools are currently emphasizing in-service education in sensitivity training (sometimes called T-Group experiences). The objective is to increase the learner's sensitivity to the needs and interests of others. These experiences actually incorporate some elements of group therapy that in the control of an improperly trained person, can create more problems than they can solve. In many cases, however, a few simple directions and precautions may be all that are needed.

What Learning Styles Are Important?

Through small-group activity, individuals may discover and develop their best cognitive style of learning. Styles of learning are defined as information processing habits that function generally for the individual. Differences among individuals in perceiving, knowing, and conceptualizing are probably as real as differences in ability levels. Individuals tend to display differences in seeing, hearing, and handling things during the learning process. Although this phenomenon is as yet imperfectly understood, the work of Frymier and his associates suggests at least three different personality dimensions that influence one's style of learning.[1]

---

[1] Jack R. Frymier, "Motivating Students to Learn," *NEA Journal* 57 (February 1968): 37-39.

Internal-external. Learning is a combination of internal and external forces. Equally motivated individuals, however, apparently differ markedly with respect to these forces. Some positively (or negatively) motivated students, for example, seem to draw heavily on internal forces. The novel and the new excite them. Ambiguity and uncertainty stimulate their quest for problem resolution. Other students, equally motivated, appear to be influenced more by the quantity and quality of external stimuli. Exciting class activities (for example, fascinating movies, interesting methods, and vivid illustrations) seem to stimulate their learning behaviors.

Intake-output. Some students are basically consumers of the world around them. They are avid readers, thoughtful listeners, and generally information seekers. "Intake" class activities have a strong appeal for such individuals. Other students, who are equally motivated, might be classified as "output" individuals. They learn readily when production activities, such as writing, talking, and doing, are stressed.

Approach-avoidance. Teacher approval, class marks, and social acceptance, for example, appeal strongly to some positively (or negatively) motivated students. Others who are positively motivated, however, tend to avoid such goals since they find them unappealing.

If Frymier's conclusions are correct, activating the desire to learn is much more complex than most teachers suspect. To appeal to two equally motivated students, class activities should be varied on the basis of individual personality.

Reflection-impulsivity. Kagan has discovered still another learning style that has a direct bearing on the reflective processes of individual learning.[2] Some students, according to Kagan, tend to weigh alternative ways of solving a problem, while others tend to group all data together and to quickly determine a solution. Both Frymier and Kagan believe that learning methods should improve the way learners process information and the speed with which they do this.

How Do Small Instructional Groups Differ from Group Therapy?

Group therapy is currently one of the most widely used methods for helping in viduals cope with their problems. Its most fundamental value can be expressed in the adage "Misery loves company." All people, especially those with severe emotional problems, seem to feel better when they realize others have the same problems.

Group therapy uses the group to change personality. The group is controlled by the therapist who typically exhibits a permissive attitude as a means of encouraging communication. The therapist must always be willing to protect any group member from excessive threat, however.

---

[2] J. Kagan et al., "Conceptual Impulsivity and Inductive Reasoning," *Child Development* 37 (1966): 583-94.

Group interaction provides the therapist with a valuable source of diagnostic information that can then be fed back to the individual either in the therapy session or in a private conference. There is no basic task goal. The individual does not surrender his or her identity; rather the identity is reinforced through group interaction. The situational events of a group enable the individual to discover the source of tensions and maladjustments.

A small group, on the other hand, emphasizes task goals. Individuals are expected to subordinate personal goals to those of the group. In becoming a part of the group, individuals surrender a part of their identity as they interact with peers in the resolution of a task problem. As in group therapy, interaction is important and should be evaluated. Unlike in group therapy, however, interaction here is analyzed from the standpoint of communication and progress toward the stated goal. While students may discuss the impact of certain contributions to group progress, they should not discuss individual feelings or attempt to analyze the behaviors of the various members.

Group therapy techniques are dangerous in the control of an untrained person. Teachers not only should prevent students from using the small group as a therapy session but also should carefully avoid diagnosing problems themselves. Through group interaction, certain tensions will be minimized, and certain minor personality adjustments may be made. Deep-seated problems, however, demand more intensive professional treatment than the classroom setting can provide. When such difficulties become apparent during small-group interaction, a psychiatrist should be consulted.

Small-Group Applications

The small group is ideally suited to processes of reflective thinking. It is *not* an approprite setting for covering content, however. In such a microcosm, students can easily discuss and analyze the practical applications of important issues. Since the small group can be used in many different ways, the applications that follow are suggestive only.

How Are Task Groups Organized?

A task (committee) group, consisting of four to eight members, solves a problem by following the same general procedures as those outlined in Chapter 8 on class and panel discussion. Unlike in other types of discussion, however, each member is actively involved in reflective processes. The tasks, roles, and assignments of members must be clearly defined and understood by all, and needed resources must be made available. In addition, a realistic time schedule must be developed, and appropriate progress reports submitted at designated points. Finally, some type of feedback activities to the entire class must be arranged. These activities may be short or long lived, depending on the nature of the task. Students themselves should be provided considerable latitude in decision making—at least with options along the way.

Since the task group represents an initial departure from purely teacher-dominated activities, students may flounder initially in their attempts to work on their own. This is to be expected until necessary skills are mastered. The following discussion guide represents the type of initial guidance that may be necessary. As students gain experience, each small group can be given the responsibility for developing its own problem.

Issue: What protection should a youth offender have under the law?

A. Analysis of the problem
   1. What basic assumptions are associated with special treatment of youth offenders in the courts? Are these assumptions valid?
   2. What are the consequences of giving a youth offender a break after he or she has committed one or more serious crimes? In many states, the judge may permit the offender to be tried in regular criminal court. Do you approve of this practice? Why or why not?
   3. As a legal institution, the juvenile court does not possess the procedural safeguards of other courts. For example, a minor may be required to testify against himself, denied the right to hear evidence, and not permitted representation by an attorney or the right to appeal the case. What are the advantages and disadvantages of such a system? What changes, if any, would you suggest?
   4. How long should a youth be held for investigation? What techniques of eliciting information are admissible?
B. Weighing alternatives
   1. For minor offenses, a youth may be released into the custody of his or her parents without a court hearing or legal disposition of the case. Police often exercise unauthorized "voluntary" supervision over the individual, sometimes collecting money in order to make restitution for damages. Some oppose such an arrangement, claiming that police officers are seldom trained for such supervision. How would you evaluate this practice?
   2. In some states, youth offenders are not photographed or fingerprinted since many employers check police records as a condition of employment. Other states, however, do photograph and fingerprint as a means of assisting them in solving future crimes. How would you evaluate such a practice?
   3. Truancy is a school problem up to a certain point. Nevertheless, it is usually specified as an act of delinquency, making the juvenile courts available for the enforcement of school attendance laws. Generally, there is no clear-cut division between the school's responsibility and the court's responsibility in the matter. What recommendations do you have in this situation?
   4. What other solutions or innovations have been tried in combating juvenile crime? (In this connection, you should investigate work forestry camps, psychiatric treatment centers, and guided group-interaction programs.)

5. Study the California Youth Authority's success in rehabilitating the juvenile offender. Would you recommend that such an approach be adopted nationwide? Why or why not?
6. Visit a juvenile court or talk with a juvenile-court judge. What impressions did you receive? What improvements, if any, would you recommend?
7. Talk with individuals who have violated the law. Do they feel that they received adequate treatment by the police or the courts? Why or why not?

Although problem-solving groups can work on any three levels—fact, value, and policy—most task group discussions should deal with all three. It should be noted that a problem of policy (illustrated above) also includes problems of fact and value. Thus we say that the first two levels are "nested" in the third. In a problem-solving discussion, the group must concern itself with all three levels; it is inappropriate to jump immediately from problem identification to problem solution.

How Are Buzz Groups Employed?

Frequently, it is appropriate to subdivide a class group into groups of four to six individuals, considered the optimum size for most effective interaction. Small *buzz* groups are usually short lived. After interacting for fifteen to twenty minutes, they "report" to the main group.

Buzz groups have been used effectively in developing group cohesion, in encouraging the timid person to speak, in devising plans germane to the total group, and in providing additional opportunities for leadership. Their most important function is to provide expanded opportunities for participation in problem-solving discussions.

Whatever the purpose, buzz groups must be oriented to the task at hand. If the task is to provide expanded opportunities for problem solving, each group must have a discussion guide. If each group is assigned a separate phase of the problem for discussion, it must clearly understand its limits and responsibilities for presenting the results of the deliberations to the main group. If each buzz group is assigned a different problem, it must summarize the problem for the total group.

Buzz-group reporting can be handled in a number of ways. Sometimes, one member from each group may serve on a panel discussion of the essential issues raised. Occasionally, individual members may be asked to present brief informal reports on group findings, or each group may list major ideas and findings on the chalkboard for all members of the various groups to discuss. Another interesting reporting technique is the group interview. Selected buzz-group reporters are asked questions by a designated *class interviewer,* designed to elicit the basic issues, problems, and conclusions derived from the experience. Since small-group work is usually limited to one or two sessions, class buzz-group reports must be brief, usually taking no more than ten minutes.

Although buzz groups have been used effectively in both small and large classes, they sometimes develop into undesirable factions. This is especially true when the same students are assigned repeatedly to the same buzz group or when the groups are too large. Moreover, it is often difficult for the teacher to detect the introduction of undesirable games or roles.

The instructor should move from group to group, offering assistance as needed, but being careful not to give students answers. Some teachers use the Phillips 66 technique. As the name implies, six persons discuss a question for six minutes. Often, the task is to formulate questions concerning a specific area of the discussion topic. This technique is more effective in raising questions for subsequent class discussion than it is in resolving problems because of the brevity of the buzz-group experience.

How Can Small-Group Clustering Be Used Effectively?

In many college classes, students are expected to demonstrate competency by completing term papers or other written projects. According to Lane,[3] valuable learning opportunities are often missed since the interaction is limited to the comments the instructor makes on the student's paper. All too often, the students never even bother to read the comments since they already have received a grade for the assignment.

Students can learn from individualized assignments by being *clustered* into subgroups of three. Lane defines clustering as "an active group exchange and/or interchange of three or more people that center their attention around a particular objective."[4] For example, if term papers or projects were due *before* the end of the term, students could exchange papers and discuss them with each other. After doing this, they could then incorporate in their papers any new and additional ideas gained from the exchange before submitting the assignments to the instructor for evaluation.

As Lane points out, this process not only expands the individual student's own thinking but also contributes to an expanded concept of the assignment. A clustering session enables the learners to review their own creations with other members of the class. Deficiencies may become readily apparent.

The instructor's role during a clustering session may vary, depending on class needs. Individualized diagnostic help may be provided, or the teacher may move from group to group, much as might be expected in most small-group situations. Following the clustering session, the class should be brought together again in order to raise questions and share ideas.

The small-group cluster context, according to Lane, can be applied in a variety of class situations. Questions, for example, can become rich material for such a session. Students can be asked to develop two or three questions, based on a reading

---

[3] Melvin Lane, "Clustering," *Improving College and University Teaching*, Autumn 1975, pp. 203-8. Much of this section is based on Lane's analysis.

[4] Ibid., p. 205.

assignment, which will then be collected for refinement by the teacher. After adding his or her own questions, the instructor can ask each cluster to select three or four for discussion, based on interest.

Short, two- or three-page handouts offer another interesting opportunity for clustering. This suggestion resembles the term paper idea previously discussed except that in this case each cluster examines the same information for criticism, position paper, or sample student paper. Whatever the handout, the task must be clearly defined.

What Function Is Served by Tutorial Groups?

Within the past decade, the use of paraprofessional personnel has received renewed attention. Indeed for many years, laboratory assistants have been used in almost every science department. It is only recently, however, that the importance of students' helping other students has been fully appreciated.

Today, use of student teaching assistants, recently popularized by the Keller Plan of individualized instruction, is one of the more promising instructional innovations.[5] Selected students who have mastered a given unit or module of work can aid in remedial instruction if given direction by the instructor, correct answers to test questions, and page numbers of corresponding textbook and supplementary sources. Student teaching assistants are often more effective than the teacher in helping class members because of their ability to relate to the students' frame of reference. In general, the Keller group has found that teaching assistants working in small groups can be effective. Some individualized attention for each member is necessary, however, if mastery is to be insured. Another alternative is to pair students having difficulty with those who have demonstrated understanding of the concepts involved. Foreign language teachers, for example, have made use of such teams in pronunciation exercises.

Using student teaching assistants and graduate assistants may not be effective unless a close liaison is developed between them and the teacher. Assistants must be able to recognize the types of problems they are not equipped to handle; thus the teacher must prepare materials outlining these problems. Psychological blocks, reading deficiencies, and incorrect use of language are but a few of the problems only the teacher should handle.

When a monetary reward for teaching assistants is not available, other rewards must be found. Fortunately, there are a number of these inherent in most class situations. Perhaps points may be awarded that count toward a final grade. For some people, merely being a teaching assistant is enough. They recognize this activity helps prepare them for a final examination. Occasionally, it may be possible to elicit tutorial help if the job exempts students from writing a term paper or doing a project.

---

[5] Fred S. Keller and J. Gilmour Sherman, *The Keller Plan Handbook* (Menlo Park, Calif.: W. A. Benjamin, Inc., 1974), ch. 4.

What Is the Purpose of Brainstorming Sessions?

For quickly accumulating a variety of possible solutions to an immediate problem, the brainstorming technique probably surpasses all other instructional methods. Treated fully in Chapter 13, the technique is especially useful in breaking down inhibitions since full participation is insured and evaluation of individual contributions, as wild as they may be, is withheld. The process demands a skillful leader and one or two people for recording the solutions suggested. Students can be quickly prepared for this recording role, however.

Brainstorming is especially useful when the problem is simple enough to permit a group to plunge into the hypothesis phase immediately. It also may be used to resolve more complex problems *if it follows an extended period of analysis and evaluation.* Evaluative statements are withheld until all possible solutions have been presented. This session can then be followed by an evaluation of the possible solutions offered, just as in any other problem-solving discussion. Brainstorming encourages creativity in small-group experiences.

What Training Techniques Are Effective in Small Groups?

Most teachers and students are ineffective in small-group experiences simply because they are unable to interact effectively with one another. Those assuming potentially destructive roles tend to divide and isolate members from one another. In assuming these roles, individuals are expressing their needs. The dominator, for example, is expressing his or her need for leadership, just as the blocker wants to be seen as a thoughtful intellectual. Similarly, the aggressor is trying to get action started, while the joker is demonstrating his or her humor and superiority. Until some group cohesion is established, however, such behaviors not only fail to satisfy the needs of the user but also render group work ineffective.

To help students develop effective group skills of participation and observation, the "fishbowl" technique is recommended.[6] While it is ideally suited to small groups, it also may be effective in groups of up to thirty-five or forty students.

The teacher divides the class into three equal groups (designated A, B, and C.). Chairs are arranged in three concentric circles. Members of Group A (in the inner circle) are paired with members of Group B. Group B members, in the middle circle, position themselves so that they can see their partners. Group C takes the outer circle in no particular order.

Members of Group A, the task group, discuss a selected problem for twenty minutes, while their Group B partners observe. Each observer partner jots down comments that will enable him or her to reflect or mirror the participant's behavior.

---

[6] This technique has been described in considerable detail by Alfred H. Gorman, *Teacher and Learners: The Interactive Process* (Boston: Allyn and Bacon, Inc., 1969), pp. 64-70; and Dorothy J. Mail, "The Fishbowl: Design for Discussion," *Today's Education* 57 (September 1968): 27-29.

The comments are in the form of "As I saw you, you ..." designed to help the participant think through his or her own group behavior.

In exactly twenty minutes, the teacher stops the action and allows ten minutes for each pair from groups A and B to confer. During this time, Group C members meet with the teacher to discuss the interacting pattern of the whole group. This group has been instructed to note who speaks most and least, who the leaders seem to be, and what behaviors produce group action, satisfaction, or dissatisfaction. It also notes the degree of cohesion of the interaction group and what seemed to be responsible for this phenomenon.

After the ten-minute critique, the groups reassemble and continue until five minutes before the close of the class period. Thereupon, each student is asked to write out his or her reactions to the experience.

At the beginning of the second session, the teacher may wish to comment on some of the written reactions. Group B is then shifted to the interaction group position. (Group A becomes the general observer group, and Group C takes its place as partner observer.) The above process is repeated. The third session proceeds in the same way with Group C becoming the interacting group.

Session four is devoted to general class reaction to the experience. By the fifth session, the class should be ready to function as a cohesive group. Although destructive roles will likely emerge from time to time, the group is at least prepared to cope with them.

Although flexible scheduling usually permits students to engage in small-group experiences only 20 percent of the time, these programs are flexible enough to accommodate special needs. A number of other class activities are somewhat dependent on the effectiveness of small-group experiences, and the fishbowl technique may set the stage for these other techniques.[7]

In addition to the fishbowl technique, informal role playing in the form of a sociodrama has been used effectively to help students develop empathy for the responsibilities of the various roles. (Sociodrama is treated in Chapter 12.) For example, it is frequently desirable to have the verbose individual assume the role of the "quiet one." Similarly, the timid person can profit substantially after the "ice is broken" in a "safe" role-playing situation. To encourage selective contributions, verbose individuals may be required to write out their comments prior to making them. Techniques for increasing attention to nonverbal expressions (for example, nods, winks, and hand gestures) also may be useful. By noting these, the chairperson or leader can often draw the individuals using them into the discussion.

How Are Small Groups Organized?

Short-lived groups are informal ones, often organized by assigning students numbers and placing those with the same number in the same group. For example, in a

---

[7] Gorman, *Teachers and Learners: The Interactive Process,* ch. 4.

class of twenty-five students, all number one students would be placed in the same group, thus making five groups of five students each. At other times, interest is the basis for determining group structure.

Long-lived groups normally have a chairperson and a leader. The chairperson is appointed or selected; the leader emerges informally as the group begins to function. The chairperson usually has specific duties to perform in order to facilitate effective operation of the discussion. These include introducing the topic, providing transitions between speakers, summarizing the discussion from time to time, and recording or having someone record the points or questions brought back to the rest of the class. In short-lived groups, a chairperson may not be needed. It is usually desirable, however, to have someone responsible for recording points and questions to be discussed later by the entire class. If small groups are used extensively, each student should have the opportunity for serving in various service and role capacities. Some training in these areas is usually needed.

How Are Small-Group Processes Evaluated?

Evaluators of small groups are primarily interested in group cohesion and its influence on group progress. Individual contributions to the group may also be evaluated. The criteria used to evaluate large groups are different from those used to assess small groups since large groups, because of their size, cannot promote face-to-face interactions.

Conventional evaluation that assesses the acquisition of knowledge and application of concepts is inappropriate for assessing small groups since their basic function is to promote group reflection or problem-solving experiences. The major aspects of critical thinking that should be tested include identification of critical issues, recognition of underlying assumptions, analysis of evidence, and drawing of warranted conclusions. Multiple-choice items from selected case or anecdotal materials are useful in this connection.

Small-group processes bridge the gap between teacher-led presentations and individualized study activities. Much individualized study features small groups of students working on common problems. Thus it is imperative that small-group activities emphasize the essentials of group interaction. These include the communication of ideas, listening activities, and group participation.

The group evaluation sheet shown in Table 5-1 is an effective device for assessing group interaction as is the group member rating summary provided in Figure 5-1.

How Can Small-Group Members Facilitate Group Decision-Making Processes?

In addition to assuming the task roles discussed previously, individuals can contribute to group progress by first not judging one another's contributions,

TABLE 5-1   *Group Evaluation Sheet* *

GROUP MEMBER RATINGS

Directions: Rate each group member, including yourself, on all four questions. Rate all members on one question before going on to the next question. To make your ratings: read the descriptions, A, B, and C for each question. Then choose and record the appropriate number from the following scale.

A			B			C		
If the person is more like A than B record:			If the person is more like B than like A or C record:			If the person is more like C than B record:		
Much More	Somewhat More	Slightly More	Almost Like A	Between A and B	Almost Like B	Slightly More	Somewhat More	Much More
⑨	⑧	⑦	⑥	⑤	④	③	②	①

1. *How clearly does he/she communicate ideas, information and/or suggestions?*

A. This person is extremely easy to understand. He/she gets to the point and is neither too detailed nor too general. An outstanding communicator.

B. This person is, generally, an adequate and satisfactory communicator.

C. This person is often hard to understand. It is because he/she often speaks in generalities—or rambles—or assumes too much—or gives too many confusing details. A poor communicator.

2. *How actively does he/she try to understand the ideas and suggestions of others?*

A. This person really tries to find out what others mean and how they see a situation whether he agrees or disagrees with them. An active and superior listener.

B. This person is, generally, an adequate and satisfactory listener.

C. This person makes likkle effort to understand what others mean. Seldom checks how well he understands what another has said. It may be because he is indifferent to others' ideas or because he assumes that he understands. He is often formulating own remarks rather than listening. A poor listener.

3. *How actively and effectively does he/she participate in the group's work?*

A. This person actively and enthusiastically pre-

B. This person usually prepares for and partici-

C. This person seldom offers his/her resources to

pares for an participates in the work of the group. He often initiates, proposes, and analyzes group tasks and goals. An excellent group participant.

pates in an adequate and satisfactory manner.

the group. He often appears silent, listless, or bored. Seldom prepares, initiates, or helps group to define or solve problems. An ineffective and passive group participant.

4. *How effectively does he/she encourage and support the participation of others?*

A. This person makes it quite easy for others to actively participate by encouraging members to speak freely and by supplying warm and supporting comments. An excellent facilitator.

B. Usually, this person adequately facilitates and encourages the participation of other group members.

C. This person makes it difficult for others to feel free to share; seldom supports others; seldom yields; doesn't seem to value others' contributions. A poor facilitator.

---

* Developed by Dr. Gerald Moulton, Associate Professor of Education, Arizona State University. (Used by permission.)

Name _____

	Group Member Names															Average
1. Communicates ideas																
2. Listens to ideas of others																
3. Participates in group work																
4. Facilitates participation of others																

Directions

1. Using the above instruction sheet as a guide, rate each member of your group including yourself.
2. Enter your name on a second summary rating form. Permit each group member to record his or her ratings of your performance.
3. Enter your average rating for each of the four criteria.

FIGURE 5-1 *Group Member Rating Summary*

especially if the judgments are negative ones. Making judgments puts the "offended" individual on the defensive and inhibits him or her from making further contributions. Acknowledging a previous contribution by linking it with a new idea is useful, however.

Second, group members should not express personal goals since doing so only confuses and delays achievement of the group task. In long-lived groups, an individual may force the group to pay attention to a personal problem. Such an individual likely needs the help of the instructor or a specialist.

Third, every group member should be willing to devote sufficient time to developing a solution to the task problem. Group deliberation cannot be rushed. Efforts to do so only result in frustration and a general feeling of resentment for what are often recognized as autocratic tactics. Impatience and the desire for faster progress can be curbed by taking "deep breaths" throughout or by doodling.[8] Occasional breaks for promoting social interaction are also useful in long-lived groups.

The Value of Small Groups

The small group provides each member with an opportunity to participate and thereby to influence decision making.

Such face-to-face learning situations promote an atmosphere of cooperation and empathy seldom achieved in other learning situations.

Empathy does not mean uncritical acceptance of ideas but rather the ability to "feel" why people believe as they do.

A basic strength of small-group techniques is their contribution to open-mindedness. Many students tend to take extreme positions and to jump to conclusions. Some experience difficulty in listening to other points of view. Small groups thus contribute to patience, tolerance, and eventually to modification of one's stand if it cannot withstand the test of scrutiny.

Small-group techniques necessitate skills in communication. Since advocacy is not a goal, ideas are not attacked. Opposing views are better expressed as questions; the right to full self-expression is assured; and differences are reconciled as nearly as possible. Consequently, clarity of expression is encouraged as well as the art of listening—actually hearing what the other person is saying.

Limitations of, and Problems with, Small Groups

Small-group techniques relegate the instructor's role to that of a recorder-observer. When used as a vehicle for problem solving, the small group forces the teacher to

---

[8] Gerald Phillips and Eugene C. Erickson, *Interpersonal Dynamics in the Small Group* (New York: Random House, 1970), p. 28.

accept problem solutions with which he or she may not agree. Some teachers have difficulty withholding judgment pertaining to matters of extreme controversy.

There is the danger of overcooperation; each member may become so solicitous of the feelings of others that direct action is avoided for fear of offending someone.

Sometimes individual members play destructive roles. Such roles, identified as blocker, special interest peddler, and aggressor, may originate from one's failure to maintain an open mind.

Small-group techniques require adequate time and resources for investigation of issues. They presuppose adequate preparation. Too little or too much structuring may be destructive to this instructional approach.

Appropriate evaluation of small-group processes is extremely difficult. The intrusion of any sort of *individual* evaluation while students are interacting in small-group situations is likely to have undesirable effects on the outcome.

Teachers must avoid group therapy since this is a task for a specialist. Small-group procedures emphasize task goals (for example, problem solving), whereas the therapy group emphasizes individual feelings and attitudes as they relate to self-concepts.

Illustrated Small-Group Experiences

I. Useful in business classes

Business letter writing

Group students into five-member committees. Each committee select a chairperson and a recorder.

A. The assignment is to invite a panel of speakers to present a topic to the class or to a school business club.

B. Committee decides on its approach, the details of the investigation, the development of the message, and the final composition.

C. Recorder types the letter.

D. Letters are exchanged, and each committee assumes the role of the invited panel of speakers. A reply must be prepared.

E. Acceptance depends on the committee's reaction to the unit. Was the invitation courteous? Were details clearly defined?

F. In addition, a short critique of letter invitations and replies is prepared by each committee.

G. Class discussion, using overhead projections of committee letters, follows.[9]

---

[9] Based on Gayle Sobolik, "Let's Move . . . to Appoint Committees," *Business Education Forum* 23 (November 1968): 20.

Since the project was recommended as a learning experience, no letter grades were given. As a follow-up activity, individual letters of invitation and reply were prepared and marked.

II. Useful in English classes

Novel study (The Scarlet Letter)

The objective is to have students understand the relevance of the book to their own lives.

A. Teacher prepares three penetrating questions for each group (of four or five each) to discuss for one or two class periods.

B. Questions:
   1. Why, after the group has tried and condemned Hester Prynne, but at the same time left her free to come and go as she pleases, does Hester, in fact, decide to stay?
   2. Why and under what altered circumstances does she at a later date settle on a plan of flight?
   3. And finally, why does the flight not materialize, or rather to phrase the question more in keeping with the novel's suggestions at this point, why is the scheme doomed even before it is tried?

C. Teacher acts as a resource person.

D. Use of student observers or video tape is employed.[10]

A general class discussion emphasizing different group responses may provide a fruitful follow-up experience.

III. Useful in science classes

A. Since the results of research often require years of study, high-school students may be grouped in pairs for the purpose of science research.

B. Each pair of students consists of the researcher and his understudy.

C. The researcher is responsible for the project, and the understudy will move into the researcher's role when he graduates.

D. The understudy, therefore, should be a year or two younger than the researcher in order that he can move into the position of researcher when the researcher graduates.[11]

This gives a continuity to research. When students pursue long-range problems, they work with the same kind of advanced research problems as studied by scientists.

IV. Useful in any class

An autolecture is essentially a synchronized coupling of a cassette tape recorder, a wide-range amplifier, a high-fidelity loudspeaker, and an overhead

---

[10] David M. Litsey, "Small-Group Training and the English Classroom," *English Journal* 58 (September 1969):920-27.

[11] B. Brown, *Education by Appointment: New Approaches to Independent Study* (West Nyack, N.Y.: Parker Publishing Co., 1968), p. 134.

projector, all capable of filling a room with a clear sound and a wall with a brilliant image, even with room lights on.

A. Makes use of programmed materials.

B. Follow with a seminar group discussion, based upon questions raised by the autolecture.[12]

    The technique has the advantage of combining many facets of instruction and all the senses in learning. The teacher need not be present during the autolecture. It is normally run by a teacher aide. He or she may or may not be present during the seminar experience.

[12] Arthur J. Bergman, "Seminar/ Autolecture," *Today's Education* 57 (December 1968): 33-36.

chapter 6

THE SEMINAR METHOD

Overview

Key Concepts

1. The seminar is a self-directed, democratically oriented method.
2. Group leadership replaces the traditional authority of the instructor.
3. Grades, if necessary, are usually based on the quality of an individually prepared seminar paper.
4. The round table discussion serves as the basic reference or focal point of the seminar.
5. Seminar reports may employ a variety of instructional techniques as long as a forum session is provided.

New Terms

1. Seminar   A small group of individuals (about twenty to twenty-five people), whose major purpose is to identify, explore, and share the results of in-depth analysis of problems.
2. Group Facilitator   An individual, usually the instructor, who has the responsibility for ensuring that the seminar will function in a democratic manner.
3. Cohesion   Free and uninhibited group interation in which total participation is encouraged. A face-to-face group is employed in a cooperative atmosphere.
4. Critique   A brief report outlining the basic concepts that will subjected to an in-depth group analysis during the seminar.
5. Seminar Report   A report discussing the basic problem-solving steps pursued by the individual writer. These steps include problem identification, analysis of data, hypotheses, and final solution. The report is usually shared with the total seminar group.

Seminar classes are offered by practically every college and university. They are also rapidly gaining popularity in both public and private schools and in private business enterprises. There are probably as many kinds of seminars as there are people who attend them. Seminars range in size from five to fifty students; they can be as short as thirty minutes or as long as three hours; they can meet once a day, once a week, once a month, or as infrequently as once a term or semester. In a few seminars, the students assume total responsibility for developing and directing the learning experiences.

The seminar method originated in the early German university that sought to "teach not simply knowledge but how to garner or create knowledge."[1] The method probably represented the first attempt to expand the professor's role from that of a provider of information to a facilitator of group reflection on information and problems. Because the term "seminar" is often used interchangeably with the terms "conference," "symposium," "workshop," "institute," "study group," and "enrichment program,"[2] no wonder there is confusion about this technique that often is responsible for its ineffective use. While not all teachers will agree with the author's analysis, a serious attempt has been made to clarify the intent, purpose, and structure of an originally viable and currently often used instructional method.

Fundamental Properties

Confusion over the seminar method can be traced, in part, to a failure to understand its theoretical basis. All too often the college professor erroneously assumes that the seminar can be handled in much the same way as a large lecture class. As should become evident from reading the following section of this chapter, the seminar method is based on a theoretical framework differing sharply from those of more traditional modes of instruction.

What Purposes Are Served by the Seminar?

Basically, the seminar is designed for those courses or experiences where an organized body of content does not exist. Its most basic function is to provide a forum for reflection on, or discussion of, problems. Both problems and essential background information are usually identified and pursued by students themselves. Preliminary reading of text materials and other common sources is assumed; sometimes this

---

[1] Hugh Hawkins, *Pioneer: A History of the Johns Hopkins University* (Ithaca: Cornell University Press, 1960), p. 225.

[2] Carolyn M. Owen, "The Seminar," *Improving College and University Teaching* 18 (Summer 1970): 203-5.

information is briefly summarized during the seminar. In short, students assume basic responsibility for their own learning.

In addition to critical examination of issues, students usually pursue reading and writing experiences of their own choice, often associated with both class and individual problems. They then share the results of their investigations with other class members. Considerable emphasis is placed on self-evaluation, a process enhanced by the organized group structure.

Most graduate or advanced seminars include an exercise in communication requiring students to describe and explain their major findings rather than to defend or support a position. (The written critique prepared by the student provides the supporting reasons or justification.) This exercise provides a basis for serious reflection on the problem. As a result, students learn valuable strategies for interacting in groups. Learning is further enhanced when group cohesion is experienced (see Chapter 5).

What Group Size and Time Limit Are Recommended?

The seminar class is usually small. The controlling factor is the specific nature of individualized and group tasks. If extensive individualized input is expected, adequate time must be made available. One way of "making needed time" is to limit group size. Groups exceeding twenty or twenty-five students are likely to become unwieldy, resulting in some loss of purpose. While there is no minimum group size, most class instructors prefer ten or more students. The group must be large enough to permit diverse points of view to be discussed. It must be remembered that each seminar member, in a sense, is a resource person.

The length of a seminar depends on the purposes sought. There must be adequate time for students to develop suitable problems, to examine them extensively, and to share their findings in a reflective group setting. Thus seminars of less than three weeks in duration are often discouraged. Certainly, it makes no sense to conduct a one- or two-day seminar. Seminars several weeks in length are quite effective since they permit adequate time for the development of group cohesion.

What Democratic Processes Are Involved?

The seminar is a problem-centered experience. With the guidance of the instructor, participants identify and clarify problems and also develop their own methods and techniques of study and investigation. At no time are they "told what to do." Emphasis is on development of individuality and leadership within the social group. Leadership is substituted for authority. Indeed, ultimate authority for the experiences may be maintained by the group.

Most seminar classes or groups are elective in nature. Grades, if given at all, are *not* based on the acquisition of a definite body of content or knowledge. Instead, the participants evolve their own assessment procedures. In short, the seminar emphasizes a learning process of experiencing, doing, and reacting under the leadership of the group itself.

What Theoretical Framework Is Needed?

Without some basic, unifying structure, the seminar becomes a disjointed group of presentations. A body of concepts must be welded into a dynamic context. Sometimes, the instructor can accomplish this by preparing an ordered list of topics for weekly discussion. All too often, however, the coherent logic linking the various facets of the experience is not clear to students. Time is needed for fitting each individual and group contribution into an overall pattern.

By requiring each student to submit a week before the seminar a brief list of concepts to be developed, the instructor can adequately provide the needed theoretical framework and also note the strengths and weaknesses of the various concepts submitted. As a facilitator, however, the instructor should withhold judgement on these concepts during the group discussion of them. The loopholes in them should be discovered by the students themselves.

Individual contributions to the seminar group usually consist of brief critiques of one or more selected problems submitted by the students to be subjected to in-depth analysis during the seminar. Even some advanced students need help in preparing critiques. For example, students sometimes confuse procedural statements with substantive statements. In reviewing a book, an individual may merely state what the author tried to accomplish or present a list of quotes with which he or she does or does not agree. A valid critique goes much further. Basic concepts are described and explained in minimum detail. The student is not expected to defend the position of the writer, but is expected to provide evidence supporting the author's views. This sets the stage for further group discussion and reflection.

What Decision-Making Processes Are Involved?

Although problem centered, the seminar basically is not a decision-making group in which complex plans of action must be developed. At certain times, however, the seminar does serve as a decision-making body, in particular early in the experience when the group must identify and clarify problems for in-depth exploration. Other needed decisions concern small-group reporting techniques and evaluation procedures, for example.

In a democratic group, each member is responsible for supplying input and objectively evaluating the contributions of others. As discussed in Chapter 5, cohesiveness is a desirable quality to have in decision-making processes and during the seminar. Balanced input, another desirable feature of decision making, is extremely difficult to achieve in interacting groups. Frequently, certain outspoken individuals dominate group proceedings and through their persuasive skills may limit the scope of the decision-making process.

The basic function of group deliberation is to deal with the assigned task. At the same time, each individual is conscious of social-emotional concerns. Actually, short periods of focusing on the problem are usually interspersed with longer periods of social distractions. Social-emotional concerns of the individual, tangential discussions, and extended drifting comments, for example, seriously impede the decision-making process. Unless carefully handled, the group may complete the task with a few highly generalized proposals that reflect only to a small degree the basic needs and desires of the seminar members.

The problem-solving process has a definite structure, proceeding from problem identification, to fact-finding, to proposing hypotheses, to reaching a consensus on the best course of action needed. Each step involves two distinct phases, namely, fact-finding and evaluation. The fact-finding phase deals with identifying problems and data sources and proposing hypotheses or possible solutions to the problem. Evaluation, if imposed too early and too rigidly, can seriously impede the decision-making process (see Chapter 13). Because the quantity and quality of group interaction vary with each phase, the selection of the instructional method is a critical decision for the instructor.

Seminar Techniques

The seminar group is a springboard for a variety of instructional activities. Almost any method may be employed to further the purposes of the group, provided the technique affords the opportunity for group reflective processes. Even a short lecture is occasionally appropriate if it is followed by a forum session. Some of the more common techniques are described in the following section.

What Is the Function of a Round Table Discussion?

The term "round table" signifies the typical seating arrangement in a seminar. This arrangement tends to discourage the use of unnecessary lecture techniques. Group discussion is held in which all group members enter into a free exchange of ideas.

The round table discussion is used to identify problems, to develop small group or individualized activities, to schedule presentations, and to provide a forum for other occasions when total interaction is needed. Assuming the role of the resource person, the instructor encourages the group to select its own leader(s) and helps to resolve any difficulties that may arise.

Although much of the work and activities of the seminar members is done in small groups, the round table always serves as the forum to which all group members are responsible for reporting their various activities and findings. Total participation is encouraged. In large seminar groups, it may be desirable to employ a steering committee for coping with special problems and for making recommendations to the total group.

What Is the Place of Small-Group Techniques?

Although the seminar group is usually limited in size to a maximum of twenty to twenty-five students, the optimum small group consists of four to six individuals. Like the family in many respects, the small group provides opportunities for face-to-face interaction needed in the pursuit of difficult problems.

The small group may rejoin the round table for purposes of sharing its findings with the total seminar group or choose one or more formal procedures, (for example, oral report, debate, or resource panel) to be followed by a round table forum.

What Written Responsibilities Are Involved?

Seminar writing usually falls into two broad categories: (1) a *précis,* or brief summary of what has been read, and (2) a *critique* of some major problem to be discussed.

As previously indicated, preparation of critiques is considerably more difficult than preparation of précis. Instead of spending time with details, the individual should get to the root of the problem and describe in concise, simple terms what the problem was, how it was pursued, and what the findings were. Supporting data should be offered but kept to a minimum. These papers should be outlined rather carefully since they may be presented to each member of the seminar prior to oral presentations. It may be desirable to use the small group as a testing ground for the oral presentations.

Sometimes, seminar writing may involve composing position or evaluation papers. One or more individuals may write a report that takes as positive a position as the data will permit. Others may write a report reflecting a negative position. Popham sees such adversary reporting as extremely beneficial because of its "partisanship-perspective" benefits.[3] He suggests that a third individual edit both reports to ensure that they contain a comparable degree of depth and analysis. Once the reports are ready, seminar decision-making procedures can be employed.

How Is the Brainstorming Technique Employed?

Brainstorming is an especially valuable technique for generating ideas on a specific problem. Indeed the term literally means "storming the brain for ideas." The technique is most effective in groups of twelve people. As illustrated fully in Chapter 13, the leader identifies a specific problem needing exploration. To illustrate: "How can we present our findings to the total seminar group." This problem is placed on the chalkboard for all to see.

Four basic rules are placed in a prominent place and explained:

1. Criticism is ruled out.
2. "Freewheeling" is welcomed.
3. Quantity is desired.
4. Combination of ideas is sought.

---

[3] James Popham, *Education Evaluation* (Englewood Cliffs, N.J.: Prentice-Hall, Inc., 1975), p. 262.

One or two recorders are appointed or selected. Ideas are accepted without evaluation. When this rule is violated, the leader may merely knock on the desk, indicating that the contribution is out of order. Ideas that relate to, or expand on, previous comments may be recognized by a snap of the fingers.

When the free flow of ideas slows down, the leader may suggest related categories within the problem area in order to stimulate thought. The session proceeds until the group "runs dry" of ideas. Afterthoughts are encouraged and added at the next session. A brainstorming session usually lasts for fifteen minutes.

Generated ideas are often combined and evaluated in a follow-through discussion. They are implemented in the manner most fitting to the purpose involved. If it is a matter of selecting a technique for presenting findings to the entire seminar group, each subgroup may work from the master list in its own way.

The brainstorming session is an extremely useful technique when full participation is desired. By eliminating evaluation until *later,* the free flow of creative ideas is encouraged. Little status hierarchy is evident. Brainstorming is probably most effective after some group cohesion is developed. At all times during the brainstorming session, the individuals must resist the temptation to evaluate or discuss ideas.

How Is the Nominal Group Technique (NGT) Used?

The Nominal Group Technique (NGT) recently has received widespread attention in decision-making business groups.[4] The term "nominal" refers to a step of the technique in which verbal communication is prohibited. The NGT combines both verbal and nonverbal stages. The technique has proven effective in situations such as the seminar in which all members share in decision making. Perhaps the most important aspect of the NGT is the opportunity it provides to develop a list of working problems for each seminar member (or small group).

The NGT proceeds as follows:[5]

Step 1: Setting the stage. The teacher provides a brief introductory explanation of the goals involved, emphasizing the importance of total participation. Flip charts or chalkboard space for accommodating the ideas from small groups of seven to nine individuals must be provided. The NGT problem must be clearly visible to all members. The problem is phrased in the form of a policy question. To illustrate, "What major ideas, in the (seminar title) would you like to examine?" If the group is larger than nine, appropriate subgroups are created, each with its own leader.

Step 2: Generation of ideas in writing. The leader(s) begins by repeating the question before the group(s), illustrating it with an appropriate example. All requests

---

[4] Andre L. Delbecq et al., *Group Techniques for Program Planning* (Glenview, Ill.: Scott, Foresman and Company, 1975).

[5] This material is summarized from Delbecq's analysis, Ibid., pp. 66-69.

for further clarification are avoided. Each member is asked to write down ideas for the task, in brief phrases or statements on three by five index cards. Five minutes are usually allowed for this task. No interruptions are permitted.

Step 3: Round-robin recording of ideas. Using flip charts or a chalkboard for recording so that all can see, each individual is asked, in turn, to present *one* idea. The process is repeated until all ideas have been offered. Simple, brief statements are encouraged. Whenever possible, the student's own words are used. New ideas that relate to or develop another person's point are encouraged. Discussion of ideas is forbidden.

Step 4: Serial discussion for clarification. Each idea is examined briefly for the purpose of clarification. Emphasis is placed on the total idea rather than on the individual words used. Although the logic behind ideas can be clarified, this is *not* the time to discuss the relative merits of the proposals. As Delbecq states, ". . . the purpose of serial discussion is to disclose thinking, not to resolve differences of opinion."[6] One should avoid forcing the originator of an idea to clarify his or her individual contribution.

Step 5: Preliminary vote on high-priority ideas. Each member is asked to select from the entire list a specific number (five, for example) of high-priority ideas and to write them on a separate card. Once this process is completed, the cards are ranked in order of priority.

The leader then asks each member to select the card with the most important idea, to write the number five on it in the lower right hand corner, and to underline the number three times. Next, the *least important idea* is selected, and the card is numbered one. In similar manner, all cards are selected and numbered.

The leader collects the cards, reassembles the subgroups, and enters the numbers on a master flip chart or chalkboard. Duplications are eliminated. Those ideas receiving the greatest number of points are selected for discussion in subsequent small-group activities.

In certain situations, increased judgmental accuracy may be desired. If so, steps four and five may be repeated until only one priority idea is selected.

How Is Panel Discussion Used?

Sometimes the small group may elect to discuss its problem in a panel format for the benefit of the seminar group. In effect, the panel is a round table discussion restricted to one small part of the total class. Attention may be directed to filling in gaps in the presentation, to raising questions, or to offering and discussing alternative interpretations of the problem.

---

[6] Ibid., p. 53.

The panel presentation has the advantage of encouraging the total participation of its members. Above all, the preparation of speeches must be avoided. Individual contributions are limited to one or two brief statements of less than one-minute duration. (This technique is described fully in Chapter 8.)

The problem for the panel can be either one of factual enlightenment or of policy resolution. (The latter likely should be emphasized in the seminar.) The panel analyzes the problem and offers valid hypotheses or possible solutions to it. In the analysis phase, lasting for about two-thirds of the panel period, facts or data are presented and evaluated. The analysis phase is followed by a critical evaluation of the possible solutions developed. All solutions must be offered before any one is evaluated.

The forum following the panel presentation is of greatest importance to the seminar group. It should not be rushed, even if it continues beyond a single class session since this is the place where total group reflection is often at its best. Additional alternatives should be encouraged.

How Is the Symposium Employed?

If a problem is easily divided into subproblems, a symposium may be desired. This consists of a series of talks given by guest speakers invited to the seminar. Presentations follow a predetermined order. There is no direct interaction between speakers or between speakers and the audience. Succeeding speakers, of course, may modify their presentations on the basis of what previous ones have said. Seating arrangement is usually in a straight line as there is no intra-group communication.

The chairman ensures that each speech relates to the preceding one and that strict time limits are observed. Speakers exceeding the time limit may be asked to summarize their points in one or two sentences.

For the symposium to be a valid seminar technique, it must be followed by a round table discussion in which the speakers participate; thus total group interaction is encouraged. This is an ideal time for integrating different points of view or conflicting evidence. The leader should work toward this end. The forum may well exceed the total time devoted to the original presentations.

One major difficulty associated with the symposium is its lack of control over invited speakers. Most guest speakers, however, usually appreciate some advance guidance. Thus the instructor might well provide a brief written outline of what is desired. This can be developed by the seminar group.

How Is Dialogue Used?

A dialogue is a conversation between two people. When used in connection with the seminar, it may involve the questioning by the instructor or designated leader of an "expert," often a resource speaker. The invited participant does not rehearse or come with prepared speeches, although the group leader may prepare a list of questions submitted by the seminar group. Questions will vary in terms of needs.

The major advantage of the dialogue is that it ensures that the purposes and needs of the group receive top priority at all times. The leader uses questions to promote clarification of difficult points and to keep the presentation moving smoothly from one point to the next. Through advance agreement with the seminar group, he or she may play the role of "devil's advocate" in order to examine ideas in depth.

Although technically the entire seminar group could accomplish the same objectives in a round table discussion, one individual is usually better able to cope with distracting elements as they arise. When the entire group is involved, somebody is likely to desire an expansion of a related issue, thus unnecessarily slowing the progress. Digression from the main purpose can be handled efficiently through introduction of a skillfully worded question from the leader.

The dialogue concludes with a forum session in which all members of the seminar participate. As in the case of the symposium, the expert may be asked to join the group discussion so that points can be clarified and additional comments discussed.

What Function Is Served by a Colloquy?

If invited experts have difficulty communicating with the panel members, it may be desirable to organize a special subgroup lay panel, or colloquy, to question the experts in detail and to enable them to provide additional information. At no time, however, do the experts engage in group discussion.

A recent modification of the colloquy is its use with a regular panel discussion. In this case, the chairperson can interrupt panel proceedings when he or she feels there is confusion by asking for comments or questions from the audience. After clarification, the panel continues with its task. The technique has the advantage of contributing to the effectiveness of the panel by enhancing communication between the panelists and the audience.

One disadvantage of the colloquy is the tendency of invited guests or the class to "take over" the discussion. The teacher or leader must adhere to rigid rules of procedure in order to stop such "discussion" when a specific point has been clarified sufficiently. This is sometimes a difficult task. One way of handling the matter is to suggest that further examination of the point can be done in the post-panel forum session.

The forum that follows a colloquy involves all group members and is often an extremely fruitful session since the special panel may have "cleared the air" for in-depth probing of technical points.

How Is the Oral Report or Lecture-Forum Employed?

The oral report is a viable technique for sharing information with the seminar group. It is given by the guest speaker or group leader. Rather than emphasize facts and details, however, the report should focus on important concepts. The same holds true for the lecture. (Lecture techniques are treated more fully in Chapter 10.)

One way of discouraging a guest speaker from dwelling on unnecessary facts and details is to provide him or her with an advance organizer (see Chapter 10). Another informal but useful technique frequently utilized is a series of key questions, submitted in advance of the occasion. The Nominal Group Technique, described earlier in this chapter, can also be useful in preventing diversions from the main issue.

What Is the Role of the Instructor?

The seminar highlights the instructor's role as a group facilitator. As such, the instructor must resist the temptation to dictate the seminar proceedings or to give solutions and answers to the class. Basically, the instructor's function is to ensure that democratic procedures are observed during every step of the seminar. Some of the professor's responsibilities as a group facilitator include:

Supplying a reading list. A few contemporary articles or books are usually needed to provide students with a common background in the area.

Preparing a sample précis and a sample critique. As indicated earlier, students need careful guidance in the preparation of written work. Carefully prepared examples, accompanied with appropriate explanations, help encourage in-depth investigation.

A précis essentially is a brief explanation of, and justification for, an article and contains one's impressions of it. A critique usually involves a listing and explanation of concepts, designed to clarify the author's contribution. The critique is often used to set the stage for a round table discussion. A critique normally is *not* used as a defense of a given position or issue. Rather it sets the stage for in-depth exploration of the problems and issues by the seminar members.

Preparing students for developing seminar papers. Seminar papers can take many forms, depending on group purposes. Even though students may be organized into small groups for investigative activities, *individual* papers are usually required. The outline of such a paper might include the following elements: rationale, hypothesis, supporting data, alternative interpretations of the data, and decision or solution reached (if possible). These papers are usually accompanied by an abstract or brief summary. Since they are often critiqued by the entire seminar group, emphasis should be placed on readability.

Preparing students for writing seminar reports. The instructor should make copies of seminar papers available to the entire group at least one week in advance of oral presentations. Thus the individual (or small group) presentation is limited to brief introductory remarks prior to group discussion. It is at this point that gaps and questionable deductions are identified and explored. In effect, the group, after being enlightened, serves as a "sounding board" for further analysis. The instructor is careful to withhold evaluation and judgement until the group has had ample opportunity for discussion of the issue.

Evaluating the seminar experience. If the seminar is a regular college class, individual grades may be necessary, usually determined on the basis of seminar reports. Grades are based on how well the task was accomplished relative to purpose and group-established standards. Norm-referenced or individual comparisons must be avoided since the essence of the seminar is cooperation rather than competition. Tests are usually not employed.

Self-evaluation is also an aspect of the seminar method. Learner independence is emphasized. A round table discussion is often employed in which group members evaluate themselves and the seminar experience. Written appraisals may or may not be needed. This form of self-evaluation has the added benefit of providing feedback to the instructor for conducting future seminars.

The Value of the Seminar Method

The seminar method is democratically oriented, placing responsibility for learning directly on the student.

The seminar features systematic student input, a factor often minimized in more traditional modes of instruction.

The seminar can be adapted to a wide variety of learning situations.

Creativity is encouraged as students actively participate in all aspects of their learning experiences.

Limitations of, and Problems with, the Seminar Method

The seminar may disorient and confuse college students who have become accustomed to being given information and knowledge.

The seminar is generally inappropriate for teaching those areas requiring mastery of an established body of knowledge.

The instructor may have difficulty fully accepting his or her role as a facilitator and may give out too much information.

The seminar approach is designed for small classes. When group size exceeds twenty to twenty-five students, the method becomes increasingly unwieldy.

The seminar demands careful group planning; an ill-prepared instructor may inappropriately identify student talk as group progress.

Illustrated Seminar Experiences

I. A panel discussion group on writing

    A. Each panelist is given a copy of the discussion problem, an outline of the discussion, and a list of sample questions. To illustrate:

Problem: What steps can I take to become an able writer?

Analysis of the problem

        1. What skills are needed?
        2. What are the rewards?
        3. What hazards exist?

Developing hypotheses

        1. Develop a work plan.
        2. Make a start.
        3. Profit from others.

    B. The panelists are introduced and rules of procedure clarified. In a regular panel discussion, the seminar members do not enter into a discussion until the forum period. The leader uses the discussion outline as a guide only.

    C. The panel discussion proceeds without interruption for twenty to forty minutes.

    D. The post-panel forum is conducted. Seminar members are asked to restrict their contributions to concise questions. Resource persons are invited to clarify and expand the discussion. This is *not* the place to challenge points made or to offer counter arguments.

    E. The post-forum discussion is conducted. After the panel is dismissed, the seminar group engages in a round table discussion. At this point any contribution made by panel members can be challenged as the group desires. Thus the panel establishes the basis for extensive group deliberation.

II. As a support method[7]

    Although the preceding chapter deals exclusively with the seminar group, the method can be used in conjunction with other types of classes or experiences for varying periods of time.

    A. Within a lecture series (two-or three-day seminar)

        Useful in (1) setting the stage for a lecture series, (2) as a vehicle for expanding understanding during a lecture series, and (3) as a culminating experience following a lecture series. To illustrate as a culminating experience:

        1. Divide students into small groups.
        2. Each group selects one controversial issue to examine in some depth.
        3. Group presentation to the class.
        4. Class forum.

---

[7]Illustrations II, III, and IV were prepared by Mrs. Betty Schiele who has studied in the German university system. The illustrations were prompted from her experiences at Phillips University, Marburg, West Germany. Used by permission.

B. Within a discussion class (or even a lecture series) for three or more weeks.

Sometimes the seminar can be useful within the framework of a semester course to establish needed background information. After the seminar, the instructor can assume that students are ready for subsequent class experiences. To illustrate from a class on nineteenth century German literature:

1. Instructor outlines the periods to be covered.
2. Students select areas for investigation (in small groups).
3. Small group research and interaction.
    a. Philosophical thought of the period.
    b. Political implications.
    c. Social aspects.
    d. Economic issues.
4. Presentation to the seminar group.
5. Postpresentation forum.

After the seminar, the instructor can assume that students are sufficiently acquainted with the different literary periods and how each influenced the authors. Study of the specific literature can then proceed, using more conventional methods.

III. As a term or semester course to test ideas

This method is currently widely used with graduate students in German universities. Each student selects a research problem for study and analysis. The problem may contradict accepted theory. The seminar is then used:

1. To test ideas and theories.
2. To exchange ideas.
3. To evaluate the methods employed.
4. To ferret out unsound concepts.

At all times the instructor serves as an observer and resource person. Group interaction in this type of seminar is restricted to the forum that follows each individual presentation.

IV. As an inter-discipline or inter-university experience

Time span may vary; a three-day minimum is recommended, however.

Two or more disciplines (such as history, sociology, and literature) or two or more universities (within the same discipline) may be studying the same period of history or a similar scientific problem. A seminar involving these groups allows deeper study of varying points of view and affords more insight into the problem area and its possible solutions.

Prior to this seminar, much preparation must be done. It is necessary to decide on an agenda. This permits all involved to gather their research materials for the stated problems and prevents wandering off into vague unprofitable areas. This type of seminar must be structured carefully. For example:

1. Prior intensive study of an area must be done.
2. Common problem areas must exist.
3. A meeting place and a specific agenda must be determined.
4. Time must be allowed for informal discussion and social contact between students. This is especially true if the groups are from different universities. Informal discussion on a one-to-one or small-group basis can be very rewarding and profitable. The suggested time schedule for a three-day seminar:

First day :   1. Arrival
              2. Introductions
              3. Discussion of agenda items and assignment of speakers for each group
              4. Formal introductory session
              5. Adjournment to a social function, informal dinner, etc.

Second day: 1. Opening of discussion of agenda items
              2. Discussion
              3. Adjournment into groups

Third day :   1. Group presentation of conclusions
              2. Summary of proceedings and conclusions
              3. Setting of a date, when appropriate, for the next scheduled seminar

Teachers serve as observers and resource persons.

V. Use of the seminar to promote basic understanding.

Seminar groups are often assembled for exploratory purposes; this is especially true in graduate school. Although students may have an overall perspective of the area, basic knowledge may be totally lacking. According to Sauer,[8] the topical seminar is an especially attractive vehicle for developing curiosity leading to discovery.

A. The leader outlines questions to be asked as well as problematical issues such as incompleteness of data, contradictory information, and gaps of knowledge or information.

B. Students volunteer to study topics they wish to explore. The leader suggests how topics might be developed and how evidence might be sought.

C. While individual inquiries are being made, the seminar meetings deal with reports on journal articles relevant to the overall topic, some of which are abstracts and others of which are critiques. These reports provide a model to the students for the preparation of their own individual papers as does the instructor's help.

D. Reports on selected topics are given. Emphasis is placed on asking significant questions and on further exploration of the issues. Presentation of information is kept to a minimum. Besides an appreciation of what others have done in the pursuit of knowledge, the learner gains an insight into what additional research is needed.

E. Additional research is conducted and may involve an examination of original reports or primary sources. As Sauer adds, such an experience may motivate students to secure missing evidence, to analyze new or alternative hypotheses, or to explore tangential problems. At this point, learners have ceased to rely on others and are on the way to becoming contributers to knowledge.

---

[8]Carl O. Sauer, "The Seminar as Exploration," *Journal of Geography* 75 (February, 1976): 77-81. This illustration is based on Sauer's analysis.

Methods and Techniques:
Focus on the Large Group

Education for all people is dependent on effective instructional groups, both large and small. While there is indeed some merit in the tutorial relationship, the costs involved are often prohibitive. Group interaction is a necessary component of life since a human being is a social animal and thus dependent for his or her existence on the cooperative effort of all people. In today's age of space exploration, traditional boundaries are becoming less important as individuals find it necessary to rely more and more on all the peoples of the world.

The class group does much more than provide a setting for instruction. It lends support, offers direction to those involved, and permits the emergence of leadership, realistic group problem solving, and the application of democratic principles to everyday living. The instructional methods and techniques described in the following four chapters have one important common characteristic: the utilization of the class group structure for enhancing learning. Although the techniques apply to smaller groups as well, they have been developed specifically for large groups of twenty-five or more people.

Chapter 7 concerns questioning strategies, techniques fundamental to all instructional methods and procedures. The entire reflective process depends on appropriately phrased questions just as it does on a well-defined statement of the problem issue. In 1970, 80 percent of all classroom questions asked by public school teachers were at the memory and procedural levels, and this pattern has held true for the last fifty years.[1] If concepts are to be derived inductively, emphasis should be on the higher levels of cognition. The questioning techniques developed in Chapter 7 are based on the Bloom taxonomy of educational objectives.

---

[1] Meredith D. Gall, "The Use of Questions in Teaching," *Review of Educational Research* 40 (December 1970): 707-21.

Chapter 8 offers a systematic approach to the two closely related techniques of class and panel discussion. Except for the lecture method, class discussion is probably the most widely used instructional approach. Students indulge in serious reflection only to the extent that the group setting is conducive to this activity. Although groups of thirty to forty are not the optimum size for class discussion, the technique can still be more effective than it is. A much less used, but often more effective, instructional tool is panel discussion. Again, the misuse of panel discussion has often produced disappointing results. Chapter 8 emphasizes panel discussion, designed to facilitate the problem-solving pursuits of the *entire* class group.

Chapter 9 concerns the student's ability to make applications to real-life situations and problems, the ultimate measure of all learning. This process is greatly enhanced when students connect class experiences to related problems. By taking a *new look* at previous learnings, the student can make important associations and develop new insights. This technique differs from traditional review and drill procedures that too often involve mere repetition of events. Effective drill or practice procedures also must approach a problem from a new angle or from a perspective different from that of the previous learning experience. The current misuse of review and practice procedures serves to underscore the urgent need for thoroughly understanding these basic instructional tools, discussed thoroughly in Chapter 9.

Chapter 10 discusses lecture methods. Teachers have been criticized justifiably for dominating the learning experience. Democratic learning methods, on the other hand, demand considerable individual initiative and independence. Perhaps the "undemocratic" stigma of lecture methods has accounted for their misuse and neglect. Nevertheless, the lecture is still the time-honored method of college and university teaching and at times is the most direct and effective one available. Although lecture methods demand considerable teacher domination, if used appropriately, they need not be stifling or oppressive, as discussed in Chapter 10.

QUESTIONING STRATEGIES

Key Concepts

1. The questioning level employed, in large measure, determines the level of thinking elicited.
2. Appropriately phrased problem questions (for example, policy questions for class discussion) set the stage for high-order questions.
3. Appropriate probing techniques encourage the learner to indulge in the higher process of reflective thought.
4. Higher-order questions necessarily incorporate the lower levels of cognition.
5. Since evaluation questions call for personal reactions, they necessarily overlap with the affective domain.

New Terms

1. Recall Questions Questions requiring the recitation of specific facts, principles, or generalizations. Usually characterized by such words as *who, what, when,* and *where.*
2. Comprehension Questions Questions requiring understanding and manipulation of data through interpretation, summarization, example, and definition. Usually characterized by such key words as *how* or *why.*
3. Analysis Questions Questions requiring taking apart data for the purpose of discovering hidden meaning, relationships, or basic structure. Characterized by using *established criteria* for discovering assumptions, motives, implications, issues, logical fallacies, and so forth.
4. Evaluation Questions Questions requiring judgments, opinions, personal reactions, and criticisms, based on the *learner's own criteria.* Usually characterized by such key words as *should, could, would, in your opinion,* and so forth.
5. Problem (Policy) Questions Open-ended type of questions, often *preplanned* by the teacher, which form the basis for an instructional experience. Often

begin with the word *what* but sometimes may begin with such key words as *why* or *how*. The word *should* or *ought* is stated or implied in the questions.

6. Probing Questions Intermediate questions, providing cues or hints or asking for clarification after the student indicates the inability to respond effectively to an initial question. Designed to lead the learner to the original question by capitalizing on existing knowledge and understanding.
7. Redirection Questions Questions directed to more than one student and often involving reasons or factors or differences of opinion.

Questions to Guide Your Study

1. Review the cognitive, affective, and psychomotor domains of educational objectives (treated in Chapter 2). Why is the question taxonomy developed in this chapter based on the cognitive domain only?
2. How would you judge the adequacy of responses to comprehension questions, to analysis questions, and to evaluation questions?
3. The bulk of any discussion should focus on comprehension questions. Defend or refute.
4. Distinguish between probing and redirection. What factors determine whether one probes or redirects?

Questioning is the heart of teaching and is involved in some way with every method and technique described in this book. Indeed, one might say that a teacher is (or should be) a professional question maker. Asking questions is one of the most effective means of stimulating thinking and learning.

Analysis of classroom discourse (of both teachers and students) reveals at least twelve areas of communication employed. Most of these areas (such as defining, classifying, comparing, evaluating, etc.) involve the use of questions. The evidence indicates, however, that the average teacher is no more skillful in this vital aspect of teaching than students or other lay people. Accordingly, this chapter provides assistance in questioning techniques, an area often neglected in instructional methods classes.

Fundamental Properties

Each instructional method is developed within a framework of critical thinking processes. The classroom question constitutes the teacher's major tool for encouraging thought processes. There are many different kinds of questions, each of which elicits different kinds of responses. If, for example, a teacher requires the recall or memorization of facts, he or she will ask one type of question. If analysis and application are to be stressed, however, a different questioning strategy will be emphasized. Fundamentally, the different kinds of questions parallel the different levels of cognition, described fully in Chapter 2. They also incorporate the affective domain. As Tanner points out,[1] the *receiving* level of the affective domain is essential in cognitive learning since no learning can take place unless the student is receptive. Similarly, the *responding* level of affective learning (interest or satisfaction) influences the quality of cognition since at the affective level, the individual develops opinions and attitudes. How, for example, can an individual examine such problems as the merits of the Social Security System without being influenced by attitudes, feelings, and emotions?

What Implications Does the Socratic Method Have on Learning?

More than two thousand years ago, Socrates developed a teaching method that is still held in high esteem by most college teachers. His fundamental concept of teaching can be expressed by the adage "There are no good answers, only good questions." Through the use of skillful questioning, Socrates was able to lead the learner to a new level of awareness and evaluation of opinions, attitudes, and values that had been taken for granted.[2]

According to McMaster,[3] other equally important aspects of the Socratic method have been almost completely overlooked by today's teacher. First, Socrates tailored his method to the discipline of philosophy. Few scholars would question the importance of self-discovery and self-analysis in value formation. In certain other disciplines, of course, the instructional task may hold few parallels with Socrates' subject field.

Another, less obvious aspect of the Socratic method can be gleaned from the circumstances surrounding Socrates' teaching, namely, that he did not charge fees or require strict attendance, yet *his students followed him.* Why? The reason is a simple one. Socrates' lessons concerned topics that were of interest to students. Indeed, students usually brought up the topic for discussion. As McMaster points out, they were assured an equal part in the ensuing dialogues. Socrates *listened* to what students had to say and probed their thinking with skillful questions. In contrast, today's instructor tends to emphasize what he or she thinks is of importance or of interest. This often varies considerably from the actual needs and interests of students. Although few educators would go so far as to suggest that students should select the topic, some attention must be given to their needs and interests in order to teach more

---

[1] Daniel Tanner, *Using Behavioral Objectives in the Classroom* (New York: The Macmillan Co., 1972), p. 54.

[2] Robert K. McMaster, "Socratic Method: More Than It Seems," *Contemporary Education,* January 1973, pp. 150-51. Many of the ideas in this section are based on McMaster's analysis.

[3] Ibid.

effectively. If this were done, Socrates' basic purpose of helping students move steadily toward the desired goal might be more readily achieved in today's college classes.

How Do Appropriate Sequencing Activities Contribute to Effective Questioning Techniques?

As emphasized throughout this book, instructional methods are merely guides to critical thinking or problem solving, and all employ questioning strategies to accomplish this end. As we shall presently see, questioning procedures usually proceed from specific to general, from simple to complex. *This hierarchy is employed in all phases of problem solving.* It is useful to divide the cognitive process of a lesson into three distinct sequences of activities: data gathering, data processing, and abstracting. As Hennings points out,[4] data gathering involves defining terms, assembling facts, providing examples, and making judgments; data processing involves drawing relationships and relating activities; and abstracting involves going beyond the data and generalizing, predicting, and concluding.

By planning questions around these distinct stages of critical thinking, the teacher can lead the learner toward problem resolution. Such a technique is especially vital since no more than a few key questions can be prepared in advance of any lesson. It provides a framework for a planned sequence of questions that essentially are formulated at the time of the actual instructional experience.

What Strategy Functions May Be Achieved through Questioning Procedures?

In addition to their use in guiding critical thinking, questioning processes contribute to the broad scheme of teaching strategy in at least two basic ways. These have been described as centering and expansion functions by Hunkins.[5] The *centering or focusing function* is used to converge student thinking on a particular topic or aspect of a topic. Perhaps the most easily recognized aspect of the centering function is the instructor's initial attempts to focus on a particular lesson. Questions are used to make students remember what they have learned and thus to develop a broad conceptual framework for the lesson. This is one way of developing an advance organizer (see Chapter 10). The centering function is also used to develop interest within a particular lesson. Discovery or inquiry techniques are applied, or an

[4]Dorothy G. Hennings, *Mastering Classroom Communication* (Pacific Palisades, Calif.: Goodyear Publishing Co., 1975), p. 143.

[5]Francis P. Hunkins, *Questioning Strategies and Techniques* (Boston: Allyn and Bacon, Inc., 1972), ch. 4.

introductory question is asked to direct attention to the topic. A less obvious, but vital, centering function is employed when questioning techniques are used to help students group data into meaningful combinations. The teacher also employs the centering function when he or she asks what processes of thinking apply and what data are considered significant in problem solving. To illustrate, "Which of these data seem to have the greatest influence on our problem?"

The expansion function is used to extend student thinking to the higher levels of cognition. After identifying significant factors to be considered in solving a problem, the teacher delays closure by asking, "Are there any other factors that might be considered?" The expansion function is employed when relationships are drawn, when information learned in one situation is applied to other situations, and when possible solutions to a problem are proposed. Often, however, when it becomes obvious that the learner is not prepared to cope with such a question, probing techniques are used. They, essentially, are centering functions, designed to guide the learner into developing the needed foundation for *expanding* his or her thinking processes. Even after drawing conclusions (a centering function), students are often encouraged to generalize (expand) them into related situations.

Another, concomitant function is *distribution*. In order to maintain a high level of group thinking, a substantial portion of the group must actively participate in the effort. Questions are distributed to stimulate thinking. In large groups, there is a tendency for a relatively few students to do most of the talking *and thinking*. Others simply drop out of the educational experience.

What Are the Properties of Recall Questions?

The process of critical thinking begins with knowledge of data or facts. Factual questions often involve the key words of *who, what, when,* and *where* and have only one correct answer. The student is merely required to recall information of facts such as dates, events, persons, and places. Also included is recall of basic principles and generalizations. It must be remembered, however, that unrelated facts are quickly forgotten and that memorized knowledge may not represent a very high level of understanding. Above all, concentrating on memory neglects other intellectual processes learned through practice. Solving problems is learned by actual practice rather than by memorizing the inductive conclusions derived by others.

Although they are a necessary starting point, the conscientious teacher is careful to avoid relying too heavily on such low-level intellectual questions. In short, recall questions most appropriately serve to guide the learner into the higher intellectual processes of thinking. As the learning experience progresses, emphasis shifts to higher order questions.

What Are the Properties of Comprehension Questions?

After the learner evidences that he or she has the essential facts well in hand, questions to determine *understanding* are asked. Comprehension questions require the learner to *manipulate* information. One must relate facts, generalizations, and definitions. Key words in this category are *how* and *why*. Whereas recall questions require remembering, comprehension questions require manipulation and modification of data. To illustrate:

1. What factors contributed to Mr. Carter's presidential victory in 1976? (Involves recall of text materials.)
2. How were the campaigns of Mr. Carter and Mr. Ford related? Different? (Involves a comparison of the two campaigns.)

The first question could be comprehensive in nature if the student were required to draw inferences from various media sources. If, however, the answer is found in a textbook or if the information has been previously presented in a lecture or report, the question is merely one of recall. Similarly, the second question may be in the recall category if the answer has been previously given to the student. Thus the *conditions of a question* must be known before the question can be accurately classified. Classification is merely a tool for recognizing the thought processes involved in answering questions. For convenience, application-type questions are included in the comprehension category since the same kind of reasoning is involved except that the student is not informed about the specific idea or concept to be applied.

Comprehension questions may be subdivided into four groups: interpretation, summarization, example, and definition. The first of these, illustrated by the preceding sample questions, asks students to show relationships between facts or ideas such as likenesses, differences, cause and effect, or comparisons. Summarization merely requires students to restate ideas in their own words. Examples call for an illustration of the idea involved. Definition requires students to develop their own explanation of an idea. (It cannot be one that has already been given.)

A major element of questioning tactics is knowing when and how to introduce higher order questions. A comprehension question, for example, may elicit a recall response or perhaps a personal reaction. In such cases, the teacher should probe for the analysis expected. Thus a series of questions may be initiated.

What Are the Properties of Analysis Questions?

The process of analysis involves taking apart information and making relationships in order to discover hidden meaning and basic structure. Students read between the lines, distinguish between fact and opinion, and assess degree of consistency or inconsistency. The science student, for example, distinguishes between relevant and extraneous materials or events. Similarly, the social science student detects unstated assumptions.

Whereas comprehension questions emphasize *understanding,* analysis questions *involve seeking out underlying relationships and organizational patterns.* Certain key words suggest analysis. Among these are assumptions, motives, implications, identification of issues, fallacies, and processes of induction and deduction. Analysis questions ask the student to solve a problem by conscious observance of *established criteria*. They follow established rules of logic and must be consistent with the known facts. The adequacy of responses is judged on the basis of their consistency with these views and conditions.

Analysis questions follow questions of comprehension. The reader will recall the comprehension question cited earlier: "How were the campaigns of Mr. Carter and President Ford different?" An analysis question could then be asked: "What *implications* can be drawn about President Ford's defeat?" (This question assumes that implications have not been drawn by others.)

What Are the Properties of Evaluation Questions?

Included here under evaluation are two categories in the Bloom taxonomy labeled *synthesis* and *evaluation.* Synthesis is the process of reassembling ideas to develop new ones. At this point in the critical thinking process, the learner offers proposals for solving the problem under consideration. Closely followed is the related aspect of evaluation in which the learner critically examines the proposals offered. Evaluation may be deferred if the objective is to generate as many ideas as possible. Frequently, however, evaluation follows immediately after an idea is proposed. Often this is accomplished by a *single student response.* For this reason the processes of synthesis and evaluation are treated as a single aspect of questioning techniques.

Evaluation questions call for responses involving judgments, opinions, personal reactions, and criticisms that are judged on the basis of stated criteria. These criteria may be imposed by the questioner or by the respondent. Such questions usually include or imply such key words as *should, could,* or *would.* Questions such as "In your opinion . . .";"What is your personal reaction . . .";"How would you evaluate . . ."; and "Do you think . . ." call for evaluations. Unless otherwise indicated, the student should state his or her opinion and then provide a basis for such views. It becomes apparent that there is no one "right" or "wrong" answer to such questions. Answers are judged on the basis of how well the response was "defended." Sometimes a teacher may ask a student to state his or her own views. In such cases, the views are defended and judged on the basis of the students frame of reference. For example, "If a presidential election were held today, *what do you think* would be the major issues?" In this case, the student would be expected to *state and support* his or her views. The question could be stated in another way, however. "If a presidential election were held today, how would you evaluate the influence of the energy shortage on the outcome?" In this case the answer must be defended from the frame of reference given by the teacher.

Evaluation questions are influenced by both intellectual and emotional considerations. Accordingly, some responses will tend to be highly biased and opinionated. While this is to be expected on occasion, continued emphasis on acceptable criteria is needed to maintain objectivity.

What Are the Properties of Problem Questions?

Although evaluation questions represent the highest order of complexity, some attention should be directed to those problem questions used as a starting point for most instructional methods. The various methods treated in subsequent chapters are developed within a broad framework of critical thinking or problem solving. Those that embody the entire problem-solving process are developed from broad problems of policy. A question of policy is an open-ended one that implies a needed change from the status quo. It often begins with the word *what* but may begin with such key words as *why* or *how*. The words *should* or *ought* are also stated or implied in the question. For example, "What action should be taken to provide compensatory education for minority groups?"

A problem of policy is most effectively treated when certain definable steps are followed. Each instrumental method has its own unique problem-solving approach. Each level of questioning, previously described, usually will be employed. To illustrate from the above example:

1. What is meant by compensatory education? (recall question)
2. Why is compensatory education needed? (comprehension question)
3. What assumptions are made about the benefits of compensatory education and minority groups? (analysis question)
4. What is your judgment concerning the availability of compensatory education? (evaluation question)

Several or even all questioning levels may be employed in each phase of the problem-solving process. Greater emphasis will be placed on certain questions at each level, however. For example, during the earlier part of a discussion, recall questions will receive considerable emphasis.

Problem questions must be carefully preplanned. If such questions are ill-conceived, the subsequent problem-solving experience is of limited value. The most common error results from confusion between evaluation questions and questions of policy. An evaluation question tends to deal with one possible solution to a problem, whereas a policy question opens the door to any number of possible solutions. In the preceding illustration, for example, one possible solution could be to make compensatory education a preschool requirement for all minorities. Sometimes the teacher, due to his or her own advanced understanding and biases, may word the problem as an evaluation-type question. To illustrate, "Should compensatory education be made a preschool requirement for all minorities?" Under such conditions, discussion tends to be limited to the merits and limitations of the one proposal. Some issues, of course, may have developed to the point that the adoption or rejection of a proposed course of action is all that must be resolved. In this case, a debate is in order. Evaluation questions, however, seldom provide an appropriate setting for discussion and related methods.

An understanding of question levels is only a small part of the art of questioning. As previously indicated, questioning techniques are directly or indirectly associated with all "logical areas" of communication. The techniques described in this section should be useful in establishing and maintaining a climate of continuous critical thinking whenever class questions are utilized.

How Is the Quality of Student Responses Enhanced?

Probing for more adequate answers is a well-known but often neglected technique. Socrates, who lived in the fourth century B.C., became famous for eliciting correct responses through probing procedures. Probing, used when an initial response is inadequate, involves asking *the same student* a series of questions. There are two principal types of probing: *prompting* and *clarification.*

Prompting involves asking a series of recall questions designed to elicit those things the student knows relative to the original question. Prior to the prompting sequence, it may be desirable to rephrase the question to insure that the student understands what is being sought. The procedure is used when the student is suspected of possessing the necessary background knowledge for handling the question. It is designed as a guide in the critical thinking processes. To illustrate:

T: How does the principle of immunization work?
S: I don't know.
T: Using a smallpox vaccination as an example, what happens if the vaccination takes? (a different question, recall in nature)
S: One usually gets sick. He runs a temperature.
T: Good. What are some other symptoms? (recall question)
S: One develops a lesion at the place of the vaccination.
T: Fine. Now what does this suggest to you about smallpox? (comprehension question)
S: That the individual actually has a mild case of the disease, I guess.
T: Your answer is basically correct. Why is an individual made immune to the disease? (analysis question)
S: The body would build up defenses against the disease.
T: That's quite true. With this in mind, why do some individuals become more immune than others from the same dosage? (evaluation question)

As the illustration suggests, the student is not told that an answer is wrong. Instead he or she is encouraged or reinforced at every step to help build confidence. Generally, one should avoid interpreting or rephrasing the student's response. In addition, a teacher should not give up on a student if an answer is not immediately forthcoming. Doing this tends to eliminate an individual from the discussion. In some cases, about 10 percent of a class may make 90 percent of the contribution.

Clarification calls for restatement or expansion of a response. It is usually used when the response is correct but still does not measure up to the teacher's expectations. Instead of giving hints, the teacher asks the student to improve his or her response. Such comments as the following are often used: "Explain." "Would you restate your answer in another way?" "What else can you add?" "Are there other reasons?" To illustrate:

T: What happens in the body when a person is immunized?
S: Well, we are usually immunized against such diseases as smallpox and whooping cough.
T: These are good examples but what actually happens in the body when we are immunized against such diseases?

It may be necessary to do some prompting if the student is unable to clarify the original response satisfactorily.

What Practices Enhance Questioning Effectiveness?

In asking a question that demands considerable thought, the teacher can suggest that an immediate answer is not wanted. This tends to discourage aggressive, hand-waving students from intimidating quieter students who, if given an opportunity to collect their thoughts, might make valuable contributions. To illustrate, "I want you to think quietly on this for a moment . . . then I will call on someone." By learning to read facial expressions (especially the faces of timid students), the teacher will be able to know when students are thinking about a question even though their hands are not raised.

Another technique for enhancing questioning effectiveness is calling on *nonvolunteers*. When students realize that they are not likely to be called on unless their hands are raised, they usually keep their hands down. The few students who do raise their hands tend to monopolize the experience. They are usually those who have a good grasp of the problem and who like the reinforcement answering provides. The teacher, in turn, is reinforced by the apparent group progress suggested by the volunteer respondents. Nonvolunteers, however, most need the experience of active participation.

Student participation is enhanced when all members of the class are asked to respond. The teacher can simply announce, "I will call on individuals whether or not hands are raised." Some teachers use a class observer whose task is to record tally marks on a seating chart for each contribution. The technique serves to remind the teacher of the need for involving as many students as possible. It also enables the teacher to objectively evaluate the participation for any given lesson.

Another way of enhancing questioning effectiveness is through *redirection*. Teacher talk can be minimized by asking questions that elicit several responses, such as those requesting several reasons or factors or in which differences of opinion exist. It may be necessary to cue the group to what is expected by saying, "This question has many parts to it. Please give only one when you answer." Redirection has the added advantage of encouraging students to respond to each other. (All too often the pattern is teacher-question-pupil response.)

Another rather obvious technique is stating a question prior to calling on an individual. The teacher should pause for a few seconds after asking the question and before calling on someone for an answer. If the teacher designates a respondent *prior* to asking the question, the rest of the class will tend to relax and may not even "hear" the question. By pausing, the teacher gives the student time to organize his or her thinking for a thorough answer. The higher level questions usually demand a few seconds for meditation.

What Techniques Interfere with Effective Questioning Practices?

Sometimes, a teacher may fall into the habit of *repeating questions* before asking a student to respond. The problem seems to be related to the teacher's insecurity. Most individuals, for example, who talk excessively have difficulty expressing themselves effectively. Suspecting this, they keep talking, hoping to add clarity with more words. Unfortunately, the end result is often increased confusion. The practice of calling on students who do not raise their hands can contribute to the problem since in order to save face these students may ask the teacher to repeat the question. In such instances, the teacher can immediately move to another student, without repeating the question. Thus the behavior is not reinforced; neither is teacher talk increased.

Answering one's own questions is another annoying habit that is unfortunately difficult to correct and seems tied to a basic psychological need of the questioner. This habit tends to be self-defeating since it definitely increases teacher talk and minimizes student volunteering. Moreover, students are likely to prepare less since the teacher will answer the questions. Students learn that if they wait long enough, the teacher will do their work for them!

Perhaps the most common obstacle to effective questioning is the tendency to *repeat student responses.* In some cases, repetition is needed for clarity or for more effective comprehension. If student answers are repeated often enough, however, students will tend to be satisfied with incomplete answers. As indicated in a previous section, incomplete answers usually call for probing techniques. Responses not heard in all parts of the room should be *repeated by the respondent.* This encourages students to speak distinctly enough to be heard.

In addition, some teachers do not listen carefully to student responses. If a pupil says a few key words or phrases, they make the assumption that the question was answered satisfactorily. This practice can seriously interfere with the reflective process. By maintaining eye contact, asking for a brief rephrasing of the response, then probing when necessary, teachers can encourage students to clarify meaning. Sometimes, students may be asked to write out their responses before answering. Sometimes too, unexpected responses are disregarded. If they were probed, they might contribute immensely to class discussion.

Teachers can easily check up on themselves by taping a lesson occasionally. When the tape is replayed, they are usually shocked when they detect their annoying habits. If a tape recording is not possible, another technique might be to use one or more student recorders. Once the teacher becomes aware of a problem, corrective action can be effected through the use of self-prompts. A game might be played in which the teacher attempts to reduce these practices with each succeeding lesson.

What Are the Characteristics of an Appropriately Phrased Question?

Many leaders encounter difficulty in developing reflective thought because of the way they phrase their questions. A question that calls for a yes or no answer usually discourages discussion. For example, the question "Do you agree with the present U.S. foreign policy toward China?" demands a supplementary "why."

Questions that reflect a given point of view or bias of the teacher are all too common. The question "Why should we embark on an energy-saving program?" begs the answer since it gives support to a stated point of view. The question "Should we allow this appalling situation to continue?" builds in a bias. Beginning teachers have been observed to ask many "Don't you think . . ." questions.

The manner of asking a question has a tremendous influence on the response. Enthusiasm, coupled with a practical, common sense approach (as opposed to textbook language), tends to prompt responses. Closely associated with wording questions properly is handling student questions (or responses) not concerned with the immediate problem or issue being discussed. In this situation, an effective technique is to accept the question as being a good one but to defer the answer for a few moments providing a good reason for doing so.

Questions tend to create considerable anxiety or fear among some students. Inadequate preparation may be an acceptable reason for not responding to a recall question, but it need not eliminate an individual from expressing his or her views on the matter after a proper foundation has been laid. Thus the teacher might well say, "Now that we have discussed some of the facts, what is your personal reaction to the suggestion that. . . ." Such a procedure is likely to make all students feel freer to respond since they realize that the recitation of textbook materials is not expected.

Still another way of breaking the traditional pattern of asking questions is to reverse roles and have students ask the teacher questions. By questioning the teacher, students are better able to perceive the importance of their responses in a chain of events leading to critical thinking.

What Is the Role of Pacing?

Employing techniques that involve students progressively in higher and higher levels of cognition is time consuming. Students need time to organize, relate, hypothesize, and generalize. Yet when the pace is excessively slow, attention soon lags; thinking processes diminish.

Research recently has focused on the relationship between the type of question asked and the "wait-time" involved. Wait-time is defined as the period between the end of one individual's comments and the beginning of another person's remarks. Thus far, evidence suggests that the level of cognition increases when teachers encourage students to pause for *three or more seconds* after asking a question or before responding to another individual's question. The mere act of employing the integrative pause in questioning seems to change the nature of questions asked from those requiring a recall response to those demanding higher level thinking.

Obviously shorter wait-times are appropriate during the data-gathering phase of a question sequence. Thus by varying wait-time, the teacher can give clues about the kind of thinking needed for an adequate response.

There are other dimensions of questioning not yet fully explored. One of these is the time needed by different individuals to complete their answers; some individuals are not as articulate as others. Sometimes individuals, subconsciously realizing an inadequacy in verbal communication, repeat their comments many times, thus generally confusing the rest of the group. This behavior often forces the teacher to interrupt the speaker so that the pace can be picked up again. These students should be encouraged to prepare brief written responses in *advance of their verbal contributions*. Again, this process takes time, but it is often time well spent, especially early in the course.

How Does Nonverbal Language Contribute to Questioning Procedures?

"Actions speak louder than words" is an adage that is almost always totally ignored by college professors. Although all professors use body language, they rarely analyze this basic aspect of communication. According to Grant and Hennings, nonverbal expressions that effectively control communication fulfill the following tasks:

To indicate participants by smiling at, focusing eyes on, orienting body toward, nodding at, pointing at, walking toward, touching a participant.

To react to a participant by using expressions of the face (a frown, a grin), shaking and nodding the head, patting . . . to express approval, making signals such as O.K. with the fingers, shrugging the shoulders, moving hands to brow, holding hands in a way that shows pondering.

To respond to a participant by shaking and nodding the head, moving toward or away from the participant, pointing.

To focus attention by pointing, moving and holding up objects, writing an answer on the board, moving toward an object or participant, shifting gaze or stance.[6]

---

[6] Barbara M. Grant and Dorothy G. Hennings, *The Teacher Moves: An Analysis of Nonverbal Activity* (New York: Teachers College Press, 1971), pp. 93-97.

Nonverbal communication can substantially reduce teacher talk. A simple nod of the head, for example, can effectively replace the question "Does anybody else have a contribution to make?" Such nonverbal acts can substantially speed up a discussion, provide a much needed change of pace, and bring an inattentive student back to attention, even while a verbal interaction is in progress. Sign language sometimes can communicate more than verbal symbols. For example, by simply making quote signs with the fingers as one talks, a person can communicate the special use intended. By smiling, nodding, or leaning or stepping toward a student, a teacher can say, "This is great!" Similarly, by frowning, staring, or rapidly shaking the head, the teacher can declare, "You'd better try again."

Since most teachers have never analyzed their nonverbal language, they usually rely on one or two specific gestures to complement verbal expressions. One teacher, for example, may be a pointer, using the finger for a variety of gestures. As Grant and Hennings suggest,[7] just as one attempts to correct overuse of a specific word by substituting other words, so should one vary body language to avoid repetition. Viewing a videotaped lesson can do much to call attention to poor teaching styles.

There is an equal number of teachers who overuse nonverbal expression. There is perhaps nothing more annoying to students than the teacher who paces back and forth so much (practically making a trail in the floor) that the students actually start counting the "trips." Equally annoying are those teachers who fidget with a pencil, glasses, or hair or constantly scratch their heads. Some men teachers constantly push their hands into the bottom of their pockets and leave them there; some women teachers constantly straighten a blouse or adjust their earrings. Even those gestures designed to contribute to the pedagogical experience may be overused to the extent that they become meaningless. The nonverbal gesture should convey the same meaning as the verbal expression associated with it in order to insure clear communication. For example, a student will become confused if the teacher says, "That's a good point, Nancy," but frowns while saying it.

How Can Students Be Encouraged to Generate Their Own Questions?

Critical thinking is encouraged through artful questioning. The ultimate goal of all instruction, however, is to develop in individuals the ability to ask and answer questions correctly. Student questions should be encouraged at all times. Unfortunately, a question session usually follows the pattern of teacher-question-student response. By asking questions with multiple answers, as described earlier, the pattern may be modified into teacher-question-student response, student response student response. A more desirable pattern would be teacher-question-student response, student response—student question—student response.

All teachers are aware of those occasions when students have carried a discussion

---

[7]Ibid., p. 164.

themselves, almost forgetting the presence of the teacher for a time. Unfortunately, such experiences are relatively rare and are rather difficult to analyze. Rosinger has developed a technique that he has found effective for expanding thinking and that he believes has great potential for eliciting student questions.[8] The approach involves taking all student answers to a specific test question and pooling them. In rewriting the answers, the teacher retains the student's language as much as possible, excluding only those comments that are clearly contradictory to the situation posed. The students are then asked to select the best answer. This tends to encourage divergent thinking as described more fully in Chapter 13. The technique could be adapted to any questioning session.

What Preplanning Is Needed?

As indicated in the illustrated lesson plan provided for each instructional method, key questions and key responses should be preplanned. Unfortunately, this is a "two-edged sword." On the one hand, the procedure tends to stultify a discussion, making it a "cut and dried" affair—leaving little room for creative imagination. On the other hand, it provides a structured sequence contributing to realization of instructional goals. The most appropriate practice, then, seems to be the development of preplanned question *samples*.

Anticipated student responses are less often needed. Sometimes, however, an anticipated answer may suggest a line of thought that can be developed. They serve other purposes as well, such as suggesting the level of questions. Analysis questions especially should be followed with probable student answers since these questions must be judged against established criteria. As a general rule, questions should not be read directly from a lesson plan; neither should one attempt to elicit those anticipated responses suggested in preplanned materials.

The Value of Questioning Techniques

Questioning techniques apply to all instructional methods. The success of any given instructional experience is largely dependent on how questions are handled.

Critical thinking is encouraged through artful questioning above the recall level.

Appropriate questioning techniques help make the learner independent of the teacher. Such growth is identifiable by a questioning pattern of teacher question—pupil response, pupil response—pupil question—pupil response.

Adequate probing techniques enable the learner to judge the adequaacy of his or her own response.

---

[8] Lawrence Rosinger, "The 'Class' Answer as a Teaching Device," *English Journal* 57 (October 1968): 1032-35.

**Limitations
of, and
Problems
with,
Questioning
Techniques**

The primary problem associated with questioning techniques is their tendency to emphasize recall only.

Teachers tend to "rush" pupil responses and to expect answers that confirm their preconceived ideas.

A common problem among teachers is their failure to involve all pupils in the questioning process.

Many teachers have difficulty developing questions that encourage discussion. A question that calls for a yes or no answer usually discourages discussion.

Teacher behaviors of repeating questions, answering their own questions, and repeating pupil responses are major obstacles to effective questioning.

**Illustrated
Questioning
Techniques
and
Applications**

The act of questioning logically proceeds from the lower levels to the higher levels of cognition. This is especially true if the total processes of reflective thinking are desired. There is a definite tendency, however, to focus on the lower levels of cognition only. Thus the illustrations that follow are constructed to depict differences between the different levels of higher order thinking. In some illustrations, all three levels of questions are given; in others only one (or two) levels are given.

    I. In different subject fields
       A. Useful in English, speech, and foreign language classes.
          1. Comprehension questions
             a. What are the merits of placing topic sentences at the beginning of a paragraph instead of at the end of it?
             b. How does Jefferson's concept of democracy compare with our present-day democratic system?
             c. Why do rules of parliamentary procedure sometimes prevent the democratic functioning of an organization?
             d. How does a study of the Spanish language contribute to an understanding of the Spanish culture?
          2. Analysis questions
             a. What do the letters RSVP on a formal invitation mean?
             b. What assumptions are suggested by the statement "Each person must do his or her own thing"?
             c. What support can you offer for implementing a planned land-use program adjacent to major metropolitan areas?
             d. What are some reasons for the Mexican-American minority's insistence that some classes be conducted in Spanish in southern Arizona and Texas?
          3. Evaluation questions
             a. What is your reaction to the suggestion that informal modes of communication be emphasized in English classes?
             b. What do you think of Langston Hughes's hip style of poetic expression?

  c. In your opinion, did the editorial focus on the basic issue?

  d. Should Spanish be taught by a person of Mexican heritage?

B. Useful in science and mathematics classes

 1. Comprehension questions

  a. How do the moon, Mars, and Venus compare in atmospheric pressure and distance from the sun?

  b. What evidence suggests that our mountains are in constant state of evolution?

  c. Why is there a move in this country to switch to the metric system?

  d. How would you define a quadratic equation?

 2. Analysis questions

  a. What techniques are being used to persuade young people to quit or not begin smoking?

  b. How are common respiratory diseases related to weather conditions?

  c. What are the implications of requiring algebra and geometry for college-bound students only?

  d. What assumptions can you make about ratio and proportion?

 3. Evaluation questions

  a. Do you think that cloud-seeding is ethically desirable?

  b. In your opinion, should overage stands of timber be harvested selectively in the nation's wilderness areas?

  c. What is your personal reaction to the contribution of modern math to a general understanding of mathematics?

  d. How would you judge the plausibility of your answer to a factoring problem?

C. Useful in social science and home economics classes

 1. Comprehension questions

  a. How has the electoral college system of electing a president been abused in modern times?

  b. What does the term "culturally disadvantaged" mean?

  c. How do the adjustment problems of growing up in the inner city differ from those of growing up in the suburbs?

  d. What are the major differences between the family of today and that of the nineteenth century?

 2. Analysis questions

  a. What were some of the motives behind our attempts to re-establish diplomatic contacts with Communist China?

  b. What are some economic implications of floating the price of gold on the world market?

  c. What are the fallacies in the argument that family size should be limited to the number of children that can be supported effectively?

 3. Evaluation questions

  a. In your opinion would the two-China policy in the United Nations General Assembly have been effective?

  b. Should an avowed communist be permitted to teach at a state university?

  c. Do you think that the Supreme Court should be permitted to reinterpret the law?

        d. What is your personal reaction to liberalized abortion laws?

  D. Useful in skills classes (physical education, art, music, and business)

    1. Comprehension questions

      a. How does a planned program of daily exercise affect the circulatory system?

      b. How might one express personal emotions and feelings with color?

      c. How do rock and western music compare with respect to tempo?

      d. How would you define John K. Galbraith's economic policy?

    2. Analysis questions

      a. What are the reasons behind the argument that each person should develop interest in some physical activity?

      b. What moods are apparent in Van Gogh's *The Orchard?*

      c. What were the motives for founding rock music?

      d. How does an advertisement depicting a famous athlete using a special hair spray create a desire in men to purchase the product?

    3. Evaluation questions

      a. Should a physically handicapped individual be exempted from physical education classes?

      b. What is your personal reaction to Paul Klee's *Girl with Jugs?*

      c. Who do you feel is the best contemporary musician in America today? And why?

      d. Do you think that tobacco advertisements should be banned from magazines?

  II. As complementary to the lecture

    Although questioning techniques apply to all instructional methods, they are most often misused in connection with lecture methods. The following illustrates how questioning strategy may be used to complement the extended lecture.[9]

Lecture problem: What conditions are aggravating the current energy crisis?

    After completing the lecture, the teacher initially asks students questions at the lower level of cognition, designed to clarify information offered in the lecture. As the question session develops, the teacher can lead students into higher processes of reflection by asking skillfully worded questions at key points. (These questions would be interspersed with student questions and discussion.)

    T: What percent of our total energy supply presently comes from coal? What is the main objection to nuclear power? What is the main impediment to the common use of solar energy? (recall questions)

    T: Why is solar energy considered the power source of the future? (comprehensive question)

    T: If (as predicted) solar energy does essentially replace other energy

---

    [9] By referring to Ch. 10, the reader will note that questions may be entertained after each main point or at the end of the presentation. Frequently they will lead into other methods dealing with the same general problem area. Sometimes, however, the question session will be all that is needed.

sources, what implications might this have on our "oil rich" neighbors and on the large group of underdeveloped nations? (analysis question)

T: In your judgment, should our people be asked to make a huge investment in solar energy research in order to hasten the practical use of solar energy? (evaluation question)

chapter 8

DISCUSSION METHODS

Overview

Key Concepts

1. Controversial issues provide a sound basis for a discussion that is intended to weigh evidence and proposals more than to resolve a problem.
2. Open-ended problems (policy problems) are most appropriate for discussion.
3. Discussion follows a logical sequence of development.
4. In discussion, student questions usually are subjected to class analysis.
5. Problem analysis and consideration of alternatives are the minimum essentials of the discussion process.
6. Discussion is ineffective with a group of more than twenty students. The optimum size ranges from five to seven participants.

New Terms

1. Problems of Policy   An open-ended type of problem, often preplanned by the teacher, which forms the basis for class and panel discussion. Often begins with the word *what* but sometimes may begin with such key words as *why* or *how*. The word *should* or *ought* is stated or implied in the question.
2. Problem of Advocacy   A question, usually beginning with the word should or ought, that limits the response to one proposed solution. Such questions enter into discussion especially when hypotheses are being considered.
3. Panel Discussion   A discussion led by students themselves, usually consisting of five to seven individuals.
4. Enlightenment Discussion   A discussion (usually panel) dealing with clarification of facts.
5. Inference   A mental leap from fact or premise to conclusion.

Questions to Guide Your Study

1. Why is an enlightenment issue sometimes appropriate for a panel discussion but generally inappropriate for class discussion?

2. Students should develop their own discussion problems. Defend or refute.
3. Why is a class discussion sometimes referred to as a pseudo discussion?
4. What are the advantages and disadvantages associated with the problem-type discussion emphasized in this chapter?
5. It has been contended that the discussion process is more important than the end product of the discussion. Why?

The students were gathered around a table drinking coffee. They were discussing the important aspects of the farm problem. The discussion was characterized by individual opinions, many of which deal with personalities.

Professor Burton was talking to her class about seventeenth-century aristocracies. She outlined the relevant facts, brought in important relationships, and drew certain conclusions. Finally, during the last ten minutes of the hour she entertained questions from the group.

Miss Killinger was questioning her biology students on their assigned readings. Most of the questions dealt with definitions and facts presented. Occasionally, a student asked about important relationships, which Miss Killinger was only too happy to explain further.

Mr. Buell was using the factual materials of an assigned lesson to help students make relationships and conclusions. It soon became obvious that few students had read the materials. Their responses, for the most part, consisted of value judgments, many of which were not related to the facts of the lesson.

While the preceding illustrations represent discussion in a broad sense, none of them characterizes the class discussion technique described in this chapter. Professor Burton is *not* conducting a guided discussion. Her method of teaching, whether it be lecture, demonstration, or something else, may be appropriate, but it does not qualify as class discussion. Nor does the method of having students recite materials from their texts, as Miss Killinger is doing, constitute a true class discussion. The rather questionable classroom practice (demonstrated by Professor Buell) of discussing anything and everything that just happens to evolve—often called "bull sessions" by the participants—certainly does not qualify as a class discussion either. *Class discussion is designed to develop group agreement through talk and reflective thinking.* Its purposes are to stimulate analysis, encourage interpretations, and develop or change attitudes. In other words, the individual is guided in reflection on a problem that involves "weighing" the evidence before a decision or opinion can be reached. Through appropriate leadership, evidence is brought to bear on the crucial issues of a problem; the evidence is analyzed and evaluated *by the group*; and certain generalizations are made.

When individuals engage in discussion, they ponder or meditate; they think critically. They *reflect* on their ideas along with those of their colleagues. Such individuals are searchers, inquirers. In effect, they say, "Here are my ideas. How do they relate to your opinions and the facts of the situation?" They are willing to alter views that seem inadequate under the scrutiny of thoughtful analysis. Views are not changed, however, on the basis of peer pressure or emotion. If the objective evidence seems to warrant reassessments of tentative ideas and assumptions, the participants are ready to adjust accordingly.

Discussion is most appropriate when areas of controversy exist. Although a rather poor means of disseminating information, discussion is ideal for evolving, sorting, and sifting facts and values essential for the resolution of problems. It is also ideally suited to attaining the higher cognitive and affective goals.

Fundamental Properites

Discussion essentially embodies the basic properties of the democratic process. It is based on the assumption that individuals, when sufficiently informed on an issue, are capable of decision making in an atmosphere characterized by a free interchange of ideas and expressions. It is the responsibility of the discussion leader to create an environment for open reflection.

What Purposes Are Served by Class Discussion?

Class discussion is ideally suited to the resolution of current problems. It may be used for other purposes, however. As Gall and Gall point out,[1] there are subject-matter discussions, issue-oriented discussions, and problem-solving discussions.

College professors often use class discussion for subject-matter mastery. The experience usually begins with some preliminary discussion on an area of common knowledge, followed by assigned readings, and concluding with a class discussion of the assigned reading material. This discussion focuses on the higher cognitive processes. If, as often happens, the discussion focuses on merely "reciting" information read, the experience is more appropriately labeled a *recitation*. A recitation is generally considered an unacceptable mode of discussion since it deals almost exclusively with learning by memorization.

The issue-oriented discussion is ideally suited for analyzing value-related activities. Several related objectives are involved. The first is to increase awareness and understanding of the participants' attitudes (beliefs, feelings, and behavior). The second is to analyze and evaluate them. The third is to modify attitudes, based on previous analysis and evaluation. The final objective is to reach a group consensus, should one be desired.[2] (This function is treated more fully in Chapter 13 dealing with creative activities.)

Class discussion engages the group in problem-solving activities. Based on a carefully worded current problem, the method essentially follows the stages of critical thinking. Although the approach can be most effective, it often breaks down simply

---

[1] M. D. Gall and J. P. Gall, "Discussion Method," *The National Society for the Study of Education Yearbook*, part I (1971): 171.

[2] Ibid, p. 172.

because the leader does not understand the essential steps involved. Thus students flounder as they get bogged down with trivial facts and related opinions.

What Basic Assumptions Are Inherent in Class Discussion?

Class discussion at its best is conceived within a framework of democracy. The leader guides, challenges, and prods students to help them deal with issues. At no time are students given answers. Inherent in this method is the assumption that there is a close relationship between it and a democratic society.

A second major assumption, according to Bormann,[3] is that every person has the right and obligation to make up his or her mind. Each individual is responsible for acquiring and processing information in such a manner as to facilitate sound decision making.

Another major assumption, often overlooked, is that each individual has the right to grow and develop within the group. Freedom of expression is encouraged, while struggles for influence and dominance within the group are discouraged. Although they are sometimes disconcerting, decisions or generalizations objectively derived are fully accepted.

A fourth major assumption associated with class discussion is faith in the human being's ability to reason and communicate. As Bormann points out, the human being is the only creature that has the ability to use language and to reason not only the present but also the past and the future. The ability of bringing reason to bear on the world's most vexing problems (through discussion) represents the unique quality of human beings.

What Ethical Considerations Are Involved in Discussion?

In translating the preceding democratic assumptions into the behavior of the discussion participants, a number of important ethical considerations become evident. In the first place, group decisions are based on total group involvement. This certainly suggests balanced participation. An individual must not pretend to agree with the group and later denounce a decision. The fact that a person does not agree with the group must be made clear at the time of the discussion. Later, a minority report must be entered.

Sometimes, an individual is not prepared for a class discussion and attempts to cover up in various ways. The responsibility of being well informed must be shared by all participants since misinformation is often the cause of a breakdown or bottleneck in the discussion. Moreover, accuracy of reporting is essential. It is easy to be satisfied with the evidence when only one data source has been examined. Such tactics can seriously mislead group deliberation.

---

[3] Earnest G. Bormann, *Discussion and Group Methods*, 2d ed. (New York: Harper and Row, Publishers, 1975), pp 62-63.

Another breach of ethics occurs when an individual distorts information for the purpose of manipulating the discussion toward his or her own ends. This can take many forms from misquoting information, to throwing out "red herrings," to making hasty generalizations, to using loaded words. An especially dangerous technique is oversimplifying by use of "either-or" thinking. Usually, there are many ways of avoiding these practices.

Although the preceding warnings were directed to discussion participants, they are even more critical for the leader, often the instructor. The teacher holds a position of high prestige in the group and can easily sway a discussion toward predetermined ends. This represents a serious breach of ethics. Whenever possible the teacher should not offer personal points of view. In those instances, when there is danger of implying a personal viewpoint, the teacher should clearly and simply inform the group, "Here are my biases on the subject; I hope you will disregard them."

What Is the Influence of Group Size on Discussion?

Group size is definitely a limiting factor in class discussion. (For a more thorough treatment of this matter, the reader is referred to Chapter 5 on small-group techniques.) Since most college classes are considerably larger than the optimum size of five to seven individuals, some compromise is necessary when the establishment of small groups is not feasible or desirable.

There are certain advantages (along with many disadvantages) to having a class discussion with more than seven individuals. For example, more people are more capable of examining a problem thoroughly; more suggestions and opinions are generated; and more resources are available. *With a skillful discussion leader*, evidence indicates that groups of as many as twelve people may be more effective for certain purposes than those with smaller numbers of people. Much depends on the thoroughness of the discussion desired. Although total participation is essential, this does not mean that total *overt* participation is necessary, even though it may be desirable. Gage and Berlinger suggest that discussion can be effective with up to twenty students, classroom teaching (a mixture of other methods with some characteristics of discussion) with twenty to forty students, and the lecture method with forty or more students.[4] Many college professors who rely heavily on class discussion report that groups of up to twenty individuals can be handled effectively in long-lived groups (extending over a quarter or a semester).

A limiting factor in all groups is the loquaciousness of some individuals. In large groups, this tendency to talk is simply magnified. Moreover, in large groups there is a tendency for members to "save up" their contributions until called on to speak. Thus they talk longer and thereby reduce the time available for other participants.

---

[4] N. L. Gage and David Berlinger, *Educational Psychology* (Chicago: Rand McNally and Co., 1975), p. 447.

Another especially limiting factor in large groups is the seating arrangement. A face-to-face arrangement is essential. Thus small groups are usually placed in a circle or a semicircle. With groups in excess of 20 people, this arrangement tends to spread individuals too far apart for effective interaction. To minimize the threat of a few talkative individuals' dominating the group, they should be placed next to each other and to the sides of the instructor. Shy students will participate more if seated near the front.

For many purposes, it is possible to divide large classes into subgroups of five students for class discussion. In some cases, large lecture classes are divided into smaller discussion groups as a matter of policy. Some professors use their imagination in various ways to achieve reasonably small discussion groups. For example, while most members of a large class are engaged in independent study, the instructor could form a small discussion group with the remaining members.

What Reasoning Processes Are Involved?

The heart of any class discussion is the process of advancing from the known to the unknown, from specific facts to inferences about facts. This mental leap from fact to conclusion occurs continually throughout a discussion. It may occur as a sudden insight, or Eureka (see Chapter 1). Usually, however, inferences are made slowly as the discussion progresses. The same mental leap, nevertheless, is involved. This process of leaping from the known to the unknown can be misleading since each person will tend to evaluate facts or data slightly differently. Since discussion problems are controversial in nature, there is likely to be considerable disagreement; *indeed, unacceptable inferences can be expected.* To evaluate inferences, one should know some of the more common bases for inferential reasoning, discussed in the following section.

Reasoning from analogy (resemblance). This technique is one of the most useful for class discussion. From beginning to end, the discussion (reflective) process involves making comparisons, or analogies to what has happened elsewhere concerning the problem. If the problem issue is national in scope, perhaps individual states or other nations have had experience dealing with it. If the issue is statewide, perhaps it has been tried in a number of localities. Such controversial issues as socialized medicine, capital punishment, birth control, and power alliances, for example, are often evaluated on the basis of how successful they have been implemented in other states or nations. The crucial test, of course, is how closely the previous experiences resemble one another. There are always differences as well as similarities. Are the differences significant in terms of the areas being considered? If so, one cannot draw analogies.

Reasoning by making causal relationships. This technique is a rather common, but quite hazardous, one sometimes referred to as the *if . . . then* type of reasoning. Often during a discussion, a participant will say, "With these facts as evidence, it is obvious that such and such causes are involved." This effect-to-cause type of reasoning is especially hazardous when one realizes that "true causes" are extremely difficult to isolate. Similarly, cause-to-effect reasoning that assumes that specific events in the past or present are responsible for generating certain events in the future is also risky. Who can fully predict what the future holds? Still another form of causal relationships is reasoning by effect-to-effect. The inference is made that one event can produce a number of effects. Although this is often true, there are usually an unlimited number of conditions (not in evidence) that may intrude to alter the effects being considered.

Reasoning by specific instances. This technique involves making generalizations from a number of specific cases. It is only useful if the cases cited are somewhat *representative* of the total group (population) under consideration. Public opinion polls, for example, are based on relatively few cases, but the cases are selected on the basis of carefully researched criteria. Have enough instances been offered to justify a generalization about the total group being considered? Are the instances offered typical of all the members of the group?

Reasoning by authority. This is probably the weakest of all types of inferences, yet the one most highly favored by college students. The assumption is made that if certain respected authorities, who are in the best position to understand the situation, favor a certain course of action, then it must be the right one. For example, the author overheard one of his students say, "Who am I to question such an authority?" What the learner often does not realize is that favored authorities are very often contradicted by equally qualified authorities, thus the competence of each authority must be carefully checked. It is common for authorities in one field to criticize conditions and events in another field in which their knowledge is no better than that of any layperson. Yet there is a tendency for the general public (and discussion members) to conclude that expertness in one field automatically renders one an expert in all fields.

What Are the Four Types of Discussion Problems?

The four kinds of problems that lend themselves to varying degrees of reflective thinking are described in the following section.

Fact. Problems of fact are concerned with the discovery and evaluation of factual information. Answers to such questions can be verified directly or indirectly. Fact questions are emphasized during the analysis phase of the problem. For example "What U.S. goods, if any, are being traded to China?" This question is in the recall category discussed in Chapter 7.

Value. Problems of value (opinion) concern matters involving value judgments. Answers to value questions cannot be verified as either true or false, but they can be examined for consistency and should include supporting reasons and implications. Value questions arising during the latter part of a discussion often call for application of accepted standards in determining the appropriateness, rightness, or effectiveness of an issue. Examples: "How well is our trade policy being administered?" "Is our trade policy interfering with efforts to keep the peace?" Questions of value arising frequently during the early phases of a discussion deal with *evaluation* of facts. Problems of fact and value usually can be identified by the presence of some form of the verb *to be*. Indeed, they are sometimes referred to as *is* or *are* questions.

Advocacy. Problems of advocacy, as the term implies, focus on finding one specific solution. Since only one solution is considered, advocacy questions tend to encourage argument rather than discussion. They often emerge when hypotheses or tentative solutions to a problem are being evaluated. It is for this reason that establishment of accepted criteria should be developed prior to weighing the alternatives. To illustrate, "Should trade with China be increased?" The question can be answered by yes or no. Wording of the question precludes consideration of other alternatives. This is the type of problem used in debate. Such questions usually begin with the word *should* or *ought*.

Policy. Problems of policy (advice) deal with matters necessitating decisions or action. Implied in the problem is the importance of exploring all possible solutions. Policy questions often begin with the words *what* or *how*. The words *should* or *ought* are also stated or implied in the question. For example: "What should be the U.S. trade policy with China?"

In resolving a problem of policy, questions of *fact, value,* and *advocacy* will be involved. The reverse does not follow, however. In formulating problems for discussion, teachers often confuse policy with advocacy questions. Advocacy questions immediately direct attention to one particular solution. Furthermore, they tend to divide a group into opposing camps.

Discussion Procedure

Individuals often find solutions to their daily problems by talking them over with others. Ask your neighbor what he or she thinks of the slate of candidates for the school board and the response will likely be, "I don't know; what do you think?" After some discussion, it is quite likely that both you and your neighbor will have clarified your views on the problem. Such informal discussion goes on continually in and out of the classroom. Indeed, it is basic to the democratic process.

To be effective as an instructional method, however, discussion must be carefully planned and executed. Although there are a number of variations and interesting modifications, the basic aims of discussion are to stimulate analysis, to encourage interpretations, and to develop or change attitudes. This section discusses a technique embodying all these aims. Through appropriate leadership, evidence is brought to bear on the crucial aspects of a selected problem; the evidence is evaluated and analyzed by *the group*; certain proposed solutions are introduced and evaluated; and finally generalizations are derived from the experience.

Although discussion for subject-matter mastery is often a rather poor technique, it is treated briefly since most college professors and business executives make use of this method at some point.

What Are the Essentials of Discussion for Subject-Matter Mastery?

Subject-matter discussions, according to Hill,[5] can be effective if a preliminary overview is established in which the total class group becomes aware of, and agrees to, the procedure. As in any type of discussion, first, important terms must be defined. In some courses, such as science, defining terms becomes a major activity. It must be remembered, however, that there is more to most assignments than a mere definition of terms. From the development of definitions, the next logical steps are to discuss briefly what the author (of the assigned reading) has attempted to accomplish and to review in detail the subtopics (major headings) of the assigned materials. It is usually desirable to transpose these subtopics into a question format (as done in this book).

After some preliminary attention to major subtopics, students are ready for the reflective processes of the discussion, in which they make applications to, and draw implications from, the content material. This is accomplished by asking them skillful questions (see Chapter 7). Students in introductory courses often have difficulty in seeing the relevance of content to related problems and issues.

Finally, students are given an opportunity to offer their personal reactions to the material. Although students readily accept this responsibility, they usually need considerable assistance in developing competence in this area. In this connection, the reader should refer to the previously developed topic dealing with reasoning processes. A conscious effort must be made to focus on the higher cognitive processes. (See Chapters 2 and 7 for a thorough analysis of the levels of cognition.) It should be emphasized that a discussion of personal opinions is *not* highly recommended and should be avoided when a problem-solving discussion is possible. (The rest of this chapter deals with the problem-solving type of discussion.)

How Is the Problem Identified in a Problem-Solving Discussion?

In nurturing the basic skills of critical thinking, problem discovery and formulation must be considered of basic importance. The individual must somehow become aware of a problem or difficulty. Perhaps inconsistencies between related facts are noted. Sometimes incomplete data or puzzling events raise problems. Often, there are questions of application involved.

---

[5]William F. Hill, *Learning through Discussion*, rev. ed. (Beverly Hills, Calif.: Sage Publications, Inc., 1969), pp. 22-23. Much of this section is based on Hill's analysis.

Problem identification has all too often been handled exclusively by the teacher. In a mathematics class, for example, the problems are carefully developed in the text or by the teacher. Similarly, in science classes, experiments are commonly defined and delineated for the student. Problem identification is indeed a difficult task—sometimes even for the teacher. Nevertheless, students should have some experience in identifying problems for themselves. This inclination toward problem discovery that characterizes the creative person is an essential aspect of democratic processes.

Certainly during the early stages of a course, the teacher may need to identify and state problems carefully for students. Later, the teacher should shift much of this responsibility to students themselves. Generally, discussion problems should be related to current issues. This will involve some application as closely related as possible to the lives of students. As indicated in the description of problem types, problems of policy are most appropriate for class discussion. Many teachers favor the practice of writing the problem on the chalkboard to promote effective discussion.

Students (and indeed many teachers) have difficulty formulating problems in a meaningful way. The problem must pinpoint the crucial issues to be resolved and in such a way as to avoid misleading students. After students have been guided in problem development, they should be assisted in developing the issues into one of policy, *prior* to the exploration and analysis of the problem.

How Does the Participant Prepare for Discussion?

An effective discussion is based on sound, solid evidence. All too often, a student has been heard to say, "It's only a discussion; you don't have to prepare for it." As Gulley points out, "An uninformed group will achieve a worthless product; an uninformed individual will contribute to an equally worthless product and a discussion under these conditions is a waste of time."[6]

A participant, of course, will bring in personal knowledge when appropriate. Indeed all such knowledge, whether it is based on personal experience, observation or interview, tends to contribute to group enthusiasm. Such information, however, must be supported with substantial library research. Although books will provide needed general information, the periodicals are the best source of current information. Many discussion problems can be divided into topical areas (subproblems) to accommodate a division of tasks and eliminate unnecessary duplication of effort, *provided* all members read certain selected sources to insure a common basis of understanding.

Preparation for a discussion demands considerable evaluation of information prior to the discussion itself. There is a tendency to automatically accept all printed matter as accurate. Unfortunately, biased individuals do write and do manage to get their biases published. As a general rule, each major concept should be confirmed by two or

---

[6] Halbert E. Gulley, *Discussion, Conference and Group Process*, 2d ed. (Holt, Rinehart and Winston, Inc., 1968), p. 80.

more sources. Since most discussion problems deal with current issues, the most recent available information should be sought. Generally periodical literature appearing during the last five years or so is the most valuable. However, basic classical data, regardless of date, must not be overlooked.

Sometimes students are not prepared for a discussion simply because they cannot find the right kind of information. A simple outline, structured around the major aspects of problem solving, can be a most valuable tool. To illustrate, What steps should be taken to reduce automobile emission pollutants?

1. What is meant by the term "automobile emissions"?
2. How extensive is the pollutant problem?
3. What kind of vehicles are the greatest contributers to pollution?
4. What are the effects of pollution on the environment?
5. What is presently being done to combat automobile pollution?
6, How does the general public view this problem?
7. What groups favor and what groups oppose suggested corrective measures?

How Is the Problem Analyzed?

As a preliminary step in decision making, the various components of a problem must be introduced and evaluated. The process leads the learner from definition of important terms to an inspection of important facts and circumstances associated with the problem. In this phase of discussion, the importance of the problem is examined; cause and effect relationships are explored; and sample analysis questions are offered for the problem. For example, What steps should be taken to minimize the use of LSD among young people?

1 What is LSD?
2. How widespread is its use among teenagers? Among college-age students?
3. What are its effects?
4. What evidence indicates the problem is likely to persist? Is there any evidence to the contrary?

How Are Hypotheses Established?

After a review and evaluation of the facts and ideas related to the problem, ways of solving the problem must be introduced. Sometimes referred to as the "idea generation" phase, this is the very heart of the problem-solving process. It is at this point that the teacher refers the group to the original question and poses the big question "What should be done?" Students offer possibilities for solving the problem, some of which may be entirely new and seem a bit wild when first introduced as is typical of much creative thinking.

Each proposed solution is followed by a brief discussion of its advantages and disadvantages. An alternative procedure and one preferred by those who emphasize creativity in teaching involves listing possible solutions *prior* to any sort of evaluation. Sometimes a fifteen- to twenty-minute brainstorming session may be in order at this point. (See chapter 13.)

How Are Ideas Tested?

For many simple problems, a brief analysis of the advantages and disadvantages of the alternative solutions is all that is needed. Through this process, appropriate action becomes obvious. Other issues are not so easily handled, however. A solution often appears the best one only because of the particular needs or frame of reference of the individual involved.

In such cases, the group must develop a set of standards, or criteria, for evaluating proposals. This may become rather difficult if the problem is close to the lives of students. If the problem is one of national or international policy, the process will be less difficult (for students) but just as essential if the issue is to be examined from as many angles as possible. For example, the problem of determining our trade policy with China should be considered from the standpoint of national security, on purely humanitarian grounds, or in relation to the policy's effects on our trade balance with other Asiatic nations. Sometimes, a priority system must be established.

How Are Generalizations Derived?

Sometimes the outcome of a problem-solving discussion is a definite plan of action. By weighing each of the suggested hypotheses, the students reach some decision concerning one or more preferred courses of action. In most classes, however, the scope of the problem will be too broad to achieve such an end.

Most class discussion experiences conclude with the derivation of generalizations. To illustrate:

1. LSD users may incur permanent brain damage.
2. While under the influence of LSD, a person loses the ability to distinguish between reality and fantasy.
3. Use of LSD may make an individual emotionally dependent on the drug.

What Is the Role of the Teacher as Discussion Leader?

Basic to effective class discussion is appropriate use of questions. Both student and teacher questions must be clearly and impartially stated. It is relatively easy for a biased leader to influence the discussion process by interjecting slanted questions from time to time. The question Why is the use of LSD dangerous?, for example, supports a preconceived point of view. A better question might be What are the effects of LSD?

An effective discussion leader must know how to handle nonrelated or remotely related questions. In the spontaneous interplay of individual reactions to issues, a variety of questions tends to emerge. The leader must continually make quick decisions about the desirability of pursuing given questions. Pushing the group too forcibly can impede or even block group reflection, while entertaining all questions can lead to a myriad of blind alleys, resulting in little or no progress. Sometimes the wise leader may simply ask the questioner, "Would you clarify for us how your point relates to our problem?" Some leaders practice putting both the problem and key questions on the board *in advance of* the discussion; this practice tends to keep the issue constantly before the group.

In class discussion, student questions are usually redirected to the group. Assuming the teacher has a fairly good understanding of the discussion problem when the discussion begins, the purpose, then, is to provide an opportunity for the group to develop an understanding by discussing the problem through to conclusion. Answering questions for the students tends to emphasize the teacher's role as an "expert." Few individuals do their best thinking when they are constantly reminded that the leader already "knows" the answers. Under such conditions, they are inclined merely to let this person think for them. Redirection of student questions tends to bring out new relationships and interpretations.

Skillful teachers generally accept pupil responses to questions. If, however, a response obviously is in error, students themselves can handle the situation if adequate time for reflection is provided. Inaccurate responses may stimulate further questions and analysis designed to evoke reappraisal of the issue. Undue pupil embarrassment should be carefully avoided, however, if reflection is to continue. A teacher can sometimes accept an inaccurate response temporarily by calling for other ideas pertaining to the issue. Usually subsequent responses will clarify the inaccuracy. (Occasionally the matter may have to be clarified before the group is permitted to advance to the next point.)

Reflection demands time! The leader can inadvertently encourage glibness by rushing responses unnecessarily. As one student expressed it, "He doesn't care what you say as long as you say it in a hurry." There are times, however, when because of a sudden insight, an individual needs to made a quick response. This is usually evidenced by the unusual eagerness of the respondent.

What Are the Qualities of an Effective Participant?

The effectiveness of class disscussion ultimately rests with the participants. Even the best leader is ineffective if the group neglects its responsibility to pull together. Above all, the leader's outline, consisting of sample key questions designed to insure an orderly development of the discussion sequences, must be respected. (Copies of it may be given to participants.) Offering a point before the group is prepared will contribute to a superficial discussion just as making a point too late in the discussion will force the group to backtrack and thus confuse it.

Full participation is desired. Since there is a limited amount of time available, individual contributions should be brief, essentially limited to one concept or idea. A few verbose individuals can ruin a discussion. It is the responsibility of both the group leader and group members to discourage such individuals. A call for supporting evidence, clarity, and examples may contribute to group progress.

In an effort to maintain a congenial discussion atmosphere, discussion members are often reluctant to challenge fallacies. Ideas must be tested, and poor reasoning abandoned. Members should be taught to expect poor or irrelevant ideas so they will not become resentful when their ideas are rejected or hesitate to challenge those of their peers.

The effective participant is constantly on the alert to illogical arguments and always acts in an enthusiastic, earnest manner. When challenging an idea, this person looks directly at the originator and diplomatically criticizes the idea, not the person. For example, he or she may say, "I see your point but have you considered. . . ?" as opposed to "I doubt that your position can be defended."

What Preplanning Does the Teacher Do?

Class discussion often breaks down because of the teacher's failure to plan a discussion outline, which contains questions dealing with the basic issues. Some teachers tend to overplan a discussion outline. They develop so many basic questions that the group in rushing from one point to another loses its ability to think creatively. The problem, as a consequence, often receives superficial study. Although the teacher should list more basic questions in the discussion outline than will be considered, the majority of questions *and* answers will come from the group. Most student questions will be redirected; the teacher clarifies, resolves different points of view, interjects summaries when needed, and leads the discussion into new areas as the occasion demands.

Some professors, on the other hand, do too little preparation for class discussion. Their questions tend to be vague and ambiguous. Too often, the student is forced to guess what the professor has in mind. Such a situation is not conducive to the processes of reflection.

A discussion lesson plan is organized around problem solving. It usually has four major subdivisions: analyzing the problem, examining possible solutions, (hypotheses), establishing criteria, and deriving generalizations. The following illustrated lesson plan is suggestive only.

DISCUSSION LESSON PLAN

Subject: World History

Unit: Population Pressures

Concept: Hunger and population pressures lead to unrest.

Problem: What steps should the United States take to improve relationships with China?

Goals: After this lesson, the students should have furthered his or her understanding of the influence of population pressures on our diplomatic relations with China, as evidenced by:

1. Contributions and questions posed during the discussion.
2. The ability to draw conclusions during a follow-up discussion of the problem.

Lesson approach

Yesterday we saw a movie that summarized the foreign relations of Communist China up to 1949.

1. What were some of the major reasons for the tension that existed?
2. What is hate? How was it propagated? What purposes did it serve?
3. What fundamental aspects of hate were implied?
4. What techniques have been employed recently in China that suggest a similar campaign against the United States?
5. Why do "hungry nations" sometimes fall prey to Communism? What are our best defenses against Communistic propaganda?
6. What historical conditions have implanted the seeds of distrust among the Chinese?
7. What bases for distrust exist in Southeast Asia? (Vietnam, for example.)

Lesson development

A. Analysis of the problem
   1. What other things happening in China and America suggest to you that we need better relations?
   2. What are some causes that led to the present tension?
   3. Why is it crucial that we establish better relations?
   4. What might be some effects if we do not establish better relations?
   5. Do you feel that China's aggressive attitude is likely to persist? Why or why not?
   6. How does the problem relate to population pressures? Do other Asiatic nations have similar problems? If so, how are they solving them?
   7. What have the Chinese done in the past to alleviate food shortages? How effective have these techniques been?

      8.   What conditions are similar (and different) in the world today?

B. Establishing hypotheses

Now in view of our discussion, what steps might the United States take to improve relationships with China? Possible solutions (suggestive only):

    1.   Develop a visitor exchange program.

    2.   Establish a military alliance.

    3.   Work out a comprehensive trade agreement.

    4.   Embark on a regional assistance and development program.

What might be some advantages and disadvantages of each of these solutions?

C. Establishing criteria

Before an acceptable solution to this issue can be established, we must examine standards that must be met. One such standard might be "Any action taken should respect friendly nations in Southeast Asia." What other standards seem important? Examples:

    1.   The effect of such action on our relations with the Soviet Union.

    2.   The effect of such action on our position in the United Nations.

D. Deriving generalizations

We have discussed one of the most perplexing problems facing the United States today. We know that the solutions we have developed can not be realized by the direct action of this class. But we do know that indirectly, through intelligent conversation with voters, we can help choose those governmental officials who feel as we do. We are also preparing ourselves to be intelligent citizens and policymakers.

Let us restate some major ideas or concepts that have emerged as a consequence of this discussion (suggestive only).

    1.   The present distrust is indirectly related to inadequate food supplies and overpopulation pressures.

    2.   Decisions relative to one aspect of the problem will influence many other areas.

    3.   Asiatic mistrust of foreigners has a historical basis.

The first portion of the lesson development, analysis of the problem, deals with definition of terms and cause-and-effect relationships. It is in this phase of the lesson that the basic historical facts are introduced and evaluated—in terms of the problem being discussed. Normally some two-thirds or three-fourths of the discussion time focuses on this phase of the experience.

The latter part of the lesson development, establishing hypotheses, focuses directly on the problem. It is designed to lead the student from the facts of the situation to a plan of action for solving the problem. Teachers who neglect formal planning all too often omit this phase of class discussion. This is particularly unfortunate since, without it, the major purpose of the class is not reached.

How Can Class Discussion Be Evaluated?

The worth of a class discussion or of any other method of teaching ultimately must be measured in terms of its original aims or purposes, for example, how well the problem has been analyzed and solved. There are other equally important purposes, however, which must be considered. For example, a teacher may have as one purpose helping students feel capable of sharing their ideas with the group. On the one hand, the leader has the task of evaluating group progress toward the goal, while on the other hand he or she must be concerned with individual progress. Both dimensions are important.

In order to evaluate individual and group progress, the teacher might prepare a chart listing every pupil and containing two separate categories—one for recording the number of contributions made by each student and the other for noting the quality of the contribution divided into four subcategories: objective sought, significant contribution, mediocre contribution, and questionable contribution. During the discussion, the teacher or appointed student observer can then tally up the number of contributions by making check marks in the numbers column and evaluate the contributions by making check marks in the qualitative column next to the appropriate subcategory. Of course, if a student observer is used, the teacher must insure that this person is competent. Although the author has found this method effective, there is the disadvantage that shy students will become more inhibited once they know their comments are being evaluated *qualitatively* as well as *quantitatively*.

The quantitative evaluation of individual contributions has considerable merit, however. The leader, by close observation, can often spot those who talk a lot but say little. This frequently suggests a conference with such individuals. The advantages associated with a *quantitative* evaluation of individual students are listed below:

1. Such a procedure encourages most members to participate.
2. The technique serves to reinforce the need for involving as many of the group as possible. A class contribution record of 75 percent can be considered good. Many teachers who have begun such a check have been surprised to discover that initially as little as 10 percent of the group was making 95 percent of the contributions.
3. Use of a class observer makes it possible to measure *individual* contributions to the class discussion *during the discussion*.
4. This measuring task can be readily performed by a student.
5. The student observer can keep a tally record while still remaining a part of the discussion group.
6. By noting extent and balance of individual contributions, the observer can determine the extent of *group* interaction.

Panel discussion involves a group of five to eight people who are seeking agreement on a problem of concern to themselves and to an audience. Like class discussion, it is usually structured around a problem of policy. Occasionally, a panel may be formed for the purpose of exploring problems of fact if the evidence is highly controversial and contradictory. Such an *enlightenment* discussion, however, must be followed with an appropriate policy problem discussion if the higher cognitive goals are to be achieved. Panel discussion contains many elements of democratic decision making. The threat of manipulation toward predetermined ends is minimized in panel discussion.

How Does Panel Discussion Differ from Class Discussion?

Upon casual inspection, one might assume that an understanding of the technique of guided class discussion can be readily applied to panel discussion. While it is true that the objectives are basically the same, the approaches are vastly different. As a matter of fact, the purposes of most teaching methods described in this book are concerned with problem solving as an avenue to learning—only the approaches differ. Some of the features that distinguish the panel from class discussion are listed below.

1. The *teacher* directs the entire class in class discussion, whereas a panel of *students* has control of the panel operation.
2. Preparation for class discussion is controlled to a large degree by the teacher, while the panel members plan and prepare for their discussion.
3. Class discussion, when used appropriately, involves the whole process of solving a problem; the panel group may discuss only one major aspect of the problem.
4. A class discussion leader is nearly always a dominant, central figure; whereas the panel leader is usually the quietest person on the panel.
5. Even in a balanced class discussion, the amount of actual participation is limited, whereas all panel members have ample opportunity to participate.
6. Class discussion is controlled and directed by an authority figure who, by student standards, can be considered an expert. The panel, on the other hand, is led by one member of the peer group who is not an expert.

How Are Panel Groups Selected and Organized?

The panel group is usually selected on the basis of expressed interest. A ten- to fifteen-minute initial planning session is necessary for the selection of a panel leader. The most enthusiastic, able, and tolerant student should be selected leader. Some groups may need help with this task. If the problem is complex, it is then subdivided into subtopics for individual research. (The leader will study all subtopics so that he or she may acquire a much needed overall view of the problem.) For example, the problem, What steps should be taken to improve game management policies on federal lands? might be subdivided as follows:

1. Forest lands
2. Park lands
2. Wildlife refuges
4. Wilderness areas
5. Bird and animal sanctuaries

Under optimum conditions, each person is equally qualified in all aspects of the problem. Time limitations and complexities of many problems, however, often render some division of labor desirable. Each member should have at least a workable knowledge of all aspects of the problem. Such background information is often attained from assigned textbook readings.

For most panel problems a group will need at least a week's preparation time. The teacher will work closely with the discussion leader. After the group has completed its investigation of the problem, it should meet briefly to discuss the major aspects of the problem to be explored. The discussion should not be rehearsed in advance, however. Many teachers limit such discussion to a period of fifteen minutes. Formulation of specific questions should be avoided.

What Are the Responsibilities of the Panel Leader?

The most important member of a panel is the leader. It is his or her responsibility to direct preplanning activities to assist any member who is experiencing difficulty, and to be a liaison between the teacher and panel members. By making the chairperson directly responsible for group progress, the teacher is relieved of many routine functions.

In addition to becoming better prepared generally than any other individual member, the leader prepares a discussion outline. This outline usually consists of a series of questions structured around the major issues to be emphasized. *Very few of these questions may be asked in a good panel discussion. They serve, instead, to guide thinking so that progress may be assured.* A simple panel guide is illustrated below.

_____

STUDENT GUIDE FOR PANEL DISCUSSION

Subject: World History

Concept: Hunger and population pressures lead to unrest.

Problem: What steps should the United States take to improve relationships with China?*

I. Analysis of problem
   A. What is meant by diplomatic relations?
   B. What are the advantages? Disadvantages?
   C. Are there problems today that make such a move especially important?
   D. Is the situation likely to continue? Why or why not?
II. Establishing hypotheses
   A. Now in view of the points which we have discussed, what steps should be taken to improve relationships with China?
   B. What are the advantages of each proposed solution? Disadvantages?
III. Establishing criteria
   A. What criteria should be used in weighing the proposals?
IV. Deriving generalizations
   A. Which of the proposed solutions best meets our list of criteria for deciding the issue?

*For purposes of comparison, the illustration is the same discussion problem as that used in the sample lesson plan for class discussion.

At the beginning of the discussion, the chairperson offers a few introductory remarks, states the problem (which also can be written on the board), and asks a question. (This is the one question that is usually written in the discussion guide; it may be memorized.) From this point on, the chairperson helps the group move toward the ultimate solution of the problem. The following guidelines should be of service to the panel leader.

First, he or she is the quietest person on the panel, allowing a free flow of ideas from the participants. The leader steers, nudges, clarifies, and summarizes in an unobtrusive manner.

Second, the leader is always mindful of his or her duties to control the remarks of the vociferous person and to encourage remarks from the more timid individuals.

It may be necessary to cut off the verbose person as unobtrusively as possible by saying, "Bill, I'm not sure we are following you. Will you briefly restate your point?" Then, when the point has been briefly restated, the leader quickly says, "Thank you. Would someone else like to speak on that point?" Another approach would be, "Wait just a minute, Bill. Let's see if we are following you. I gather you to mean that . . . . Who else would like to speak on that point?" At other times, it may be necessary to avoid calling on this talkative person.

The quiet person usually poses a more difficult problem. Sometimes he or she can be drawn out by a skillful question. To avoid possible embarrassment, however, the question usually should be of a general nature, for example, "Would you like to react to Bill's point, Joe?"

Third, the leader should keep the discussion as reasonable and as informative as possible. Here the leader's preplanned outline will be useful. What is the evidence? Is the speaker's conclusion warranted by the facts? Such comments as the following can do much to aid the group.

"You have heard Bill's point. Does anyone have any data that may support it?"
"Bill, why do you hold that opinion?" (This may remind Bill that he was actually voicing a value judgment.)
"Bill, has reached a conclusion. Do you go along with him?"
"Bill seems to be accepting the assumption that. . . . Is this a valid assumption to make?"

Fourth, the chairperson summarizes periodically, briefly restating the points or emphasizing areas of agreement. Whenever the leader believes it time to move to another point, a short summary can provide a ready transition, especially if it ends with, "Are there other aspects of this problem that need consideration now?"

Fifth, the leader keeps the discussion on the topic. This is sometimes a difficult function to perform since the relationship may be clear to the participant but not clear to the leader. The leader can tactfully handle the situation by asking, "How does your point relate to our problem?"

Sixth, the leader provides smooth transitions from one aspect of the problem to another. Frequently, a comment from some member can be used to bring up another aspect of the problem. For example, "John has just mentioned. . . . Perhaps we should examine his point a little more closely." The leader usually avoids such remarks as "Johnny, what did you find out about the topic?" or "Jack, would you like to begin our discussion of your topic?" At no time should the audience know that a certain aspect of a problem has been assigned to an individual. While individuals will probably make more specific points when their areas of investigation are under consideration, the other panelists will be asking questions and reacting to statements and proposals.

Seventh, the discussion leader summarizes the discussion. The summary will not be a restatement of points made, but a reminder of what the group has accomplished. Points of agreement will be stressed. The final summary is usually very brief—often not more than two or three comments.

Finally, the leader directs the question session that follows the panel presentation. Questions are addressed directly to the leader who, in turn, directs them to some member of the panel.

What Are the Responsibilities of Panel Members?

After selecting an aspect of the problem for exploration, each panelist should give some attention to the entire discussion problem before examining his or her specific assignment. In studying a particular aspect of the problem, the panelist is mindful of purpose: What is the present state of affairs? What weaknesses seem apparent? What step(s) might be taken to improve existing conditions? Why would such action be desirable? Notes will be brief but to the point. References will be noted. Occasionally one's source of authority will have a decided bearing on the final outcome. Some teachers like to have students submit their study notes after the discussion is completed. This enables the instructor to diagnose difficulties in the collection and evaluation of data.

During a panel discussion, the members actually are exchanging ideas among themselves. *They are doing this, however, for the benefit of an audience.* For this reason, it seems desirable to have the panelists arranged in a semicircle in front of the class, with the chairperson occupying a position near the center of the panel group. The objective is to have the participants partially facing each other, the chairperson, and the audience.

The amount, manner, and quality of participation is of utmost importance. First and foremost, the group must remember that *central to a panel discussion is reflective thinking necessary in solving a problem.* It is the function of the panelists to present information *only when it is necessary to reflect on the issues.* Consequently, prepared speeches are not in order. Students should thoroughly understand the following responsibilities of panel members.

1. Seldom will it be appropriate for a panelist to make a contribution longer than one minute's duration. The objective is to bring out enough of an important point to elicit further discussion and questions.
2. The best panelist develops an inquisitive attitude during the proceedings. This does not mean, however, that one becomes argumentative. Instead, the panelist probes assumptions, asks for clarification, points out hidden weaknesses, and the like.
3. The participant follows the discussion carefully. By listening (and actually hearing what others have to say) one's own thoughts are stimulated so that contributions fit the situation. Some panel discussions are characterized by brief silent periods, which may be indicative of reflective thinking.
4. The panel participant relates remarks to what has been said. Examples: "Bill's point relating to the effects of dumping wheat on the world market seems to be a good one. Here is another reason why it might be worth our serious consideration. . . ." "I think your point on the costs involved is well taken, Charley, but how would it solve the problem of surpluses? For instance. . . ." "The argument that the Secretary of Agriculture should be empowered to change price controls at his own discretion seems a bit hazardous to me. What would happen if . . . ?"
5. Tact is essential in reaching an agreement. Disparaging remarks and uncomplimentary labels tend to divert the discussion from the problem to personalities.
6. Flexibility is basic to any agreement. The panelist is always ready to consider new points of view and to alter views when warranted. He or she is willing to compromise but does not do so just for the sake of agreement.

How Can the Audience Profit Most from the Presentation?

Teachers who have been most successful with the panel method have found that the student audience generally enjoys panel presentations. There is enough time to enable students to analyze the problem along with the panelists. Instead of taking notes, as some students will try to do, they are instructed to jot down questions that are prompted during the course of the discussion.

Taking notes during a panel presentation is to be discouraged for several reasons. First, some data presented may be irrelevant to the resolution of the problem. Second, some points will not be sufficiently supported, while others may be purely personal opinions. Furthermore, occasionally misinformation will come before the group. In the course of the deliberative process, most of these fallacies will be corrected. Sometimes, however, the instructor will need to correct certain misleading assertions during the class discussion that follows. In order to avoid the taking of notes during a panel discussion and to prevent a few students from losing interest, some sort of individual panel evaluation technique should be used. (One such technique is described in detail in the topic which follows.)

When the panel presentation is completed, the chairperson invites members of the audience to ask questions. The audience is advised to make questions brief and to the point. Similarly, the respondents make their answers short. Nothing is more discouraging than a five-minute discourse when several people have questions to ask.

In most cases, the panel discussion experience can be divided as follows: five to ten minutes for class routines and panel introduction, twenty-five to thirty-five minutes for actual discussion, five to ten minutes for student questions, and about five minutes for the teacher's critique of the panel process. Most panel leaders want the instructor to determine when the discussion phase of the operation should be ended. They may request a five-minute time signal. Following the question period, the leader should compliment the panel group and make two or three general suggestions to guide future groups.

How Is Panel Discussion Evaluated?

Students often object to the teacher's acting as sole judge and jury of a group presentation. In the first place, they realize that the teacher is unqualified to judge that aspect of the job performed behind the scenes. For instance, the individual who worked hardest during the preparation phase may not communicate as adequately as the person who made the best showing during the panel presentation.

The author has used peer evaluations to supplement that of the teacher. First, each member of the audience evaluates the participants; then the panelists evaluate each other; and these evaluations are averaged with a teacher evaluation.

Prior to the panel presentation, each member of the audience is given an evaluation form on which he or she evaluates both quality and quantity of participation and the personal characteristics of the participants (see Figure 8-1). Each panelist's name is placed at the top of one of the rectangles, and each panelist is given a number, placed below the square.

Every contribution is evaluated *at the time it is made* by placing a tally mark in the appropriate column. For example, if in the opinion of a student observer, Paul introduced a new idea or made a significant clarification of the discussion purpose, he would be credited with a tally mark in the major category (see Figure 8-1). In case of doubt, the student is instructed to enter the point as a minor contribution. There will be relatively few major contributions and even fewer passive or doubtful contributions during a good panel discussion. As the chairperson is not evaluated on the same basis as a regular participant, a big X is drawn through his or her column on the participation chart. The evaluation forms are not signed.

When the discussion period is ended (or sometimes during the discussion), the rating scale is marked by each member. To save time, *only the extremes are indicated.* One can assume that most individuals will have an average rating. For example, if Michelle were characterized by a lack of stress throughout the presentation, her number (2 in Figure 8-1) would be entered to the right on the line representing voice quality and stress. Similarly, Paul's number (1) would be entered in the appropriate place on the scale for "Enthusiasm" if he were *either strong or weak* in this category. Since only the extremes are marked, usually there will be relatively few numbers appearing on the rating scales.

Since the chairperson is not evaluated by the audience, he or she takes the forms and analyzes them out of class. This involves little more than tallying points and assigning weights to the different categories of contribution as the group or the instructor suggests.

While the group is completing its evaluation of the panel participants, each panelist (including the chairperson) is given an evaluation form such as appears in Table 8-1. After leaving the group, panelists rate all group members, except themselves. Ratings are submitted the next day, thus keeping the evaluations confidential.

After each participant is ranked on the basis of points, the three evaluations (class, panel, and teacher) are averaged for individual marks. Although the preceding description may seem complicated and time-consuming, this is not the case. By maintaining an adequate supply of forms and assigning the leader the task of tallying the class forms, a teacher need only combine the three evaluations; this can be accomplished in five or ten minutes.

Such an evaluation procedure has many advantages, some of which are as follows:

1. It makes use of the peer group and thus reduces the tendency of some students to object to the teacher's evaluation. (In practice, the instructor's evaluation is usually as high, and sometimes higher, than that of the peer group.)
2. The evaluation makes the group realize the importance of the group deliberation process.
3. Students are prevented from taking notes or losing interest in the proceedings.
4. Use of peer evaluation, in this case, tends to add reliability to the evaluational

CONTRIBUTION

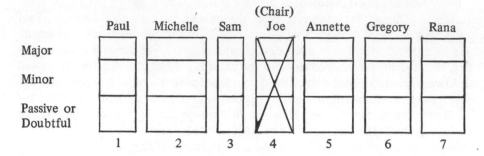

Major Contribution—Introduction of a new idea or significant clarification of the goal.

Minor Contribution—Keeping others on the topic, clarification of ideas already presented, minor addition to idea.

Passive or Doubtful Contribution—Statement of dubious value.

PERSONAL

1. *Voice Quality and Stress*

Emphasized points in speaking.	Occasionally stressed points but frequently spoke in a monotone.	Stress lacking. Mumbled.

2. *Knowledge of Subject*

Well informed. Used information to advantage.	Evidence of some information. Not especially well organized.	Little preparation indicated. Resorted chiefly to personal opinions.

3. *Enthusiasm*

Appeared to be highly interested and alert throughout the entire period.	Some interest indicated.	Lack of interest. This was just another job to do.

4. *Degree of Flexibility*

Willing to accept new evidence and to admit weaknesses of a contribution.	Some evidence of adaptability.	Unwilling to accept new evidence and to admit weakness of a contribution.

Quotes:

Comments:

FIGURE 8-1 *Audience Evaluation of Panelists*

TABLE 8-1 *Panelist Evaluation Form*

Directions: Rate all other participants on the panel, *including the chairperson.* Assign each participant a rating for *each* criterion. Several persons may be assigned the same rating on any one point. (Your rating, to be done in private, will be held strictly confidential.)

5 Superior   2 Below Average
4 Above Average 1 Poor
3 Average

(In case of doubt, assign mark of 3!)

	#1	#2	#3	#4	#5	#6	#7
	___	___	___	___	___	___	___
1. *Preparatory Activities* Attended and contributed in preliminary planning sessions. Did his share of reading in the area.	___	___	___	___	___	___	___
2. *Contribution to Panel Progress* Facilitated panel progress by adhering to discussion pattern, asking thought-provoking questions and assisting others in making key points.	___	___	___	___	___	___	___
3. *Value of Contributions* Depth of understanding; authoritative support for comments; reasoning ability.	___	___	___	___	___	___	___
4. *Discussion Attitude* Objectivity-openmindedness; goodwill toward others; contributed to "groupness."	___	___	___	___	___	___	___
5. *Communication Skills* Listened to others, effective voice control; courteous to others.	___	___	___	___	___	___	___

Total

Key to Identification:
(Names)

1_____   5_____
2_____   6_____
3_____   7_____
4_____

procedures. Generally speaking, as the number of subjective evaluations increases, the "halo effect" decreases.[6]

5. It enables a person to receive credit for thorough preparation which may not have been evident to the observers. In most cases, each member of the panel group is well aware of what has gone on behind the scenes.

What Functions Does the Follow-through Discussion Serve?

The teacher leads the group in a follow-through discussion in which students are expected to derive key generalizations from the experience. Most of the generalizations should come from the members of the audience rather than from the panel members, whose role is to clarify points. The teacher also may want to expand or introduce neglected points.

One should review the panel experience, especially when other groups are to follow. Could all members be heard? Was there enough probing? Was proper balance achieved? The instructor usually jots down key questions and comments as the discussion progresses, noting the students who make them.

The Value of Discussion

Group discussion involves the process of compromise essential to a democratic system.

Prejudices and biases are frequently modified when subjected to the scrutiny of the peer group.

When individuals in a group pool their ideas they are much more likely to correct deficiencies in evidence and reasoning than they could on their own.

The processes of discussion involve cooperation and sharing of ideas; thus judgments tend to improve.

Group discussion tends to make the leader and participants progressively less dependent on the teacher.

Limitations of, and Problems with, Discussion

Discussion presupposes adequate preparation.

The permissive characteristic of discussion tends to encourage digression.

The discussion leader may be unable to maintain an open mind.

Even when carefully organized, discussion is unpredictable.

Group agreement or consensus does not insure accomplishment of goals.

---

[6] The "halo effect" is the tendency of a rater to evaluate all characteristics on the basis of one impression.

I. Useful in biology, general science, and health classes

Unit: Microorganisms

Concept: Respiratory diseases are transmitted in many ways.

Problem: How can the transmission of respiratory diseases be minimized?

Sample analysis questions

1. What are some common respiratory diseases?
2. What are airborne mocroorganisms?
3. How are they transmittcd?
4. Why is this problem of more concern today than in the past?

Some possible solutions to consider

1. Pass strict laws on air pollution.
2. Require inoculations against disease.
3. Require medical checkups.
4. Require regular chest X-rays.

II. Useful in U.S. history, government, American problems, and sociology classes

Unit: The Beginnings of the American Tradition

Concept: Thomas Jefferson's political ideals provided the foundation of American democracy.

Problem: How can we best apply Thomas Jefferson's ideals of democracy to today's democracy?

Sample analysis questions

1. What were some of Jefferson's ideas of democracy?
2. How did he define aristocracy?
3. What did he mean by a "natural aristocrat"?
4. How do our president and vice-president fit that definition?

Some possible solutions to consider

1. Employ tests designed to classify public candidates for office.
2. Limit campaign funds.
3. Investigate family and background.
4. Consider leadership potential.

148   *METHODS AND TECHNIQUES: FOCUS ON THE LARGE GROUP*

III. Useful in U.S. history, government, American problems, and sociology classes

Unit: Birth of Democracy

Concept: The system of checks and balances is an integral part of all forms of democratic life.

Problem: What steps should be taken to change the method of electing a U.S. president?

Sample analysis questions

1. What is the electoral college? Why was it established?
2. What purposes does it presently serve?
3. What difficulties have been experienced in using it?
4. What hazards are involved in its continued use?

Some possible solutions to consider

1. Use electoral college votes based on a percentage of popular vote in each state.
2. Abandon the college, using percentage of popular vote only.
3. Use state vote only.
4. Use one electoral vote for each congressional district, plus two for every state.

IV. Useful in home economics and sociology classes

Unit: Marriage

Concept: There are many valid reasons why couples may or may not marry.

Problem: What factors should be considered in selecting a mate?

Sample analysis questions

1. What are some of the sources of mutual attraction?
2. What is meant by the phrase "love is blind"?
3. What is the purpose of the engagement period?

Some possible solutions to consider

1. Age, religion, and cultural background.
2. Values.
3. Life goals.
4. Physical features.

V. Useful in art and home economics classes

Unit: Color Relations

Concept. An individual can control color when he or she has the ability to analyze color relationships.

Problem: How might one use color in creating a work of art?

Sample analysis questions

1 What are the essential properties of color?
2 How did Albrecht Dürer use color in his painting *Young Hare?*
3 How did Paul Klee use color in his painting *Around the Fish? Girl with Jugs?*
4. How did Van Gogh use color in *The Orchard?*

Some possible solutions to consider

1. Give spatial quality to the pictorial field.
2. Create mood and symbolize ideas.
3. Express personal emotions and feelings.
4. Attract and direct attention as a means of giving organization and composition.

VI. Useful in earth science, biology, and general science classes.

Unit: Our Dynamic Earth and Its Materials

Concept: The sequential order of events enables us to reconstruct the earth's history.

Problem: What procedures should one follow in interpreting geologic history?

Sample analysis questions

1. How are "first events" identified in the earth's crust? later events?
2. What does the angle of beds mean in the history of rocks?
3. How does pressure contribute to the ordering of events?

Some possible solutions to consider

1. Submergence and disposition.
2. Emergence and erosion.
3. Igneous activity, dikes, and stocks.

chapter
9

REVIEW AND PRACTICE
PROCEDURES

Overview

Key Concepts

1. Although recall is a basic aspect of review, it merely sets the stage for the extension of original learnings.
2. A review emphasizes application of concepts to related problems.
3. Related problems are merely *identified* in a review lesson; they are not analyzed extensively.
4. Review and practice often are used informally in conjunction with other instructional experiences. A carefully planned concluding review is an essential experience, however.
5. Practice is an effective method for improving mental or motor skills; it is generally ineffective for improving cognitive and affective learnings, although commonly misused in this way.
6. Review is most effective in increasing retention of that which has been learned.

New Terms

1. Review A new look at previous learnings for the purpose of guiding the learner in applying original learnings to new situations.
2. Initial Learnings (for review) Previously learned concepts (ideas) that form the basis for review.
3. Retention One's ability to remember (and use) that which has been learned.
4. Drill Commonly used in connection with the teaching of mental skills. In this chapter the terms "drill" and "practice" are used interchangeably.
5. Practice Commonly used in connection with the teaching of motor skills.
6. Initial Learnings (for drill) Basic cognitive understanding or perception of the skill to be learned.
7. Varied Contact Preliminary practice of the skill being developed.

8. Repetitive Practice   That practice designed to correct minor details (problems) associated with a skill. Often referred to as "polishing" the skill.

9. Kinesthesis   Usually used in connection with motor skill development, the term refers to muscular sensation or the "feel" for a desired movement. Verbal and visual kinesthetic cues are most useful in the early states of learning, gradually giving way to internal cues as the skill develops.

10. Overlearning   Learning beyond the point of basic mastery. Up to 50 percent overlearning is recommended. Thus if basic mastery is achieved in thirty minutes, fifteen additional minutes could be profitably devoted to practice.

11. Specific Transfer   Application or extension of basic habits and associations to related areas. Mostly limited to skills type of learning.

12. Nonspecific Transfer   Application of principles and attitudes to future learning situations.

13. Reminiscence   The tendency of the mind to "continue on" (to learn) after a given learning experience has been terminated.

14. Negative Transfer   The interference of one learning with another similar learning.

Questions to Guide Your Study

1. Review and practice may be used interchangeably. Defend or refute.
2. Why must students assume major responsibility for a review discussion?
3. How does concept learning contribute to effective review?
4. Why are review lessons (as typically conducted) so often dull and boring?

Dr. Krupp was looking forward to today's review lesson in world history. For some time now, he had concluded each unit with at least one period of review, prior to his unit test. Even those students who had shown relatively little interest usually paid attention during the review proceedings.

As usual, he began by asking the class to submit questions on points needing clarification. Mary immediately opened the session by asking, "What do you think was the most important cause of World War I?" The instructor countered with, "How would *you* answer the question, Mary?" Thereupon, Mary proceeded to review two or three causes of the conflict which were mentioned either in the text or in previous class periods. After hearing responses from four more people, Dr. Krupp stated what he considered the major cause of the war. (Many of the class members made a note of this point, in preparation for the next day's test; the succeeding questions were handled in a similar manner.)

Note that the session was "carried" by five individuals. Most of the instructor's questions were designed to determine if students could *repeat* important points studied, whereas the students' questions were primarily concerned with the opinions of the instructor on important points. Toward the end of the hour, the group became quite restless. Some students apparently attempted to get Dr. Krupp off the topic into more interesting avenues of thought.

Dr. Krupp's review is representative of many such experiences. While it does contain some aspects of an appropriate review experience, its effectiveness is of little lasting value. The students obviously were interested in receiving help in passing a test. Instead of extending their associations in the area, they were *repeating* or *practicing* factual material that had already been covered. Dr. Krupp's lesson violated all the basics of a good review.

In the first place, repetition or drill generally is inappropriate for such a lesson. The recall content material does not ensure application. In fact, it has been demonstrated that such an experience often impedes the making of worthwhile associations. Both students and teacher have a tendency to think in terms of factual-type tests only. Like most other teaching methods, the review experience appropriately deals with the resolution of important problems. The only problem being solved during Dr. Krupp's lesson was preparing students for an examination. An important function of review is the *extension* or *transfer* of previous learnings to other areas.

Because he had no specific purpose, Dr. Krupp limited contributions to a few individuals. In most cases of this nature, these are people who will excel on written examinations. Even when there is a worthwhile purpose involved, interest tends to lag unless variety is introduced. Instead of discouraging attempts to digress, Mr. Krupp should have encouraged them—so long as they dealt with inferences and relationships concerning the lesson topic.

The term "review" is almost as ambiguous as the term "class discussion." Teachers speak of reviewing *for* a test, reviewing the *results* of a test, reviewing important words or terms, reviewing the major points of a lesson, and so on. Too often a review is little more than a repetitive practice, or drill. While there is a definite place for such an exercise, when drill is *substituted* for review, the results *must* be disappointing. Review, literally, means a re-view or a re-look at something. This review might be better called a new view, that is, a view of some problem from a new angle. It is a technique for guiding the student in applying original learnings to related situations.

Fundamental Properties

Review and practice, or drill, are old, time-tested techniques of teaching. They are essential to every subject area. Unfortunately, however, they have been grossly misused. Near the end of a long, illustrious career William Burton stated that although he had seen several hundred reviews in progress, practically none of them amounted to anything more than drill.[1] Yet in a recent analysis of the functions of a review lesson, Moynehan does not even mention drill when he says, "We visualize the review class as a time for consolidating previous learning, bringing a fresh perspective on that learning, and providing a basis for further learning. These classes are most successful if they . . . use factual information as a basis for developing broad conceptual understandings."[2]

The general inadequacy of review and practice reflects a basic misunderstanding of the fundamental psychological processes involved. This section emphasizes those fundamentals having a critical influence on review and practice.

What Is the Role of Review and Practice in Retention and Transfer of Learning?

Concepts learned in the classroom must be applied to related out-of-school situations. (The classroom is a contrived situation designed to illustrate a few applications.) Review and practice contribute substantially to retention and transfer of learning, provided the basic psychological processes involved are observed. At least three theories warrant brief examination.

1. The formal discipline theory. This theory proposes that memory, attitudes, judgments, and imagination can be strengthened through academic exercise. Because of this theory, geometry and Latin were once defended for their contributions to training one's reasoning faculties. Many studies, however, have contradicted this theory, stating that it is impossible to strengthen one's power of critical thinking, memory, and perceptions through academic exercise.

2. The identical elements theory. Experimental investigation consistently has revealed that the more two activities or situations are similar, the more training in one is likely to affect performance in the other. This has led to an emphasis on vocational training courses. In many instances, educators today emphasize a set pattern of responses that one should expect to apply in real-life situations. Psychologists, however, now place greater emphasis on the learner's *perception* of identical or similar elements rather than on his or her knowledge that they are alike or similar.

3. The generalization theory. This theory, an expansion of the identical elements theory, reemphasizes the complexities of that which has been learned. An internaliza-

---

[1] William H. Burton, *Guidance of Learning Activities,* 3rd ed. (New York: Appleton-Century-Crofts, Inc., 1962), p. 460.

[2] William J. Moynehan, "The Review Class," *Today's Education* 63 (November 1974): 78-79.

tion of broad understandings, skills, attitudes, and values may influence one's behavior in an infinite number of ways. As a result, concept formation can be related to other experiences in many ways other than the mere recognition of similar or identical elements.

In general, the skills type of learning is most likely applied to new situations under the following conditions: (1) when the initial responses are well learned, (2) when the learning situation closely resembles the potential out-of-school situation, and (3) when the learner can perceive the range of situations for which learning is applicable. For other types of learning, transfer to related situations is enhanced through students' encountering concepts, principles, theories, values, and attitudes in a variety of ways and through their actively seeking applications for the learning under consideration.

At this point, it might be well to *review* some basic psychological principles of retention and transfer of learning common to most educational psychology textbooks.

1. *Initial learning experiences tend to be retained best.* For this reason, it is imperative that first reactions be checked for accuracy. Incorrect responses are difficult to correct.

2. *The original learning sequence is easiest to recall.* This principle applies especially to mental and motor skills. Learning experiences, such as sequences and combinations, should be varied as much as possible.

3. *Generally, students retain about one-third of the material studied one year after taking the course, and forgetting continues, though at a much slower rate.* The degree of forgetting, however, is influenced by thoroughness of learning, along with its functional nature. The rate of forgetting is always greatest immediately following learning. Despite this factor, relearning is readily achieved.

4. *Recalling specific facts is much more difficult than recalling their existence or the attitude and method associated with them.* In those areas where concepts are to be learned, it is not necessary to stress recall of specific facts. An all too common error is the tendency to provide extensive drill in content areas. If the main ideas are clear, there is little or no need to retain specifics for any length of time.

5. *Learning beyond the point of basic mastery (overlearning) increases retention.* Generally about 50 percent overlearning is recommended. If, for example, one hour is necessary for basic mastery, an additional half hour might be devoted to practice of the material learned. Full attention must be directed to the task.

6. *Learning interrupted or stopped just prior to mastery improves recall after a brief interval of no further learning.* Known as *reminiscence,* this phenomenon suggests that the mind probably "continues on" until the learning sequence is completed. Later, additional practice may be desirable. When an initial learning process is completed, introduction of new material to "fill in" the rest of the class period should be discouraged.

7. *Numerous practice sessions varying in length of time are more effective in promoting prolonged recall than is one lengthy session.* Material crammed into one long session tends to be forgotten quickly. Practice sessions of decreasing

length, coupled with rest periods of increasing length, are preferred. A rest period is defined as any activity different from that being practiced. Because frequent short tests force distribution of practice, they are also effective in encouraging recall.

8. *Transfer of learning (from the classroom to related life situations) is more likely to occur when there is conscious teaching for transfer.* Although students (especially bright ones) will transfer to some extent on their own initiative, this process is greatly enhanced if the instructor makes a deliberate effort to encourage it.

9. *Concepts, methods, and attitudes are readily transferred to new situations; specific facts are transferred to new situations only if the new situations contain the same facts.* Since specifics are not retained as well as generalities, emphasis on recall is appropriately limited to the area of mental and motor skills.

10. *One learning may interfere with another, similar learning (negative transfer).* The greater the similarity between the two learnings, the less transfer there is likely to be.

11. *Negative transfer (the interference of one learning with another) is decreased when the corresponding elements are separated in time and context.* Thoroughness of learning, even to the extent of overlearning, tends to minimize negative transfer.

What Major Functions Are Served by Review and Practice?

As implied in the previous discussion, review and practice help learners apply original learnings to related life situations. The specifics (facts) of original learning provide a *basis* for this extension process. Through practice, learners perfect the mental or motor skills they have learned. Relearning, if it becomes necessary, is always an extremely difficult task since the initial learning pattern becomes "imprinted" in one's mind, and the skill is performed incorrectly from habit.

Prior to engaging in any form of practice, an individual must develop a basic cognitive understanding of the skill to be mastered. This usually involves some preliminary reading, participation in a discussion, or listening to a lecture presentation, for example. In the motor skills area, the importance of basic cognitive understanding is readily apparent; in the mental skills area, however, the problem is much less obvious. Drill, in the absence of basic understanding, is often confusing and usually a waste of time.

Cognitive understanding in the skills area may be greatly enhanced through a modeled demonstration. Such an experience must be as consistent as possible with basic understandings. All minor discrepencies should be clarified. The learner is then able to mimic his or her observation in the preliminary stages of application.

Review, likewise, is facilitated by recall of some specifics. In review, however, the specifics essentially consist of the recall of originally derived concepts. To assist students in recalling major ideas or concepts, the teacher should mention the context from which they were developed. Consequently, the experience may begin with the question "What have we done during this unit?" When an activity is mentioned (for example, class discussion), attention will be directed to the major idea(s) that evolved from the experience. Each major unit concept is identified in a similar manner. (They are usually listed, providing a basis for subsequent review activities.) Instead of recalling these concepts as ends in learning, however, students should relate them to other concepts previously learned. Factual recall plays a negligible role in review techniques.

What Are Some Occasions and Conditions for Review and Practice?

Review and practice occur constantly during the instructional process and at the end of a unit. Even tests, when appropriately constructed, provide excellent review and practice experiences.

Regardless of when review and practice occur, they serve the basic functions previously described. Because of the informal nature of a substantial portion of all review activities, however, there is a tendency to "slide over" the activity carelessly. At definite points during a lesson, assessments of learning transfer should be made. Questions such as "How can this idea be applied?" and "What implications do you see?" should be asked. Figure 9-1 depicts this learning transfer process.

Even though the teacher may initially emphasize concept learning it is likely to be minimal if the review and tests stress recall questions. Students study for tests. If they anticipate basic knowledge-level questions, they will make little or not effort to think in terms of applying concepts.

Daily short drill, or practice, sessions are needed to maintain the skill. Especially in the area of mental skills, the learner soon becomes exhausted. Fifteen- to thirty-minute sessions are most efficient. When an individual becomes exhausted, the frequency of mistakes increases. If repeated often enough, the mistakes may become "stamped-in" and thus extremely difficult to correct. Although the same principle holds in the area of motor skills, it may be necessary to gradually lengthen practice sessions for the purpose of developing "polish." This is especially true in the competitive sports area, where individuals frequently must play under exhausting conditions.

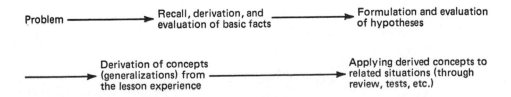

FIGURE 9-1   *The Learning Transfer Process*

Daily practice is recommended. Less practice is not efficient for maintaining efficiency. The polish phase of skills development represents overlearning (learning beyond the point of basic mastery). Drill in up to 50 percent overlearning is recommended. For example, a foreign language skill that requires one hour to learn may be efficiently drilled for one and one-half hours. Although the same principle holds for motor skills, the coach of a competitive sports team may emphasize drill beyond the point of minimal efficiency to produce team excellence.

Why Is Drill, or Practice, an Individualistic Process?

In translating any cognitive learning into somatic movements, each individual is unique. In skills development, orthodox approaches are encouraged. Ultimately, however, those practice exercises necessary for learning "the correct strokes" become an individual matter.

Similarly, in teaching a verbal skill, it may be necessary for an entire class to sound out certain words in unison in the early stages of drill. Otherwise, drill is something that each learner must perform individually. The same principle holds for a motor skill. Even though several members of a team may be on the field at the same time, the coaches must observe the progress of each student in perfecting the skill. For this reason, drill outside the class setting is usually encouraged.

Review, on the other hand, is tremendously enhanced in group settings. For example, one individual's insightful application often serves as a catalyst for other students. Such a review lesson contains many elements of creativity.

What Is the Role of Feedback in Skills Development?

Skills development basically consists of solving mechanical problems. Basic to this process is immediate knowledge of results. In the early stages of skills development, the learner should receive feedback from each exploratory try. In learning a motor skill, for example, students must realize what their muscles are doing *and* what the muscles *should be doing* to perform the skill properly.

Although verbal feedback is reinforcing, visual feedback is more reinforcing. By videotaping exploratory trys and playing the tapes back immediately, teachers enable students to analyze their performance and make necessary adjustments. Once an adequate record of the movement is established, the learner can use memory to guide performance. Verbal and visual cues are gradually eliminated.

What Is the Role of Kinesthetic Sense in Motor Learning?

In the early stages of skills development, motor patterns are developed through "trial runs." Varied trys at performing the skill call attention to certain patterns. Accuracy is not important at this point. With practice, however, each movement is refined partially by "feel"; that is, the learner begins to internalize the movement(s).

Less conscious effort is required to perform the task than originally needed. The degree of effort varies with the individual and the particular skill involved.

As skills development progresses, the "feel" or "touch" for various movements becomes increasingly evident. In order to enhance this experience, continued use of visual cues is desirable. Films and demonstrations help learners "sharpen their mental image" of the skill to be mastered. Some teachers reinforce the kinesthetic sense of the learner by calling attention to sounds, such as the "crack" of the bat or the "swish" of the tennis racket. This feedback assists the learner in developing appropriate associations between sound and movement. In the advanced stages of motor learning, kinesthetic sense becomes internalized.

Motor skills sometimes are developed inappropriately prior to any organized instruction. Relearning thus becomes extremely difficult since a new set of guidelines (cues) must be established for developing the correct "feel" for the movement. The learner may revert to his or her old (outmoded) patterns without even becoming aware of the process. Even so, this kinesthetic sense accompanies learning and provides necessary feedback for the learner.

What Is the Role of the Teacher in Review and Practice?

Practice techniques demand some teacher guidance in order to establish basic patterns for subsequent practice. In the motor skills area (for example, the tennis serve), certain basic steps must be followed. Until a basic pattern is established, constant teacher guidance is essential. Similarly, in the mental skills area, the teacher must make sure that the principle, axiom, or postulate (as in mathematics) is correctly applied.

Review techniques are also facilitated when the teacher points out related applications. Quite early in the process, however, the emphasis must shift to the students' making their own applications. Thus the teacher guides students and asks them probing questions that will direct them toward their own applications (see Chapter 7 for an analysis of this process).

How Does Review Differ from Class Discussion?

In a class discussion, a problem of policy is studied, with the hope that some sort of resolution of the difficulty might be reached. As a *result of this experience,* students should attain certain concepts or centralized ideas useful in the resolution of related problems. The review is also a problem-solving process. Unlike class discussion however, it deals with problems that are closely related to original learnings. The following serves to further clarify this distinction.

Dr. Anderson's U.S. history class was concerned with the Jacksonian era. A substantial portion of the text material dealt with the "spoils system" first popularized during the administration of President Andrew Jackson. Recognizing the historical significance of the subject, Dr. Anderson decided to guide students in the discussion problem by asking, "What steps should our government adopt concerning vested interests among public officials?"

In the analysis of the problem, the past history of the situation was thoroughly developed. Thus the "spoils system" for the Jacksonian era was brought to bear upon the resolution of a current difficulty.

In a later (review) lesson, Dr. Anderson wanted to help students broaden and extend their understanding of the problem. Above all, she hoped they might apply these concepts to related situations. This time, instead of a broad question of policy, she formulated key questions of advocacy (actually restricted policy questions) definitely related to, but not identical with, previous questions in the area.

1. Should businessmen be barred from public office?
2. Should U.S. congressional representatives be required to relinquish share holdings in corporations when elected to office? If so, should the same ruling apply to state and local officials?
3. Should our local government establish civil service requirements for elected public officials? (This might cause the class to check further into the history of the civil service law, first enacted under President Chester A. Arthur's administration.
4. Should members of the President's cabinet qualify under civil service regulations?

Because Dr. Anderson drew their attention to such related problems, the students were able to associate isolated learnings with a number of important issues. From the preceding examples, four important distinctions between review and class discussion procedures are evident.

1. The review lesson deals with issues related to those resolved in one or more class discussions (or some other method). It is, in essence, a means of applying initial learnings to related problems.
2. The major thrust of a review involves questions of advocacy, whereas class discussion deals with all question levels as students deal with one basic problem of policy. In discussing a broad question of policy, a group attempts to decide *what* course of action is preferable. The more restricted advocacy question is concerned with one alternative. It is related to the resolution of a debate but, unlike debate, pertains to problems very closely related to previous class learnings.
3. Because of the nature of the activity, a review lesson can introduce a number of difficult issues. The guided class discussion typically treats only those problems pertaining to the resolution of one major difficulty or issue.
4. The outcome of a review is not so much the resolution of related issues as it is the recognition of those issues. Class discussion, on the other hand, emphasizes the *entire problem process* along with its end products. In class discussion,

emphasis is on the students' resolution of problems; in review, the emphasis is on *associaion* of given learnings to related issues.

How Does Drill, or Practice, Differ from Review?

Practice and review are alike in that they both supplement initial classroom learnings. Moreover, there is a substantial amount of recall in review procedures. It must be remembered, however, that in review, a minimum amount of time is devoted to the recall of basic concepts and that these concepts serve as a *means* of focusing on the major issue to be resolved. "What problems seem to relate to the things we have learned?" Furthermore, both practice and review, when properly used, ensure more permanent learning. The deeper understandings and association gained through review, like the polish developed through practice, tend to make learnings more functional, thus increasing retention.

As previously indicated, although practice techniques are most effective in teaching skills, they are not effective in teaching concepts in cognitive and affective domains. In these areas, reviews are needed. Whereas review involves the process of *group* deliberation or problem solving, practice techniques for the most part do not rely on group processes. Practice, or drill, can be considered an extension to the *group* problem-solving process—one of refining the *products* of deliberative processes. Another important distinction between the two techniques is that a review lesson involves the entire class group but practice or drill procedures must be individualized. In a review lesson, for example, the relationships and associations developed by one member can be especially helpful to the other class members. Practice, or drill, however, usually is much more effective when individualized. Most of us can remember instances when the class was asked to repeat something in unison. Perhaps it was the letters of the alphabet or a rule of grammar. Recent investigation, however, has discredited such practices. One junior high school teacher even questions the time-honored practice of pledging allegiance to the flag as a result of her having had students write out what they were actually saying. Lack of understanding was readily apparent from such expressions as "One nation under guard"; "I pledge a leagence."

Review Procedure

Once an individual has resolved an issue (facilitated through some other teaching method), a review can help him or her acquire new meanings, understandings, and attitudes from original concepts or generalizations. Psychologists tell us that transfer of learnings to related situations occurs to the extent that the learner is able to recognize identical or similar elements in both situations. *Review, then, is a technique for guiding the student in the application of original learnings to related situations.*

Although it is recognized that a *re*-view or *re*-look is important at any point during a lesson, the emphasis in this chapter is on review lessons that occur at the end of a unit or block of work. The basic essentials, however, can be readily applied to other review situations. Those who have been most successful with the technique usually direct their attention to the steps that follow.

What Is the Role of Recall in Review?

Recall is a fundamental aspect of review. Basic unit concepts are brought together in one lesson for the first time. As a means of assisting students in recalling major ideas or concepts, it is often desirable to recall the context from which they were developed. Consequently, the experience may begin with the question "What have we done during this unit?" When an activity is mentioned (for example, class discussion), attention will be directed to the major idea(s) that evolved from the experience. In like manner, each major unit concept is identified. (They are usually listed, providing a basis for subsequent review activities.)

It should be noted that the major unit concepts, developed by students during a review, will not be identical to individual lesson generalizations. Rather they will be similar to *unit* concepts developed by the teacher in preinstructional planning activities. (Each lesson is normally based on one such concept.) The teacher does *not* provide the learner with his or her own list of unit concepts, however. Unit concepts, derived by students, are likely to more closely parallel actual learnings than those sought by the teacher.

This phase of review involves clarifying, in some cases for the first time, the major ideas (concepts) of the unit. Since the ideas are based on a number of lesson generalizations, the process of abstraction, in addition to mere recall, is involved. There is a natural tendency, however, to expand lesson generalizations into broader concepts. This process should be encouraged. To illustrate from an art class concerned with color relationships:

Lesson generalizations

1. Light, bright colors evoke a happy, gay mood.
2. Dark, somber colors generally evoke a depressing mood.
3. Different colors have different emotional impacts. (Red, for example, is happy, exciting.)
4. Colors symbolize ideas. (Blue, for instance, is associated with loyalty and honesty.)

In recalling these generalizations, students might be guided in evolving the following unit concept: "Color may be used to create mood and symbolize ideas." The reader will note that the mere recall of specific facts is not an essential aspect of review.

How Are Unit Concepts Extended to Related Problems?

Basic unit learnings are broadened when the student perceives how they can be applied to related problems and situations. This application process is the heart of every review lesson. Expansion of original learning is achieved through a process of skillful questioning.

In this phase of review, the higher order questions are emphasized. Advocacy questions beginning with the word *should* are often asked. An advocacy question directs attention to one particular solution to a problem. Sometimes, *how* or *could* questions are also asked. For example, the teacher might ask an art class studying color relationships "How can use of color improve our homes?" Possible responses might include the following:

1. Light, cool colors make walls seem to recede.
2. A single dark wall may be used to correct the proportions of a large, square room.
3. Single light-colored walls give focus to a large, square room.
4. Dark, warm colors may be used to make large barnlike rooms cosier.

Each suggested application is discussed briefly for the purpose of clarifying the idea. No effort is made to resolve issues in a review lesson since its purpose is *to determine related problems for expansion of knowledge.* (In some instances, of course, such problems may reveal the need for further consideration of basic issues. In such cases, other appropriate techniques will be employed.)

In a review lesson, students should assist in recall of basic generalizations and in derivation of concepts; they should bear the major responsibility for extending these learnings to related areas. It may be necessary for the instructor to offer a few suggestions in order to prepare students for further analysis. There is a decided tendency to rush students through a review lesson, under the assumption that most of the important relationships are obvious. Evidence quite clearly suggests, however, that students transfer learnings only to the extent to which they are taught to transfer. Two or three class periods might be profitably devoted to such activities.

How Is the Review Lesson Evaluated?

The review lesson, designed to extend learnings to related problems, is closely akin to evaluational experiences. An appropriate review generates considerable enthusiasm and creativity. When individuals understand how their school experiences can be applied to out-of-school problems, they develop and maintain a high degree of interest. The teacher also becomes more conscious of the importance of transfer of learnings to related situations.

The effectiveness of a review lesson, perhaps more than with any other method, is reflected in a written unit test. Frequently, however, students complain if teachers emphasize the application of broad concepts in review and then give examinations based largely on specific details. Such inconsistency seriously undermines the effectiveness of instruction. Tests, however, must also include additional problems not introduced during reviews since their purpose is to determine if students can make associations and relationships on their own.

What Preplanning Is Needed?

A major factor contributing to poor review lessons is inadequate planning. Teachers quite naturally are interested in clarifying facts and principles; oddly enough, they are often less interested in extending them to real-life applications. Yet, it is through extension and association of ideas that adequate understanding is best revealed. The following illustrated lesson plan suggests how a review of a unit may be treated.

LESSON PLAN FOR AN ART OR HOME ECONOMICS CLASS IN BASIC DESIGN

Unit: Color Relationships

Concept: (The concepts are stated as point A,B,C, and D under lesson development.)

Problem: How can we relate what we have learned about color relationships to different situations outside the realm of fine arts?

Goals: After this lesson the student should have furthered his or her understanding of the basic principles underlying color relationships as evidenced by:

1. The ability to identify related problems in class review.
2. The ability to apply basic principles to related problems.
3. The ability to draw parallels with problems previously studied.

Lesson approach

During the past few weeks, we have emphasized the principles underlying color relationships. We have analyzed the properties of color, and we have seen how colors may be used to give spatial quality to the pictorial field, to create mood and symbolize ideas, to attract and direct attention, to organize a composition, and to accomplish aesthetic appeal. We have seen that color is one of the most expressive of art elements because its quality affects our emotions directly and immediately.

Although we have spent the last few weeks exploring color relationships in the fine arts area, color is not restricted to this domain. Actually, colors permeate every area of our lives. Today, we will take a look at some of the areas outside the realm of fine arts, areas where carefully controlled color solves numerous problems.

Lesson development

I. Recall of basic unit concepts
   What generalizations evolved during our study of this unit?
   A. Color may be used to give spatial quality to the pictorial field.
      1. The warm colors (red, orange, and yellow) will, in general, bring the pictorial field forward.

   2. The cool colors (containing blue), such as green, violet, and blue-green, will usually make the pictorial field recede.

  B. Color may be used to create mood and to symbolize ideas.

   1. Light, bright colors evoke a happy, gay mood.

   2. Dark, somber colors generally evoke a depressing mood.

   3. Different colors have different emotional impacts; for example, red evokes a happy, exciting mood; blue suggests a dignified, sad, or serene mood.

   4. Colors symbolize ideas. Blue is associated with loyalty and honesty; red with bravery, passion, or danger; yellow with cowardice; black with death, green with life, hope, or envy; white with purity or innocence; and purple with royalty or wealth.

  C. Color may be used to direct attention and to organize a composition.

  D. Colors properly combined are aesthetically appealing.

 II. Recall of how the major concepts were derived

  A. Each student created a collage of simple flat shapes overlapping in space. These flat shapes were cut from colored paper and pasted on a neutral background. The colors were chosen to establish spatial position of the forms.

  B. Each student executed three small paintings using color, not subject matter, to express (1) a happy mood, (2) a sad mood, and (3) either an angry or dangerous mood.

  C. To illustrate color organization in a composition, each student executed three small paintings: (1) monochromatic, (2) analogous, and (3) complementary in color.

  D. To illustrate aesthetic appeal, we discussed harmonious color combinations. We discussed selection of hues and arrangement of them in a pictorial field. We also discussed variety and repetition and dominance. These activities were followed with a critique on the finished paintings and collages.

 III. Extension of unit concepts to related problems

  With our ideas before us, let us briefly consider other areas to which they may apply.

  1. How can we use color to improve our homes?

   a. Light, cool colors make walls seem to recede, giving a small room a more spacious impression.

   b. A single, dark wall may be used to correct the proportions of a long, narrow room.

   c. A single, light-colored wall gives focus to a large, square room.

   d. Dark, warm colors make walls appear to close in. They are often used to make large, barnlike rooms seem cozier.

  2. How can we use color to improve our clothing?

   a. Color in everyday clothing can correct the physical disproportions of individuals.

   b. Color in theatrical costumes can set a mood and help symbolize ideas.

3. How can we use color to improve industry?
   a. Illumination may be improved through the use of color.
   b. Frequencies of color may be lowered with use of color.
4. How could we use color to improve hospitals?
   a. The psychological effects of different colors are used.
   b. Visual variety is considered essential in the care of hospital patients.
5. How can we use color to improve architecture?
   a. Color is used to make buildings more aesthetic.
   b. Color is used to control heat reflection.
6. Should we use color to improve restaurants?
   a. Bright, cool colors make a restaurant appear clean.
   b. Warm, subdued colors place the customer at ease and presumably increase the size of his check.
7. How can we use color to improve sales?
   a. Colors attract attention to packaging.
   b. Colors can make advertising more emphatic.

Deriving generalizations

From our treatment of related problems, what big ideas seem to stand out?
1. Color, when carefully controlled, is capable of improving every area of our environment.
2. Color deals with facts and principles that can be scientifically utilized.

It should be noted that the last phase of the illustrated plan (deriving generalizations) involves a further abstraction of unit concepts. Although this is not an essential aspect of a review lesson, it may be useful as a means of clarifying the basic theme of the unit.

As in any method of teaching, there are certain steps that, if followed closely, will greatly accelerate development of effective skills. Although the perfection of motor skills depends to some degree on innate ability, these skills seldom will be fully realized in the absence of an effective training program. A basketball team, for example, may be limited by the innate abilities of its players, but these abilities certainly can be improved by effective coaching. The same principle holds for other skills. Teaching, for example, is a complex of skills that can be developed. Although some teachers possess more natural abilities than others, appropriate instructional procedures can be of invaluable assistance to most of them. The cliché that "teachers are born and not made" has been thoroughly disproved. Perhaps as a consequence of the earlier and false notion that skills cannot be taught, they were for a long time left to chance. Even today, some teachers make relatively little systematic effort to develop mental skills among students.

Drill, or Practice, Procedures

As a result of extensive investigation, educational psychologists have been able to offer many useful clues to the effective development of skills. Three steps contribute greatly to the development of skills: (1) development of initial learning, (2) varied contact, (3) and repetitive practice. These are discussed in the following sections.

How Are Skills First Introduced?

A skill, like any other learning, is first introduced by explaining to the student its purpose. Once the purpose is thoroughly understood, verbal instruction on the rudiments of the skill is given, often accompanied by a demonstration of the skill, in order to promote full comprehension of the purpose of the activity and the general form and sequence of events to be followed.

Detailed explanations or demonstrations should be avoided at this point. If more than the rudiments of the skill are presented, thinking processes may become confused. A speech teacher, for example, first introduces the art of speechmaking with a brief description of the following points:

1. Introduction—attention-getting
2. Body—two or three main points to be developed
3. Conclusion—restatement of the major theme of the presentation

This description can be followed by the teacher's giving a five-minute speech that illustrates these points.

What Function Does Varied Contact with the Skill Serve During the Early Phase of Its Development?

After being briefly introduced to a skill in a functional situation, the learner must have direct contact with it in a variety of meaningful situations. The learner must be given an opportunity to engage in exploratory trials, ask questions, observe skilled performers, and inspect diagrams, for example. In terms of the problem-solving process, this phase might be called *evaluation of alternative proposals* since during this phase, students develop and test their own ways of performing the skill. This is indeed the *creative* aspect of skills development.

The teacher can **be** especially useful in the exploratory phase of mastering a skill by helping students capitalize on strengths and minimize weaknesses. By pointing out their strengths and weaknesses, the teacher can aid learners in diagnosing their own problems. Recognizing the importance of reinforcement or reward in learning, the teacher should make critiques as positive as possible.

One of the greatest problems a teacher will encounter in skills development is getting learners to see their mistakes. For example, the mere act of telling a person that he or she has a flat, nasal voice may have absolutely no effect for the simple reason that we have no difficulty hearing our own voices but we do have difficulty

playback of a selected presentation, however,
results. Similarly, it may accomplish little to
or that their posture detracts from their
the back of the room, however, the problem

at verbal instruction is all that is needed to
once a person understands how a skill is
rocess through individual initiative. An
found in the teaching of instructional
ities. The complaint is often heard, "We
achers how to teach, but they tend to
." A more accurate statement would be
prepared to utilize the skills involved. They
with skills under controlled and closely supervised conditions that
approach actual situations as nearly as possible. Simulated teaching experiences in a
methods course cannot produce proficiency in the skills needed, but they can broaden
understanding and perception of the intricate relationships involved. If a teacher is to
use review, drill, sociodrama, and class discussion effectively, verbal explanations,
demonstrations, and varied direct contact with the skills, prior to actual teaching, are
needed. Polish can be achieved later in intern teaching situations, for example.

How Does Repetitive Practice Contribute to Acquisition of Skills?

A skill must be repeated often for the purpose of refining it. The *conditions* under
which it is performed, however, should be varied as often as possible in order to
prevent boredom and, more importantly, to enhance the likelihood of its transfer to
related situations. Let us take an example from the area of foreign language. A group
of students in a beginning Spanish class could practice speaking the language by
discussing a topic in class, by visiting the Spanish consul's office, by planning an
imaginary trip to some South American country, or by inviting some Spanish-speaking
people to class. The vocabulary drill should be similar in all situations, but the
situations should be varied.

Although repetitive practice is essential for perfecting a skill, forcing students to
practice will have little positive results. Students must be self-motivated to improve
their skills through practice. Following a period of accelerated learning that results
from early practice sessions, many learners reach a plateau in their progress. This
probably indicates a need for a more thorough understanding of the relationship
between certain details and the total skill. At this point, added encouragement and
direction from the teacher is extremely useful. A chart showing the individual's own
progress tends to contribute to continued interest and improvement.

Practice or repetition can become monotonous very quickly, even under the most
favorable circumstances. When individuals practice for purposes very important to

them, motivation can remain high for long periods of time. To ██████████
classroom problems are more remote to the learner than might b█████████
nature of the materials sometimes accounts for this difficulty. ██████████
terminology and sequences of events, for example, may be important █████
very interesting. Short games offer excellent opportunities for motivat█████
Games can be created in which winning is not essential in order to encou███
students who really need the practice.

The Value of Review

Review facilitates application or transfer of learnings to related situations. It has long been recognized by psychologists that individuals apply or transfer learnings to new experiences to the extent that they are taught to make this transfer.

The formulation of new associations and relationships, through review, renders learning more permanent.

Review enables the teacher to correct misconceptions and misunderstandings that inevitably arise in group-learning situations.

Review procedures are extremely flexible. They may range from the informal five-minute review at the end of a class period to extended reviews of one or more class periods.

The Value of Drill, or Practice

Drill, or practice, is the basic instructional method for acquisition of mental and motor skills.

The individualistic nature of the method is conducive to direct pupil involvement. Especially in the motor skills area, interest is easily maintained.

Drill, or practice, when spaced appropriately, can reduce the rate of forgetting and contribute to continued development of the skill.

Practice develops habits. Thus desirable habits developed during the adolescent years tend to become a part of one's life style.

Limitations of, and Problems with, Review

Review has been widely misused. Recitation sessions in which learners have been expected to recall specific facts for a test have been often substituted for review.

Conducting a review session before students have developed a thorough understanding of the material is pointless.

Review is deceptively easy. Even when review is used for the purpose of expanding learning, it is extremely easy to get bogged down on some related issue. If this occurs, review purposes may be impossible to achieve.

The written test following a review must cover the material discussed in the review; that is, it must contain questions that evaluate the student's application of knowledge to real-life situations and not the student's recall of isolated facts.

Drill, or practice, in the cognitive domain usually is inappropriate.

Since early drill, or practice, is largely exploratory, diagnosis is essential. Misguided drill, or practice, may impede appropriate skills development.

In the early stages of skills development, accuracy, rather than speed, should be emphasized. Because skills development is largely individualistic in nature, it is sometimes difficult to achieve a balance between speed and accuracy.

Repetitive drill, or practice, may become monotonous unless a variable learning environment is provided.

Overlearning in the later stages of skills development is desirable. Since the degree of overlearning will depend somewhat on the learner's purpose, it may be difficult to work out appropriate practice sessions with each individual learner.

Limitations of, and Problems with, Drill, or Practice

Illustrated Review Problems

I. Useful in history, government, and social studies classes

Unit: Population Pressures

Problem: How can we relate what we have learned in this unit to other problems in the Far East?

Unit concepts

1. Many conflicts are indirectly related to inadequate food supplies.
2. Basic religious differences account for much strife within and among many nations of the Far East.
3. Problems of population control reflect religious, educational, and cultural concerns.
4. Asiatic mistrust of the West is related to past colonial problems.
5. Communism tends to have a special appeal to impoverished peoples.
6. Regional development is hampered by long-standing disputes and mistrust between neighboring countries.
7. Underdeveloped nations often assume that the wealthier nations have a moral obligation to provide economic assistance.

Extending concepts to related areas

1. Should we withdraw support from those nations that violate human rights?
2. Should we pressure certain nations into accepting the will of the majority?
3. Should we encourage the establishment of birth-control clinics in nations like India and Pakistan?
4. Should we develop regional assistance programs in return for crude oil shipments?

II. Useful in U.S. history, American literature, and social studies classes

Unit: Responsible Individuals Make Up a Democracy

Problem: How can we relate what we have learned in this unit to other problems involving decision-making processes?

Unit concepts

1. Mature decision-making is part of becoming a responsible adult.
2. People both as individuals and as part of a group have responsibilities for the democratic judicial process.
3. In a democracy, one must not be politically disinterested.
4. Duties and privileges in a democratic family unit parallel those of all citizens.
5. Participation in the arts is a privilege and responsibility of all citizens.

Extending concepts to related areas

1. Should the citizen try to influence television programming toward higher aesthetic levels?
2. Should an individual expound an unpopular personal philosophy?
3. Should an adult let children share equally in family decisions?

III. Useful in physical education, group guidance, and sociology classes

Unit: Teamwork in Sports and Society

Problem: How can we relate what we have learned about teamwork to our lives as a whole?

Unit concepts

1. We are on teams all our lives.
2. Each player has a responsibility to the team.
3. It is as important to bring others into team participation as it is to make an individual contribution to the team.
4. Principles of teamwork are readily transferred to teamwork in society.
5. All people must be competent team workers to function effectively in society.

Extending concepts to related areas

1. How can teamwork be used in civic clubs?
2. How can we use teamwork principles in church groups?
3. How can we use teamwork principles in the family?
4. How can we use teamwork principles at work?

IV. Useful in mathematics classes

Unit: Equations and Formula

Problem: How can we relate what we have learned about equations and formulas to everyday situations?

Unit concepts

1. Parentheses must be cleared before any action is taken outside the parentheses.
2. There are three types of equations: true, false, and conditional.
3. Every equation possesses roots which must be clearly understood for effective use.
4. Equations and formulas represent ways of expressing equivalence.

Extending concepts to related areas

1. How can one find solutions without using parentheses?
2. How can equations be used to solve distance problems?
3. How can equations be applied to navigational problems?
4. How can equations be used to help us save money?

V. Useful in chemistry classes

Unit: The Gas Laws

Problem: How can we relate our learning about gas laws to practical aspects of living?

Unit concepts

1. Pressure is defined as a force per unit of area.
2. Temperature is based on arbitrary scales.
3. Volume is a three-dimensional quantity.
4. Pressure is inversely proportional to volume.
5. Volume is directly proportional to pressure.

Extending concepts to related areas

1. How can we transport more electric power to existing power lines?
2. How can the power of electric magnets be increased?
3. How can living organisms be preserved for future use?

Illustrated Drill, or Practice, Techniques

I. Useful in any motor skills area

Videotaped explorations

Prepare for five-minute skills-teaching sessions by having students select either a progressive or a repetitive task sequence. Then tape their performance of the skills involved.

Immediately following the experience, replay the tape for study and analysis. Have students analyze themselves in terms of delivery, continuity and sequences, and specific techniques and styles used. Finally, have students identify different ways of performing key phases of the experience. (This tends to expand thinking, thereby encouraging new insights in the area.)

II. Useful in foreign language (or almost any mental skills area)

If, as has been emphasized in this chapter, mental skills development involves a form of mechanical problem solving, the traditional drill procedure may need to be lengthened.[3]

A. The teacher reads aloud the first line of the drill (often about four or five lines long) plus the cue word for the next line.

Model sentence:	The chair is in the room.
Cue:	Table
Response:	The table is in the room.
Cue:	Book

(This exercise is repeated until students learn the vocabulary.)

B. Students provide sentences from the drill in any order without cues.
C. Students take turns suggesting sentences that are grammatically similar to those in the drill but which contain other vocabulary.
D. Students use sentences derived from the previous steps that hopefully will draw reactions from the teacher or other students.[4]

Such an experience tends to make drill sessions less teacher centered and has the advantage of encouraging pupil reflection, thereby broadening and expanding original learning.

III. Drill teams (for the practice of both mental and motor skills)

After the rudiments of the skill are understood, gross body movements follow. The participant must progress through a stage of "shaping" body movements or vocal patterns. Another student (who possesses basic understanding) can be extremely useful in providing much needed feedback and diagnosis.

Following short practice sessions and critiques (perhaps repeated once), the roles of the team members are switched. The technique permits the instructor to concentrate on common problems and unusual difficulties as he or she moves from one drill team to another.

IV. Use of games (for the practice of both mental and motor skills)

Games are so often used to teach motor skills that it is difficult to think of them in any other context. Oddly enough, games as a vehicle for teaching mental skills have been strangely neglected even though the basic instructional method is the same for both mental and motor skills.

---

[3] For a thorough analysis of how this process is related to transactional psychology, the reader is referred to Earl W. Stevick, "The Meaning of Drills and Exercises," *Language Learning* 24 (June 1974): 1-22.

[4] Ibid., pp. 16-17.

A. Useful in foreign language, business, or mathematics

Set up a party in a foreign country. Assign students specific roles such as hosts and hostesses, visiting celebrities, young and old adults, and children. Have each participant plan an aspect of conversation that will offer a challenge to others.

Set up a mock business where shorthand must be taken (and dictated) under a variety of trying conditions. Include typists who must prepare manuscripts under a variety of pressure situations. Also include office workers and other personnel who might be found in any large business firm.

Develop a mock business situation involving mathematicians, accountants, tax specialists, and sales personnel. With imagination roles can be established for a variety of skill levels.

B. Useful in industrial arts and home economics

Turn the school shop into an imaginary industrial shop. Accept a variety of orders from customers in the local area. Contract these jobs out to students, according to their various skill levels. (Such a "game" will not only spark considerable interest but results in a wide range or projects.) If additional equipment is needed or additional skills must be developed, make the necessary arrangements as would be expected in any such firm.

chapter 10

LECTURE METHODS

Overview

Key Concepts

1. For many years, the lecture method has been misused at all levels of instruction.
2. The informal lecture (lecturette) is basically a means of clarifying or expanding information; other supplementary methods must be employed to complete the reflective process.
3. The lecturette is short, usually lasting for less than thirty minutes.
4. The lecturer must provide a structural framework for connecting new material to existing concepts.
5. The lecturer employs visual aids and repetition in order to increase understanding and retention.

New Terms

1. Formal (Extended) Lecture   A presentation lasting for a whole class period, designed to offer information and solve problems *for* the learner. In conventional college classes, the lecturer is usually assisted by one or more graduate assistants. (When used in connection with flexible scheduling, the lecture is designed to set the stage for small-group activities and independent study. In such a context, it is usually referred to as large-group lecture.)
2. Informal Lecture (Lecturette)   A short presentation designed to inform or clarify points that may be temporarily impeding the processes of reflective thinking.
3. Advance Organizer   Introductory comments and materials designed to provide anchorage with existing concepts.
4. Overview and Summary   Techniques for emphasizing and simplifying the main points of a lecture.

Questions to Guide Your Study

1. Why should extensive use of the extended lecture be discouraged?
2. The lecture method is an easy method to employ. Defend or refute.
3. Reflective thinking processes are at a minimum level during an extended lecture. Defend or refute.
4. What techniques for improving listening do you consider most practical?
5. What are the functions of questions and discussion following a lecture?

The lecture is currently the most widely used, yet the most highly criticized, instructional method in colleges and universities. It was popularized in the medieval university during the fifteenth century, prior to the development of moveable type. The lecturer, possessing the only book available, read to students. The term itself is derived from the Latin word *legere* (past participle, *lectus*), which means "to read." Lecturing eventually became synonymous with teaching. Times changed more rapidly than instructional procedures, it seems, since teachers continued to base their lectures on text materials long after books became available to all class members.

Though cognizant of criticisms of the method, most professors continue to lecture, partially because of habit and tradition and partially because of certain assumptions about the method. One underlying assumption is that lecturing enables students to share with the teacher the process of reflective thinking. Another is that the presentation of facts leads to independent problem solving by the learner. While these assumptions are valid to a limited degree, they are certainly questionable in many situations. Certainly, it makes no sense to give students information they can readily obtain and understand from reading their textbooks. Yet, this is precisely what happens in too many instances.

The short informal lecture, or lecturette, on the other hand, serves a distinctly different function. It is merely an auxiliary technique used in conjunction with other instructional methods to clarify and expand ideas. Like the extended lecture, however, the lecturette is often misused. This chapter is designed to clarify the appropriate use of these two basic lecture methods.

Fundamental Properties

Classroom learning is maximized when certain conditions are present. Some of these are especially critical to the success of a lecture presentation. For example, without careful planning, much of a lecturer's effectiveness may be lost. Feedback also is essential. Yet in their desire to cover a certain body of information, teachers often ignore student questions and comments.

Why Are Lecture Methods Preferred?

Wesley and Wronski suggest four purposes appropriate for employing lectures; these are to motivate, to clarify, to review, and to expand contents.[1] In general, lecture presentations are preferred under the following circumstances:

1. When the needed background information is not readily accessible to students.
2. When the facts or problems are conflicting or confusing in nature.
3. When the unique experiences of an individual (teacher, student, or resource person) will substantially contribute to clarification of issues.
4. When time is of the essence and the sources of data are widely scattered.
5. When a change of pace is needed. Many oral reports and demonstrations fall into this category.
6. When the best way to understand a topic is through oral presentation. Movies and demonstration, for example, are often informative. Sometimes "viewing" material is the best way to understand it.

Why Is Objectivity Important?

The lecturer can be a powerful force in shaping the views and thoughts of others. For example, consider the power of television advertising. Though employing a variety of techniques, all TV commercials attempt to be "objective." Sometimes "research" is cited; at other times there is an appeal to "give the product a try and judge its effectiveness for yourself." The classroom lecturer, unlike the TV advertisement, does not attempt to persuade an audience through propaganda techniques. Rather he or she maintains objectivity through an orderly presentation of the pertinent facts. If private opinions intrude, the lecturer must label them as such. Whenever possible, the lecturer offers a balanced treatment of the problem by encouraging further investigation where there is controversy. Highly controversial issues are usually avoided. (They are best handled through other techniques, such as debate.)

What Are the Essentials of Learner Readiness?

An inherent threat to the extended lecture is the tendency of students to take down the words of the lecturer and memorize them for a test. Such rote learning is often devoid of meaning and is, quite understandably, quickly forgotten.

To prepare the learner for the lecture, the teacher should provide a conceptual framework for the new material that links it with previously learned ideas or concepts, introduces the main new ideas, and defines new terms.

Placing points on the chalkboard can serve as an immediate framework for the

---

[1] Edgar B. Wesley and Stanley P. Wronski, *Teaching Social Studies in High School*, 5th ed. (Boston: D.C. Heath & Co., 1964), p. 367.

presentation. In addition, a map of the United States, for example, can facilitate learning of factual material about our country.

Since all meaningful learning essentially is a reduction of specific information to main ideas or concepts, the advance organizer, overview, and even the summary can serve as learning facilitators. Moreover, they set the stage for needed repetition and review of salient points.

What Is the Role of Pacing?

Pacing, the rate at which new lecture material is introduced, assumes a key role in all expository techniques. Most college lecturers tend to cover all materials at a constant rate. Moreover, they are likely to omit steps that seem obvious. Sometimes, they rely almost completely on verbal explanations when symbolic or visual aids would be more appropriate. Because of this reliance on verbal explanations, student comprehension of the first few ideas in a lecture tends to be relatively high and then drops off considerably as the lecture progresses. The learner retention pattern is depicted in Figure 10-1.

During the early part of the lecture while curiosity is high, learner comprehension is also usually high. As ideas are added, however, learners tend to lose their understanding because there is insufficient time for them to organize the points into a sequential pattern. Thus repetition of important points during the body of the lecture presentation is extremely important.

The rise of retention near the end of a presentation is dependent on the effectiveness of the lecture. By using key summary phrases (for example, to sum up or conclude), the teacher can help the learner review and understand major concepts. Thus the retention pattern tends to rise again.

The introduction and conclusion of a lecture presentation should be as carefully planned as the body of the presentation. To make the body of the presentation as effective as possible, the lecturer should change pace frequently by introducing

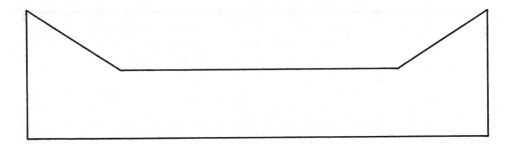

FIGURE 10-1 *Learner Retention Pattern*

examples, visual illustrations, and the like. Some limited verbal feedback from students also may be desirable.

Another aspect of pacing involves the distribution of lecture presentations, within the time period needed to complete a particular course. Many college classes meet for approximately one to one and one-half hours two or three times a week. Night school classes, however, often meet only once a week, whereas summer school classes commonly meet daily. Although the relative impact of pacing patterns has not been fully explored, it is recognized that the learner requires adequate time to reflect on the lecture. Moreover, there must be adequate time for practice so that consolidation of new information can be effected. Thus lectures might well be interspersed with other methods designed to facilitate integration of major concepts.

Why Are Visual Aids Desirable?

The skillful lecturer, realizing the limitations of verbal communication, uses a variety of visual material to supplement the presentation (for example, chalkboard, pictures, color transparancies, and diagrams). An effective lecturer, for example, frequently outlines major points on the chalkboard and then proceeds to develop each point by offering numerous illustrations and examples. By outlining major points on the chalkboard as the lecture develops, the teacher gives students the time they need to take notes. In addition to their impact on learning, visual aids serve as points of focus that tend to be remembered. Furthermore, they become useful reference points for subsequent questions and comments. There is certainly some truth in the adage that "a picture is worth a thousand words."

What Is the Role of Nonverbal Feedback?

The assumption that a lecture is a form of one-way communication is erroneous if the lecturer is fully aware of the audience. By establishing eye contact with the audience, the lecturer can communicate with it. Nonverbal behavior from the audience (such as nods of the head, chuckles, and facial expressions of understanding or perplexity) can tell the lecturer whether he or she is being effective. Restlessness on the part of several students should cue the lecturer to change the activity. Perhaps, a short question session is in order. Sometimes, an entirely different method may be needed.

The attention span for an oral presentation is shorter than generally suspected. Seldom, if ever, should an informal lecture exceed twenty or thirty minutes. Extended lectures may continue for as long as an hour. Even so, they should be interspersed with periods of learner activity. In conventional class settings, for example, an extended lecture may be broken into two time periods, separated with a lively question-and-answer session.

What Is the Role of Verbal Feedback?

Techniques for eliciting student feedback are limited only by the teacher's imagination. One teacher, for example, structured key questions into his lecture presentation at various intervals. After a few minutes of this activity, the teacher proceeded with the lecture until the next planned question session. The effect was a break in the activity in addition to valuable cues for directing the next lecture phase.

Ideally, questions should be handled as they arise. It takes considerable skill, however, to answer questions effectively and still maintain control and continuity of the lecture. To maintain interest and comprehension during the presentation, some teachers introduce a question period *prior* to the summary. This technique, according to Morrisey,[2] encourages the learner to remember the lecturer's ideas rather than someone else's ideas. One might say, for example, "I'll be glad to answer your questions now, but would like to reserve the last two or three minutes for a summary."

Although, in many respects, the worst time to have a question session is after the presentation, this may have to be done for the purpose of continuity. One way of building interest is to deliberately leave out some key information, thus prompting a question about a key point.

The question session is often impaired by the argumentative individual. It is probably best to respond to such a person by briefly answering or summarizing a point and then offering to discuss the point in more detail later. Regardless of how verbal feedback is handled, it remains a vital aspect of lecture procedures.

Extended Lecture Techniques

Large-group instruction, in this chapter, is discussed in terms of the extended formal lecture that characterizes many college classes. During the presentation, the learner may be given a few opportunities to ask questions or interject comments. The length of the presentation is usually forty to sixty minutes.

When used in conjunction with modular scheduling,[3] the lecture is often an essential part of a three-dimensional instructional program involving discussion in small groups and independent and semi-independent study.

What Constitutes an Appropriate Lecture Problem?

The answer to this question, in part, can be derived from the basic functions of informational techniques described in the first part of this chapter. There is much

---

[2] George L. Morrisey, *Effective Business and Technical Presentations* (Downey, Calif.: North American Rockwell Corporation, 1968), p. 82.

[3] Modular scheduling is frequently referred to as team teaching.

more to the problem, however, when the extended lecture is used to provide a base or enrichment for further learning. Almost unwittingly, the instructor can provide too much information, leaving little for the student to accomplish.

The following discusses some appropriate topics for extended lectures. In teaching civil liberties, the lecturer might well develop an organized account of court decisions rendered subsequent to those discussed in the textbook. In the natural resources area, the lecturer might want to present certain aspects of the energy crisis, not treated in current social science texts. Sometimes, it is necessary to lecture for the purpose of clarifying text materials. Thus the trigonometry teacher may want to present additional examples and illustrations in support of a difficult mathematical concept. The science teacher may want to clarify the nature of scientific proof.

The basic criterion of an appropriate extended lecture is its success in *raising further questions*. While it is true that it is designed to *answer* immediate questions that perplex students, these are viewed as merely intermediate questions along the way to more complex problems. Recall that most expository techniques merely supply data essential to resolving larger, more basic issues. A lecture, then, must result in learner activity. In modular scheduling, small-group discussion is designed especially for this purpose. As described in Chapter 5, the discussion leader often pinpoints a basic issue. Effective resolution of the issue, however, is dependent on the learner's repertoire of background information. The lecture constitutes one important source of this information.

How Are Advance Organizers Developed?

Advance organizers are introductory materials, offered in advance of the body of the lecture to link the lecture material with previously learned ideas. Organizers are always more general and comprehensive than the content of the lecture that is to follow.

According to Ausubel and Robinson,[4] there are two kinds of organizers. If the material is completely new to the learner, an *expository* organizer would be needed. Such an organizer makes use of whatever relevant ideas might exist in the cognitive structure of students. For example, in introducing the concept of photosynthesis, the lecturer might briefly summarize how different materials are used in the manufacture of carbohydrates. This idea would then be connected to the concept of photosynthesis. The lecture presentation itself would contain specifics.

If the material is not completely new, a *comparative* organizer would be used. As Ausubel and Robinson point out, this type of organizer has two purposes: to integrate new ideas with existing concepts and to point out their similarities and differences. Suppose, for example, that students already know that the primary center of plant

---

[4] David P. Ausubel and Floyd G. Robinson, *School Learning* (New York: Holt, Rinehart and Winston, Inc., 1969), pp. 145-46.

growth is at the end of a plant's stem. The lecturer would point this out and also remind students that sometimes new growth begins at any point on the stem as a result of special conditions, such as injury to the stem. The lecture itself would then focus on such specifics as size of leaves, length of internodes, and nature of growth cells, for example.

Organizers seem to be most useful for helping students learn factual material and less so for helping them learn concepts; in fact, they may not be needed at all if the content contains its own built-in organizers.

What Techniques of Presentation Are Preferred?

The forceful lecturer has materials well organized and is an effective speaker. These qualities apply to all techniques of exposition and are more fully described in the lecturette techniques section of this chapter. At this point, attention will be given to those techniques that apply specifically to large-group lectures. Students often need copies of the lecture outline. It not only helps them follow the lecturer but also enables them to note areas of doubt and misunderstanding. Usually, they will want to jot down questions that arise along the way. Some lecturers like to conclude their lecture outlines with one or more basic questions that relate, at least indirectly, to anticipated small-group discussion. The question may be written directly on the lecture outline or posed orally as the lecture is brought to a close.

Student questions can be handled in a number of ways. They may be left for subsequent small-group experiences. Frequently, however, the large-group lecturer may want to react to them in a subsequent presentation. This may be especially important if the second lecture is a continuation of the first one. In this case, a question box may be useful. Sometimes, a lecturer resolves the problem by entertaining a few key questions during the lecture. Rather than risk the danger of becoming bogged down with insignificant questions, the instructional team may agree to interject key questions along the way. One interesting innovation, described by Nussel and Villemain,[5] has been characterized as the "Dual Socratic Method." The system is based on a minimum of lecture material. At any time, an instructional team member is free to ask for clarification, to prod, or simply to goad. Nussel and Villemain have found the technique especially useful in capturing and holding the attention of college students. A related technique is to switch instructors after a few minutes. This can be prearranged or it may occur if a team member leaves out an important point. In this way, the team members can serve as a check on each other. This technique has the added advantage of breaking up the lecture since the attention span of the average listener is rather short.

Attention also must be given to audio-visual techniques. Too often, the lecture is

---

[5] Edward J. Nussel and Francis T. Villemain, "The Dual Socratic Method in College Instruction," *Journal of Teacher Education* 17, no. 4 (Winter 1966): 452-55.

used in unimaginative, inefficient ways. Large groups increase the problems of communication substantially. Use of the cross-media approach is recommended by Morlan.[6] The lecture outline, for example, may be presented on one screen while graphs and pictures are projected on another. This enables the lecturer to take advantage of the best media available for illustrating specific points.

What Preplanning Is Needed?

A good lecture outline helps insure a smooth presentation. Usually, the lecturer's outline will be considerably more detailed than the outline made available to students. With slight modification, the lesson plan illustrated for the lecturette (see page 188) can be used effectively in large-group presentations. The major difference is that student questions are likely to be entertained (if at all) in a different manner. The length of the presentation usually will determine the length of the plan.

With the help of fellow team members, the lecturer decides on the major aspect to be emphasized in the outline. Some lecturers prefer to enter the content materials in one column and the materials and equipment needed in a second column. The lecture presentation is then built around the major concept(s) to be presented. Time estimates for each major point help insure content coverage in the allotted time.

The equipment needed for the extended lecture should be carefully worked into the outline. Visual aids must be arranged in the order in which they are to be used and should be numbered chronologically. The lecturer should also insure that all machines and equipment are in satisfactory working order.

There is seldom an occasion when a lecturer will read a presentation. Thus a lecture need not be written out. The lecture outline is usually preferable. It includes key words and phrases that help the lecturer recall the examples and illustrations to be employed. A lecture walk-through is advisable. Some teachers prefer that this walk-through be done in the lecture hall itself. This "dress rehearsal" enables the lecturer to establish the sequence and order of the presentation and to develop realistic time estimations for each point to be developed.

What Is the Purpose of a Postlecture Forum?

Whereas the lecture question session helps students clarify key lecture concepts, the postlecture forum helps them derive implications. All too often, the typical college lecture is followed immediately by another lecture. Students need some assistance in making appropriate connections, associations, and applications of basic lecture concepts. This process is greatly facilitated when they become actively involved.

The length of a postlecture forum will vary in accord with the length, nature, and

---

[6] John E. Morlan, "The Team Approach to Large Group Instruction," *Audio-Visual Instruction* 9, no. 8 (October 1964): 520-23.

purpose of the preceding lecture. Most lecturers let forum sessions run for approximately one half the length of the preceding lecture. Sometimes, two lecture sessions will be followed with one session devoted to forum work.

How Is the Large-Group Lecture Evaluated?

The absence of student response during a lecture robs the lecturer of his or her most useful evaluation method. There are many indirect evaluation measures available, however.

If a teaching team is used (a highly recommended method), a team member or graduate assistant might walk down the aisles in order to observe how students are taking notes. Particular attention should be given to students who are known to have physical handicaps, such as hearing deficiencies.

One of the most accurate assessments of a lecture presentation can be made in subsequent small-group sessions. Such sessions may be opened with unanswered questions from the lecture. If a major portion of a session must be devoted to clarification, one can infer that the lecture was not fully effective.

As in informal lectures and demonstrations, student evaluation is also desirable. Evaluation can be done at any point. Some teachers prefer to have students do an evaluation at the end of each unit or module of study. Although student evaluations have their limitations (for example, faking answers), they are valuable assessment tools when their purpose is thoroughly understood and when they are done anonymously.

What Basic Instructional Team Decisions Must Be Reached?

Effective large-group presentations are the result of extensive team planning. The process of providing for both large- and small-group instruction necessitates modification of traditional instructional procedures. The professor and his or her assistants must work together to reach decisions. This demands a spirit of compromise.

One important decision concerns *who is to be responsible for specific presentations.* Some teams rotate this responsibility, while others leave such responsibilities to the senior professor. A concern sometimes overlooked is the effectiveness of large-group presentations. The best qualified individual may not be the most skillful lecturer. Student feedback may be used as one basis for placing team members where they can be most effective.

Another important decision concerns the *number and length* of large-group presentations in each curriculum area. For example, fewer large-group lectures will be needed weekly in a skills course than in an academic course. Length of formal lectures will also vary. Excessively long lectures should be interspersed with periods of direct student involvement.

A final decision concerns how large-group presentations will be *integrated* with small-group discussion and independent study. Major points of each lecture must be evaluated by the team in view of anticipated subsequent learning experiences.

Although discussion leaders can handle small groups in their own way, they must operate within the framework provided by large-group presentations. Even though an individual discussion leader may not fully agree with the content of lecture presentations, he or she must not "strike out on a new course." Following the format of the lecture presentation is essential.

Informal Lecture (Lecturette) Techniques

Techniques for informing others include the informal lecture, or lecturette, the demonstration, and the oral report. While the techniques differ in certain respects, their functions are identical; hence, they are treated together in this section. Important differences in technique are noted.

Although these techniques are sometimes employed in connection with modular scheduling, emphasis here is on their use in conventional classes. They range in length from one to two minutes of spontaneous explanation to a preplanned twenty- to thirty-minute presentation.

How Does the Lecturette Differ in Purpose from the Extended Lecture?

As previously defined, the lecturette emphasizes telling, explaining, and showing. Its basic purpose is to prepare the learner for solving problems. The same description might be given to the extended lecture used in large groups. The basic differences, then, are found in their applications.

Whereas the lecturette may take place for varying lengths of time at any point in the learning process, the extended lecture is scheduled for a fixed period of time. The lecturette usually is given when it becomes obvious that students can profit from expert or at least outside assistance. Some lecturette sessions are planned in advance, although most occur spontaneously. They are usually short, enabling the learner to proceed with his or her own activities as soon as possible.

Unlike the lecturette, the extended, or formal, lecture may be used to present *basal content* or to present enrichment material. In modular scheduling situations, it usually focuses on the presentation of basic content. In any event, the lecturer must determine *in advance* the amount and kind of information needed for subsequent small-group and independent-study activities. There is a minimum of pupil involvement during the presentation since questions from the audience tend to prevent adequate coverage of basal content needed for subsequent experiences. A certain amount of informal lecturing is expected in both small-group and study activities. It is expected, however, that the background presentations will minimize this need considerably.

Another contrasting application is the way individual needs are met. During a lecturette, students may be helped immediately, or if the problem is too involved for on-the-spot analysis, they may receive assistance within the same class period following the presentation. The formal lecture, on the other hand, assumes that all students have the same needs and that all will profit equally from the presentation. Problems, ideally, are jotted down by students for later clarification.

How Is the Lecturette Topic Selected?

Sometimes, teachers utilize informal lecture or demonstration simply because of apathy or inability to plan other activities. Not only is the experience likely to suffer from insufficient planning, but the problem may not lend itself to the particular technique. Individual presentations, for example, are likely to be of little value if the aim is to change feelings or attitudes or to develop skills and habits. On the other hand, abstract ideas or principles can be taught appropriately through some sort of verbal presentation. Demonstrations are usually most appropriate when independent dimensions and spatial relationships are involved. A "look at the real thing" is usually far superior to words alone. Purpose, then, determines the nature of the learning activity to be employed.

Basically, the informal lecture, demonstration, or report is employed to enhance critical thinking. The information that is supplied and evaluated further prepares students for resolving a critical issue presently being considered or one that is to be considered in the immediate future. For example, a report problem might be appropriately formulated as "What factors contribute to the American Indian's continued difficulty in coping with life in the United States?" It should be noted that the problem is one of fact or value only. Subsequent class experiences might deal with possible solutions to a more basic problem in the same general area. Thus the experience merely sets the stage for a full problem-solving experience.

How Is the Lecturette Presented?

Oral instructional techniques are usually ineffective unless the speaker captures the imagination of the listeners. One can do this by beginning a presentation with an unusual or startling statement. One student, for example, who was reporting the effects of fluoridation began the presentation with "I hate dental appointments." The student then continued by saying:

> Your teeth are as old as a forty-year-old man. A man who has lived forty years has lived almost two-thirds of his life; a tooth which has lived sixteen years has lived approximately two-thirds of its life. But with the help of flouridation, the average tooth may chew well for you. . . .

This speaker made an unusual comparison to capture interest and then explained in more scientific terms the benefits of fluoridation.

It is in the *attention* and *needs* phase of the lecturette that one introduces the topic of discussion. Usually three or four statements will suffice. The speaker must avoid lengthy introductions.

It is in the *satisfaction* phase of a presentation that one discusses main points of the lecturette. The speaker can greatly increase the effectiveness of this phase by adhering to the following simple outline.

1. Initial summary. This consists of a brief enumeration of the main points. It is often desirable to write these points on the chalkboard. The initial summary should provide a basic conceptual framework for the presentation. Sometimes, an advance organizer may be needed. If so, it precedes the initial summary (see page 180).

2. Detailed information. Here the speaker brings in supporting facts, examples, and illustrations to clarify the issues. Usually it is desirable to show the relationship between the major points.

Some individuals have difficulty determining what the main points will be. The speaker may break his or her topic into such categories as time sequence (past, present, future), cause-and-effect relationships, interested parties involved, and anticipated problems and their solutions.

The speaker completes one point before proceeding to the next one. By referring to the original points listed on the chalkboard, one is able to move from one area to another without losing the audience.

3. Final summary. The speaker concludes by restating main points and important conclusions that have been developed.

The student who reported on the effects of fluoridation broke the presentation into three parts: causes of tooth decay, benefits of fluoridation, and the permanence of fluoridation treatment. After placing main points on the board for the benefit of the class, the student presented facts and examples designed to clarify each of the main points.

Essentially then, the lecturer relies heavily on repetition. As a speech teacher once said, "You tell your listeners what you plan to say, say it, and then tell them what you have said." Repetition through the use of examples has a vital role in the body of the presentation. Overuse of illustrations, however, should be avoided. Examples and illustrations are used merely to clarify difficult points.

What Presentation Techniques Are Recommended?

The effective presentation of a lecture, demonstration, or report embodies all the characteristics of effective speaking. First of all, the speaker must be heard. One must vary voice and pitch in such a way as to drive home important points. The good speaker is enthusiastic about what he or she has to say and looks directly into the eyes of the listeners, talking "to" them rather than "at" them.

Techniques of delivery can be found in any basic speech textbook. The following elements of effective communication are basic. The lecturer should:

1. Speak in a conservational manner.
2. Observe audience reactions.
3. Maintain poise at all times. Some teachers violate this rule by sitting on the desk or leaning on a speaker's stand. In an attempt to appear casual or relaxed, they may appear sloppy or lazy.
4. Avoid annoying mannerisms. One may develop "little habits" that detract seriously from what is being said. Often, the lecturer is unaware of these annoyances. Some teachers periodically provide students an opportunity to indicate the nature and extent of such mannerisms. Anonymity is essential for valid suggestions.

How Is Listening Improved?

One of the most difficult problems facing the lecturer is educating a group to listen effectively. It is easy enough to spot the student who is disturbing the class, but often, it is practically impossible to detect the individual who has let his or her mind wander to more pleasing avenues of thought. On the other hand, some individuals who attempt to listen carefully have difficulty forming the mental images essential for comprehension.

In many life situations, listening is voluntary. This is often not the case in ordinary classroom situations. Attention, however, is enhanced when listeners realize they are to become directly involved in subsequent activities. Ways to involve students include:

1. The day before an examination, a teacher summarized the highlights of the course by saying, "I want you to pay especially close attention for the next few minutes because I am going to ask you to describe what you see."
2. A teacher explained a mathematics problem, including principles necessary for doing the assignment.
3. The class leader issued final instructions before the start of an extended trip.
4. Mary gave a report on the mountain rattlesnake that the group was likely to encounter on a science excursion.
5. The physical education teacher demonstrated techniques of artificial respiration prior to practice by each student.

Listening is also enhanced when the speaker shares personal experiences with the audience. A person who sees the task as more than just a job to be done will provide anecdotes, sometimes making his or her presentation almost a life-or-death matter.

Thus far, consideration has been given to the speaker's efforts to gain attention from the audience. Communication, however, is a joint process between the speaker and the observers. Listeners also have definite responsibilities in addition to placing themselves within hearing range of the speaker and assuming the proper listening pose. One who listens pays attention to what is being said; that is, he or she is "at tension." This state of mind suggests that the person is focusing on what he or she expects to receive from the experience. In short, one *listens with a purpose*. In an expository type of presentation, the hearer is interested in the soundness of the presentation and in the relationships between the facts and ideas presented. This, in turn, will facilitate purposeful listening. After all, there always will be reports and lectures that are poorly organized. However, it may still be possible to profit from the experience, despite the speaker's limitations.

What Functions Are Served by the Postlecturette Question Session?

The question or discussion period following a lecturette (or demonstration or report) is of utmost importance, even when some questions are answered during the lecture. Certain aspects of a presentation will usually need some clarification. By having this opportunity for clarification, the lecturer gets a chance to judge the effectiveness of his or her initial presentation. A five- or ten-minute clarification session will usually suffice for a twenty-minute report.

The teacher then leads the class in a brief *review* of the main points made and brings them to bear on the solution of a problem. (For the extended lecture, this may involve a postlecture forum.) The reader will recall that an informal lecture or report is often used to provide a *basis* for resolving a problem. It is concerned with the data-gathering (factual) step. There remains the evaluation of the data and their bearing on an appropriate solution to the problem under consideration. In the process of review, both students and teacher can bring related information to bear on the problem.

A similar review session after an oral report can be valuable training in evaluation of data. Students need assistance in assessing the validity of both the spoken and written word. Fallacies, improper deduction, and outright distortion of facts are among the most prevalent weaknesses of oral discourses. College students are prone to confuse the issues by expressing their own value judgements in conjunction with the facts.

What Preplanning Is Necessary?

Lecture presentations must be carefully planned. Students are painfully aware of teachers who "can't explain very well" or those who "are confusing or difficult to follow." Likewise, students and teachers recognize the difficulties that many students experience when asked to present oral reports. Most of these difficulties are related to inadequate planning. It is hoped that the illustrated plan that follows will clarify the problem somewhat. The plan is suggestive only.

LESSON PLAN FOR A LECTURE

Subject: Due Process of Law

Concept: Legal safeguards, based on the Bill of Rights, have been modified through various Supreme Court decisions.

Problem: What are the legal safeguards of the accused?

Goals: After this lesson on civil liberties, the student should further understand the impact of recent Supreme Court decisions on one's protection under the law, as evidenced by:

1. The ability to relate recent court decisions to basic constitutional guarantees.
2. Questions asked in the subsequent discussion on what protection should a youth offender have under the law.
3. The application of the basic lecture concepts to a subsequent case analysis involving procedural safeguards.

Lesson approach

Catch title. "The thief is guilty; let's go on with the hanging!" These words ring out repeatedly from our favorite cowboy movies and TV shows. Almost without exception (in these shows) the "thief" is not hung; his innocence is established—usually at the last moment.

Advance organizer and initial summary. In our study of civil liberties, we have made reference to the constitutional foundations of our legal safeguards, emphasizing the guarantees contained in the Bill of Rights. Through the study of cases, we have seen how the basic constitutional guarantees are implemented through our federal and state governments and how the Fourth Amendment serves both the ends and means of justice.

We will now direct our attention to the "innocent thief" who usually barely escapes hanging in the cowboy movies. The rights of the accused are being continually reinterpreted through Supreme Court decisions. I am going to interpret some of these at this time. You will note that several of these decisions have been rendered since our textbook was written. Rights of the accused generally fall into two major areas. They consist of pretrial rights and rights during the trial. I will develop both of these areas. (Place main points on chalkboard.)

Lesson development

I. Pretrial rights
  A. Preliminary hearing
    1. Differences between federal and state courts (our own state practice).
    2. Arraignment—pleads guilty or not guilty.
  B. Grand Jury (if serious case)
    1. *Purpose* To determine if the evidence warrants holding for trial (indictment).
    2. Not all states have one.
    3. Federal—consists of 16-24 local citizens; serve as long as 18 months.
    4. Majority decision only.

      5. *Cassell* v. *Texas* (1950)—must not exclude important racial groups.

  C. Bail bond (in most cases)

      1. Purpose.

      2. Eighth Amendment—no excessive bail.

      3. *Stack* v. *Boyle* (1951).

  D. Right to counsel prior to arraignment

      1. *Escobedo* v. *Illinois* (1964)—right to a lawyer while being interrogated.

II. Rights during the trial

  A. Assurance against self-incrimination

      1. Fifth Amendment.

      2. Not sufficient grounds if just fear of being ridiculed by friends.

      3. Can be held in contempt of court.

  B. Coerced confessions

      1. Another application of the self-incrimination privilege.

      2. *Definition.* A confession made after one's will has been broken down.

      3. Can't be used—considered untrustworthy.

      4. Techniques in obtaining confessions.

         a. *Chamber* v. *Florida* (1940)—no brutality permitted.

         b. *Colombe* v. *Connecticut* (1961)—no psychological coercion.

         c. *Miranda* v. *Arizona* (1966)—all questions must be preceded by warning of rights.

  C. Can't be required to testify at one's trial

      1. *Malloy* v. *Hogan* (1964)—extended the Fifth Amendment to state courts (through the Fourteenth Amendment). Thus no penalty for remaining silent.

  D. Counsel for indigent defendants

      1. Approximately two-thirds of those charged with serious crimes cannot afford to hire a lawyer.

      2. State courts (until recently) required to provide counsel for capital offense cases only.

      3. *Gideon* v. *Wainwright* (1963)—required free counsel for all indigent defendants charged with serious crimes.

Deriving Generalizations

In this presentation the rights of the accused *prior to* and *during* a trial have been emphasized. From the preceding cases cited, a number of important ideas stand out. They include the following:

1. The United States Supreme Court, in effect, makes law by rendering decisions that are consistent with the changing social climate.

2. Legal safeguards for the accused are basically derived from the Bill of Rights.

3. The law is designed specifically to protect the accused.

4. The law shall not discriminate on the basis of wealth or social standing.

The preceding lesson plan is more detailed than preferred by many teachers; it is perhaps not detailed enough for others. The primary purpose of this plan is to provide information not readily accessible. The information is useful (along with the four basic concepts) in providing a factual *basis* for resolving fundamental issues in the area of civil liberties. Certain aspects of the lecture undoubtedly touched on in text materials were *reorganized* and re-presented in the lecture. These aspects, of course, would be merely mentioned in the presentation.

How Are Oral Presentations Evaluated?

One of the most difficult and controversial aspects of oral presentations involves evaluation. Indeed, some teachers attempt to judge such presentations on the basis of purely general impressions. Some authorities, however, would seriously question or even deplore such a technique. Whether we like it or not, evaluations of oral discourses are highly subjective. Thus they are affected by certain predispositions of the evaluator. The personal factor involved can be substantially reduced by (1) having a number of people participate in the evaluation and (2) by establishing a number of bases for such an evaluation. Whenever practical, both techniques should be utilized.

Since reporting procedures are designed to facilitate the presentation of facts, students usually will be busy in making notes of the main points, jotting down questions, and the like. Therefore, the teacher is the most logical person to make a formal evaluation. There are at least three criteria that can be used to judge a presentation.

1. A presentation can be judged on the basis of the group's response. Do students seem interested in the report during the actual presentation? Are there a number of appropriate questions following the report? Do students keep referring to the speaker's points in the forum session?
2. A presentation can be evaluated in terms of the techniques employed. Was there evidence of planning? of proper body and voice control? Was eye contact maintained throughout?
3. A report can be judged on the basis of content coverage. Did the speaker present the facts fully? Was he or she able to maintain the role of an impartial observer?

The fallacy of using audience reaction as a sole basis for evaluation is readily apparent. Many topics, for instance, may provoke enthusiasm because they are of immediate concern to the group. Or they may happen to support the convictions of many listeners. Sometimes the speaker may be especially well liked by the group. Enthusiasm expressed under such circumstances can be high, even though the content may be poorly stated or even invalid.

The immediate disadvantage of relying solely on techniques of delivery is inherent in the purpose of the talk. A report is designed to inform a group of people. Although recommended speech techniques correlate with effective communication, it is possible that the criterion of objective techniques will not be an effective measure for a particular individual.

Likewise, completeness and accuracy of content can be lost to the group if oral communication is ineffective. Many research specialists are weak in this respect. They often make up for the deficiency, however, by making copies of the report available to each member of the group. Under these conditions the desirability of having the report read in the first place might be questioned. In any event, the ordinary class report is dependent on adequate communication of ideas.

It can be seen, then, that all three bases of evaluation are needed. Few teachers can maintain a very high degree of accuracy by relying on general impressions only. Many teachers utilize rating scales that can be checked during and immediately following oral presentations.

The rating scale in Table 10-1 illustrates essential evaluation criteria. Note that all three bases for evaluation are included in the rating scale. In addition, there is a category called general effectiveness. After the teacher completes the evaluation, he or she weighs the relative balance between the check marks that fall above and those that fall below the average category (between the vertical lines in Table 10-1). From this, an informal assessment or grade may be derived. Different teachers, of course, favor different evaluation methods.

How Can the Quality of Oral Reports Be Improved?

Oral reports are easily assigned and can be easily presented. The process sometimes receives a highly superficial treatment, but teachers can do a lot to correct this tendency by offering guidance along the lines suggested in the preceding portion of this chapter. Even so, many teachers have not been overly satisfied with the results obtained. Why is this? No one seems to be sure! There undoubtedly are many psychological factors involved. Poor performance can be a result of poor examples set by some teachers and students. Or the problem may result from an attitude that content, rather than technique, is of paramount importance. There are undoubtedly many other causes of poor reports.

One teacher, despite repeated efforts to correct the problem, kept getting poor oral reports from students. He first noticed the difficulty at the junior high school level; later, at the high school level; and, still later, at the college level. After three or four years of college teaching, this teacher discovered an approach that resulted in a consistently higher quality of oral reports. The technique was amazingly simple, as the following instructions to students indicate: "You will be allowed twenty minutes for your presentation. The only restriction is that you cannot just lecture; you must also ask and answer questions."

By the time the students had time to ponder the problem, they were guided into the topic by the introductory questions the speaker asked. They then briefly asked the speaker to explain existing ideas or understanding on the subject. This paved the way for a short presentation of the information. Actually, the students were giving an

TABLE 10-1   *Rating Scale for Oral Presentations*

Directions: Place a check mark next to the category that most accurately represents your evaluation of the point. The space between the vertical lines will be roughly equivalent to an average rating. Check only those points that fall outside the vertical lines.

I. Delivery

A. *Lesson Beginning*

Attention-getting indicative of general content.	Beginning apparently planned, but effectiveness somewhat lacking.	Beginning poorly given; rambling statements; apologies.

B. *Audience Contact*

Looks directly at listeners.	Depends heavily on notes, apparently does not "see" listeners.	Reads from notes or looks above heads of listeners.

C. *Enthusiasm*

Intensely interested in topic. Stress is natural or spontaneous.	Some interest evident. Occasionally lapses into a monotone.	Lack of interest, just another job to be done.

D. *Use of Communication Skills*
(voice, posture and gestures, grammar, spelling, penmanship)

Communication skills above reproach.	One or two of the communication skills need further development.	Several communication skills need immediate attention.

II. Content

A. *Major Points*

Major points stressed and supported with pertinent examples.	Major points not very clearly defined and developed.	Content of the presentation confusing or extremely vague.

B. *Objective*

Distinguishes between facts and opinion.	Sometimes difficult to distinguish between facts and opinion. Tends to overemphasize own opinions.	Facts and opinions generally indistinguishable. Apparently unaware of projections.

III. *Audience Reaction*

Students attentive; take notes and ask pertinent questions.	Some audience interest evident. Note-taking and questions are brief.	Little evidence of interest. Only occasionally does a student take notes. Few questions.

IV. *General Effectiveness*

High overall effectiveness. Appropriate balance maintained.	Presentation reasonably effective.	Presentation generally ineffective. Lacks needed punch.

informal lecture. Through skillful questions, however, the group was psychologically prepared for the presentation, and the actual lecture was reduced to a bare minimum.

Asking listeners to participate tends to "awaken" both speaker and students. The presentation becomes more of a cooperative endeavor and is more directly associated with the needs and thoughts of the audience. Furthermore, answering questions forces the speaker to give some consideration to the audience. By focusing attention on the audience in this manner, the speaker is prepared to apply the techniques outlined in the preceding pages. There is the ever-present danger, of course, that the speaker will let the question-and-answer period block his or her purpose—that of presenting information. To prevent this, the teacher should put a time limit on this discussion period.

The Value of Lecture Methods

Lecture methods are economical in terms of time and materials.

They serve to channel thinking of all students in a given direction.

Demonstrations, especially, enable the class leader to utilize activities that would be too dangerous for pupils to perform themselves within the ordinary classroom.

Lecturettes, and to some extent reports and demonstrations, are easy to prepare, as they are usually based on the specialized knowledge of the leader. Large-group instruction increases the accessibility of especially competent leaders.

Limitations of, and Problems with, Lecture Methods

Information-giving methods encourage the retention of facts as ends in themselves.

Lecture methods, by themselves, are inadequate for teaching certain types of concepts. (Attitudes, feelings, and skills, for example, are not learned through pure telling or showing procedures.)

Some teachers have difficulty adapting their presentations to the comprehension levels of their students. (A passive audience is less able to indicate its lack of understanding.)

Social learnings are minimized during oral presentations.

The lecture approach to teaching tends to encourage acceptance of the teacher as the final authority. Because of this factor, a teacher's bias and prejudices may be accepted at face value.

Exposition processes are extremely difficult to adapt to individual differences among students. Superior students, for example, frequently complain of boredom "after about the fifth explanation." Similarly, less able students often charge that lectures present too much information too quickly.

I. Useful in art, home economics, and psychology classes

Unit: Color Relationships.

Concept: The artist utilizes color in many ways.

Problem: How is color used to create mood, symbolize ideas, and express emotions?

Main points:

1. Plastic quality of color.
2. Emotional quality of color.
3. Aesthetic quality of color.

II. Useful in English literature, world history, and social studies classes

Unit: The Aspiring Mind

Concept: The fusion of classical forms of literature with the English context of exuberance (in the Elizabethan era) brought about a mature and artistic drama.

Problem: What are the basic elements of the drama in literary works?

Main points

1. Story line.
2. Conflict.
3. Plot structure.
4. Character development.
5. Interpretation.

III. Useful in industrial arts classes

Unit: Precision Measuring Instruments

Concept: Precision measurement is essential to today's complex industrial system.

Problem: What methods do we use to measure units smaller than one sixty-fourth inch?

Main points

1. Basic parts.
2. Working principles.
3. Different sizes.
4. Different types.

IV. Useful in history classes

Unit: Imperialism

Concept: China's relations with the West have been typified by one misunderstanding after another.

Problem: What were the circumstances and consequences of the first opium war?

Main points

1. Causes
2. British bombardment of Chinese ports
3. Results

Methods and Techniques: Focus on Affective Learning

Education at its best is a contrived experience designed to help the learner cope with professional responsibilities following the college experience. One purpose of education is to provide students with the cognitive understandings and skills needed to perform professional responsibilities. Another, equally important purpose is affective in nature, that is, to provide students with an understanding of the complexities of human interaction so that they will be able to develop effective relationships with others—a prerequisite to success on any job. The chapters in this unit are addressed to this vitally important, but often neglected, aspect of teaching.

Chapter 11 concerns the case-method approach to teaching, which requires the learner to solve a real-life problem involving human emotion and conflict. Usually, a case is limited to a single incident or a series of closely related incidents. Through the study of actual life incidents, learners are able to project themselves into the situation.

Chapter 12 discusses the sociodrama, which is closely related to the case approach. This technique goes one step further than the case method, however, in enabling the learner to enter directly into the situation through role play. Sociodrama is usually based on a single, relatively simple incident in which a spontaneous enactment provides the basis for study and analysis. Simulation games add complexity through a series of related events in which several vital decisions must be made. Usually involved is a payoff of some kind.

Chapter 13 treats an area that has long been neglected at all levels of education, namely, creativity. Originality, a basic ingredient of creativity, is often discouraged simply because it tends to upset the teacher for it often interferes with instructional techniques and carefully prepared assignments and projects. Although definitely related to the normal processes of cognition, creativity is also linked with intuitive thinking and emotion.

Methods and Techniques

Cooperative Learning

Overview

ANALYZING REALITY:
THE CASE METHOD

Key Concepts

1. The case approach may be used to resolve problems and to derive principles.
2. Because it emphasizes emotional reaction to a given situation, the case approach closely parallels reality.
3. The short incident case (structured around a single conflict situation) is recommended for class use.
4. Case analysis focuses on three dimensions: facts, feelings, and relationships.
5. The incident case, based on a single unit concept, is most appropriately developed by the teacher.

New Terms

1. Incident Case A short sketch (100-200 words) of an incident involving a misunderstanding or conflict that actually happened to two or more parties. Students are usually given a specific frame of reference for working on the case.
2. Types of Cases Manner of presentation of case data. Includes such classifications as the vignette, historical narrative, and original documents and research data.
3. Issue Case Commonly contains one or more problems, along with background material necessary for understanding the setting for the case. No indication of what was done to resolve the major problem is provided. Students choose from among a number of alternatives which may be implicit or explicit in the case.
4. Descriptive Case Features one or more problems, along with relevant background material, and a statement or hint of how the problem was resolved. Students may be asked to evolve concepts by generalizing from specific events.

5. **Case Report**   After the major issue has been fully clarified, each student may be asked to write a report on the case that provides a solution to the case problem and a justification for selecting it. This report may be done during the regular class period or assigned as homework in preparation for the next analysis session.

Questions to Guide Your Study

1. What are the psychological advantages associated with the case method?
2. Why is the short incident case preferred?
3. Students should be given the actual solution to an issue case after they have completed their own analysis. Defend or refute.
4. Why should teachers develop their own cases?

Clarence Earl Gideon, a 53-year-old drifter and ex-convict, sat slumped over a half pint of vodka in a dingy bar on Florida's Gulf Coast when he was arrested for the burglary of a poolroom on skid row that had occurred about an hour earlier at 10:00 P.M. A few minutes later when interrogated by the police, Gideon couldn't remember much except to say, "I've never done anything drunk that I didn't remember when sober." Nevertheless, as someone had reported seeing Gideon prowling inside the establishment earlier that June day, his denials carried little weight, especially since he had spent most of his adult life in jail.

Gideon asked the court to provide him with a lawyer but was refused. Under Florida law, he was not entitled to one. Serving as his own lawyer, the man was tried and convicted by a six-man jury. A maximum sentence of five years was imposed.

Gideon did not particularly mind the jail sentence since prison was more or less his home, but for once he actually believed he was innocent. Furthermore, he thought that a fair trial should have entitled him to the services of a lawyer. After the Florida Supreme Court denied Gideon's petition for a writ of habeas corpus, he decided to appeal to the U.S. Supreme Court. Although handwritten and full of misspellings, his petition was taken seriously. The court ruled that he, in fact, did have the right to counsel. A new trial was ordered. This time, with the services of legal assistance, Gideon was set free.

What are the historical roots of basic liberties in this country? Why is the Supreme Court able to upset state court decisions, as in the Gideon case? Why would a "poor risk" like Gideon be permitted to go free since his freedom could pose a serious danger to the life and property of the community at large? What basic civil liberties are involved?

This case might be used in a general business class. In all probability, the reader developed immediate interest in Gideon's problem. Indeed most readers probably caught themselves pondering the key questions posed. Why is this? Why do we, after reading an account of less than 200 words, want to analyze the problem? The answer, of course, is that Gideon's problem is real—one that many of us have faced in some way at one time or another. Furthermore, the case involves common emotions and values. The element of human interest captures our imagination.

The case method is not new. Indeed, it dates back many centuries and has been used by such outstanding teachers as Jesus (parables), Aesop (fables), and Grimm (fairy tales). Oddly enough, however, it has only recently received the attention that it deserves.

Its use as an instructional technique has been accepted for many years in law schools, medical schools, and graduate shools of business administration. More recently, the case approach has been used in public administration, guidance, social work, and educational administration. Today college teachers in almost all areas are finding the case approach an effective means of relating to real-life applications.

Fundamental Properties

A case is an account of a realistic problem or situation experienced by an individual or a group of people. It includes a statement of the problem along with a description of the perceptions and attitudes of those who are facing it. Cases can be fictitious accounts of realistic situations or recordings of events that have actually happened. If possible, it is best to use a case reporting an actual situation.

What Is the Case Approach to Teaching?

Case-oriented instruction focuses on application of general principles or concepts to specific problem situations. While lecture methods concern the transmission of theoretical or factual material, the case approach focuses on the application of concepts to the solution of real-life problems. The learner must decide which data are relevant and how they relate to the problem. Eventually, a decision must be reached. Decisions, in some instances, may be based on two or more alternative solutions developed or implied in the case. At other times, learners are expected to develop their own list of alternatives prior to reaching a decision.

What Are the Purposes of the Case Approach?

The case approach focuses on the actual relationships of people. By studying such selected life episodes, learners should improve their own relationships with people in similar situations. Case analysis is a search for common denominators, or those kinds of problems that keep reappearing in everyday life. Eventually, learners realize that each case, in some way, is related to all other cases involving human interaction. After considerable experience in case analysis, they are often able to view their own problems in a detached manner. "What would I recommend that another individual do in my situation?" In addition, by analyzing several interested parties, each with a somewhat different motive and frame of reference, learners are able to look beyond their own immediate rationale and thus to empathize with others.

What Are Some Types of Cases?

There is no one particular kind of case. The assumption that there is *one* kind of case, according to Newmann and Oliver,[1] has led to much confusion and ambiguity. They believe that the common characteristics of every case are outweighed by the important differences among them.

One case type is the familiar story or *novel* that portrays specific events, human behavior, dialogue and feelings and has characters and a plot. The story style, according to Newmann and Oliver, is especially effective for involving students emotionally. Closely related to the story is the *vignette,* a short portrayal of human experience with no completed plot.

Another case type is the *historical narrative,* written like a news story. Such a presentation makes no effort to develop a plot to describe the emotions and feelings of the people involved. It is merely a straightforward account of an event (often eyewitness).

Documents, another case type, include court opinions, speeches, letters, diaries, transcripts of trials, and laws, for example. Still another kind of case is *research data,* sometimes used as the basis for deriving valid generalizations. As opposed to primary data offered in research, these data describe public movements, organizations, or different groups of people, for example. A textbook writer may use this kind of case to illustrate generalizations.

What Distinct Case Approaches Are Used?

Cases are used for two distinctly different instructional needs: (1) to illustrate previously developed conclusions, or (2) to provoke controversy and debate on issues for which definite conclusions do not exist (the issue-case approach). Both categories permit the study of descriptive issues (factual material) *and* prescriptive issues (what ought to be).

In those cases that deal with previously developed conclusions, specific facts, definitions, or concepts may be presented in the form of an exciting narrative that supports the conclusion reached. Thus by furnishing the learner with a realistic situation, abstract theories and concepts become more understandable. These cases are also useful in helping students generalize from specific events. Unfortunately, these cases may also be used by the instructor to support prescriptive conclusions or moral lessons, and thus become a vehicle for dogma.

---

[1] Fred M. Newmann and Donald W. Oliver, "Case Study Approaches in Social Sciences," *Social Education* 31 (February 1967): 108-13.

As a method for stimulating inquiry on unresolved problems, the issue case probably has no equal. The objective of such a case is to provide a basis for reaching a decision from a specific situation. All solutions to the case problem are carefully withheld until the case is solved by the students. Students analyze the facts available, determine a course of action and finally accept the responsibility for the consequences of the proposed action. Quality of performance is based on reasonable justification for the position taken rather than on mastery of facts.

What Analytical Skills Are Needed?

It is difficult to analyze a case, even one involving a relatively simple problem situation. The process consists of studying information in order to gain perspective on the entire problem. Since case materials are complex and based on a misunderstanding or conflict, there are always confusing and conflicting elements to be considered.

First of all, one should search for leads from key words or phrases. The following offer valuable clues to analysis: "repeatedly disregarded," "continued to disobey," "several times entered late," "often argued," and "usually could be heard over all others." Such clues help to uncover those attitudes and feelings that are the causes of action taken. Often what happens *in* people is more important than what happens *to* them.

Second, one should consider the organizational relationships of the various parties involved. An employee, for example, is expected to play an assigned role in certain contexts. Because of this, the chances for this person's making an objective decision are not very good. Similarly, a business executive, a school superintendent, a principal, an interested parent, a teacher, a departmental chairperson, and a student would all look at any given problem from a slightly different perspective.

Third, one must pay attention to role assignment, an often neglected aspect of case analysis. In the process of decision making, the learner may be expected to assume the role of a given party to the conflict or misunderstanding. Sometimes, this is not clearly stated in the case materials. Thus the student should ask, "Who am I supposed to be?"

Finally, the quality of analysis (and synthesis) is enhanced when the reasons for a recommended alternative action are given. For example, the decision to provide an individual with a trial might be defended by, "In our society an individual is considered innocent until proven guilty; an individual is entitled to a hearing in cases of dispute." In addition, preparation of written analysis prior to stating a solution is often desirable for adding clarity to a case-analysis discussion.

How Are Issues Clarified?

Conflict resolution is often hampered because of uncertainty over what constitutes the crux of the problem(s). Many times, the immediate issue is merely a symptom of a more basic problem. Although case materials lead up to an impending decision, the real issue may be submerged in the organizational relationships among the parties to the dispute. Thus a close look at relationships is an essential aspect of case analysis.

Based on extensive investigation at the Massachusetts Institute of Technology, Pigors and Pigors have found that " . . . a formal issue for arbitration is easier to see clearly and to state precisely than the kind of issue which often confronts an administrator, who must make a decision after the incident."[2] They recommend starting off with cases that define the issue in question. In other types of cases, asking students "What is at stake here" is one way of helping them focus on the basic issue involved.

What Time Factors Must Be Considered?

Case analysis takes time. The process of evolving concepts and general principles from specific case data demands considerable reflection and analysis. In-depth analysis required of mature students cannot be achieved in less than two hours. Classes in case analyses should be held once or twice a week for three hours. Three hours may be a little long, however, unless other activities such as small-group work are also engaged in.

Total time needed for adequate concept development through case analysis will vary with the maturity of the group and with the type of problem. Many teachers favor following up each case study with two or three class periods of related discussion. Certainly, it is extremely difficult for students to assimilate difficult concepts from case analysis week after week; some time for reflection is necessary. Using three nonrelated cases in a three-day workshop should be avoided.

Although the case approach has been used as the only method for teaching some subjects (as in business management), it can also be used effectively with other methods. In large lecture classes, for example, the lecturer can use the incident-case approach to relate abstract points to real-life problems. A few class sessions can be devoted to case analysis even in large lecture classes if space will permit division into subgroups of twenty to twenty-five students. Short case reports, of course, provide excellent subject matter for written papers and examinations in any class.

How Does the Case Approach Differ from Simulation Techniques?

The case method in a sense is a simulated experience. Rather than experiencing reality as it happens, the learner analyzes reports of reality. By analyzing the facts, emotions, and feelings of a situation, the learner grasps the intellectual *and emotional* framework of the actual event. By studying the experience, the student may acquire the skills to cope with similar situations.

---

[2] Paul Pigors and Faith Pigors, *Case Method in Human Relations: The Incident Process* (New York: McGraw-Hill Book Co., 1961), p. 169.

In contrast, simulation techniques actually involve learners in the event by requiring them to role play, to act it out. (These techniques are treated in a separate chapter.) Like the case method, they portray human emotions for the purpose of analysis and synthesis. One simulation technique, the sociodrama, is a spontaneous enactment of a specific incident. As such, it captures a microcosmic aspect of reality. The case report, on the other hand, usually portrays a larger slice of reality by emphasizing the feelings and attitudes of parties involved in a conflict or by including a series of successive incidents. Another technique, the simulation game, features a complex situation in which a number of related decisions must be made. Sometimes, the case is portrayed through role playing. Still another technique of simulating reality is through the use of case films.

Each technique of simulating reality may serve similar purposes and often can be used interchangeably, according to the particular preference of the teacher. The case method, however, seems to be uniquely suited for capturing the different and sometimes remote aspects of a complex situation. Furthermore, it seems to be most useful for developing broad concepts.

Essential Case Procedures

Teachers sometimes confuse case methods with studies that they perform for the purpose of understanding certain students. Occasionally, they confuse the method with research undertaken on students over a considerable period of time (sometimes known as case, or longitudinal, research.) Each of these methods is likely to require long hours of preparation and analysis. The incident-case approach, emphasized in this section, is a relatively simple instructional approach, however. Each case incident may vary in length from one short paragraph to one or two typed pages. Any teacher with a minimum of imagination can prepare his or her own cases; or if preferred, especially prepared cases can be used.[3]

Although in-depth cases receive emphasis at some institutions, the incident case is usually preferred. Since in-depth and incident cases involve problem solving, both will be emphasized in this chapter. The in-depth case will be treated as a series of related incidents. Generally those techniques that apply to one will apply to the other.

How is the Case Presented?

As with other teaching procedures, the case method must be integrated with other methods. Because case material presupposes a background in the subject area, it should be used to supplement textbook material. The study of banking, in a general business

---

[3] Dean Donham was largely responsible for initiating the case approach at the Harvard School of Business Administration. For a report of this project, see Malcolm P. McNair and Anita C. Hersum, eds., *The Case Method at the Harvard Business School* (New York: McGraw-Hill Book Co., 1954.) The Harvard cases are based on actual events.

class, for example, can become much more meaningful if supplemented with a case problem dealing with the borrowing of money.

Copies of the case are usually given to students. (Occasionally a short case may be read to them.) The case may be presented as an assignment for the next class period or it may be presented for immediate reading and reaction. This will depend somewhat upon the basic purpose to be served and the length and complexity of the case. Following the case presentation, three or four key case questions are usually asked to provoke stimulating thought.

In some subject areas, case analysis may be based on a single incident. In other areas, analysis may be based on a number of sequential incidents designed to reveal a number of related concepts. If a single incident is to be used, care must be exercised to include necessary details. Each sequential incident is designed to encourage the processes of induction. Pertinent questions are answered by the instructor or through additional case materials. The case which follows is offered for illustrative purposes.

THE SMYTHE PARKING INCIDENT

Promptly at 9:00 A.M., May 18, 1978, Professor Smythe was admitted to the campus traffic court hearing room. The university committee (composed of three professors, one departmental chairperson, a member of the dean's advisory committee, and a student representative) had convened to hear Professor Smythe's case on campus parking violations.

Quoting from the record, the committee spokesperson pointed out that Professor Smythe had been cited twelve times within the past four months for parking in an unauthorized parking lot. On each occasion, he was supposed to pay a five-dollar fine and complete a form stating his reason for violating standard parking regulations. Smythe had ignored all these procedures. Once when the dean asked Smythe about the matter, Smythe said, "Oh, that morning I was late for class; the regular parking lot was full; so I didn't really have any choice."

When asked to corroborate the record, Smythe nodded in agreement and then added, "I want to go on record as being strongly opposed to this sort of harassment. As a professor, I must leave and re-enter the campus frequently. When the nearest faculty parking lot is full, I have to park elsewhere if I'm to meet my professional responsibilities." He then added, "I refuse to pay all traffic fines given to me under such circumstances."

1. What is the major issue?
2. What basic rights are being violated, if any?
3. Was Professor Smythe justified in his behavior?

After reading the case materials, students begin asking questions, some of which are answered by the instructor:

Q. Does Professor Smythe have permanent status (tenure)?
A. Yes, he does.

Q. Did his professional group help establish parking rules?
A. No, they were established by higher administrative officials.
Q. Have other professors violated parking procedures?
A. Yes, but in each case, they apparently settled the matter with officials.
Q. Does Smythe's behavior deprive others of needed parking space?
A. Yes, he used a student and a visitor parking lot both crowded during rush hours.
Q. What is the specific responsibility of the campus traffic court?
A. It is responsible for making specific recommendations to the dean of the college.

During the proceedings, the instructor provides a map of all parking lots at the university. It soon becomes apparent that another large faculty parking lot, within one-quarter mile of Professor Smythe's office, is available.

Each member is then asked to write out his or her decision, supported with reasons; thus eventually the entire deliberative process is completed. One possible option would be to analyze another incident(s), indicating what action was taken and postpone further action until the case is appealed. The next level of appeal would be the university grievance committee, followed by the president's advisory committee, and finally the board of regents.

How Is the Case Problem Analyzed?

The discussion analysis is initiated when the teacher asks, "What is the issue or problem in this case?" It is essential that students know precisely what the difficulty is. In complex cases, there may be three or four minor problems, but usually it is relatively easy to identify the basic issue from which the other difficulties originate.

The second step is the analysis of facts in the situation. *Here, the emphasis is on what actually happened rather than on one's personal opinion of the facts.* The purpose of this phase of the discussion is to get the case facts into the open, making sure that all important bits of information are considered. Some teachers find it desirable to put these points on the chalkboard for all to see. If the case is somewhat complex, each student may be asked to prepare a written analysis prior to the experience. Such a technique tends to promote an atmosphere of uninhibited discussion. Explanations of *why* the behavior occurred can be gained from analyzing what case participants actually said. Key phrases may be jotted down for future reference.

Next, the discussion might turn to the relations between the people involved. To whom is the party responsible? Is there evidence of a hidden allegiance? What are the established channels of communication?

The final step is the analysis of *beliefs and attitudes.* A word of caution is in order, however. It is important to distinguish between attitudes and feelings expressed in the case and those inferred by students who are participating in the case analysis.

How Are Hypotheses Derived?

After case activities, relationships, and sentiments and beliefs have been thoroughly explored and evaluated, attention turns to decision making. "What needs to be decided and done, right now?" It is helpful to consider decision or action in terms of *each party* to the conflict. This usually results in more than one proposal. Pigors and Pigors suggest a technique that they have found most effective.[4] First, each member of the group (working independently) jots down a decision and outlines the reasoning behind it. The student signs the paper and presents it to the discussion leader. Next, the class is assembled in separate opinion groups for the purpose of comparing notes and consolidating reasoning. The strongest possible argument for a given decision is prepared. Then, a spokesperson is selected to present and argue this case briefly before the entire class. (Sometimes the various decisions may be role played.) Thus tentative decisions are tested from the standpoint of each party to the conflict. Sometimes, depending on the frame of reference accepted and the basic assumptions made, it becomes apparent that more than one decision is best.

How Are Generalizations Derived?

As a concluding activity, students are encouraged to derive generalizations from the experience. These are the basic ideas that they are expected to transfer to related situations. As Pigors and Pigors so aptly express, the process involves "looking back, looking up, looking about, and finally looking ahead."[5] Reflecting on the case as a whole (along with other cases previously studied), the student once again assumes a position "outside" the case. He or she examines the fundamental issue explored, reflecting on those behaviors that appeared to be highly effective (or ineffective) in the situation. For example, the teacher might ask, "How could this conflict have been prevented? How could more have been accomplished?" This process naturally leads to *looking up* to the level of general ideas and principles. Thus the teacher might ask, "What guiding concepts can be distilled from our case analysis?" This, in turn, leads to *looking about* for other situations that are similar to the present one. "How do the general ideas in this case apply to other cases?" Finally, the basic concepts are *thrust forward* to problems that might be reasonably anticipated. It must be emphasized that the basic assumption underlying use of the case method is that the fundamental concepts derived from particular cases are applicable to a variety of similar situations. The teacher must assist the learner in this knowledge expansion process. In psycho-

---

[4] Paul Pigors and Faith Pigors, *Case Method in Human Relations: The Incident Process,* p. 144.
[5] Ibid., p. 145.

logical terms, one might say, "Transfer of learning is enhanced when the student is taught to transfer."

What Role Does the Teacher Play?

The heart of the case method is discussion analysis. As in a problem-solving discussion, the teacher must establish an atmosphere conducive to student analysis. In order to do this, the teacher must play many roles and change roles frequently. He or she questions, restates problems and issues, voices opinions, and draws on his or her own knowledge. The appropriate combination of these can only be acquired from direct experience.

The instructor often opens the discussion by asking students to identify the basic problem, sometimes using the questions that often accompany a case report. The written questions accompanying a case report are designed to provoke thinking *in advance of* the discussion analysis.

Perhaps the most basic principle of case discussion is cooperative leadership. In their attempt to solve selected case problems, both teacher and student must recognize that wise decisions are sometimes based on personal and social values as much as on factual information. They must recognize, however, that their own hunches as to the best solution may not stand the test of critical analysis.

A critical aspect of productive leadership is keeping the discussion in focus. At any given moment, for example, the entire group should be centering its attention on the same idea or point. Furthermore, all members should adhere to the same level of abstraction at any one time. For example, the student who proceeds into the realm of general ideas while others are discussing specific facts should be asked to cite specific illustrations of his or her point of view.

The leader must resist the urge to offer his or her own solution to the problem. On the other hand, this individual must not withhold needed knowledge or points of view. It occasionally may be important, for example, to suggest alternative proposals, not because they are better than those suggested by the group but because they will further stimulate productive thinking of the group. Above all, the leader must help the group make decisions on the basis of evidence, rather than merely judge the characters in the case.

Planning for Case Analysis

In addition to preparation of case materials, a lesson plan must be developed. The lesson plan employs a problem-solving approach and includes key questions to be used to develop thinking along appropriate channels.

LESSON PLAN ILLUSTRATION FOR CASE ANALYSIS (biology class)

Problem: How can each of us assist in the control of microorganisms?

Concept: Adequate health safeguards are the responsibilities of all people.

Goals: After this lesson in microbe diseases, the student should have furthered his or her understanding of the problems as evidenced by:

1. The ability to distinguish between fact and opinion in case materials.
2. The ability to discuss deterents against diseases and their importance.
3. The ability to justify case decisions from given points of view.

Lesson approach

Following preliminary investigation of the basic essentials of microbe diseases as provided in textbook materials, students will be provided individual copies of the case "The Inoculation." Students will be asked the question "Have you ever seen a person who is dying of lockjaw?" Then they will be told a brief story of a person dying of lockjaw. Students will be asked to read and take notes on the case materials and to reflect briefly on the key questions following the case.

THE INOCULATION

Jeff Jones is a freshman college student. He participates in school athletics and for a hobby works on automobiles during the weekend. He is the eldest child from an average-income family that includes two other children—one son and one daughter. During his senior year in high school, Jeff was injured in athletics and, as a result of his injuries, was hospitalized twice last spring. Jeff hates to have inoculations and tries his best to avoid them.

All athletes at Jeff's college must receive a tetanus booster at least once a year. Dr. Adams, the school doctor, gives the athletes their tetanus shot at the beginning of each sport season. The only charge to the student is a twenty-five cent fee to cover the cost of the antitoxin and syringe. If the student cannot afford the twenty-five cents, the doctor will give the shot free; the only way Jeff can avoid the shot is to present a waiver form from his family doctor stating that he has received a tetanus shot within the last three months.

Bill Smith, Jeff's best friend, has known Jeff since first grade. They live a block away from each other, and Bill participates in the same sports as Jeff. When Jeff finds out about the tetanus shot requirement, he asks Bill to forge the doctor's signature on the waiver. Bill refuses, so Jeff forges the signature himself.

Bill is the type that usually lets a person do as he wishes, and this is especially true when it comes to his relationship with Jeff. On the other hand, Bill takes pride in the fact that he has, on several occasions, gone against Jeff's will for Jeff's own protection.

On the way to school, a week before physicals for football, Jeff tells Bill that he has forged his doctor's name on the waiver. Bill seems to be disturbed by Jeff's action and doesn't immediately say anything to Jeff.

Lesson development

A. Initiating the discussion
   1. What is the basic problem in this case?
   2. What might be done to make Jeff understand the necessity for the inoculation?
B. Analyzing the problem
   1. What are the facts in the situation?
   2. Why is a tetanus shot important?
   3. What is the relationship between Jeff and Bill?
   4. How does Bill feel about Jeff's actions?
C. Weighing alternatives
   1. In view of the facts, relationships, and feelings just discussed, what action, if any, should Bill take?
   2. What might be the consequences of such action? (Each of the possible solutions will be discussed until alternatives are reduced to two or three likely courses of action.)
   3. At this point, jot down your own preferred course of action, along with specific reasons supporting it.
   4. We will now divide into discussion buzz groups, corresponding to the different decisions reached. A representative will prepare the best possible case for your proposed course of action.
   5. We will now reassemble, and each spokesperson in the group will briefly debate his or her group's case for the class. Questions may be interjected by others as needed.
D. Deriving generalizations
   1. What similar situations have you encountered?
   2. What general principles seem to apply? Examples might include:
      a. Discussing value questions with others who have had wider experiences in the area.
      b. Discussing similar problems with friends in your own age group.
      c. Discussing the case with your family doctor.

This lesson plan illustrates what can be done with a very brief case. Often, the case will be more involved, depicting conflicting feelings and emotions. Regardless of the length and complexity of the case, however, similar planning principles apply. Case analysis will vary considerably, depending on the wishes of the teacher and the nature of the case. Frequently, the teacher will have students evaluate proposed alternatives without first dividing the class into subgroups. On the other hand, the teacher may demonstrate the effects of a decision by having students role play or engage in a sociodrama.

Basic to the preparation for a case analysis is mastery of the case facts. The instructor must be prepared to think with the students as they explore any number of side issues. If the case is complex, the teacher should summarize pertinent facts in the lesson plan and ask key questions that lead students toward the main goal of the lesson.

How Is Pupil Progress Evaluated?

One of the most effective means of evaluating student mastery of case analysis is to give them a case similar to the one they have been studying and then ask them to answer questions about it. The case incident that follows illustrates one way of testing for the acquisition of principles.[6]

Ben has been dating Sue for a year and they are considering marriage. They have not, however, reconciled all of their ideals and standards. Ben regards himself as a "liberal" in his sex standards (morals) in that he thinks everyone should make decisions about "how far to go" according to his own convictions. Ben, however, sets high standards of sex ethics for himself, and he has chosen Sue because she too is strict in her observation of moral codes. Sue, on the other hand, has pronounced ideas of what is "right" and "wrong" for everyone and she has no patience with persons who are more "liberal." She thinks Ben is too tolerant.

What position would you take if you were involved to the extent of Ben or Sue? Why? (You may choose as many as you wish.) (Circle the number of your choices.)

1. Decide not to discuss the issue any more?
2. Recognize that to me there is a rightness about morals but that people of different circumstances and experience might view morals differently in terms of "right and "wrong"?
3. Recognize that under certain circumstances you could believe and behave differently?
4. When the subject is brought up just ignore it?
5. Point out that it is hurtful as well as shocking to realize that some people have such morals?
6. Attempt to change the other person's viewpoint to coincide with your own?
7. Recognize that "right is right and wrong is wrong" and anyone should know the difference?

---

[6] Helene M. Hoover, "Concept Development of College Students Exposed to Systematic, Organized Learning Experiences in Family Relationships" (Doctoral dissertation, Oklahoma State University, Stillwater, Oklahoma, 1966) pp. 148-49. Used by permission of the author.

8. Try to recognize and appreciate what makes the other person feel as he does?
9. Read about the background and experiences of people with different moral standards from your own?
10. Acquaint one's self with people of different moral standards and try to understand their viewpoints?

Now check the behaviors which you feel would develop empathy.

An alternative way of testing students is to have them write an analysis of the case. This technique has been employed extensively in college classes, where the case approach has been employed as the basic instructional procedure.[7] Four criteria for evaluating written case analysis have been offered by Estrin and Goode. They include:

1. *Insight.* Ability to grasp material and to see relationships and patterns. Ability to synthesize the disparate facts of the case and to see the whole.
2. *Relevance.* Deals with central problems, rather than periphical ones. The concepts and theories should be relevant to the case.
3. *Thoroughness.* Uses all pertinent facts and useful tools of analysis and synthesis.
4. *Organization.* Follows some logical plan.[8]

Attempts to evaluate an ongoing discussion often have been discouraging. When students know they are being evaluated, their discussion behaviors tend to be affected markedly. Use of an observer for evaluating group progress has been effective, however.

What Case Sources Are Readily Available?

Many teachers would make more extensive use of the case approach to teaching if they had ready access to prepared cases in their fields. Fortunately, a number of prepared cases are available in several fields. These include, among others, the fields of business,[9] science,[10] and home economics.[11] Delta Pi Epsilon, the honorary graduate fraternity in business education, for example, has assembled a source book of 100 cases, collected from secondary business teachers from all parts of the country. These

---

[7] Kenneth R. Andrews, *The Case Method of Teaching Human Relations and Administration* (Cambridge, Mass: Harvard University Press, 1953) pp. 122-37.

[8] Herman A. Estrin and Delmer M. Goode, *College and University Teaching* (Dubuque, Iowa: William C. Brown Co., 1964), pp. 185-87.

[9] Delta Pi Epsilon, *The Business Teacher Learns From Cases* (Chicago: South-Western Publishing Co., 1957).

[10] Leopold E. Klopfer, *History of Science Cases* (Chicago: Science Research Associates, 1964).

[11] Jessie Bernard, Helen E. Buchannan, and William M. Smith Jr., *Dating, Mating and Marriage* (Cleveland, Ohio: Howard Allen, Inc., 1958).

cases are based on actual experiences of secondary students. A somewhat different approach has been taken in the field of science. Klopfer has prepared a number of historical narrative cases containing quotations from scientists' original papers, pertinent student experiments and activities, marginal notes and questions, and space for students to write answers to questions. Bernard and his colleagues, on the other hand, have prepared a series of documentary case analyses in the area of male-female relationships.

The big disadvantage of using prepared cases, however, is that they very often do not fit the needs of the class. Also, they may not be realistic enough for the group involved. *Thus teachers should acquire skills in preparing their own cases.*

The Harvard Business School for many years has collected its cases by sending out case writers, who record problems that they actually witness in business firms. Some of the materials are produced from actual interviews with the executives and employees involved. Based on these experiences, three general guidelines have been offered: (1) most cases describe one or more current events; (2) the author should present some background on the people and the problem; (3) the case should conclude with questions for a follow-up discussion. By adhering to these simple rules, teachers can develop their own file of cases on student problems and behavior.

The development of complex cases in a content area can be a bit more involved than the "incident technique" commonly used. A technique for developing such cases in history has been developed by Morosky. He recommends that the teacher first prepare an outline of the information to be presented, as illustrated below:

1. If a role is to be assigned, designate what role the class will assume.
2. Identify the period as soon as possible.
3. Give a background sketch.
4. Discuss the problem influences.[12]

Morosky then recommends that each of these areas be expanded to become the case study. Whenever possible, he would have the writer follow the three basic rules cited in the preceding paragraph. Morosky's technique is well worth further investigation by any teacher interested in developing proficiency in the preparation of cases. How may a teacher acquire skill in developing cases?

Any teacher can quickly prepare a short, incident case by following the procedure outlined below.

First, one should identify the unit concept to be portrayed. As indicated in Chapter 1, the concept will incorporate or imply a real-life application.

The first paragraph or two should include a brief description of the individual(s) with which the case reader is to identify. Included will be background material (both

---

[12] Robert L. Morosky, "The Case Method Approach to Teaching History," *Social Studies* 57, no. 5 (October 1966): 199-204.

facts and feelings) and a description of the current situation. An occasional quote, designed to dramatize feelings, provides an added touch of realism.

The next paragraph or two will include a brief description of the opposing individual(s) involved in the situation. Again, the writer will provide background information and portray basic feelings and relationships.

Finally, a paragraph or two will be devoted to the basic problem of the case. This will clearly portray clashes, differences of opinion, or issues aggravating the problem. Immediate facts, feelings, and relationships will dramatize the conflicting conditions. This paragraph will end with a statement concerning the final decision to be made.

The case material usually ends with three or four case questions, designed to provoke reflective thinking prior to the actual case analysis. As discussed earlier, the questions usually will emphasize the higher levels of cognition.

In teaching case-writing techniques to prospective teachers, the author has effectively utilized selected photographs portraying complex or ambiguous situations. Students develop cases in class based on these photographs, which are shown on overhead projectors. Some students can develop two such cases within a single class period. After a careful analysis of each case, prospective teachers are usually able to develop their own cases with little difficulty.

The Value of the Case Method

The case approach is realistic. Analyzing a portrayal of reality is about as close to the real thing as possible.

By treating human emotion and feelings, the case approach captures the interest and imagination of the learner.

The case has an advantage over other simulated techniques (e.g., sociodrama and role playing) because it can deal with a larger slice of reality. For example, factors leading up to a conflict and the interrelated aspects of conflict can be readily analyzed.

Case analysis treats feelings as facts. Some instructional approaches (for example, discussion methods) tend to strip cognitive facts from their affective components.

By capturing and analyzing real problems, the student is able to bridge the gap between school and real-life experiences.

Limitations of, and Problems with, the Case Method

Although the case is a portrayal of reality, it is *not* reality. Actual decisions are sometimes reached on the basis of intangibles that cannot be captured in a case portrayal.

Because someone selects the case, it runs the risk of favoring a particular point of view, as King points out. [13]

---

[13] David C. King, "Using Case Studies to Teach about Global Issues," *Social Education* 38 (November 1974): 657-63.

The case technique tends to collapse time and space dimensions. Consequently, it tends to emphasize positive action. Sometimes in real-life situations action may not be justified. A solution may not be feasible.

The case approach is time-consuming. If used extensively, it will definitely limit the content material that can be covered.

Preparation of cases is an art that must be learned. Use of cases not specifically designed for the material being taught may limit the effectiveness of the learning experience.

The learner tends to overgeneralize from studying only one case. This probably can be minimized by providing statistical data to accompany the case material and by using a variety of cases on a given topic.

Illustrated Cases

I. Useful in history, government, and social studies classes

Concept: A man is innocent under the law until proved guilty.

Jack Phillips grew up in a wealthy section of Chicago. Even though his parents provided him with toys and games during his childhood, he began to steal comic books and candy from the local stores. As soon as he reached the age of sixteen, with his parents' reluctant consent, he quit school and began to work as a stock boy in a local sporting-goods store. In addition to his earnings from his job, he received an allowance from his parents. This enabled him to flaunt his wealth and, as a result, he had few, if any, friends.

During the first few months of his job, he found it easy to steal sports equipment and to sell it. However, his boss, beginning to notice that certain items were missing from stock, notified the police. After watching Phillips for a number of days, the police entered his home, searched it, and, after finding some sports equipment there, arrested him. He was sent to jail to await trial.

Jack's family, sparing no expense, immediately contacted a prominent lawyer, who agreed to defend their son. After examining his client's case, the lawyer claimed that several of Jack's constitutional rights had been violated and that he should be released from jail.

Questions

1.   From the description of this case, what rights do you feel might have been violated?
2.   The events described all occurred before Jack Phillips appeared before a jury for trial. Do you feel that the case should come to trial?
3.   In view of the wealth of the Phillips family and the fact that they spent money on their son, how might you explain Jack's desire to steal?
4.   Do you feel that Jack's family has any *legal* responsibility for his actions?

II. Useful in home economics, group guidance, sociology, and psychology classes.

Concept: Empathy is essential to a successful marriage.

Jane and her husband, Bill, live in a middle-class suburb. They have three small children, all under school age. Bill is not a college graduate but is capable and ambitious. Jane indicates that she values these traits in her husband. He is a salesman for a large company, but his work is largely confined to his home state. Sometimes he is away for two or three days and he often gets home late at night. Occasionally his work interferes with their weekends.

Lately Jane has been complaining about his being away so much and getting home so late. Bill explained that he had made several contacts which he considered good prospects for a sale and that it was difficult to break up his conferences to come home at a regular hour. Besides, he sometimes had paper work to do when he got back to the office. Bill feels that she should appreciate his efforts for the family. Jane said that he was always about to make a sale, which usually fell through, and that he should spend more time with his family. Moreover, financial support, she says, is not the only kind of support she needs. She would like help with the children.

Questions

1. What is the problem?
2. What incidents show lack of empathy?
3. What are some understandings about Jane's feelings that Bill needs in order to empathize, and vice versa?
4. What are some specific ways in which Jane and Bill can develop empathy?
5. If the present relationship continues, what type of family life will they likely have? Give the principles that explain your answer.

III. Useful in speech and social studies classes

Concept: Each group member must contribute to group progress.

Ron Powell a freshman college student lives with his divorced mother. He is a lonely only child, having little opportunity to participate in small-group activity. Ron does have a few close friends, however, who have persuaded him to become a student council representative. Ken Goodwin is also a member of the student council. He is the oldest child in his family of six. He is usually quite tactful in his relationships with others but does have a hot temper.

Every September, the student council holds a workshop; the representatives break into committees to discuss problems and plans for the coming semester. This year the workshop is being held in the gymnasium, and the committees are seated in groups about the room. Several faculty advisers are also present.

When the committees are formed, Ken and Ron and two other students are assigned to the same group. Ken, the discussion leader, is trying his best to establish some rules that will be acceptable to both the students and the faculty. Ron keeps trying to tell the group about his week at summer camp. They listen reluctantly, wanting to continue with their business. Ken tries again to get some ideas from the group. Ron cuts in and begins to tell about his dog. Ron continues to monopolize the conversation, talking on completely irrelevant subjects.

Questions

1. What is the major problem in this case?
2. What are the issues involved?
3. What action would you take if you were a member of the group?

IV. Useful in laboratory science classes

The case that follows has been used successfully in chemistry classes.[14] The author of the case suggests that while the case describes a realistic situation, class discussion need only focus on the available options.[15] (Certainly, discussion soon is impeded if too much emphasis is placed on case facts.) For less mature students, Jones favors the listing of facts (as illustrated in his case) over the narrative form.

LEAD—A CASE STUDY

In this case study, the problem is to develop a position on lead pollution for a politician campaigning for an approaching election. Thus, in addition to the chemistry of lead and lead poisoning, aspects of political science, economics, mass communications, and medicine will have to be considered.

You are on the staff of a United States Congressman from a district in which a large chemical company is located. It is the fall of 1975 and the Congressman wishes to take advantage of the popular concern about the environment by running on a plank involving lead pollution. Your committee has assembled the following facts and now, using only these facts, you must put together a good position for the Congressman to take. The Congressman has instructed you to do the following:

—Decide the best issue concerning lead pollution for the Congressman to use. This will be the theme of the campaign plank. A number of good issues are possible.

—Using the chosen issue, propose at least three positions from which the

---

[14]Richard F. Jones, "Lead—A Case Study," *Chemistry* 48, no. 3 (March 1975): 12-15. Used by permission of the author and the publisher. Copyright © 1975 American Chemical Society.

[15]Personal correspondence with Richard F. Jones.

Congressman may choose. Your positions should include all reasonable solutions to the problem you have chosen to highlight.

—Analyze the probable consequences of each solution giving its pros and cons.

—Select the most favorable position and give your reasons for the choice.

—Propose a detailed plan of action for the Congressman to follow during the coming campaign. This should include the arguments the Congressman will use, how he will address his audience, to which audience he will appeal.

In preparing your case, you will have to balance contradictory goals with data that are less than perfect. Need to obtain the backing of the strong environmental groups with what they consider an ecologically correct plank must be balanced against the need to obtain money to finance the campaign. The Congressman will be wary of doing anything that might disrupt the economy of the region. Environmental issues are often complex and you must ensure that the average voter will be able to understand the issue and its importance to him.

Some of the facts which follow will be useful, some will be irrelevant, some will be contradictory (numbers in parenthesis indicate reference and page). Part of your task is to evaluate each fact and decide which to use. Information that you might want may be missing; nonetheless additional research is not allowed. As is often the case in real life, your decision will have to be made with incomplete information. Thus your task involves risk-taking in that judgment is at the center of your case decision. There is no single correct answer: This is often the way it is.

Lead pollution fact sheet

—The surface waters of Earth's oceans today contain 10 times as much lead as they did before man learned to smelt lead (3, 68).

—The early Romans, in their quest for silver, smelted large amounts of ore that contained lead. About 400 tonnes of lead were recovered for each tonne of silver.

—Mining and smelting were done by slaves, who undoubtedly often died of lead poisoning. The Romans used lead for a wide variety of purposes, including roof sheathing and cooking and wine vessels. Because the ruling classes used leaden vessels most, they were the group most poisoned. The result was a declining birth rate and an impairment of their creative and governing ability (3, 68).

—During the early years of the 20th century, lead poisoning was common among house painters (3, 68).

—Convulsions, delirium, coma, severe and irreversible brain damage, blindness, paralysis, mental retardation, and death can result from lead poisoning (3, 69).

—Lead content of the Greenland icecap, traced back to −800, shows an explosive increase during the last half century (3, 69).

—Low-compression engines get fewer high-speed kilometres per litre of fuel (3, 70).

—Unlike many other pollutants, lead is a cumulative poison (3, 70).

—Most lead entering the human body does so through food. This lead, which enters the stomach, is rather inefficiently absorbed by the body, and only about 5 to 10% of the lead actually enters the blood stream (3, 69).

—The United States now consumes more than half the world's production of lead—about 1.3 million of the 2.2 million tonnes (3, 70).

—The Environmental Protection Agency (EPA) recently reported that lead-free gasoline could be available across the country by 1975 at an additional cost to the motorist of between 0.05 and 0.23 cents per litre of fuel (3, 75).

—Governors of the Massachusetts Bay Colony in New England outlawed the distillation of rum in lead vessels in order to prevent what were called the dry gripes (3, 68).

—Lead inhaled from automobile exhaust is dangerous because the fine particles retained within the alveoli of the lungs are absorbed by the body with an efficiency of about 40% (3, 69).

—The total daily intake of lead in the food and drink of an individual American is typically about $300\mu g$ (3, 69).

—The level considered indicative of lead poisoning in healthy males is 0.8 part of lead per million (ppm) parts of blood (3, 69).

—Grass harvested from alongside highways has been found to contain as much as 100 times the lead concentration of grass not exposed to automobile exhaust (3, 69).

—There is some evidence that emission of aromatic hydrocarbons increases as lead content of fuel falls (3, 70).

—Man's manufacturing, use of pesticides, combustion of coal, incineration of refuse, and use of leaded gasoline are the leading sources of lead in the biosphere (2, 42).

—The maximum lead concentration allowed in drinking water by the U.S. Public Health Service is 0.05 milligram per litre (2, 42).

—To achieve the same octane rating in lead-free gasoline, more aromatic hydrocarbons are needed. These additives are expected to produce in exhaust more 3,4-benzopyrene, which is known to cause cancer in laboratory animals (4, 178).

—There is a very high correlation between lead in rainfall and sales of leaded gasoline (2, 42).

—Lead is a cumulative poison and its continued use will eventually build up dangerous levels in the environment (4, 178).

—Lead exhausted by automobiles originates in the antiknock ingredient in the gasoline (2, 43).

—Significant sources of naturally occurring lead in air include silicate dusts from soils and particles from volcanoes (2, 42).

—Removal of lead from gasoline means that engines would run on fuel of a lower octane rating than that for which they were designed. Thus engines would run less efficiently, producing more carbon monoxide and oxides of nitrogen and spewing more unburned gasoline into the air (4, 178).

—The main inorganic compounds in automobile exhaust are lead bromochloride and three species in which lead bromochloride is combined with ammonium chloride. Very small amounts of the lead alkyls in the gasoline escape to the air by evaporation (2, 43).

—Concentrations of lead aerosols in a sampling of urban areas were 1 to 5 μg per cubic metre (μg/m^3); air in rural areas contained a few tenths of a microgram per cubic metre (2, 43).

—The air pollution threat was worse in Los Angeles in 1970 despite the virtual elimination of industrial pollution and the requirement of pollution control devices on all new motor vehicles since 1965. Increases in the number of cars wiped out gains made by technological improvements (4, 178).

—About two thirds of the lead consumed in gasoline is exhausted to the atmosphere, and 25 to 50% of that amount becomes airborne (2, 54).

—The atmosphere of the Northern Hemisphere contains about 1000 times more lead than it would if man were not a contributor (2, 42).

—In a major study of the lead in urban air, annual concentrations of lead averaged 1 to 3 μg/m^3. Average concentrations of lead over relatively short periods of time in heavy traffic ranged from 14 μg/m^3 in a vehicular tunnel (2, 42).

—Lead used in electric batteries, solder, and pewter can be recycled (3, 70).

—Today the average American's blood lead concentration is about .2 ppm (3, 69).

—In midtown Manhattan average values of 7.5 μg/m^3 of lead in air have been reported (3, 69).

—Theoretically, but as yet not practically, lead particles can be removed from the exhaust stream by special filters and separation devices (3, 70).

—Of the many methods proposed to control the amount of hydrocarbons, carbon monoxide, and oxides of nitrogen leaving the exhaust pipes of automobiles, one of the most discussed is the catalytic converter. The catalytic converter uses filtering by porous material having a large surface area in proportion to the volume occupied. The pores in the material fill rapidly with lead particles when leaded gasoline is used, and the process of converting other pollutants to their harmless constituents is blocked (3, 70).

—Ethyl Corp. and Du Pont, the primary makers of tetraethyllead (the gasoline antiknock additive), contend that continued use of lead in gasoline will provide needed engine lubrication and avoid a controversial phenomenon called valve seat pound-in, which may cause rapid wear of valve seats in cars using unleaded gas (3, 70).

—The average city dweller experiences an atmospheric lead level of about 2 μg/m^3. He inhales about 20 m^3 of air per day (3, 69).

—T. J. Chow of Scripps Oceanographic Institute recently reported that in San Diego average values of lead are now 8 μg/m^3 of air; he noted that the concentrations are rising at a rate of 5% per year (3, 69).

—The most commonly used indicator of exposure to lead is its concentration in the blood (3, 69).

—Heavy metals owe their toxicity primarily to their ability to react with and inhibit sulfhydryl (—SH) enzyme systems such as those involved in the production of cellular energy. For example, 2 glutathione + metal ion (M^{2+}) → M (glutathione)$_2$ + 2H$^+$ (5, 409).

—The average human rids himself of about 2 milligrams (mg) of lead a day through the kidneys and intestinal tract (5, 411).

—Lead, like mercury and arsenic salts, can affect the central nervous system (4, 178).

—Even though lead-pigmented paints have not been used in this country for interior painting during the last 30 years, children are still poisoned by lead from old paint. In 1969, about 200 children in the United States died of lead poisoning and untold thousands suffered permanent damage (5, 411-12).

—Probable upper limits for the intake of lead are shown in the table below (5, 412).

—Surveys in Massachusetts have shown that in all cities and towns where there has been extensive testing of children, between 5 and 10% of the children have some degree of lead poisoning. In older districts (where there is likely to be more old paint) 20 to 30% of children were poisoned (1, 3).

—It has been suggested that airborne lead particles could combine with iodine vapor to form lead particles that could seed clouds and thus modify climate (2, 44).

—There is little direct evidence of the composition (type of compounds) and reactions of lead aerosols in the air (2, 43).

—Though it has been illegal to make leadbased paint for indoor use for many years, most houses built before 1950 have several old coats of lead paint under the new nonlead paint. If the paint chips, the old layers chip off too (1, 3).

—No national standards now exist for emission of lead compounds by automobiles (2, 54).

—The amount of lead used in gasoline averages 0.6 gram of the metal (as tetraethyl- and tetramethyllead) per litre (2, 54).

—A simple finger prick blood test can be used to determine if a child is suffering from lead poisoning and to what degree (1, 3).

—Extensive research on nonpolluting octane improvers for gasoline has failed to produce any that approach lead in overall effectiveness (2, 55).

—In 1967, the four U.S. producers of lead alkyls made 308 million kilograms of tetraethyl- and tetramethyllead valued at $254 million (2, 55).

—Petroleum refiners now increase octane ratings and otherwise upgrade their feedstocks by manipulating molecular structures of the gasoline itself (2, 55).

Probable Upper Limits for Intake of Lead (5)

	Mg/Day
Solid Food	1200.0
Air	0.225
Water	0.200
Beverage	0.030

—Paint can be tested for lead in just a few minutes using a small portable X-ray fluorescent analyzer (1, 4).

To approximate more closely a real life situation, students should work in teams of three or four. In class, each team will present its proposal to the Congressman (the instructor). The rest of the class will act as members of the Congressman's staff. With each member actively participating, the presenting team should take about 15 to 20 minutes to give their case to the class. Then, the class will debate with the team the merits of their platform plank. Purpose of the class discussion is to provide a forum for the testing of the case study against opposing views and to experience group decision making.

Criteria of evaluation are: familiarity with the case facts; worth of the issue chosen; completeness of the alternative positions, consistency in the handling of the facts; cogency of presentations (written or oral); and participation in class debate and team presentation.

References

(1) Braver, Barbara, "Lead Paint Poisoning called 'Hidden Epidemic' by State," "North Shore '74" supplement in *The Daily News*, Newburyport, Mass., January 5, 1974.
(2) "Cleaning Our Environment: The Chemical Basis for Action," 1969, The American Chemical Society, Washington, D.C.
(3) Craig, Paul P., "Lead, The Inexcusable Pollutant," *Saturday Review*, October 2, 1971.
(4) Hill, John W., "Chemistry for Changing Times," 1972, Burgess Publishing Co., Minneapolis, Minn.
(5) Jones, Mark M., Netterville, John T., Johnston, David O., Wood, James L., and Blackburn, John R., "Chemistry, Man and Society," 1972, W. B. Saunders Co., Philadelphia, Pa.

chapter 12

SIMULATION TECHNIQUES

Overview

Key Concepts

1. A simulation is a close representation of reality.
2. A simulation of reality may be superior to reality itself for instructional purposes.
3. Role playing is a vehicle for portraying selected problem situations.
4. Sociodramatic problems must be relevant to the lives of those involved; one does not play his or her own life role, however.
5. Simulation games involve a complex of interacting problems: a number of decisions must be reached.
6. A simulation game has its own payoff, or reward system.

New Terms

1. Spontaneous Acting naturally without preparation. Sometimes used interchangeably with the term "extemporaneous."
2. Role Playing The practice of spontaneously acting as somebody else in a contrived situation. This spontaneous quality distinguishes role playing from a dramatization. As used in simulation techniques, role playing helps develop insight into the motives and relationships of others in enacted situations.
3. Sociodrama A relatively simple, spontaneously enacted situation, based on a partially structured social problem. With the exceptions of the task, setting, and roles (merely suggested), the enactment develops spontaneously as the situation develops.
4. Model A set of interrelated physical or symbolic factors organized so as to depict accurately a process, event, or theory. The factors are limited to those necessary for the portrayal of reality.
5. Simulation Game An operating (as opposed to a static) model of a comparatively complex situation involving conflict of interests. Flexible

(game) rules and sequences are established for enabling the players to achieve specific objectives.

Questions to Guide Your Study

1. How might one develop a sociodramatic situation around an issue that is considered "too hot to handle"?
2. Students should select their own sociodramatic situations. Defend or refute.
3. Since simulation games cannot capture the whole of reality, they may be misleading. Defend or refute.
4. What advantages and disadvantages are associated with the payoff of a simulation game?

Simulations . . . are learning exercises that place students in roles similar to real world roles and, in playing the game, require them to make decisions as if they were part of those real world situations. [Simulations] are fun and students enter eagerly into the world of not-so-make-believe. Within the classroom this imitation of reality can teach important things about the real world, because we all learn from our experiences.

Simulation [techniques include] . . . several experimental teaching techniques . . . [e.g.] role playing, sociodrama, and values clarification, which increasing numbers of teachers are using. These techniques are gaining popularity because they can make schooling more effective by relating activities within the school to reality outside.[1]

This quote expresses the optimism of a sizable number of college professors who are becoming increasingly excited about the possibilities of simulation techniques. By placing students in simulated situations representative of the real world, teachers can make the learning experience more relevant for them.

Fundamental Properties

Simulation techniques are based on the premise that contrived reality provides an ideal setting for learning. Because these techniques merely simulate reality, they do not contain the threats of physical and psychological damage that may be inherent in the "real" situation. They operate under the assumption that once the learner can deal with simulated experiences, he or she is better able to cope with the broader problems of the real world. The following section offers a fundamental framework for those who desire to use simulation techniques for the first time.

---

[1] Mark Heyman, *Simulation Games for the Classroom* (Bloomington, Ind.: The Phi Delta Kappa Educational Foundation, 1975), p. 10.

What Is the Relationship among Role Playing, Sociodrama, and Simulation Games?

Role playing provides practice in how to behave in selected situations. Hence, it is often called "reality practice." In role playing, hypothetical but representative circumstances involving interpersonal relationships are established. Its purpose is to enable students to understand the attitudes, feelings, or situations of those persons whose roles they assume. As opposed to a *dramatization* for which students prepare by practicing assigned roles, role playing is done spontaneously.

Sociodrama involves acting out a situation in order to find a solution to the problem it poses. The situation is a relatively simple model of reality in which the "actors" react spontaneously to the events as they arise.

A *simulation game* is an artificial, condensed representation of reality. Governing the conduct of the game are rules limiting or prescribing the actions of the players. Rules are usually incorporated into a *game* of some type for the purpose of introducing the elements of competition, cooperation, and conflict as they normally occur in real life.[2]

Rules of a simulation game perform three distinct functions:

1. They specify the distribution of resources among the players once the game begins.
2. They state relationships among the various elements of the game, including players, resources, moves, and winners or losers.
3. They describe the sequence of play.

A simulation game is a relatively complex problem since it includes a number of interacting problems. Like sociodrama, a simulation game is based on some elements of social conflict. The objective is usually much broader, however, such as finding a solution to some business, social, or political problem. Solution(s) must be acceptable to the majority of the group members. Unlike sociodrama, the simulation game introduces the element of competition. Thus there are winners and losers. Figure 12-1 depicts the close relationship among role playing, sociodrama, and simulation games. As Figure 12-1 illustrates, role playing is the least structured of the three techniques, and simulation games are the most structured.

What Purposes Are Achieved by Simulation Techniques?

In many ways, simulations of reality may be superior to reality. From a practical standpoint, for example, one cannot create a serious accident for the purpose of studying the necessary first-aid treatment. Nor is it practical to rush students to an

---

[2] Dale M. Garvey, *Simulation, Role-Playing and Sociodrama*, The Emporia State Research Studies, vol 16, no. 2 (Emporia, Kans., November 1967), p. 11.

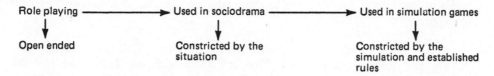

FIGURE 12-1 *The Relationship among Role Playing, Sociodrama, and Simulation Games*

accident so that they can practice first aid. Simulation techniques enable the instructor to provide a safe setting and thus to avoid costly errors of judgment while students are gaining valuable practice and insights.

Simulation techniques have the added advantage of condensing and reducing complexities to manageable learning units. An actual accident, for example, is often a scene of confusion since many conflicting events occur simultaneously. By reducing events to manageable proportions, simulations help the learner establish necessary priorities. Similarly by condensing time, simulations enable students to study events that otherwise would take many months to develop completely.

Frequently, however, events cannot be studied in their totality. Consider the elements of the universe, for example, and the relative position and functional processes of the sun, moon, and other heavenly bodies. Similarly, the real situation may be too dangerous to deal with until a certain amount of skill has been achieved. During World War II, the military service developed the Link Trainer to study reaction time of aviation cadets. Obviously, the error of a cadet was less costly in men and materials than a crash of a multimillion dollar aircraft.

Finally, simulations permit the reproduction of a chain of events that might not ever occur naturally. A simulation of an atomic war, for example, is about the only means possible for understanding the destructive potential of such an event. Similarly, the numerous problems of space travel cannot be solved except through simulation techniques. When war or even neighborhood conflicts are at stake, simulating social and political events provides a safe study environment.

How Does Simulation Contribute to Empathy?

As an anonymous English author once said, "To emphathize is to see with the eyes of another, to hear with the ears of another, and to feel with the heart of another." Empathy enables us to experience someone else's feelings. Through role playing, we can assume the positions of others by projecting ourselves into their lives. When accomplished, the individuals experience certain physical and emotional changes. For example, spectators at a football game may experience these changes when they cheer for their favorite player. When empathizing with another, an individual experiences a vivid sense of closeness with the other person.

Empathy is most readily given to those who are close to us personally. As Katz points out:

> . . . we empathize with relatives, with friends, and others who are like us and who have had similar experiences. . . . We empathize with our fellows because we experience the same social rejection. If we are teen-agers, we have a language of our own and a special feeling for the appetites and dreams of our peers. . . . The husband and wife who have long experienced the give and take of married life often enjoy an almost automatic empathy; one can read the mind of the other.[3]

On the other hand, it is quite difficult for us to empathize with those with whom we have little in common. Grandparents, for example, can readily empathize with their children and grandchildren, but children have great difficulty empathizing with adults.

Simulation employs role playing to help the learner develop an empathic understanding of emotional situations. Included are both subjective feeling and objective analysis. Although the portrayed situation may be relatively simple, the degree of involvement can be remarkably intense. In this way, a simulation goes beyond the cognitive into the realm of affective learning. For the first time, students may fully comprehend why logic is apparently so often ignored in the interactions of individuals and groups.

What Constitutes a Realistic Representation of Reality?

As Raser points out,[4] the question of relevance can be determined only within the framework of a particular goal. Intelligent abstraction and simplification are critical elements in preparing a simulation for enactment. Which elements, relationships, and processes should be included can be answered only when the total picture or theory is envisioned. Since a perfect replication of reality is impossible, the criterion must be a *representation* of reality in terms of the purpose sought.

How Does Simulation Contribute to the Generation of Theory?

All fields of study rely on theory to provide meaning to isolated bits of information. A theory is a set of statements about some aspect of reality. It attempts to describe the elements of that reality and to clarify the nature of the relationships among the component parts.[5] Theory usually deals with those aspects of reality that are not readily apparent from the facts. Essentially it "digs beneath the facts" for underlying principles.

---

[3] Robert L. Katz, *Empathy: Its Nature and Use* (New York; Free Press of Glencoe, 1963), pp. 5-6.

[4] John Z. Raser, *Simulation and Society* (Boston: Allyn and Bacon, Inc., 1969), p. 11.

[5] Ibid., p. 6.

In the physical science fields, theory is often expressed by means of a model. This is merely an easy way of depicting the essential components and their relationships. A model is static, as if time stands still. A model becomes a *simulation* when functional relationships are introduced, thus making it a dynamic representation of a process over a specified period of time.

A simulation contributes to the generation of theory by forcing one to explicitly formulate his or her assumptions, to state the underlying values, and to clarify relationships among variables. Thus fuzzy or illogical concepts tend to stand out in sharp contrast to the logic of the theory system.

By dealing with many different aspects of a problem, a simulation tends to contribute to an expanding context. In describing certain relationships, for example, the instructor is likely to uncover other "hidden" relationships that must be considered. Thus one tends to think in terms of the total system and to grasp the interconnecting elements that make static events a part of an unfolding, dynamic process. In the social sciences especially, theoretical formulations tend to be vague. The simulation can pinpoint such areas and thus may contribute to needed clarification.

How Does Simulation Contribute to Decision Theory?

Decision theory is based upon the assumption that in order to understand how an organization functions, one must first comprehend the roles, personal traits, and environment in which decisions are made.[6] Although official roles assigned in actual life situations may be clear-cut ones, the intangibles of personality and organizational environment weigh heavily on how these roles are played and on how decisions are made.

For creating a learning experience that permits a study of all three factors (roles, personality, and organization) in a dynamic situation, the simulation game is the best technique to use. Although a simulation game is never complete enough to capture completely all these key factors, it does incorporate the crucial aspects needed for intelligent decision-making experiences. Indeed, the validity of a simulation game rests on its ability to capture these intangibles for study and analysis.

Sociodrama Procedure

The students in Professor Kim's secondary instructional methods class were more than a little disturbed. Although various principles of good classroom behavior had been emphasized, they were not being observed. Finally, a student asked, "Why don't we set up a situation and actually act it out so that we can get the 'feel' of the

---

[6] Ibid., p. 52.

problem?" Professor Kim agreed and divided the class into subgroups for the purpose of developing problem situations. One of the groups suggested the following problem:

> Mr. Jones caught Jane cheating on the midterm examination in senior English class. Other students also noted the behavior. Jane was a reasonably capable student who had just returned to school after a brief illness. Mr. Jones planned to talk with Jane, now that the term was over.

This is an appropriate problem for a sociodrama. The sociodrama should be developed in a series of steps necessary for a successful learning experience. Since the method focuses on human emotions, careful planning is essential if a sound psychological climate is to be maintained.

How Is the Problem for a Sociodrama Defined and Delineated?

The sociodramatic experience incorporates role playing in order to depict one fairly simple conflict situation. The occasion for a sociodrama may arise naturally from regular class experiences. Such remarks as the following suggest the need for such an experience:

> "I believe I can intellectualize your point but still have difficulty seeing how it would apply in a situation."
> "Your comments are clear enough, but for some reason I'm still confused."
> "Can you show me how this would apply in our college?"
> "How does one know if the idea will work?"

To clarify the problem, the instructor should introduce the sociodrama approach through a series of carefully worded questions. For example, let us suppose the general problem is how to conduct a class discussion. The immediate problem might be, How should one handle a student who forcefully challenges a point made by the teacher and another student? In introducing the problem, the teacher might proceed as follows:

> "From your experience, what factors are most likely to cause a discussion breakdown?" (Someone will refer to a student who tends to dominate the discussion.)
> "What makes an individual dominate a discussion?" (Someone will probably suggest that this individual desires attention.)
> "How can one discourage such an individual?" (Various solutions may be mentioned.)
> "Will they work?" "How can we know?" (Students will probably state that much depends on how the situation is handled.)
> "Well, then, why don't we set up a situation to help us understand the dominating individual?"

The teacher should ask students to help select the problem since the effectiveness of the sociodrama is directly dependent on its realism to the students.

Once the problem has been defined, the teacher should explain that no participant is to be criticized or judged on his or her acting ability and that those who volunteer to assume the roles will receive the most benefit from the experience. The teacher should also emphasize that no one is to play himself, but a role assigned to help solve the problem.

How Is the Situation Developed and How Are the Players Prepared?

Let us assume that the group has decided to enact the problem. How should Mr. Jones, a teacher, cope with Henry, a student who challenges his comments and those made by other students? Through careful guidance, the group establishes details of the situation. The following points should be clarified:

1. Where does the encounter occur? (It is usually desirable to begin with simple situations involving two or three individuals only.)
2. When does it occur?
3. What are the participants doing?
4. How long has Henry been in school?
5. What seems to be his general attitude toward school?
6. Does he particularly enjoy or seem interested in sports?

The situation, fully developed, might produce the following details:

Henry is a loner. He does not participate in the sports program. Seldom does he participate in class discussions, but when he does, he tends to be argumentative. His school work is reasonably good, consisting of mostly B's and C's.

On the day the class was discussing the problem of how air pollution can be controlled, Henry almost lost control when someone suggested that motorcycles should be banned.

The next scene takes place after school between Henry and Mr. Jones. Mr. Jones helps Henry understand an individual's responsibility in a problem-solving discussion. This situation is developed in some detail by the group. *The individual roles, however, are left to the actors.* It is desirable to let class members volunteer for the roles; otherwise, they may have difficulty identifying with their parts. Students are sometimes rather reluctant to "stick their necks out," but if sufficiently prepared by the teacher and given a few minutes to think about the situation (not too long a time or the students will become uneasy), they will usually want to participate. It is often advantageous to divide the class into small groups for a role-playing practice session before asking for a volunteer to perform before the entire group.

When the roles have been assigned, the participant with the lead part is asked to leave the room while the class members define more clearly the situation and the roles of the other participant(s). In the example case cited previously, Henry would remain in the room; Mr. Jones would be asked to leave. The persons who remain in the classroom function much like interviewers in a counseling situation in their asking questions of Henry. Henry, like any other student his age, has certain interests, abilities, and problems that must be defined and that probably are not known to Mr. Jones. One class added the following circumstances after Mr. Jones had left the room.

> Henry, who lives in a rather poor section of town, owns a motorcycle. He has had it tested at a state inspection station twice this month. The vehicle failed the test both times. His father is pressuring him to get rid of the vehicle.

Henry is instructed to begin the conversation with a slightly suspicious attitude, as might reasonably be expected under such circumstances and *to react as Mr. Jones makes him want to react.* For example, if Mr. Jones makes Henry more suspicious or even resentful, Henry should act in this manner; if Mr. Jones makes Henry feel like warming up to the situation, Henry should do so. Only if he desires, should Henry discuss his special interests or problems with Mr. Jones.

Finally, in preparation for the enactment, Mr. Jones is called in and the players prepare for their roles by asking Henry such questions as:

"Exactly what time of day is it?"
"How old are you?"
"What class is involved?"
"How did you get to school this morning?"

How Is the Audience Prepared for Intelligent Observation?

Teachers should instruct class members to ask themselves the following questions:

1. When an interest or hobby was suggested, did the person leading the situation follow up the lead?
2. What questions or comments seemed to cause the person being interviewed to become a bit resentful or to warm up to the situation?
3. Did the approach pave the way for goal accomplishment?
4. Who did most of the talking and why?

Group members should also be asked to jot down comments and behaviors that seemed significant.

Different sections of the group can be assigned specific observational tasks, for example, observing specific characters, looking for conflict situations, and noting the facial expressions of the players. Whether such a systematized approach to observation is desirable depends on the purpose and nature of the situation being portrayed.

What Factors Need Attention during Role Playing?

Above all, the actors should play their assigned roles without interruption, according to their own feelings at the time. The teacher normally lets the role-playing scene continue until the purpose has been achieved. It is easy to defeat the purpose by letting the scene continue beyond its usefulness. In a simple situation, involving two or three people, the drama seldom continues for more than ten minutes.

The action is cut when enough of the scene has been portrayed to enable the audience to analyze the problem or when an impasse has been reached. When one of the participants starts making repetitious comments or when it becomes obvious that emotional responses are getting out of control, the scene obviously should be stopped. Occasionally, a player will try to psychoanalyze another. When this happens, the scene should be stopped immediately. Psychodrama, unlike sociodrama, is an instrument that should be reserved for specialists; it has no place in the average classroom.

How Is the Sociodrama Analyzed and Discussed?

The discussion that follows the enactment concludes the experience. It is at this point that many meaningful learnings are achieved. Without careful guidance, however, students are likely to be criticized for their acting. It is worth repeating that the discussion should focus on the situation rather than on the players. The teacher should begin the discussion by asking the group if the enactment was realistic. Then the players are asked how they feel about their roles. At all times role names are used to emphasize the character rather than the actual person involved. Finally, members of the audience are asked to analyze the character who was interviewed in the sociodrama. For illustrative purposes, reference is made to the case of Mr. Jones and Henry.

To Henry and Mr. Jones. "How did you feel, Henry, as the situation developed?" ("I began to feel more resentful until near the end.") "Did you feel as if you were getting anywhere, Mr. Jones?" ("Not exactly. He didn't seem to open up very well.")

To the audience. "What clues did you note that might have caused Henry to feel this way?" "How did Henry react when he was asked where he lived?" "Why did Henry resent the question?" "Did Henry drop any clues about his special interest?" "Why or why not?" "What factors could have accounted for Henry's changed reactions toward the end of the scene?"

Following a thorough analysis of the situation, alternative approaches should be discussed. The reader will recognize here the similarity to the "alternative solution" step developed in the class discussion method. Once the group has reached some agreement on *another* approach, the situation then can be re-enacted to illustrate applications of the new insights. The roles should be reversed; this forces the players to put themselves in the other person's place. Whether replaying is to be done depends on the circumstances involved. In any event, emphasis is placed on *other* ways of doing the jobs, questions *which might have been asked,* and so forth. At no time should the recommendations imply *better* ways of approaching the situation.

How Is the Sociodrama Evaluated?

Regardless of how much the group may have enjoyed the experience (Most groups usually do!), the sociodrama was a waste of time and effort if no new insights were developed. Situational-type test items can be used to determine how much was learned from the enactment.

Perhaps the best index of the validity of such experiences is the degree of change evidenced in social situations arising from actual classroom situations. The eagerness with which a group enters into succeeding role-playing experiences is an indication of a satisfying first experience. If the players become defensive during the discussion following the sociodrama, the instructor might well do a bit of introspection. "What questions did I ask which made the actors feel they were being criticized personally?"

What Preplanning Is Necessary?

The sociodramatic experience demands intricate planning. Although the experience can be satisfactorily completed during a fifty-minute class period, there is little time to waste. Since there are so many aspects in the process, the recommended time limits for each step in the illustrated plan should be followed carefully.

LESSON PLAN FOR SOCIODRAMA

Subject: Methods of Teaching

Unit: Group Participation

Concept: Balanced participation in class discussion is needed.

Problem: How can balanced participation in class discussion be achieved?

Goals: After this lesson, the student should have furthered his or her ability to perceive the feelings associated with who dominates class discussion, as evidenced by:

1. Participation in discussion following the sociodrama.
2. The ability to offer alternative solutions to the problem enacted.

Lesson approach (ten minutes)

In previous simulations, we have had reasonably balanced class participation. None of our group members has become argumentative or tried to force ideas on others. In real life, however, things sometimes do not develop in this manner. Occasionally, a student will challenge the points that a teacher or other students make. While some argumentation is acceptable in class discussion, excessive amounts can destroy a discussion. It is the teacher's responsibility to control this kind of behavior as diplomatically as possible. This means that the teacher must develop some empathy for the offending student.

Today, we will enact a situation involving a student who challenges the teacher and class members.

Lesson development (thirty to thirty-five minutes)

Immediate problem: How can Mr. Jones cope with Jane, a good student whom he discovered had been cheating on exams.

Broad situation

Mr. Jones caught Jane cheating on the midterm examination in senior English class. Other students had obviously noted the behavior. Jane was a reasonably capable student who had just returned to school after a brief illness. Mr. Jones is about to talk with Jane now that the class period is over.

Details of situation (class establishes)

Threat reduction: In this type of experience, no one is to be criticized for his or her acting ability. (One should not be permitted to play his or her real-life role, however.)

Selection of players: Call for volunteers.

Class analysis of situation

1. Send leading character from the room (Mr. Jones).
2. Fill in additional details.

Guide to audience observation

1. Jot down key words and phrases that seem to affect feelings—either positively or negatively.
2. Note expressions on students' faces.

Warm-up exercise

1. How old are you, Jane?
2. What is your favorite subject?

Enactment (not more than ten minutes)

Follow-up discussion

1. Was this situation realistic?
2. How did you feel? (to each of the players in turn)
3. Why did you have these feelings?

Re-enactment (if needed)

Derivation of generalizations (five to ten minutes)

What guiding concepts or principles seem to emerge as a consequence of this experience?

Examples

1. Look for clues to behavior.
2. Permit an individual an opportunity to "save face."
3. Attempt to appease opposing points of view.

What are some similar situations involving these principles?

Illustrations

1. People who have difficulty working in subgroups.
2. Individuals who represent different cultural backgrounds.

Sociodrama can be used as an instructional technique for dealing with problems of human interaction in the subjects of business, family living, sociology, education, psychology, and history and in group guidance classes. Suppose, for example, that a political science class is discussing the concept "Paternalism seldom contributes to a harmonious relationship." The major problem is, How should our nation help emerging nations to become economically independent? The immediate question for a sociodrama is, How does a paternalistic relationship make others feel? Any situation close to the lives of students could be developed for enactment. Figure 12-2 depicts the process of applying principles that occur during a sociodrama.

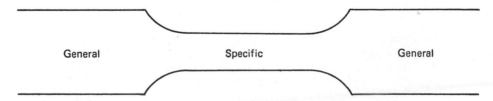

General   Specific   General

FIGURE 12-2 *Process of Applying Principles in a Sociodrama*

As Figure 12-2 indicates, many broad problems have specific applications. The sociodramatic experience can be used to help learners understand the impact of emotion on problem resolution. Most concepts are not fully understood by students until they are applied to their immediate lives; sociodrama make this application possible.

Simulation Games

In studying a unit on communication, . . . a social science class might treat the problems of network television at a presidential nominating convention. The networks want to attract viewers by playing up the sensational side of the news. At the same time, they must avoid broadcasting false or distorted reports—especially if these reports might cause civil disturbance or lead to slander suits. A game might include three teams of network broadcasters and an audience. By drawing information cards, news from on-the-spot reporters and from the wire services could be fed to the broadcasters. Each team of broadcasters would judge the reports for interest, reliability, and importance and then decide which to pass on to an audience. The audience rates the presentation of each team on a point system for interest and for social responsibility.[7]

As the preceding quotation demonstrates, simulation games can be used to solve complex problems confronting our society. Unfortunately, however, the design and use of simulation games are too often left to hit-or-miss procedures. Many individuals have written about their experiences with simulation games, but few have suggested the specific steps to be followed in using them. Like sociodrama (and indeed most methods of teaching), the simulation game is another approach to problem solving. Unlike most other methods, however, the simulation game usually involves a complex situation necessitating the *resolution of several problems* as the situation develops. (Most instructional methods approach a problem from a single framework of decision making.) The steps identified in the following sections should greatly facilitate the appropriate application of this method.

How Is the Problem Identified?

The initial step when considering use of a simulation game is to identify those concepts that need clarification. The concepts will have many subtle relationships that should be projected and developed during the game. To illustrate: Conflict is a natural outgrowth of competing desires; dissent is expressed within established ways; compromise is essential in a democratic system.

---

[7] Norris Sanders, "Simulated Games," in *Special Studies Curriculum Development: Prospect and Problems,* ed. Dorothy M. Frazier (Washington, D.C.: National Council for the Social Studies Yearbook, 1968), pp. 164-65.

A simulation game will vary in length from one to five or six class periods and should embody at least two or three closely related unit concepts. Basic to the simulation game are the development and resolution of conflicting forces or desires. Like other methods, the simulation game is based on one or more unit concepts (see Chapter 1).

How Is the Simulation Game Developed?

Using the identified basic concepts as a guide, the teacher develops a rough outline of the game to be played. The game may be based on a hypothetical or real situation. In any event, it must be a selective representation of those elements necessary to achieve objectives. If it is too complex, students will become frustrated and may lose sight of the purposes entirely. If overly simple, the game may have little motivational value and may mislead students by understating the complexities of actual events.

Above all, the teacher must explore in depth the essential elements to be utilized in the simulation. In evaluating the potential value of the proposed simulation, the teacher should ask, "Do the elements to be portrayed look like the real thing?"

Creating a rudimentary outline for the simulation game is the "giant step" in the process. It is at this point that creative imagination is essential. Once the broad aspects of the experience have been created, the details can be readily developed.

How Are the Actors or Teams Identified?

Identification of roles to be played is determined from the basic concepts previously identified for the situation. Class size, of course, is a practical consideration that will influence role assignments.

Especially in the area of social or political relations, decision making is usually an outgrowth of group effort. Subgroups of five are ideally suited for these games. Thus, if five political or social groups are involved, five teams of five each can be established. Since decisions in political social games often influence the public, the game may require two or three students to assume the roles of reporters. If there are more than twenty-eight students in a class, the number of groups can be expanded accordingly. In a business simulation game, the office model would be organized around an office staff, including company officers and secretaries. If, however, the roles to be played are fewer than the total number of students in class (as is often the case in commercially developed games), two or more independent simulations may be conducted simultaneously, assuming there are classroom facilities and competent teachers or teacher aides.

Roles are further identified by group task assignment. For example, in a political game, it may be necessary to communicate with rival groups. If so, a group representative (ambassador) is elected for this purpose. The election of a national president may be called for. In this case, a candidate is advanced by each subgroup or by one or more subgroups working jointly. In short, the organizational structure of each subgroup is dictated by the overall situation.

Role assignment may be made on a purely random basis to avoid teacher bias and the formation of undesirable cliques. Random assignment tends to make leadership a function of the role(s) involved. Student choice, on the other hand, capitalizes on natural interest and motivation associated with the portrayal of certain roles. Sometimes, of course, the success of a simulation is largely dependent on one or more key roles. Thus, student assignment on the basis of ability may be desirable. Perhaps a combination of all the preceding should be considered, depending on the nature of the group and simulation involved.

How Are Game Resources Identified and Allocated?

The relationships among the elements in a simulation game are sometimes made realistic through an exchange of the external resources (troops, money, votes, etc.) the players use to compete with one another. Although a precise quantification of power is not always evident in real life, most educational simulations attempt to assess precise values of resources exchanged. We often say, for example, that the President is more powerful than Congress in certain contexts. By providing units that correspond to power, this important concept can be fully understood. Units may be internal resources like persuasive capabilities and military capabilities, which enable students to assess progress at given points and also provide a basis for a "win" or "lose" evaluation at the end of the game. Cards are provided for this purpose, or the units may be reproduced on the chalkboard.

Basic to any simulation game is appropriate use of audio-visual materials. Such media are most useful for creating the simulated environment. In a political party nominating convention, for example, posters, noisemakers, state costumes, and balloons can add much needed drama to the experience. In a portrayal of a legislative session (that has actually taken place), copies of the proposed legislation, supplemented with simplified rules of procedure, might be employed. In games involving international crises, large strategic maps may be provided for ready reference.

How Are the Sequences of Play and the Final Payoff Identified and Developed?

A game is played in well-defined cycles, each structured around a particular event. Students must know the precise goals to be achieved in each session and fully understand the rules of procedure to be followed. Rules define the actions of the players.

Action begins with a "crisis" or impending decision of some kind. The first phase of the first cycle involves developing strategy. Each subgroup confers to decide what it will do in the situation. Communication with other groups is *not* permitted during this phase. The session is brief—perhaps five minutes long.

The next phase, negotiations, involves sending representatives to confer secretly with other representatives. It is here that compromise and strategy develop. "My group will support your group if. . . ."

The third phase usually involves group action of some kind. In effect, the strategy, planned and developed in the previous phases, is now put into action.

The final phase focuses on the consequences of action taken in the preceding phase.

Some games consist of only one cycle, others may incorporate three or more such cycles. The nature of the phases within a cycle depends on the nature of the game. They usually involve a sequence of planning, negotiation, action, and consequences.

How Is the Simulation Introduced?

Games usually begin with a brief, written description (scenario) of the necessary background information essential to the experience. If a crisis-type game is to be enacted, for example, a historical description of the situation is essential. Descriptions of the various groups and their objectives and resources and of the rules governing the behavior are also included.

The following scenario represents a simple, brief simulation that can be completed in a single (or several) class period. (Most commercially developed games are more complex.) Developed by a college professor to depict the complexities that often enter into the selection of new faculty, the scenario includes all essential elements of a simulation game.[8] A fundamental understanding of interdepartmental relations and of the balance of power may emerge clearly from the scenario. Table 12–1 provides a lesson plan for teaching the scenario "Day of Decision."

DAY OF DECISION

Scenario. The class represents members of a faculty of a small residential liberal arts college seeking to fill an instructor's position. The college is dedicated to providing excellence in teaching and prides itself on its academic standards. Although research and publication are valued, the primary focus is to fill the position with a person who is well grounded in his or her field and can relate well to students and colleagues. Affirmative action policies have been met, and those identified for final interviews meet all qualifications in this area.

For the purpose of this simulation, a five-member search committee is elected to interview two students who play the role of job applicants. (It is helpful to allow the students in the role of applicants to apply for the job in their own subject field.)

Various constituencies are represented by each member of the search committee.

Member # 1. Represents the conservative element among the faculty. These people support a strong emphasis on general education, curve grading, research in all areas, and a straight lecture approach in the classroom. They favor, through a strong testing program, elimination of students of inferior academic achievement. The

---

[8] This scenario was prepared by Dr. Susan Cummings, Associate Professor, Arizona State University, Tempe, Arizona. Used by permission.

TABLE 12-1 *Lesson Plan for Simulation Game*

Subject: Secondary Education Methods Class

Unit: Interview—Day of Decision

Concepts:
1. The interview is a process of gaining employment in education.
2. The real-life interview may be less emotional and more valuable for the future teacher.
3. Practical application through simulation is a valuable experience.

Problem: What is the value found from the interview as it applies to real life?

Goals:
1. Completely and accurately fill out an application for employment.
2. Pick sound education references who will speak favorably about him.
3. Better understand the procedure of the educational interview.
4. Formulate a plan of attack for responding to the first interview barrage of questions.
5. Function with poise and confidence while under pressure during the interview process.

Lesson approach: In this lesson, it is the intent to provide a situation of an educational interview which has been taken for granted in the past. It is now apparent to methods teachers in education to leave no stone unturned in providing the future teacher with background experiences necessary for employment.

This lesson will provide each class member an opportunity to participate. Role playing is the means used for providing the actual experience. Every member of the class will have some input before the game ends.

Each class member will be given a specific role to play. The people who are the applicants will be given the chance to rate and then accept or reject the job offered. Even the community observers will have a say about the applicant.

Lesson development: The scenario will take place in the board meeting room. Each member should read the role to be played and be familiar with the overall setting.

Phase I: The situation begins by the teacher asking for two volunteers to be applicants for the job. (This can be any teaching job according to the methods class being taught.) He/she also picks two references at this time.

Phase II: While the applicants are filling out the application, the class will elect a superintendent, board of education, president of the board, and a principal.

Phase III: The board is now ready to hear from the first applicant and his references who speak instead of submitting a written reference.

Phase IV: The board hears out each applicant and reference, plus they ask questions they have formulated. Each applicant and board member has a rating card which they fill out at the end of the interview. The job is offered to an applicant and he has the task of accepting or rejecting the job.

Post-game discussion: Processing will be used to see how each student felt about the experience. What value was the interview to each class member? Do you feel any different about your role as an applicant?

This plan was developed by Edward W. Wuch, Missouri Southern State College, Joplin, Missouri.

purpose of higher education is to acquire factual information and demonstrate ability to write theses.

Member # 2.   Represents the liberal contingency. These faculty members feel that with proper guidance, most young people can succeed at the college level. They feel professors should motivate students to learn, develop an inquiring attitude, and stress communication and problem-solving skills. The purpose of higher education is to promote human growth and develop self-actualizing individuals.

Member #3.   Represents the minority factions of the community. They are concerned with providing "culture fair" education. Special consideration should be given to provide opportunities for "disadvantaged" racial minorities and women. Students should be made aware of sociological and political issues and become actively involved in the community-at-large.

Member #4.   Represents the element which supports and promotes extracurricular activities. They feel the resident life of the student provides at least as important a learning situation as the classroom. Each faculty member should devote time to the social life on the campus. Recreational activities and student government should be stressed as an important facet of college.

Member #5.   Represents the athletic enthusiasts. They have a great concern that student athletes be given every opportunity and perhaps extra consideration to maintain their required academic level of competence. Competition, the basis of the free enterprise system, is best demonstrated through athletics. Esprit de corps is the measure of success of a student body.

The class may be divided into groups reflecting the roles of the members of the search committee; after a thorough discussion of the position of the role, each group picks a representative to sit on the search committee. The whole class or the search committee then elects one of its members as chairperson to preside over the interviews.

Two candidates are selected to apply for the job vacancy. They, in turn, select two individuals who will provide oral references in contrast to the usual written references. The candidates may be "themselves" or choose to play a role. Each fills out an appropriate application form [see Table 12-2] and prepares a resumé. A "plan of attack" is discussed with his or her references.

While the candidates prepare their positions, each constituent group will discuss with their representative search committee member the criteria they deem most important in selection of a new professor. They will also create a list of questions which will be most useful in drawing pertinent information from the candidate.

Candidates present their applications and references and make a brief presentation on the behalf of each. The final scene of the simulation is the meeting of the search committee in which each applicant is interviewed in turn. After the interview search committee members and applicants fill in appropriate evaluation sheets [see Tables 12-3 and 12-4]. The search committee presents its decision as to which will be offered the position, and the selected applicant responds in turn with acceptance or rejection.

TABLE 12-2 *Sample Application*

Name _____ Age _____

Address _____ Phone _____

Demographic Data:

(Optional) Sex _____ Race _____ Religion _____

Age _____ Marital Status _____

Number and Ages of Children _____

Health _____

Educational History

High School _____ Graduation Date _____ Grade Point _____

College	Major	Degree	Graduation	Grade Point
_____	_____	_____	_____	_____
_____	_____	_____	_____	_____

Subjects Certified to Teach   Number of Hours

_____   _____

_____   _____

_____   _____

Associated Activities   Offices Held

_____   _____

_____   _____

_____   _____

Awards _____

_____

_____

Work Experience   Dates

_____   _____

_____   _____

_____   _____

_____   _____

Philosophy of Education _____

_____

_____

_____

_____

Remarks _____

_____

_____

References: Name   Position

_____   _____

_____   _____

_____   _____

_____

Prepared by Dr. Susan Cummings, Associate Professor, Arizona State University, Tempe, Arizona. Used by permission.

TABLE 12-3   *Evaluation of Applicant*

	Rank: 5=Superior, 1=Poor				
Appearance	1	2	3	4	5
Knowledge of Subject	1	2	3	4	5
Knowledge of Adolescents	1	2	3	4	5
Related Experience	1	2	3	4	5
Attitude	1	2	3	4	5
Communication Skill	1	2	3	4	5
Interpersonal Relations					
Peers	1	2	3	4	5
Superiors	1	2	3	4	5
Students	1	2	3	4	5
Public	1	2	3	4	5
Commitment	1	2	3	4	5
Related Skills (Coaching, club)	1	2	3	4	5
Maturity	1	2	3	4	5
Open-minded	1	2	3	4	5
Reliability	1	2	3	4	5
Other:					
_____	1	2	3	4	5
_____	1	2	3	4	5
_____	1	2	3	4	5
_____	1	2	3	4	5
_____	1	2	3	4	5
_____	1	2	3	4	5

Score:

Prepared by Dr. Susan Cummings, Associate Professor, Arizona State University, Tempe, Arizona. Used by permission.

A follow-up discussion should include consideration of the differences and similarities between the simulation and reality, evaluation of the means of eliciting information from both sides, the adequacy of the data engendered, and analysis of feelings elicited.

What Are the Essentials of the Post-Game Discussion?

A thorough post-game discussion is potentially the most valuable aspect of simulation since it offers students an opportunity for assessing how closely the game mirrored reality. In the scenario illustration, for example, tokens could have been awarded to represent units of power gained or lost. In real life, however, several other factors would have been involved such as implied threat to various curricular offerings,

TABLE 12-4 *Evaluation of Job*

	Rank: 5=Superior, 1=Poor				
Philosophical Agreement	1	2	3	4	5
Working Conditions (climate)	1	2	3	4	5
Salary	1	2	3	4	5
Fringe Benefits	1	2	3	4	5
Administrative Support	1	2	3	4	5
Faculty Cohesiveness	1	2	3	4	5
Academic Freedom	1	2	3	4	5
Clarity of Job Expectations	1	2	3	4	5
Opportunities for Promotion	1	2	3	4	5
Opportunities for Professional Growth	1	2	3	4	5
Released Time	1	2	3	4	5
Other:					
_____	1	2	3	4	5
_____	1	2	3	4	5
_____	1	2	3	4	5
_____	1	2	3	4	5
_____	1	2	3	4	5
_____	1	2	3	4	5
_____	1	2	3	4	5
_____	1	2	3	4	5
_____	1	2	3	4	5
_____	1	2	3	4	5
_____	1	2	3	4	5
_____	1	2	3	4	5

Prepared by Dr. Susan Cummings, Associate Professor, Arizona State University, Tempe, Arizona. Used by permission.

pressure from administrative personnel, and economic problems. Since a simulation cannot include all aspects of reality, the experience must be analyzed thoroughly for distortions of reality.

As with sociodrama, the portrayed experience should be generalized to other contexts. A local election, for example, is very similar to national elections, to international organizations like the United Nations, and to treaty alliances since the same democratic principles apply. The teacher should guide students in their derivation of concepts or generalizations since the process of becoming thoroughly involved in a conflict situation may cause them to lose sight temporarily of the basic purposes involved. The concepts students derive may not correspond to those identified by the teacher during preplanning but they should be similar to them. The following are key questions that contribute to an effective post-game discussion:

1. What real-life events were portrayed?
2. What effects did your basic decisions have on the game?
3. What factors and events influenced your decisions?
4. What kinds of relationships were formed among the different parties involved?
5. What pressures, if any, were experienced?
6. What feelings emerged as you interacted with others?
7. As you look back, what would you do differently if you could replay the game?
8. How do you think this game compares with reality? How and why is the real world different?

The Value of Simulation Techniques

Simulation enables one to learn directly from experience.

By playing games, the student develops an understanding of complex social situations or systems that influence decision-making processes.

Simulation promotes a high level of critical thinking, involving such processes as developing alternative strategies, anticipating those others will suggest, and assessing the validity of important decisions.

Through role playing, an individual learns to empathize with the real-life person being portrayed. Realism is maintained without the fear of exposing one's personality— always present in real-life situations.

Simulation provides feedback on the consequences of actions and decisions made. "Hidden" interconnected relationships frequently emerge.

The simulation game usually involves both cooperation (within groups) and competition (between groups).

Simulations can be conducted for relatively short periods of time (as with sociodrama) or for extended periods of time (as with simulation games).

The post-simulation analysis enables teachers and students to uncover misconceptions and misinformation since it requires them to assess the realism of the simulation.

Simulation techniques help motivate students. Simulating life is always interesting and exciting. In the case of a simulation game, there is the additional motivation of a reward.

Limitations of, and Problems with, Simulation Techniques

Since simulation involves a portrayal of selected events, it may result in a simplistic view of reality.

The approach demonstrates how people *may* behave rather than how they *will* behave.

Simulation techniques are not appropriate for teaching factual information.

There is a tendency to use the results of a single simulation as the sole basis for generalization.

Simulation games can easily become overly complex, leading to confusion.

Because simulation games are time-consuming, they may impede coverage of a specific amount of content.

The traditional role of the teacher is changed from a provider of information to a facilitator of learning. Thus the teacher may tend to interfere with learning as events unfold.

Commercially developed simulation games are expensive. Teacher-made games, however, are inexpensive and relatively easy to develop.

Illustrated Simulations

I. Sociodramatic situations

    A. Useful in home economics, group guidance, sociology, and psychology classes

        Unit: Family Finances

        Concept: Budgeting procedures demand a definite plan of action.

        Broad situation

        Two eighteen-year-old girls, Kathy and Betty, meet at a local soda fountain. Both earn about fifty dollars per week. Betty cannot seem to budget her money and asks Kathy for help.

    B. Useful in speech, general communications, and social studies classes

        Unit: Sharing Ideas with Others

        Concept: Encouragement from the peer group may help one overcome shyness.

        Broad situation

        Sue, a shy, quiet girl, is disturbed because of a student council ruling. John, her student council representative, learns of her distress and wonders why she failed to voice her feelings when he asked for them. Sue states that she was afraid to do this in front of the class.

    C. Useful in American or English literature, history, and sociology classes

        Unit: Conflict

        Concept: Traditional behavior must be viewed in terms of the times; as times change, so do customs.

        Broad situation

        A selective boy's club is holding its annual freshman initiation. The initiates traditionally have been subjected to considerable discomfort.

One boy is usually selected at random to carry out a difficult task. This year Tom's assignment is to steal a car. He is discussing his feelings with the initiation committee.

Unit: Ambition

Concept: Insincere persuasion or flattery is often misleading. (based on *Julius Caesar*, Act I, Scene II, by William Shakespeare)

Broad situation

Two seniors, Mike and Paul, are members of the student senate. Mike is the leader of a small group of students who want to get an unpopular bill through the senate. Mike wants to make sure that Paul is on his side and approaches him for support.

D. Useful in home economics classes

Unit: The Family

Concept: Emotional family stress can break down family ties.

Broad situation:

Ted Smith has just spent two days in the hospital. His parents have brought him home. Ted knows his parents are upset and that he is the cause of their distress. He decides to discuss his feelings with them.

E. Useful in social science classes

The following presents a more complex sociodramatic situation than did the preceding examples.[9]

The students should be divided into groups of eight to ten people. The task will be to arrive at a decision. Twenty minutes should be allowed for the decision-making process, and the remaining class time should be used for discussion. Breaking the class into several small groups allows for comparison of behavior between groups.

Two members of each group should be asked to leave the room. The remainder should form a circle leaving two chairs empty on opposite sides of the circle.

The task should be explained to the groups.

You belong to a travel club at the university and are trying to decide whether you want to spend spring vacation skiing at Aspen or swimming at a Caribbean island. The cost will be the same so cost should not be a

---

[9] From Paul F. Kaplan and Clovis R. Shepherd, *Doing Sociology*, (New York: Alfred Publishing Co., Inc., 1973) pp. 132-33.

deciding factor. You must reach a decision today, or the trip will be cancelled.

Two members will be at the committee meeting today. They are very different in terms of power and prestige. One is a popular faculty member who will serve as a chaperone for the trip and the other is a freshman who is an expert either in skiing or water sports (depending upon which vacation you choose).

The new members will not know that they differ in terms of prestige. So it is important when addressing them not to refer to the professor as professor or doctor.

It should be predetermined which empty chair will represent the professor and which the freshman so that when they return and sit down you are able to determine which is the professor and which the freshman.

Remember they will not know this.

The two students outside should be briefed on what the committee meeting is about and should decide which type of vacation they will support. They should take opposite positions.

After the decision has been reached, discussion can be held around the following areas.

1. How did the two new members feel? Were they aware of any differential treatment?
2. Discuss the behavior of the individuals in the group. Did they behave differently to the two new members? If so, how?
3. How was the decision arrived at? Did you choose the location that the professor supported?
4. How does the status of the individual affect decision making in groups to which you belong?
5. Do you think that status really affects decisions? If so, in what situations is this likely to occur and why do you think it occurs?

II. Simulation games

The following is a simulation game designed to stimulate students' thinking about the educational process.[10]

COMPU-EDUCARE

A taped set of directions sets the stage and prescribes the activity for this simulation. Students should be divided into groups of four to five individuals. The groups discuss the topics suggested while the teacher acts as process observer.

After the simulation, the teacher should summarize the responses of the various groups so that students will have the opportunity to compare their views.

---

[10] This simulation game was developed by Dr. Susan Cummings, Associate Professor of Education, Arizona State University, Tempe, Arizona. Dr. Cummings offers a course in gaming in which students develop at least one game in their area of specialization.

Tape script of compu-educare

BUZZ. . . . This is COMPU-EDUCARE, the computer printout voice of education. An international catastrophe has just occurred. The educational systems all over the world have just disintegrated. There are no more schools, no more teachers, no more texts, and no more programmed materials. Because you are educators of the past representing all nations of the world, you have been selected to recommend to the World Council what shall be done about education for the future.

First, what shall be the purpose of education? You have ten minutes to reach a decision. (Turn off tape.) BUZZ. This is COMPU-EDUCARE; I am ready to receive your reports on the purpose of education. Each group will have one minute of computer time. Begin now. BUZZ. Thank you for your reports. Your second task is to determine who shall be educated and when they shall be educated. You have ten minutes to reach a decision. (Turn off tape.) BUZZ. This is COMPU-EDUCARE; I am ready to receive your reports on who shall be educated. Each group will have one minute of computer time. Begin now. (Turn off tape.) BUZZ. Thank you for your reports. The World Council is concerned with how education will take place. You will have ten minutes to arrive at a decision. (Turn off tape.) BUZZ. This is COMPU-EDUCARE; I am ready to receive your reports on how education shall take place. Each group will have two minutes of computer time. Begin now. (Turn off tape.)

Summary by teacher

I would like to summarize the responses from each group. Would you please check what I have done against your perception of what has been presented to insure its accuracy?

Survival is the main purpose of education. There should be basic education for all people. Beyond this level, special learning should be available to meet perceived needs of the individual. Education should be a life-long process with greater opportunities for both young children and adults. An open-access approach should provide opportunities for individuals to choose their path more freely in a more flexible framework.

Families, educational establishments, and businesses should cooperate in the overall educational system.

Examinations should serve essentially to compare skills under varying conditions. They should not be viewed as final determinants but as starting points in helping individuals assess the effectiveness of their own study methods.

Finally, institutions and services of a new kind (language laboratories, technical training laboratories, information centers, libraries and related services, data banks, programmed and personalized teaching aids, and audio-visual aids, for example), intended to help people teach themselves, should be integrated into all educational systems. Computers will inevitably play a more significant role in the educational process.

Ultimately, the educational system should be concerned with enabling each individual to learn to relate to others and to become self-directing.

Is this an accurate representation of the various results? If so, I must confess that rather than summarizing your remarks, I have encapsulated the recommendations published by a special committee of UNESCO in 1972, under the title, "Learning to Be." The Internal Commission on Development of Education included representatives of seven major nations, including the United States and the United Soviet Socialist Republic.

What you have done this evening is a small sample of the type of exercises we shared with educators of sixty-six nations of the world. The results too were indicative of the conclusions we reached as we compared our hopes and dreams and goals with others from vastly different cultural backgrounds—those from developing countries as well as those from established western nations.

In a world in which we are constantly bombarded by disagreements and even open strife between Arab and Jew, Catholic and Protestant, Capitalist and Socialist, and Black and White, to mention only a few, such an experience, indeed, represents a kernel of hope—a seed to be nourished since we found commonality among educators far superseding what appeared to be petty differences among them.

We agreed not only on the ideals we hope to achieve in education but also that education should ultimately become the vehicle that will carry us to a peaceful world. Peace, we agreed, is defined not as a lack of war or even harmonious coexistence but rather as a state in which each person enjoys a symbiotic relationship with every other person—a multicultural world.

As anthropologist Margaret Mead expressed so well, "We are now at a point where we must educate people in what nobody knew yesterday and prepare in our schools for what nobody knows yet, but what some people must know tomorrow."

The time is now. The responsibility for "Learning to Be" is up to you and me. Education is not a panacea; thus it should not shoulder the blame for all the varied woes of mankind. But surely it can represent "the hope of the world" and provide the tools for achieving individual growth and success, interpersonal compatibility, and international community.

For this, indeed, is "Learning to Be."

chapter
13

ENCOURAGING CREATIVITY

Overview

Key concepts

1. Creative teaching essentially provides a release from some restrictions (especially evaluation) during the processes of reflective thinking.
2. All individuals are potentially creative; levels of creativity vary with each individual.
3. Students who possess the highest ability for school work may not be the most creative.
4. Highly creative individuals tend to experience educational and personal adjustment problems in conventional school settings.
5. Creativity, though an individualized experience, may be cultivated in group (class) settings.
6. Characteristics of the creative process differ markedly for different types of creative tasks.

New Terms

1. Convergent Thinking Emphasizes reproduction of existing data and adaptation of old responses to new situations in a more or less logical manner.
2. Divergent Thinking Characterized by flexibility and originality in the production of new ideas. Sometimes such thinking is characterized by a sudden "flash" of insight (illumination).
3. Detachment The ability to put a problem aside temporarily, to suspend judgment until one has sufficient time to think through the problem.
4. Incubation The period in which little or no conscious effort is put into problem solving; the subconscious apparently makes connections and associations that may be blocked out during periods of concentrated effort. Some believe that the incubation process is merely a means of escaping "mind sets" concerning the problem.

5. Illumination A sudden flash of insight that may occur during a brainstorming session or after the problem has been put aside.
6. Brainstorming A group process designed to amass as many solutions to a problem as possible in the absence of restraints or evaluation.
7. Synetics A thinking process that involves making metaphors in order to gain insight by joining together different and apparently irrelevant elements. Often used in connection with the brainstorming procedure.

Questions to Guide Your Study

1. What are the differences between creative problem-solving processes and conventional problem-solving processes?
2. What is the place for convergent thinking in creative endeavors?
3. Why is deferred judgment considered essential to creative-thinking processes?
4. Most conventional instructional methods tend to impede creative thinking. Defend or refute.
5. Why does the creative individual sometimes pose a threat to the college professor?

An abundance of evidence indicates that different instructional methods have varying effects on achievement of different students. Some students who make relatively little progress under one mode of instruction quickly become star performers when instructional methods are changed. This phenomenon, in part, is a function of how an individual copes with problems. At least two distinct ways of thinking have been identified: *convergent* and *divergent.* In illustrating the extreme differences between convergent and divergent thinking, E. Paul Torrance offers an interesting analogy.

This analogy comes from my personal experiences with pets and their learning problems. As a child ... I managed to train [dogs] ... so that they became reasonably well productive killers of rats, mice, and moles ... Essentially, I punished undesirable behavior and rewarded desirable behavior. Dogs, anxious by nature to please, respond to this kind of treatment.

In recent years ... I undertook to train Hazel, my first cat, in very much the same way that I had, as a child, trained dogs. I still bear some of the physical marks of this error and I suppose Hazel still bears some of the psychological scars of my inhumane treatment. The more I punished undesirable behavior, the worse she misbehaved; the more I rewarded desirable behavior, the worse she behaved. In time I began to gain insight into the ways by which cats learn and I changed my treatment of Hazel accordingly. She is now a well-behaved, apparently happy, loyal and affectionate cat. She is definitely curious, independent, proud (sometimes appearing haughty and self-satisfied), possessed of great dignity, manipulative, experimental, playful, quiet, adventurous, highly sensitive to ridicule or criticism, energetic, persistent, yet affectionate and considerate.... In the main, dogs tend to learn by authority. They are anxious to please and respond favorably to the stimuli provided. Cats, on the other hand, tend to learn creativity—by exploring, testing the limits, searching, manipulating, and playing. They have been noted throughout history for their curiosity and venturesomeness.... The cat and the creative.., [student] ... both need a responsive environment more than a stimulating one....[1]

Torrance then goes on to define a responsive environment as one that "... involves absorbed listening, fighting off criticism and ridicule, stirring the unresponsive and deepening the superficial. It requires that each honest effort to learn meet with enough reward to insure continued effort. The focus is on potential rather than norms."

Although the processes of creative or divergent thinking are still imperfectly understood, mounting evidence suggests that they are often stifled and criticized. Indeed, Thomas A. Edison, one of the world's greatest inventors, was declared mentally "addled" by one of his early teachers. Thereupon, his mother withdrew Tom from school and taught him herself. Edison contributed numerous inventions even after he was eighty-years old.

Although the processes of creativity, like other modes of thought, are individualistic in nature, they are often imitated and developed in group settings. Thus the technique of group brainstorming is emphasized in this chapter. Creativity can be furthered through any of the group methods discussed in this chapter. *In many instances, however, creativity is not fully exploited, simply because the teacher is unaware of those factors that tend to block creative processes.*

Fundamental Properties

An idea is creative when it brings a new insight to a given situation. The process of creativity includes the ability to change one's approach to a problem, to produce ideas that are both relevant and unusual, to see beyond the immediate situation, and to redefine the problem or some aspect of it.[2]

All individuals to some extent are creative, although some are much more creative than others. While a small part of this difference may be due to heredity, a large part likely results from the failure of individuals to express their creative potential. In fact,

---

[1] E. Paul Torrance, "Different Ways of Learning for Different Kinds of Children," in *Mental Health and Achievement,* eds. E. Paul Torrance and Robert D. Strom (New York: John Wiley & Sons, Inc., 1965), pp. 260-62. Torrance has done some of the foremost research on creativity and creative teaching.

[2] George F. Kneller, *The Art and Science of Creativity* (New York: Holt, Rinehart and Winston, Inc., 1965), p. 13.

many essential attributes of creativity are all too often discouraged in the typical college classroom.

What Cognitive Style Characterizes the Creative Individual?

From intensive investigation of creative processes, it is becoming increasingly apparent that there may be several kinds of creativity. Donald N. MacKinnon, for example, has outlined three different kinds of creativity used as a basis for research at the Institute of Personality Assessment and Research Laboratory, (IPAR), Berkeley, California.[3] The first is artistic creativity that reflects the creator's inner needs, perceptions, and motivations. The second type is scientific and technological creativity that deals with some problem of the environment and results in novel solutions but exhibits little of the inventor's personality. The third type is hybrid creativity, found in such fields as architecture, that exhibits both a novel problem solution and the personality of the creator.

In studying creativity, the IPAR group, along with most other research groups, assumed that all kinds of creativity shared common characteristics. Indeed, this assumption seems to be true. For example, it appears that most creative persons are relatively uninterested in small details or facts for their own sake; they are more concerned with meaning and implications. Creative people have considerable cognitive flexibility, communicate easily, are intellectually curious, and tend to let their impulses flow freely.[4]

The creative act often occurs suddenly and is short lived. This moment of insight usually occurs after a prolonged period of searching, sometimes comprising months or even years of observation and search. It seldom immediately follows a period of intensive reflection; rather it occurs much later, when least expected.

What Are Some Basic Attributes of Highly Creative Individuals?

The attributes of highly creative individuals are not theirs alone. However, certain characteristics do seem to make such individuals "stand out" from their peers.

Originality. The ability to produce unusual ideas, to solve problems in unusual ways, and to use things or situations in an unusual manner is the essence of originality. Sometimes, originality is viewed as uncommonness of response—the ability to make remote or indirect connections. Creative individuals, being skeptical of conventionl ideas, are willing to take the intellectual risks associated with creative discovery.

---

[3] Donald W. MacKinnon, "IPAR'S Contributions to the Conceptualization and Study of Creativity," in *Prespectives in Creativity,* eds. Irving A. Taylor and J. W. Getzels (Chicago: Aldine Publishing Co., 1975) p. 75.

[4] Ibid., p. 77.

Persistence. Creative people are usually persistent individuals who are willing to devote long hours to a given task and to work under adverse conditions, if necessary. Above all, creative people are willing to face failure. Frustrations seem to motivate them on to increased effort.

Independence. Creative individuals are independent thinkers who look for the unusual, the unexpected. Such people notice things that other people do not such as colors, textures, and personal reactions. Frequently these people explore ideas for their own sake to see where they may lead.

Unlike the nonconformists who flout convention because they feel a compulsion to be different, independent thinkers maintain a balance between conformity and nonconformity. Unlike conformists, creative persons are open to experience and confident in the worth of their ideas, although they are often their own most severe critics.

Involvement and detachment. Once a problem has been identified, creative persons quickly become immersed in it, first researching how others have tried to solve it and becoming acquainted with its difficulties and complexities. Thus involvement sets the stage for their own creations. Creative individuals soon become detached enough to see the problem in its total perspective. By setting work aside temporarily, creative persons give ideas the freedom to develop.

Deferment and immediacy. Creative persons resist the tendency to judge too soon. They do not accept the first solution but wait to see if a better one comes along. This tendency to defer judgement seems to be an attribute of an open-minded person, one who is unwilling to reach a decision prematurely.

Incubation. By putting the problem aside temporarily, creative persons allow the unconscious mind to take over, making various associations and connections that the conscious mind seems to impede.

The incubation period may be long or short, but it must be utilized. Sleep or almost any change of activity helps to encourage illumination. This period of purposeful relaxation permits the mind to run free.

Illumination. After a long period of frustrated effort, creative persons may sometimes suddenly solve a problem. This sudden flash of insight is the fruits of unconscious inner tensions. It may be that the powers of association are enhanced when the mind runs freely on its own. The flash usually occurs after a period of incubation when individuals are not actively pursuing the problem.

Verification. Although illumination provides the necessary impetus and direction for solving a problem, the solution must be verified through conventional objective procedures. Sound judgment must complete the work that imagination has set in progress. Indeed, a flash of insight may be partially if not totally unreliable and merely serve as a catalyst for liberating the creator from a restricted approach to the problem. Sometimes, one flash of inspiration will precipitate others that must be verified.

What Is the Relationship between Creativity and Intelligence?

For many years, it was assumed that creativity and intelligence were closely related. The incidences of highly creative individuals (for example, Edison, Chuchill, and Einstein) who at some time experienced difficulty in school, however, led to closer examination of this issue in the 1960s. One of the most widely publicized studies was done by Getzels and Jackson who produced evidence that creativity and intelligence were largely independent traits.[5] In an effort to reproduce the Getzels and Jackson study, Hasan and Butcher found creativity and intelligence so highly correlated that they were almost indistinguishable.[6]

These and other conflicting studies have made the issue of creativity and intelligence a controversial one. Perhaps, the most prevailing view today is that beyond a minimum level of intelligence necessary for mastery in a given field, additional intelligence offers no guarantee of a corresponding increase in creativity. Thus the idea that the more intelligent individual is necessarily the more creative person is fallacious. According to Reeves and Clark,[7] all available tests of creativity suggest there is merely a relationship between intelligence and creativity. In no way do they suggest that one causes or necessarily contributes to the other. Even the best known creativity tests today are still somewhat invalid because of the subjective nature of the elements they measure and the lack of any predetermined right answer.[8] Intelligence as measured by IQ tests must be distinguished from how one uses that intelligence. As far as creativity is concerned, one's defense mechanisms, mode of repressing and suppressing ideas, and motivational variables all probably play a vital role in determining its nature and extent.

How Are Cognitive-Affective Aspects Integrated in Creative Behavior?

It has been emphasized throughout this book that learning, basically, involves processes of reflective thinking or problem solving. There are some notable exceptions

---

[5] J.W. Getzels and P.W. Jackson, *Creativity and Intelligence* (New York: John Wiley & Sons, Inc., 1962).

[6] P. Hasan and H.U. Butcher, "Creativity and Intelligence: A Partial Replication with Scottish Children of Getzels and Jackson's Study," *British Journal of Psychology* 57 (February 1966): 129-35.

[7] Thomas C. Reeves and Richard E. Clark, "Research on Creativity," *Educational Technology* 17: (February 1966): 57-58.

[8] These are the Torrance tests of creativity. See E. Paul Torrance, "Examples of Rationales of Test Tasks for Assessing Creative Abilities," *Journal of Creative Behavior* 2 (February 1968): 165-78.

to this broad generalization, however. Teachers and students everywhere are aware of the rote learning still all too common in college and university classes. As indicated in Chapter 2, this type of learning represents a very low level of cognition. Although still imperfectly understood, creativity may offer another exception to the processes of reflective thinking. At least creative thinking and learning do not seem to fit into the usual processes involved in learning.

The reader will recall (from Chapter 2) that learning is classified into three broad domains: cognitive (understanding), affective (appreciation, values, and interests), and psychomotor (skills and habits). Although these domains overlap, achievement in one domain offers no guarantee of achievement in the other domains. Processes of problem solving usually emphasize all levels of cognition; at the upper levels of this domain (synthesis and evaluation), considerable affective learning is evident. Creativity, it seems, places even more emphasis on affective learning. Indeed, creative processes may represent an extension of the more familiar problem-solving or cognitive processes. Crutchfield seems to suggest this in his statement that "both divergent and convergent thinking are required in any creative task; only the proportions vary widely."[9]

Certainly, the processes of creativity require an openness to hunches, guesses, emotions and intuitive feelings about intriguing facts. These personal-motivational factors, according to Williams,[10] are crucial, resulting in an individual's operating on feeling as much as on logic. The creative person is able to deal with fantasy, imagination, and emotion and has the courage to become a risk taker. This individual is curious about possibilities and alternatives generally considered inappropriate by someone less creative.

Similarly, the psychomotor domain is prominently involved when the learner applies imagination at the *adapting* level of this domain. Dance and the art areas, for example, hold little meaning in the absence of creativity.

The hierarchical nature of each domain suggests that the higher levels build on the lower ones. Thus instruction, designed to achieve objectives at all levels below the *synthesis* level of the cognitive domain (knowledge, comprehension, application, and analysis), would offer no guarantee of achieving creative objectives. This point holds for the *valuing* level of the affective domain as well as for the *adapting* level of the psychomotor domain.

What Are the Relative Merits of Individual and Group Creative Experiences?

For many years, educators viewed creative thinking as a process that could only be pursued on an individual basis. Recognizing the innate developmental quality of

---

[9] Richard S. Crutchfield, "The Creative Process," in *Creativity: Theory and Research*, ed. Morton Bloomberg (New Haven: College and University Press, 1973), p. 55.

[10] Frank E. Williams, "Models for Encouraging Creativity in the Classroom," *Educational Technology* 9: (December, 1969): 7-13.

creativity, educators placed relatively little emphasis on furthering and enhancing creativity through group-teaching methods until Osborne and his associates developed the brainstorming technique for sales personnel in the 1950s and early 1960s.[11] Today's widely known Synetics Education Systems Laboratory of Cambridge, Massachusetts, is devoted exclusively to techniques for class use. Like all attributes of learning, creativity can be developed through carefully selected class experiences, although like other approaches to problem solving, much individualized instruction is also needed. Creative problem solving in carefully organized group situations is not only effective but also an economical use of time. Evidence suggests that individuals working in groups exercise deferred judgment as much as they do when working independently.[12] Thus *both* group and individual creative experiences should be emphasized.

What Are the Differences between Convergent and Divergent Thinking?

Convergent thinking is characterized by its reproduction of known concepts and its adoption of known responses to new situations. Divergent thinking, on the other hand, involves fluency, flexibility, and originality and is essentially concerned with production of large numbers of new ideas.[13]

Both convergent and devergent thinking are essential to the problem-solving experience. When convergent thinking is applied during a divergent thinking phase of the problem-solving process, however, the latter may be seriously impeded. When students are developing possible solutions to a problem, for example, evaluation of each solution as *it is presented* tends to inhibit the flow of ideas.

Most IQ tests measure convergent thinking almost exclusively. In essence, such tests require the student to apply what he or she has learned to new problems or to abstract some rule from previously developed examples. Usually, there is only one correct answer. Correctness is determined on the basis of logic, rules, or laws.

To illustrate: Which of the following words is least like "new"?

1. Old.
2. Big.
3. Shiny.
4. Satisfactory.

The respondent is expected to notice that "new" denotes something's age. Thus the word is the opposite of "old" that also denotes age. The divergent thinker, however, could reason that "new" tells about some condition of an object and so does "old,"

[11] Alex F. Osborn, *Applied Imagination*, 3rd. rev. ed. (New York: Charles Scribner's Sons, 1963) pp. 166-96.

[12] Sidney J. Parnes and Harold F. Harding, *A Source Book for Creative Thinking* (New York: Charles Scribner's Sons, 1962) pp. 238-90.

[13] A.J. Cropley, *Creativity* (London: Longmans, Green and Co., 1967) p. 2.

"shiny," and "satisfactory." "Big," on the other hand, relates to size; thus it must be the right answer. Indeed, the process of combining, recombining, or transposing in a novel or adaptive way represents the essence of the creative process.

Individual Techniques for Encouraging Creativity

Basically, creativity is an individualized process. It involves breaking away from established modes of thought. Each person does this in his or her own way.

The natural processes of problem solving involve the creation of patterns used over and over again in critical thinking. New information is fitted into one of these patterns. Patterns, of course, can be easily manipulated by extending or combining related elements. Although useful, the patterns of thought themselves may become restrictive. The creative thinker skips, reverses, and in many other ways alters established channels of thought. In many specific and subtle ways, a teacher can encourage this process.

How Does the Creative Thinker Uncover Problems?

Until recently, most studies of creativity have focused on the problem-solving aspect of creative behavior. Certainly, it is clear that the divergent thinker solves problems differently from the convergent thinker. The question of how the divergent thinker, or creative person, *finds* problems, however, has not been given much attention. Is the process essentially one of evolving a new solution to an old problem? Or is it more likely to be finding a new solution to a *new* problem, discovered by the creative person? On the basis of some two decades of research, Getzels and Csikszentmihalyi believe that the way in which a person discovers problems is the essence of the creative process.[14] They have identified three problem situations in which the learner is given a problem to solve and also a method for solving it. For example, to find the area of a rectangle, multiply side a by side b.

The second is the situation in which the learner is given a problem, but not a method for solving it. For example, find the area of a rectangle. Here the individual must engage in reasoning and analysis in order to solve the problem.

The third situation is one in which the learner is given neither a problem nor a method for solving it. For example, How many important questions can you ask about a rectangle? Thus the problem solver must become a problem finder. Once problems have been formulated, solution(s) must be sought.[15]

---

[14] J.W. Getzels and M. Csikszentmihalyi, "From Problem Solving to Problem Finding," in *Perspectives in Creativity* pp. 102, 103, 114.

[15] At this point, the reader should review the evaluation level of questioning strategies, offered in Chapter 7. Note that these questions have no established criteria; the learners must develop their own.

Getzels and Csikszentmihalyi believe that many potentially creative learners prefer to work on problems they discover themselves. Others may be more comfortable in more structured situations. Certainly, problem finders have been sorely neglected in our institutions of higher learning, possibly at the expense of society as a whole.

How Can an Individual Develop Creative-Thinking Powers?

Tremendous creative potential is often lost by inadequate planning. The typical student tends to postpone term projects until the last moment. When he or she does get started, it is necessary to rush through, perhaps borrowing heavily from established sources. Any ideas or insights that may emerge are quickly pushed aside to save time. Although there is no established pattern for activating the imagination, there are a number of guidelines that many creative people have found effective; the following lists some of these guidelines.

1. *Making a start.* Too often, a person defers action until the mood strikes, or until one can "find the time." There is no substitute for getting started!
2. *Taking notes.* Most really creative individuals carry a pencil and note pad with them at all times. Whenever they attend a lecture or meeting of any kind, they take notes.
3. *Setting deadlines and quotas.* In a sense, this is a form os self-discipline. Deadlines and quotas intensify emotional power since we fear the failure of not meeting our goals. The pressure of deadlines tends to force one to become more efficient in carrying out daily routines that take time away from creative effort.
4. *Fixing a time and place.* We should take time for thinking up ideas! This activity should take precedence over our daily routines. By setting a time and place for such cognitive thought, one may "lure the muse." Some people allow ideas to *incubate* by napping, listening to soft music, or just sitting quietly in a dark corner. Of course, sudden illumination can come at *any* time, even in the middle of the night. Here again, a handy pencil and note pad ensures retention of an idea.[16]

The instructor must assume responsibility for guiding learners into creativity. Although originality and creative imagination are private, individual virtues, guidance and training *can* substantially increase the learner's output, as in any other area of education. Too often, teachers concentrate on the less motivated student at the expense of the truly creative individual. By setting up intermediate check points for term projects, for example, the professor can see that students make an early start.

---

[16] Alex F. Osborn, *Applied Imagination*, pp. 215-21.

How Are Alternatives Generated in Creative Thinking?

One of the basic characteristics of creative thinking is finding different ways of viewing problems. In convergent or logical thinking, the process of searching for alternatives usually stops after a few approaches are suggested and one is selected as the final solution. All unreasonable or far-fetched approaches are summarily dismissed.

In creative thinking, one deliberately searches for as many alternatives as possible. A promising solution suggested early in the process is acknowledged and put aside for later reference. The generation of other alternatives continues. Unlikely—indeed wild or unreasonable—possibilities are tentatively accepted without evaluation (done later). Basically, the objective is to delay a final decision by loosening up fixed patterns of thinking. Most problems can be solved in a variety of ways. While a logical approach(es) may seem ideal, there is no guarantee that it is the best solution. A deliberate generation of alternatives enables one to consider those possibilities that appear unacceptable at first.

In addition to generating alternatives in group problem-solving processes (described elsewhere as brainstorming and synetics), individualized assignments for generating them can be developed in a variety of ways. According to deBono,[17] geometric figures are ideal since they can be developed in an unequivocal form. The student is merely asked to generate different ways of describing a figure. As students find out what the generation of alternatives is all about, according to deBono, they can move on to less artificial situations.

Pictures also provide another useful way of generating alternatives. Students are requested to describe what they think is happening in the picture. The different interpretations are then used to disclose alternative ways of seeing things. According to deBono,[18] there are several different levels of description: what is shown, what is going on, what has happened, what is about to happen. He suggests that the teacher leave the assignment quite open at first but later require more specific descriptions.

Brief anecdotes also provide excellent sources for generating alternatives, especially when the anecdotes concern different people or animals. The assignment thus becomes one of asking for a point of view from each of the parties concerned. To illustrate: A boy and his dog are watching a squirrel in a tree; in the background are a man and a woman; describe what is happening from the viewpoint of the boy, girl, squirrel, man, and woman.

Again, the variety of responses can be used to illustrate differences in perception. Sometimes, a favorable description of an event may be changed to an unfavorable

---

[17]Edward deBono, *Lateral Thinking: Creativity Step by Step* (New York: Harper and Row Publishers, 1970), p. 65.

[18]Ibid., p. 82.

description by merely altering the emphasis given to the various facts, but not the facts themselves.

What Role Does Creative Thinking Play in Challenging Basic Assumptions?

Any ideas (principle or truth) deemed self-evident is referred to as a basic assumption. In solving problems, one must begin with basic assumptions. They provide the foundational structure for problem solving. Moreover, they set boundaries for reducing problems to manageable proportions. If one or more basic assumptions are false, however, the reulting solution will also be false. Many assumptions are handed down by tradition. To challenge them may be considered unfair, sacrilegious, or downright stupid. Certain verifiable false assumptions were held above suspicion for years. At one time, for example, the tomato was considered poisonous. For years scientists were thwarted in their attempts to learn about the human body because it was considered sacrilegious to examine cadavers. Some of our female ancestors (in the Unites States) were burned at the stake for being witches.

In a similar manner, the boundaries imposed on problem solving often lead to faulty conclusions. These boundaries, often self-imposed, are rarely challenged since the represent a "natural" structuring process of the human mind. If someone steps outside the boundaries and solves the problem, this person is considered to be operating unfairly. Yet the boundaries are arbitrarily imposed.

In challenging basic assumptions, both the limits and validity of individual concepts should be questioned for the purpose of restructuring established patterns of thinking. This can lead to different and sometimes improved results. A useful exercise for helping the learner abandon traditional modes of thinking is illustrated in Figure 13-1.

The problem in Figure 13-1 is impossible to solve if one stays with a self-imposed boundary of not extending lines beyond the outer line of dots. If one can break through this arbitrary assumption, however, the problem is easily solved, as Figure 13-2 demonstrates.

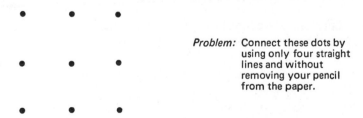

Problem: Connect these dots by using only four straight lines and without removing your pencil from the paper.

FIGURE 13-1   *An Exercise in Creative Thinking*

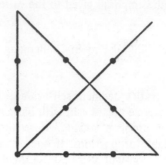

FIGURE 13-2   *A Creative Solution*

How Does the Practice of Suspending Judgment Contribute to Creative Endeavors?

Basic to the processes of cognitive thinking is evaluation. At every step, ideas are evaluated for the purpose of facilitating the problem-solving process. Continuous evaluation does, however, limit the generation of ideas. A suspension of judgment enables one to further examine seemingly wild or impossible ideas. *Wrong ideas may be right in the final analysis.* Emphasis shifts from the validity of a particular point to its usefulness in producing new arrangements or patterns. Withholding judgment enables an idea to survive long enough to generate other ideas and encourages those who may have useful input but are afraid to state their viewpoints for fear of being wrong. This technique can be used in a variety of ways in the classroom. For example, a quota on hypotheses could be established and judgment of each suggestion withheld until the quota has been met.

Professors often discourage creativity by emphasizing the mistakes on written exercises. A better procedure would be to call attention to what was done well and then to point out sources of difficulty, leaving the student with the task of discovering the exact mistakes. The student can then rework certain assignments for credit.

How Can the Restrictive Influences of Labels or Categories Be Minimized by Creative Processes?

By using labels, one risks misrepresenting information. It is convenient to function with relatively few categories, but this often results in polar thinking. For example, one must be either "right" or "wrong." Even those categories that at one time were rather functional tend to become outdated over time. The label remains permanent, however, and thereby contributes to rigid thinking. All young adults, for example, are aware of the restrictive influence of the term "son" or "daughter." It is appropriate to supervise young children closely; when children get older, however, close supervision may even be harmful. Some parents fail to realize that the reality behind the fixed term is changing constantly. They may even seek to control a young person's behavior even after he or she has entered college.

Despite the problems they present, labels or categories are necessary. They can be used effectively if qualified. For example, an individual can be "partially right" and "partially wrong," not for or against something but some place in between. One learns to use labels cautiously by engaging in experiences designed to challenge them, to do without them, or to establish new ones. Teachers might ask students to pick out certain words in the newspaper that seem to generalize or categorize ideas and concepts. For example, students might examine how the words "justice", "equality," "disadvantaged youth," "women's liberation", and "patriotism" are used. A class debate also provides an excellent opportunity for examining how certain labels can be used to influence listeners.

Sometimes, it may be useful to devise experiences that call for dropping certain labels temporarily. The pronoun "I," for example, is often overused. What impact could it have on a persuasive speaker's argument? The reasons for using this pronoun might be the basis for a lesson in English or speech class. Similarly, students might replace old labels with new ones to determine if they make ideas more functional and realistic.

How Can Creativity Be Encouraged Informally in the Classroom?

Creative processes can be encouraged in all instructional activities. All instructional methods discussed in this book involve some form of both creative and reflective thinking as well as skills for generating ideas, the very core of the problem-solving process. If the stage is set for "bold guessing," such experiences will be more effective than when such activities are inhibited.

Experts on creativity repeatedly stress the importance of discovering *both* problems and solutions. Original ideas should be actively sought. For example, a student assigned an oral report might be encouraged to add a personal evaluation and to employ any unique techniques that he or she wishes. Too often, correct thinking requiring one solution and one method has been emphasized. Alternative solutions to a problem need not have been previously suggested by others to be viable. Indeed, alternatives, not found in textbooks should be solicited from students. These can be encouraged by establishing quotas on alternatives; thus students are forced to advance beyond the first one.

Creativity can be encouraged by establishing a class environment that accepts and reinforces new ideas. Such ideas can be weighed on their own merits. It should be emphasized that most creative achievements seem revolutionary when first introduced, as Osborn points out:

When John Kay invented the flying shuttle, it was considered such a threat to labor that weavers mobbed him and destroyed his mold. When Charles Newbold worked out the idea of a cast-iron plow, the farmers rejected it on the grounds that iron polluted the soil and encouraged weeds. In 1844, Doctor Horace Wells was the first to use gas on patients while pulling teeth. The medical profession scorned his new ideas as a humbug. When Samuel P. Langley built his first heavier-than-air machine—flown by steam—the newspapers dubbed it "Langley's folly" and scoffed at the whole idea of self-propelled planes![19]

Rather than present fact or theory, the teacher should place students in situations where they are forced to seek out the information for themselves.

Above all, creativity involves self-direction. From time to time, students should be placed on their own to work on projects, to make their own mistakes, to toy with ideas, and to follow up hunches that may not seem promising at first. Students, in turn, will be encouraged to evaluate for themselves the fruits of such endeavors. Curiosity motivates one to analyze problems that others have taken for granted. By constantly probing with such questions as What would happen if . . . ? curiosity can be enhanced.

Perhaps, the greatest deterrent to creativity is the conventional teacher. Ideas tend to "pop up" at any moment, often catching the teacher by surprise. All too frequently, instructors may view this behavior as the student's impertinence or criticism of their teaching methods. Actually, such a suggestion may merely reflect an individual's "brainstorming" an idea. Such brainstorming may be encouraged by permitting the individual (and the group that may be involved) to develop a plan for putting the idea to work.

Group Techniques for Encouraging Creativity

The precise relationship between creative imagination and problem solving is not fully understood. Most writers suggest, however, that too much emphasis on the formal structure of analytical thought processes is detrimental to creative (sometimes called intuitive) thought. Routines of any sort seem to be detrimental to the creative process. Bruner, in stressing the complementary nature of the two, concedes that through "intuitive thinking the individual may arrive at solutions or problems which he would not achieve at all, or at best more slowly, through analytic thinking."[20] He points out, however, that ideas reached intuitively must be checked and refined by analytic methods. The procedures described in this section enable the learner to exercise considerable creativity within the broad framework of the problem-solving process.

As the following discussion points out, brainstorming and synetics procedures involve a careful combination of individual judgment and development of ideas as well

---

[19] Alex F. Osborn, *Applied Imagination*, p. 54.

[20] Jerome Bruner, *The Process of Education* (Cambridge, Mass.: Harvard University Press, 1961), p. 58.

as group thinking. Flashes of insight often are provoked by others. Group techniques introduce *additional* creative effort to conventional problem-solving procedures and individual development of ideas.

Brainstorming literally means *using the brain to storm a problem.* Using this technique, a group attempts to find a solution to a specific problem by amassing all the ideas spontaneously contributed by its members. Brainstorming is a technique involving applied imagination or creativity.[21]

How Are Problems and Participants Prepared for Brainstorming?

In preparation for a brainstorming session, the leader selects a *specific,* as opposed to a general, problem. The problem How can I write a better term paper? is too broad. To narrow the problem two or three subproblems might be formulated: How can I improve my paragraph structure? How can I create and hold interest? How can I pinpoint major ideas?

When the problem has been reduced to its lowest common denominator, the selected subproblem(s) is posed as a concise, definite question. Questions of what, why, where, when, who, and how often serve to stimulate the creation of ideas. For example: Why is it needed? Where should it be done? Who should do it? How should it be done?

New participants need to be conditioned for their initial session. A warm-up practice session on a simple problem will stimulate the production of ideas. For example: How could our classroom seating be improved?

The group should be given a background memo of not more than one page in length at least two days in advance of the session. The memo serves to orient participants and to let them ponder over the problem in advance of the experience. Contained in the memo is a statement of the question or problem and a few examples of the type of ideas desired. For example:

Problem: How can I pinpoint major ideas?

1. *In the classroom.* Write out my thought before expressing it.
2. *In written papers.* Use short subheads.
3. *In conversation with friends.* Enumerate my points.
4. *In my room.* Imagine that I am my own most interested listener.

Participants should not be permitted to read their lists of ideas, however. These lists should be handed to the leader in advance of the activity.

---

[21] Alex F. Osborn, *Applied Imagination,* pp. 283-90.

What is the Leader's Role in a Brainstorming Session?

In preparation for the actual brainstorming session, the leader explains and writes out four basic rules that must be faithfully followed.

1. *Criticism is ruled out.* Judgment of ideas must be withheld until later.
2. *Freewheeling is welcomed.* The wilder the idea the better; it is easier to tame down than to think up.
3. *Quantity is wanted.* The greater the number of ideas, the greater the likelihood is that ideas will be useful.
4. *Combination and improvement are sought.* In addition to contributing ideas of their own, participants should suggest how ideas of others can be turned into *better* ideas or how two or more ideas can be combined to form still another idea.

The setting for brainstorming is informal and relaxed. The leader begins the session by explaining the problem, writing the four basic rules on the chalkboard, and indicating that when a rule is violated, a special signal will be used to stop the violater (for example, a knock on the deck or the ring of a bell or buzzer). Only one idea is to be offered at a time. The leader especially encourages ideas precipitated by previous ones. Perhaps, a snap of the fingers can designate such association ideas. If several people desire to speak at the same time, participants are encouraged to jot down ideas before they are forgotten. Because ideas tend to be contagious and many persons often desire to speak at the same time, groups of about ten to fifteen people are preferred. Much larger groups, however, have been effective under the direction of expert leaders.

Sometimes, the leader may need to repeat ideas to encourage additional creative thinking and to suggest solutions or new categories of thought if the flow of ideas slows down. The objective is to "milk the group dry of ideas." In addition to opening up new channels of thought, the leader keeps prodding with statements such as "What else?" "I cannot believe that you have expressed all your ideas." Short silent periods are to be expected as participants try to think up new ideas. It is usually in the final stage of the session that the most unique and useful ideas emerge. All ideas suggested are written down by a student recorder to ensure they are preserved. Most sessions will not exceed fifteen minutes. If the group is large or if more than one subproblem needs exploration, two or more subgroups may be formed and led by experienced students.

How Are Afterthoughts Utilized?

In closing the brainstorming session, ideas generated should be counted and reviewed. This serves to stimulate individuals to think further on the problem. The recorder(s) can quickly scan ideas for categories. Usually, there will be from three to five classifications of ideas. Collecting afterthoughts the next class period is an essential aspect of the brainstorming process. Essentially, this process combines individual with group creativity. Such an incubation period produces some of the most valuable ideas. This individualized phase of the brainstorming process can be further stimulated by asking students how they might adapt, magnify, minify, rearrange, or combine their ideas or substitute new ones.

Students have reported that their most valuable ideas often came as flashes of insight when they were making no conscious effort to think. Oddly enough, sleep seems to induce this sudden flash of illumination. It is extremely important that such ideas be recorded at the time or they may be forgotten entirely.

How Are Ideas Evaluated?

After all ideas (including comments about them) have been reviewed, they are screened, edited, and placed in appropriate categories. While this may be done by the entire group, it is usually preferable to have a committee of three to five students do it. The teacher usually will want to assist in this process. Criteria for evaluating the ideas should be established. One group established the following criteria:

1. The idea must be stated concisely.
2. It should be feasible.
3. It should possess some element of the unusual, the novel.

The committee must be careful about eliminating ideas. Sometimes, it may be desirable for the committee to brainstorm one or more of these "wild" ideas that are not readily understood by the group. Indeed, Sidney Parnes of the Creative Problem-Solving Institute, Buffalo, New York, suggests that it is possible to "do the necessary idea-stretching . . . in all stages of the creative problem-solving process rather than emphasizing it only for idea-generation as such."[22] He points out that equal emphasis is now placed on creativity in the difficult phases of evaluation, development, and implementation.

How Are Ideas Implemented?

How a group uses the ideas of a brainstorming session is largely dependent on its purpose. For example, the purpose may be to develop techniques of oral or written expression in art, literature, or music, or it may concern novel ways of obtaining proper physical exercise, of memorizing, or of doing some chore. It may even deal with certain aspects of human relations such as how to maintain poise when one is angry. Whatever the purpose, ideas must be implemented. This may be accomplished on an individual basis or in subgroups. Sometimes the results of brainstorming sessions may be shared with the class; on other occasions, they may not be shared with anybody

---

[22] Sidney J. Parnes, "Aha," in *Perspectives in Creativity*, p. 240.

except the instructor. For example, as an individual exercise, students might be asked to write a paper employing the ideas generated earlier and containing a brief statement about how they are used. Several such experiences might be necessary for enabling individuals to discover those techniques most beneficial to them.

As a concluding experience, the group should draw generalizations, based on various action programs. This enables all members to profit from the experiences of many. Certain experiences may set the stage for the enactment of one or more selected situations for further study and analysis. Sociodrama has been most useful in this connection.

What Preplanning Is Necessary?

Although the brainstorming session is an informal one, it must be carefully planned. The plan illustrated below, indicates one way of stimulating a group to creative activity. Since the creative act is in itself a unique experience to the individuals involved, the brainstorming method will take on many different dimensions, depending on the purpose being served.

LESSON PLAN ILLUSTRATION FOR A BRAINSTORMING SESSION (art class)

Concept: The expressive power of a linear statement is limited only by the artist's imagination.

Problem: What everyday sights can be expressed in terms of line?

Goals: After this lesson the student should further appreciate the role line plays in artistic creations, as evidenced by:

1. The generation of ideas in the brainstorming session.
2. The use of these ideas in his or her own artistic creation.

Lesson approach

As has been previously pointed out, a line is defined as a point moving through space. Line is distinguishable from shape in that length is greater than breadth. Therefore, line tends to emphasize movement or direction. In the course of everyday experience, we come across many beautiful and interesting expressions of lines. Frequently, however, such experiences are so commonplace that they go unnoticed. Have you ever thought of common visual experiences in terms of line alone? Today, we will attempt to describe the variety and moods of the line, which compose the structural essence of beauty, as we perceive them in our everyday lives. The experience should stimulate us for later development of our own artistic creations.

For the next few minutes, we are going to "storm the brain" for ideas involving line. (Appoint two recorders, one from each side of the room to write down each section's ideas.) This is a "fun" type of experience if we abide by four simple rules (put on the board).

1. Criticism is ruled out.
2. "Freewheeling" is welcomed. (the wilder the idea the better.)
3. Quantity is desired.
4. Combination and improvement of ideas are sought.

I will knock on my desk when a rule is violated. Just snap your fingers when you desire to comment on a previous idea.

Lesson development

What everyday sights can be expressed in terms of line? Suggested categories follow (to be offered if the flow of ideas diminishes).

1. *Motion.* The line following the path of a football player as he tumbles through the air is viewed by a slow-motion TV camera shot.
2. *Silhouette.* The scene of a distant horizon at sunset.
3. *Flight:* The line formed by an eagle soaring in the sky.
4. Sound (or heat) waves. The line created by an auctioneer as he calls for bids.

Reviewing ideas (first day)

Now that you seem to have exhausted all ideas, let us determine how many have been generated in the last fifteen minutes. (Ask recorders to give the number and to suggest categories.) I would like you all to develop some more ideas.

Utilizing afterthoughts

Write out the problem and the categories suggested by our recorders. Keep the problem in mind until tomorrow when I will call for your additional ideas. Just keep your mind open, jotting down ideas as they occur. Such ideas may occur to you when least expected; so keep pencil and paper near at all times.

Processing ideas (second day)

(Collect lists of additional ideas and pass along to the recorders.)

I am appointing a committee of five to screen, edit, and categorize your ideas on how line can be expressed. (Instructor will assist the committee as needed.) You will each receive a copy of the committee's list. You may want to do some more brainstorming in connection with this activity.

Implementing ideas (third and fourth days)

Study the list of ideas and select two or three ideas that you wish to use for the following assignment.

Assignment

Your task is to produce at least one drawing from a suggested idea. The idea may be expanded and altered as you apply your imagination to the problem. You should write out the original idea on the back of your drawing, however. I will then ask the class to relate your drawings to the list of ideas.

Deriving generalizations

As a result of this experience, a number of principles or ideas concerning line are evident. Let us list some of these.

1. Line expresses life.
2. Line exists in everything that we can visualize or perceive.
3. Line exists in infinite variety.
4. Perception of line may set the stage for artistic expression.

How May Synetics Be Employed in the Ideation Process?

A technique for developing ideas somewhat related to brainstorming procedures has been employed for many years by the Arthur D. Little Company, Cambridge, Massachusetts. Originally under the direction of William J. J. Gordon and sometimes known as the "Gordon Technique," the approach was designed to emulate the procedures that inventors employ.[23] Synetics means the joining together of different and apparently irrelevant elements. Although used with a group, like brainstorming, it can also be applied to solving problems on an individual basis.

As an operational procedure, synetics depends heavily on two mechanisms: making the strange familiar and making the familiar strange. The objective is to rid one of conventional or habitual ways of viewing problems. As George Prince, the chairman of Synethics, Inc. (Cambridge, Mass.), points out, "The synetics process focuses on two basic and interrelated approaches: first, procedures that aid imaginative speculation and second, disciplined ways of acting so that speculation is not reduced but valued and encouraged.[24] He later adds, "Any activity that increases speculation will increase the probability of getting ideas. Whatever decreases speculation decreases probability."[25]

When confronted with a new problem, the strange may be made familiar by searching for parallels with known situations. Is not this actually an old problem in

---

[23] For a thorough description of the technique, the reader should consult William J. J. Gordon, *Synetics* (New York: Harper and Brothers, Inc., 1961).

[24] George M. Prince, "Creativity, Self, and Power," in *Perspective in Creativity*, p. 254.

[25] Ibid., p. 257.

disguise? Seeing even partial resemblances may lead to an application of familiar methods in solving the new problem. A new and difficult biological concept, for example, usually is based on known concepts.

Making the familiar strange is a way of eliminating preconceptions and habitual patterns of thought. In a speech class, for example, a conventional problem might be, How can enunciation be improved? An unusual, but perhaps equally fruitful, problem might be, How can one communicate without enunciating?

To attain the goals of making the familiar strange and the strange familiar, four main approaches have been employed: personal analogy, direct analogy, symbolic analogy, and fantasy. *Personal analogy* involves identification of oneself with an object, event, or thing. To illustrate, "If I were an automobile without wheels, how would I go from place to place?

Direct analogy is perhaps best illustrated by Alexander Graham Bell's description of his invention of the telephone.

> It struck me that the bones of the human ear were very massive, indeed, as compared with the delicate thin membranes that operated them, and the thought occurred that if a membrane so delicate could move bones relatively so massive, why should not a thick and stouter piece of membrane move my piece of steel . . . and the telephone was conceived.[26]

Symbolic analogy, as described by Gordon, is usually a visual image. He uses the following example: "How to invent a jacking mechanism to fit a box not bigger than four by four inches yet extend out and up three feet to support tons?"[27] Thus the principle of the hydraulic jack was born.

Fantasy as used in synetics involves freeing the imagination from the bounds of a given word or concept. For example, What would happen to a given land formation without the influence of the pull of gravity?

The Value of Creative Approaches

Cultivating imagination in the college classroom substantially increases levels of learning.

Group techniques, such as brainstorming and synetics, help prepare students for truly creative individual effort.

The brainstorming session minimizes inhibitions that block creativity.

Brainstorming and synetics are useful techniques for generating many alternatives to the resolution of problems. They are also useful in the processing and implementation stages of creative experiences.

---

[26] William J. J. Gordon, *Synetics,* p. 132.

[27] Ibid., p. 57.

Group experiences generate enthusiasm for learning. Once their imagination is activated, most students progress at an accelerated rate.

Limitations of, and Problems with, Creative Approaches

Despite the many values of group creative activities, individual exercises are usually more valuable. Actually the group process does incorporate both individual and group ideation in a three stage approach: individual creation of an idea, group verification of the idea, and then development of the idea to its conclusion.

The effectiveness of a brainstorming session is dependent on the appropriateness of the problem employed. There is a decided tendency among teachers to select complex problems.

Production of ideas through brainstorming sessions is merely an initial phase of creativity. Analytical problem-solving techniques must complement this process.

Brainstorming and synetics place the leader (teacher) in a new role. Instead of passing judgment and giving direction, he or she must develop an atmosphere free from inhibitions. Some teachers (as well as students) experience difficulty in making such a transition.

Illustrated Applications for Different Subject Fields

I. Illustrated brainstorming outlines
   A. Useful in history, government, art, and social studies

   Concept: Man's history is recorded in art.

   Problem: How can man preserve history for succeeding generations?

   Suggested categories

   1. *In space.* Equip a special space capsule and put in an earth orbit.
   2. *On earth.* Construct and equip a special cave with typical artifacts of our civilization.
   3. *In polar regions.* Construct a model city under the ice pack.

   B. Useful in home economics, child development, sociology, and psychology classes.

   Concept: *Through play, the child develops an ability to create, to reason, and to talk.*

   Problem: How can playing with dolls contribute to growth and development?

Suggested categories

1. *Role playing.* Child may assume roles of family members.
2. *Social development.* Child learns to share dolls with other children.
3. *Intellectual growth.* Child develops skill in communication by talking to dolls.
4. *Physical development.* Child learns grooming techniques by bathing doll and combing its hair.

C. Useful in English, speech, and drama classes

Concept: Voice projection is a basic aspect of communication

Problem: How can one project one's voice?

Suggested categories

1. *With facial expressions.* Exaggerate formation of key words
2. *With the diaphragm.* Talk by expanding the chest cavity.
3. *With body expressions.* Use hands to emphasize verbal expressions

II. Illustrated applications of creativity
   A. Forced relationships[28]
      Select anything in one's perceptual field of awareness and attempt to relate it to a specific problem.
      To illustrate: A small group of people desire to use a small table as a focal point for entertainment. They wish to make the dinner as intimate as occasion as possible.
      Their task: Focus on a tree outside the window for suggestions.
   B. Useful in mathematics[29]
      A U.S. Department of Agriculture report says that an average American family of four spends $30 per week for groceries with 9¢ of each food dollar going for the package. Each person in the U.S. throws away about 577 pounds of packaging material (boxes, plastic wrap, paper, and so on) in one year. Disposing of this packaging costs approximately $50 per person per year. On the average, each American also throws away about 5.3 pounds of garbage per day. It costs about 4.5 billion dollars ($4,500,000,000) per year to collect and dispose of this waste for 200,000,000 people in the U.S.
      Make up as many questions as you can concerning the math situation, questions that can be answered from the information in the paragraph.

---

[28] Based on Sidney J. Parnes, "Idea-Stimulation Techniques," *Journal of Creative Behavior* 10 (July 1976): 126-291.

[29] Reprinted from Donald A. Balka, "Creative Ability in Mathematics," *The Arithmetic Teacher* 21 (November 1974): 633-36. Used by permission.

Criteria for measuring such a creative experience include:

1. The ability to formulate math hypotheses concerning cause and effect in selected math situations.
2. The ability to determine patterns in math situations.
3. The ability to break from established mind sets to obtain solutions in a math situation.
4. The ability to consider and evaluate unusual math ideas, to think through their consequences for a math situation.
5. The ability to sense what is missing from a given math situation and to ask questions that will enable one to fill in the missing math information.
6. The ability to split general math problems into specific subproblems.

C. Useful in science classes

Situation for reaction: The tundra biome

Describe the tundra and then ask, "If you were trying to live in the tundra, what life form that you have seen would you try most to imitate to survive?" (Discussion will move toward the smallest, the least metabolically active forms of life.) Eventually *seeds* are discovered. "The closer you are to being a seed, the better off you will be in the tundra winter."

Thus the characteristics of seeds, once discussed and listed, are used as a standard for measuring the survival power of all other life forms in or near the tundra biome: How close are such forms to being seeds?[30]

(The above demonstrates that a potentially vast and confusing amount of information can be contained within a very simple framework for study and analysis.)

D. Useful in English and journalism classes

Image-forming exercise (need prior to writing a composition)

You are sitting at a table when suddenly you feel something rub against your leg. You reach down and move your hand over what you think is a dog. Your hand glides from its nose to the tip of its tail. In five sentences describe the *feel* of the dog. Remember you cannot see it; you do not know its color or even what kind of dog it is.[31]

You are sitting in an old trunk in the attic, examining its contents. Suddenly, the lid falls down and locks. In five sentences describe the *fear* you feel when you realize you are imprisoned and no one is around to rescue you.

---

[30] From Jacques Jimmez, "Synetics: A Technique for Creative Learning," *The Science Teacher* 42 (March 1975): 33-36.

[31] From A. D. Alley, "Guiding Principles for the Teaching of Rhetoric," *College Composition and Communication* 25 (December 1974): 74-81.

Assessment Techniques

Measurement and evaluation techniques have been recognized as the weakest aspect of the instructional process. Some professors recently have even made a plea for the abolition of tests and grades. They point to the general poor quality of many teacher-made tests and the frequent arbitrary use of grades. Measurement and evaluation techniques and devices, however, need not be poor in quality. When used appropriately, they become an indispensable aspect of the instructional process.

When instruction is based on basic concepts and predicted behavioral outcomes, measurement and evaluation become an integral part of the instructional process. Reflective thinking, then becomes a basis for assessment experiences. Indeed, multiple-choice and essay test items can be constructed to involve the learner in similar processes of reflection.

The two chapters in Unit V discuss necessary components of sound measurement and evaluation techniques. The reader will recognize that some aspects of measurement and evaluation are difficult to achieve effectively. The writing of appropriate situational test items is not only difficult but also time-consuming. Nevertheless, it is a task that must be accomplished if criticisms of tests are to be negated. Like other instructional skills, such techniques can be mastered with experience. In the final analysis, the quality of measurement and evaluation determines the quality of the learning experience. Students quickly anticipate how they will be evaluated and will react accordingly.

MEASURING INSTRUMENTS AND DEVICES

Overview

Key Concepts

1. A valid test must be reliable; a reliable test, however, may not be valid.
2. Specific behavioral outcomes, derived from instructional goals and basic concepts, provide the basis for measurement and evaluation.
3. Tests generally should emphasize the higher levels of cognition (see Chapter 2).
4. Multiple-choice items tend to be superior to other test items.
5. Test-taking behavior involves definite skills that have a marked impact on test scores.

New Terms

1. Measurement   A quantitative evaluation of some experience, such as a test score.
2. Evaluation   The quality of an experience, often based on some measure.
3. Validity   The trustworthiness of a measure. For example, Does it measure what it is supposed to measure?
4. Reliability   The consistency of scores on a given measuring instrument.
5. Situational Test Item   An item that thrusts the student into a contrived situation. Designed to determine how well learnings may be applied.
6. Performance Test Item   An item that requires the learner to actually do (perform) a specified skill.
7. Modified or Qualified Test Item   Usually a supplementary question designed to probe understanding or frame of reference of a major test item.
8. Subjective Test Item   An item open to more than one type of response, dependent on the frame of reference of the individual involved.
9. Objective Test Item   An item that can be scored objectively.
10. Item Analysis   A technique for determining which test items do and do not contribute to test reliability.

11. Criterion-Referenced Measures Measures that evaluate achievement in terms of a predetermined standard (criterion) of preference, without reference to the level of performance of other members of the class.
12. Norm-Referenced Measures Measures that evaluate achievement in terms of an individual's position relative to other members of the class.
13. Minimum-Essentials Measures Those criterion-referenced measures used to assess mastery or competence in specifically defined areas. Such measures are usually most appropriately used in the skills areas; a minimum passing score of 85 to 90 percent is usually established to allow for sampling and personal errors.
14. Developmental Measures Measures used to assess a class of behaviors (often in the cognitive domain) that represent achievement beyond the minimum-essentials level.

Questions to Guide Your Study

1. Measurement and evaluation have been described as the weakest aspect of the instructional process. Why?
2. Since memory and recall are necessarily involved in the higher levels of cognition, recall test items are not necessary. Defend or refute.
3. Why are modified or qualified test items recommended?
4. The kind of test students anticipate determines the extent to which they will try to learn. Defend or refute.
5. It has been said that objective test items are not objective. Explain.
6. Mastery (minimum-essentials) test items tend to be at the lower levels of cognition. Defend or refute.

Fundamental Properties

Measuring instruments and devices are often difficult to construct and score. They are as much a part of the instructional process as any other aspect of teaching, however. In fact, measuring instruments often determine the nature of learning that will occur when students study for tests. Thus a thorough understanding of their fundamental properties is essential if measuring instruments are to be effective.

What is the Role of Concepts in Measurement?

As indicated in Chapter 1, module or unit concepts, extrapolated from basic course content, represent the basic structure on which all instruction is based. Quite naturally then, the teacher uses them as a basis for the development of appropriate measuring instruments. By referring to Table 14-1 (see page 291), the reader will note that unit concepts constitute one set of evaluation specifications and instructional objectives form the other. (Note also that the unit concepts developed in conjunction with unit planning in Appendix A are identical to those used in Table 14–1.) In actual practice, preplanned module or unit concepts are modified in accord with the actual instructional experience. Some concepts may not be achieved; other concepts should be added to the list.

What Is the Role of Behavioral Outcomes in Measurement?

As indicated in Chapter 2, behavioral outcomes set the stage for all instructional and evaluational activities. Once a basic concept has been incorporated into an instructional goal, the teacher is able to predict (in terms of actual performance) both the en route and terminal behaviors that will signify progress toward goal achievement. Such anticipated behavioral outcomes provide the basis for all evaluational activities. As emphasized throughout this book, learning must be *applied.* Applications are made during basic learning experiences, during review experiences, and again when progress is being evaluated. Consistency in each of these aspects of instruction is essential. Testing students for recall of facts, for example, would be grossly unfair (invalid) if the instructional activities emphasized application and other higher level goals. Moreover, such an experience would seriously undermine the whole instructional experience since students tend to gear their learning to anticipated evaluational procedures.

Behavioral outcomes reflect the levels of cognition anticipated. This is especially evident in the action verbs used. An outcome stating that the student will be able to *name, list,* or *order* certain data, for example, would likely be at a low level of cognition (probably recall or memory only). Other action verbs, such as *develop, construct,* and *analyze* suggest a relatively high level of cognition (for example, application, analysis, synthesis, or evaluation). The skillful test maker must decide the level(s) of cognition that should *actually* be achieved, based on the instructional experience. If application has been emphasized (as it should be), most test items should also emphasize application.

What Is a Valid Test?

A valid test is one that measures what it is supposed to measure. If, for example, ten major concepts have been identified and emphasized during a module or unit, the test must be based on these concepts. Although it is appropriate to include some items dealing with specific facts pertaining to concepts, major emphasis must be focused on the learner's ability *to use* the concepts in related situations.

The number of test items pertaining to any given concept should correlate with the emphasis given to the concept during the instructional program. If, for example, three class periods were devoted to concept A while a single class period was devoted to concept B, three times as many tests should be given on concept A as on concept B. Although time is not the only barometer of emphasis, it serves as a useful guide.

More tests are generally needed for assessing minimum-essentials objectives than for assessing of developmental objectives.

What Is Meant by Reliability?

Every teacher is concerned with the trustworthiness or consistency of test results. Does Joe's poor mark, for example, indicate a general lack of understanding in the area, or does it merely reflect errors due to chance and poor test items? How much would his score change if the test were administered several times without the influence of previous test experiences?

Although it is impossible to eliminate all errors of chance, a simple item analysis will reveal those sources of inconsistency due to poor and ambiguous items. An accurate index of item difficulty and discrimination between good and poor students can be obtained by determining how well a given item is related to success on the test as a whole. The most accurate procedure entails contrasting the responses of the highest 27 percent of the examinees with the lowest 27 percent.[1] The procedure is long and laborious, however.

It is possible, nevertheless, to conduct an item analysis in ten to twenty minutes by passing the corrected tests to students and having them call out their scores. This slightly different procedure, as described by Paul Diederich,[2] involves separating test papers into two piles, representing the highest and lowest scores. Use of test *halves* renders small and less obvious differences since some papers will fall into one or the other half by chance. On the other hand, the procedure has the practical value of involving *all* students while the analysis is being made. In contrast, the top and bottom *quarters* analysis leaves one-half of the class idle during the procedure since it excludes the middle 46 percent of the papers.

The difference between the high and low *halves* should be 10 percent, that is, 10 percent more of the top half papers should contain a correct answer to an item than those in the bottom half. In a class of forty students, for example, at least four more students in the top half than in the bottom half should select the correct response. The minimum acceptable high-low difference of 10 percent (for halves only) is accurate for the *middle range* of item difficulty; that is, 25 to 75 percent of the students respond correctly to the item. This approximation is reasonably accurate until one reaches items that fewer than 20 percent or more than 80 percent of the class answered correctly. In a class of forty students, the 20 to 80 percent range (for which the 10 percent discrimination difference is reasonably accurate) would represent between eight and thirty-two students. Any difference of four or more within this range would

---

[1] This percentage applies to norm-referenced tests only. Since score variability is assumed, it does not apply to criterion-referenced (mastery) test items.

[2] Paul Diederich, *Short-Cut Statistics for Teacher-Made Tests*, Educational Testing Service, Bulletin no. 5 (Princeton, N.J., 1960) p. 7.

be reasonably acceptable. As noted earlier, most items that fall outside this range would be considered too hard or too easy.

All scores that fall above the median (midpoint) are handed to one half of the class. Those that fall below the median are given to the other half of the class. The teacher is now ready to conduct an item analysis. He or she must obtain four figures for each item, labeled and defined as follows:

H=the number of "highs" who got the item correct
L=the number of "lows" who got the item correct
H+L= "SUCCESS"—total number who got the item correct
H−L= "DISCRIMINATION"—the high-low difference

As the teacher calls out the item number, selected students indicate, by a show of hands, the number of correct responses, thus enabling the teacher to do the necessary adding and subtracting.

A teacher will soon discover that the high-low difference for some of the items will be zero. This indicates that the better students are doing no better, or perhaps worse, on an item than the poorer students. Accordingly, the item can be improved prior to its use on a subsequent test. Eventually, one may be able to build up quite a reservoir of test items, designed to discriminate the good from the poor students.

There may be two or three multiple-choice items on a test that did not discriminate satisfactorily for no apparent reason. When there is time, a teacher may want to subject these to a second stage of item analysis (assuming they are multiple-choice items). This may be accomplished by determining how many of the "highs" and how many of the "lows" chose each response. Thus a response that tended to confuse the "highs" may be easily identified. Perhaps this group suspected a trap or thought it too obvious.

What Is Meant by Objectivity?

A test item is objective if it is clearly stated. Most words have several meanings. Therefore, it is important for a teacher to clarify questions so that all students will understand them in the same way. Both essay- and objective-type items run the risk of being misunderstood. The *qualified* essay item, described later in this chapter, tends to be much more objective than the traditional essay item. Similarly, *modified* multiple-choice and true-false items enable the student to indicate his particular frame of reference when responding to them.

Another aspect of objectivity is associated with scoring procedure. Use of a scoring key reduces the effect of personal bias. A scoring key usually consists of acceptable responses and the various weights to be assigned to each item.

What Should Be the Range of Difficulty?

The difficulty range of criterion-referenced (mastery level) items must be quite different from that of norm-referenced (developmental level) items. In the former, student achievement is assessed in terms of the type of behavior or performance a student is capable of demonstrating. Level of performance, usually predetermined, is stated as a part of each behavioral outcome (see Chapter 2). In this manner, an absolute standard (criterion) is established for assessing an individual's achievement. *One's position relative to other students in the class is not a factor.* In testing for minimum essentials, mastery within reasonable limits is expected. Thus a spread of scores is not expected. The difficulty of a test item (or task) should correspond to the difficulty of the performance task described in the specific learning outcome.

The range of difficulty becomes an important concept in all norm-referenced and criterion-referenced measures at the developmental level. Here one is interested in the student's relative standing in class. Achievement is assessed in terms of how the learner's performance compares with those of other students. Thus a spread of scores becomes important. Since complete mastery is not expected, a range of item difficulty is needed if one is to assess relative degree of progress toward a given objective.

Norm-referenced items chosen for maximum discrimination tend to have a range of difficulty of approximately 50 percent; that is, one out of two students will respond incorrectly to the item. Allowing for chance clues and the like, the point of optimum discrimination usually is placed slightly higher. Although an item ideally will be answered correctly by 50 to 60 percent of the students, it may be desirable to include a few easy items (for encouragement) and a few hard items for the purpose of discriminating among the top students. Since a few easy and a few hard items are included, a minimum level of about 70 percent is usually considered a "passing" level.

A criterion-referenced test must accurately determine the range of criterion behavior involved. Rather than give students such a test before the learning experience begins, teachers often arbitrarily determine the range themselves. Perhaps, a better technique would be to administer the test both before and after the learning experience. Although only a few students would be expected to answer any given item correctly on the preassessment test, most of them should respond correctly on the postassessment test. An overall score of 80 percent or higher should be expected.

What Time Limitations Should Be Observed?

There are two types of tests with respect to time: power and speed. A *power* test provides the student with ample time to respond to all items, whereas a *speed* test limits the amount of time allowed for separate sections or the total test time. Most teacher-made tests are designed as power tests. In attempting to include as many items as possible within the limits of a class period, tests are sometimes too long for poor students. Thus a power test, in effect, becomes a speed test for *some* students. Such a condition may produce unreliable test results.

In those areas in which criterion-referenced items can be used, the problem becomes especially critical. A representative sample of a student's performance within a given area is necessary. If numerous skills are involved (as in mathematics), each separate skill must be tested. Gronlund suggests that at least ten items for each instructional objective be included.[3] In order to keep these tests of reasonable length, subunit tests, involving a week or two of class time, may become necessary.

What Functions Do Tests Serve?

Tests can serve a variety of purposes that contribute to the learning process. Perhaps the least used but potentially the most valuable is the *pretest.* A pretest can be extremely useful in assessing the learner's readiness for the material to be learned. If, for example, one does not possess the needed entry level skills, he or she has little chance of success until such skills have been mastered. A pretest can also reveal those portions of an instructional unit that students have already mastered. In addition, a pretest can serve as a baseline for assessing an individual's progress. For most pretests, an individual's standing relative to his or her peers is not important.

Tests perhaps serve their greatest function as an instructional activity for improving learning. Tests designed to improve learning are called *formative* tests and may be administered at intervals throughout a given unit. Such tests may be self-administered; sometimes they take the form of open book tests. Occasionally, a teacher may permit students to grade their own papers. If basic essentials are involved, the tests are given again until mastery is achieved.

Diagnostic tests are somewhat similar to formative tests in that they measure learning but, in particular, attempt to discover common errors that students make. It is essential that these errors be analyzed in terms of degree of complexity. Thus such tests tend to be somewhat longer than formative tests.

Tests given at the end of a unit or course for the purpose of assigning grades are often called *summative* tests. Such tests may consist of both mastery and developmental level items, separated into two parts and arranged by instructional objective. In those cases where it is necessary to report test performance in terms of letter grades, Gronlund suggests the following:

A—achieved all mastery objectives and *high* on developmental objectives.
B—achieved all mastery objectives and *low* on developmental objectives.
C—achieved all mastery objectives only.

Students who failed the mastery portion of the test should repeat the instructional process until mastery has been achieved. If this is not possible, letter grades of D and E must be assigned.

What Test Preparation and Test-Taking Behaviors Are Important?

As indicated, teachers must follow a carefully outlined procedure in order to develop valid tests. This entails testing in terms of instructional goals and anticipated

---

[3] Norman E. Gronlund, *Preparing Criterion-Referenced Tests for Classroom Instruction* (New York: The Macmillan Co., 1973), p. 14.

behavioral outcomes. Test items should be so constructed to emphasize the higher levels of thinking. If the student is *unable* to demonstrate these levels of learning, however, the best test is useless. In order to minimize failure, appropriate test-taking behaviors must be emphasized. As in any other aspect of learning, there are certain essential skills involved.

In the first place, there is no substitute for thoroughness. Careful preparation above all else, tends to eliminate examination panic. By distributing review sessions evenly throughout the week preceding the examination, the teacher can help insure that students not only know the material but feel they know it.

Some students mistakenly associate thoroughness with "cramming," that is, spending long hours the night before the examination going over and over the materials. On the contrary, evidence clearly indicates that cramming is not desirable; instead, one should probably stop studying the day prior to the test. Daily working, eating, and sleeping habits should be continued as usual.

In addition to thorough study, allowing students to bring notes to the examination makes them more confident, since they know they can check a question just prior to the exam, if necessary. Students should avoid the temptation of discussing material with other students just prior to the exam, however. *Panic is contagious!*

Test takers should just answer those questions that they obviously know. Those items that pose some uncertainty should be checked and answered tentatively (on a separate piece of paper). Those that are confusing or apparently not known should be checked for later reference. Above all, students should avoid pondering over items during the first time through the test.

After responding to the items clearly understood, test takers should reread those items that they think they know and compare answers with those made the first time through the test. (The first impression is often best.) Finally, they should deal with all baffling items. It often helps to phrase the question in one's own words and then compare the rewording with the original version. Many times, confusion is a result of misreading the item.

Since words often carry many meanings, one must avoid thinking too hard about an item or its alternatives. Bright students especially tend to read meaning into items that was never intended. For those items that remain in the "unknown" category, students can usually increase their chances of answering them correctly by looking for test clues. An alternative that is longer or shorter than the other choices is often the correct one. In addition, such qualifying words as *usually* or *sometimes* tend to denote correct choices, whereas such words as *always* or *never* often suggest incorrect responses.

In responding to essay items, one should set up a time schedule, allowing a few minutes at the end of the period to answer each question after first reading all of them. (Six incomplete answers usually will receive more credit than three complete ones.) In reading the questions, one should note answers that come to mind with key words, to serve as cues for later reference.

As with confusing objective items, students should put confusing essay items in their own words and then compare the rewording with the original phrasing of the question. Doing this substantially increases the chances of deriving intended meaning. It also helps to briefly outline a proposed answer and then expand this outline as one answers the item. This not only contributes to thoroughness and accuracy but also tends to make a favorable impression on the evaluator. The practice of beginning to write in the hope that the right answer will somehow appear is wasteful and usually unproductive. Finally, one should check for misspelled words, grammatical errors, and misleading or dogmatic statements. In emphasizing the importance of qualified answers, it is better to say, for example, "toward the end of the nineteenth century" than to say "in 1896," when you cannot remember whether the date is 1886 or 1896. If the test contains both essay and objective items, the essay items should be answered first.

Adequate test-taking skills often make the difference between letter grades; they sometimes make the difference between passing and failing. For the teacher who is interested in increasing the validity of test results, providing instruction in test-taking skills is of utmost importance.

Techniques of Measurement

The teacher uses a variety of measuring instruments to help in evaluating a student's progress. For some purposes, tests afford reliable data, as in the case of understandings related to academic achievement. For other purposes, as in the case of attitudes and appreciations, observation will produce the most reliable results. Through measurement, a *quantitative amount* of some experience is assembled, as in the case of test score. Evaluation, on the other hand, attempts to assess the *value* of the quantity to be measured. Measurement in and of itself is meaningless; it can do no more than facilitate the ends of evaluation. To cite a previous example, a score of 80 on a test must be *evaluated* in terms of the goal or purpose involved. Evaluations made with inadequate or improper measuring instruments serve no useful purpose and lead to erroneous conclusions.

How Are Concepts and Goals Identified?

The reader will recall that the first step in the instructional process is concept identification. Each unit concept (usually six to ten per unit) provides a basis for the development of unit goals and their accompanying behavioral outcomes. As illustrated in Chapter 2, the outcomes are usually more useful as guides to instruction than as guides to evaluation. When behavioral outcomes are first identified, the instructor is quite naturally most interested in those intermediate behaviors that indicate *progress toward* goal achievement and concept attainment. To illustrate the point, refer to the following goal illustration from Chapter 2.

After this unit in American literature, the student should further appreciate the social inequalities resulting from a social class structure, as evidenced by (1) realistic *responses* in a class discussion of what should be U.S. policy toward migrant workers (2) willingness to examine reactions resulting from a sociodrama designed to portray feelings in a specified social situation, and (3) greater cooperation with underprivileged students in class and in society.

Note that outcomes one and two are to be elicited during the instructional process. Although the third outcome is a *terminal* behavior, it cannot be used for evaluational purposes in its present form.

To be useful for evaluational purposes, behavioral outcomes must be redefined as *terminal* behaviors. Such behaviors must be much more explicit than the intermediate behaviors described in Chapter 2. For example, the first outcome from the previous illustration, "realistic responses in a class discussion of what should be U.S. policy toward migrant workers" would be restated as "What should be U.S. policy toward migrant workers?" In answering this question, one might expect the learner to evaluate evidence in the area and to draw warranted conclusions from the evidence available. The unit concept "A social class structure produces social inequalities" would be used as a guide for constructing test items designed to determine how well the learner can evaluate evidence and draw warranted conclusions in the area. Similarly, the second outcome, concerned with the learner's willingness to examine feelings portrayed through a sociodramatic experience, must be stated more specifically for evaluational purposes. The instructor should determine what will result from this examination of feelings. Perhaps, it will be increased empathy or increased skill in interpersonal relationships. Test items and other evaluational tools are then constructed for assessing progress in this direction. The third outcome, although already stated as a terminal behavior, must be more specifically qualified if it is to be used for evaluational purposes. (As a terminal behavior in the affective domain, it does not directly serve instructional purposes.) Further refinement of the outcome can be achieved by specifying the important *conditions* under which "greater cooperation with under-privileged students" might be expected. One condition, for example, might include the learner's willingness to accept these students in specific group activities. Such an outcome is probably most appropriately evaluated through direct observation.

How Are Instructional Objectives, Behavioral Outcomes, and the Content Outline Integrated

Prior to actually developing test items, one must assemble instructional unit goals (which end with anticipated pupil behavioral outcome samples). Instructional goals, of course, are evolved from basic unit concepts. All these are developed in pre-instructional activities and must be modified, on the basis of the actual instructional experience. Utilizing the Bloom taxonomy as a frame of reference,[4] unit goals are

---

[4] Benjamin S. Bloom, ed., *Taxonomy of Educational Objectives, Handbook 1: The Cognitive Domain* (New York: David McKay Co., Inc., 1956).

listed from simple to complex. The essential elements only are listed. The list that follows is illustrative only. The reader may want to identify his or her own major field by filling in the blank spaces provided.

OBJECTIVES FOR A UNIT IN ⎯⎯⎯⎯⎯

1. Knows important facts or terms.
   a. Reproduces word meanings.
   b. Matches terms that fit given definitions.
   c. Uses terms correctly in describing ⎯⎯⎯⎯⎯problems.
2. Understands ⎯⎯⎯⎯⎯principles.
   a. Derives ⎯⎯⎯⎯⎯concepts from class experiences.
   b. Describes ⎯⎯⎯⎯⎯principles in own words.
   c. Transposes ⎯⎯⎯⎯⎯selections into own language.
   d. Points out the relationship among ⎯⎯⎯⎯⎯principles.
3. Applies ⎯⎯⎯⎯⎯principles to related situations.
   a. Identifies the ⎯⎯⎯⎯⎯ factors needed to solve a practical problem.
   b. Relates practical life problems to the⎯⎯⎯⎯⎯ principles involved.
   c. Uses⎯⎯⎯⎯⎯ correctly in selected problem situations.
   d. Predicts the probable outcomes of an activity involving ⎯⎯⎯⎯⎯principles.
4. Interprets ⎯⎯⎯⎯⎯data.
   a. Distinguishes between facts and assumptions.
   b. Formulates appropriate problems from provided data.
   c. Identifies bias in provided data.
   d. Differentiates between essential concepts and related details.
5. Synthesizes ⎯⎯⎯⎯⎯concepts.
   a. Derives hypotheses from provided data.
   b. Compiles the essential properties from selected class experiences.
   c. Reconstructs basic ⎯⎯⎯⎯⎯concepts from provided materials.
   d. Creates a new story, formula, music selection, etc., from provided data.
6. Evaluates the adequacy of⎯⎯⎯⎯⎯ principles.
   a. Justifies point of view, based upon sound⎯⎯⎯⎯⎯ principles.
   b. Compares contrasting views within a given context.
   c. Appraises the adequacy of data.
   d. Derives logical conclusions from provided data.

Although a completed outline of instructional objectives applies generally to the subject matter of a course, it does not describe specific content material. Under the objective of *knowing*, for example, the specific items to be learned are not identified. As Gronlund points out,[5] this makes it possible to apply such an outline to various subject areas and thus to various units within a given course.

Recall that some behavioral outcomes must specify the conditions under which the behavior is to be exhibited and the minimum level of performance expected. Such

⎯⎯⎯⎯⎯⎯⎯⎯

[5] Norman E. Gronlund, Stating Behavioral Objectives for Classroom Instruction (New York: The Macmillan Co., 1970), p. 40.

a procedure is desirable for minimum-essentials outcomes but not appropriate for developmental outcomes. The preceding outline is representative of the latter. Although items designed to test for minimum-essentials outcomes may be included in it, they must be evaluated separately.

The next step in preparation for a test is to develop a table in which behavioral outcomes are related to the basic concepts of the unit. These concepts will correspond to those that were developed for instructional purposes. They must be modified in accord with the actual experience, however. Table 14-1 is based on the concepts developed in the illustrated teaching unit offered in Appendix A.

The concepts identified in Table 14-1 represent the major content emphasis, while instructional objectives correspond to the six categories of Bloom's taxonomy.[6] The numbers in each column are the number of items to be prepared at each level for each concept. Note that emphasis is placed on the higher levels of cognition. If instructional methodology is based on processes of reflective thinking (as assumed in this book), this is a valid point of emphasis. Moreover, it must be remembered that the higher objectives necessarily involve attainment of the lower ones. The total number of items in each column indicates the relative emphasis to be given to each of the concepts. Since concepts B and F are to receive the greatest emphasis in the test, they should also receive the strongest emphasis during the instructional process.

How Are Test Levels and Types Selected?

After the terminal behaviors for each unit concept have been identified, the instructor must decide which of these can best be examined through the use of test items and then ascertain the level of goal achievement expected. By referring to Chapter 2, the reader will note that the cognitive domain contains six levels, the affective domain five, and the psychomotor domain four. The three domains range from the simple to the complex, and the lower level objectives are each necessary for the attainment of each succeeding higher level objective. In terms of the actual instructional experience(s), the teacher decides what level of goal attainment might be expected. If, for example, oral reports were employed as the basic means of attaining a given concept, the teacher must judge how effective they were. If they were not as effective as anticipated, test items dealing with the specific concept(s) involved might be restricted to the knowledge or comprehension levels of the cognitive domain.

Identification of goal achievement level provides a sound basis for ascertaining the type of test item to be employed in each case. As indicated in the sections that follow, different test types correspond broadly to the goal levels identified in each of the three instructional domains.

---

[6] Progress toward affective goals is usually best measured by actual observation of behavior. This will involve various techniques of observation, for example, rating scales, checklists, and anecdotal records.

TABLE 14-1 *Specifications for a Sixty-Item Test on a Unit in General Business*
(Sales Promotion and Advertising)

Unit Concepts	Instructional Objectives						Total
	1 Knows Basic Terms	*2* Understands Concepts and Principles	*3* Applies Principles	*4* Interprets Data	*5* Synthesizes Principles	*6* Evaluates Principles	
A. Customer satisfaction is the most important product.	1	4	3				8
B. Customer needs are the prompters for purchasing decisions.			5	5	4	2	16
C. Advertising can be an effective means of preselling products.	2		2	4			8
D. Advertisements use customer motives that can be restated in the personal selling approach.		1	3		3		7
E. The customer market is in a state of constant change and therefore requires continuous study to stay abreast of current developments.	1	1		2	3	2	9
F. Sales appeals must be consistent with ethical standards of advertising.	2		4	3	3		12
Total number of test items							60

How Are Performance Test Items Constructed?

For many years, one of the leading controversies in the area of test construction has been the level of item difficulty needed to determine progress toward goals. Some teachers have assumed that a knowledge of the essential facts in given areas should be sufficient evidence of goal achievement. Others, pointing out the wide gap between knowledge and application, have suggested that more than retention is needed. Although some indication of learning can be ascertained from how well one knows the facts, most teachers would readily agree that the best indication of learning is application to real-life situations.

Especially in the area of motor and mental skills, it is relatively easy to develop tests that demand actual life applications of the concepts involved. The illustrations that follow suggest the wide applicability of performance test items to different areas of specialization.

- Adds fractions correctly.
- Prepares and delivers persuasive speeches effectively.
- Recognizes plant species in the local area.
- Summarizes effectively.
- Speaks in a foreign language.
- Selects art objects that portray a given mood.
- Plays music according to directions.
- Analyzes current events in terms of selected concepts gleaned from history.
- Types _____ words per minute with a maximum of two errors.

It is evident from the preceding illustrations that performance test items can be employed in most subject fields. In skills subjects, some tests are entirely concerned with performance. The items are relatively easy to construct once the desired application has been identified. The major task is to establish the conditions and criteria of acceptable performance. For example, how many plant species in the local area should a student be able to identify and under what conditions? How well must a student speak a foreign language and under what circumstances? How many words per minute should a pupil type?

How Are Situational Test Items Constructed?

Unfortunately, it is not always possible to measure behavioral changes directly. In the first place, the instructor may not have an opportunity to see each pupil in a realistic situation that demands a direct application of the learning involved. Frequently, the outcome will not be applied to any real-life situation for several weeks or even months, simply because learners will not find themselves in a situation demanding such application. The teacher, in an effort to determine degree of understanding, will have to resort to less direct measures. In such instances, one can do no better than to *simulate* an experience involving an appropriate application. For example, in a unit on first aid, one evidence of understanding the principles involved would probably be "The student recognizes a case of shock and administers first aid properly to the victim." It is impractical to induce a case of actual shock for test purposes; it is possible, however, to simulate or act out the experience. Since it is impractical to ask every individual in a thirty-five member class to simulate this experience, providing students with a written description of a realistic situation is the next best alternative. Thus students are measured on the basis of what they would plan to do in the situation rather than on their actual behavior in the situation. Such a procedure obviously is a compromise with what is desired, because people do not always behave the way they plan to behave. For instance, in the previous illustration, a student might provide an adequate plan of action, although in the actual situation, he or she might become hysterical and do nothing. Despite the exceptions, however, an indication of what a person *thinks* he or she would do in a lifelike situation is a reasonably sound prediction of what the individual actually will do. For this very reason, people plan ahead.

Multiple-choice test item.   The multiple-choice item can be readily adapted to the problem-solving situation. Most difficult problems involve making choices between known alternatives. The choices made in relatively simple problem situations often materially affect degree of success and happiness in life. This is not greatly different from the problem a student has in choosing between alternatives on a multiple-choice test item. Experience over many years has convinced test developers of the generally superior versatility and convenience of multiple-choice items. Although other forms can be used effectively in special situations, the multiple-choice is more widely applicable and generally effective.

The multiple-choice question consists of a base question or statement and four or five responses, only one of which is the best answer. The other answers are usually referred to as foils, or distractors. In essence, the base item poses the problem situation, and the possible answers represent the alternative solutions. The student "solves" the problem by making a choice. All the foils, or distractors, should be plausible even to those who lack the necessary understanding of the concept application involved. Some teachers include distractors that all seem quite acceptable, that is, they are accurate statements. Only one of the possible answers is best, however, *in terms of the situation posed.* In general, the possible answers should include *one preferred* answer, a distractor that is almost the correct answer, and another that is clearly erroneous. The remaining distractors tend to fall some place between these two extremes. Teachers sometimes make use of the distractors "all of these" or "none of these." These responses can be used effectively only when the question calls for a highly specific answer that is either completely correct or incorrect.

There are likely to be a number of reasons why students make inappropriate selections for a multiple-choice test. They could misunderstand the base item or any one of the distractors; they could interpret the question in a unique way; or they simply may not possess an adequte understanding of the concepts necessary for the application. If the first two reasons are involved, the item is not valid for *that particular individual.* Sometimes, a teacher desires to achieve greater validity by giving the student an opportunity to qualify or otherwise justify an answer. This enables the instructor to give credit for a choice that might have been justifiably selected *from the student's point of view,* even though it ordinarily would have been considered incorrect. Ultimately, however, the teacher must decide whether or not the reason given is sufficient to warrant either full or partial credit for the response.

A modified, situational form of the multiple-choice test is illustrated below.

Subject: Art

Concept: Color is derived from light.

Item: A. Suppose you were asked to paint a desert landscape that will convey the impression of intense heat, extreme aridity, and yet contain a beauty. How would you choose the colors you would use?
1. Hold your palette up close to the sand and then hold it close to a cactus in order to mix the exact colors of the objects you are painting.
2. Mix your colors according to directions in a book that gives precise formulas for mixing a sky color, a desert color, and a cactus color.
3. Take a photograph of the desert and match the colors in the photograph.
4. Study the color of light reflected on the desert at various times of the day before deciding what colors you will use.
5. Study the color of the sand, rocks, and several different varieties of cactus before deciding what colors you will use.
B. Defend your answer.

Subject: American literature

Concept: Realities of life are not always consistent with ideals.

Item: Crevecoeur's view of "the American Dream" expressed a concern for the people's ideals. Assuming that ideals can act as a force to help overcome harsh realities, which of the following would be most consistent with Crevecoeur's views? (Indicate a reason for your choice, which should be consistent with the idea that ideals can be a force overcoming harsh realities.)

1. Setting our goals as high as possible.
2. Accepting reality as it is, eliminating the stress of striving.
3. Setting concrete and absolute goals for which to strive.
4. Setting our goals at the upper limits of what is reasonable and attainable.

Note that the second item is to be answered in terms of Crevecoeur's views. Teachers should not ask students to respond without providing a specific frame of reference. Doing so forces the student to "outguess" the teacher. The correct answer, under such conditions, is based on the opinion of the teacher only.

If during the instructional process, the teacher did not discuss the same specific situation employed in the items, then the test questions will probably demand knowledge of the facts *in addition* to application of basic ideas (concepts). Thus the student must "go the second mile" to respond properly. The "defend your answer" part of the items serves to probe, still further, one's understanding.

Essay test item. Like the multiple-choice item, the essay item is readily adaptable to a specific situation. Unlike other test item types, it may elicit a detailed written response, involving the making of complex relationships, the selection and organization of ideas, the formulation of hypotheses, the logical development of arguments, and creative expression.

The essay item is particularly vulnerable to unreliability, especially in terms of how it is scored. To some extent, a student's mark is dependent on the reader rather than on the actual quality of a response.

The essay item can be made more reliable if constructed to elicit an application of learnings to new or different situations. Test reliability can be improved by giving directions concerning the structure of the answer expected. Sometimes this is called the *qualified* essay question. Illustrations of the *situational* essay, in which the answer is somewhat qualified, follow:

Subject: Art

Concept: Color is derived from light.

Item: Every color can be described in terms of physical properties: hue, value, and intensity. Discuss the color blue in terms of these properties.

Subject: U.S. History

Concept: Bitter feelings between individuals and nations (for example the Allies and the Central Powers following World War I) make peaceful relationships difficult to establish and maintain.

Item: Wilson urged "peace without victory" at the Versailles Peace Conference. How does this statement relate to our relationships in the Middle East today? Be sure to tie in Wilson's statement with the attitudes and feelings of other members of the peace conference and relate your ideas on the situation to the problems in the Middle East today.

Scoring reliability is substantially improved if the teacher develops an answer key in advance of marking the questions. Sometimes, it is desirable to underline or otherwise call attention to key points. Students also may be asked to underline key phrases. In addition scoring reliability can be increased if the teacher does not know whose paper he or she is correcting until *after* all items have been marked. This may be accomplished by asking the individual to enter his or her name on the back of the test paper. In addition, marking each essay item on each paper without interruption instead of marking each paper completely before proceeding to the next one may greatly enhance scoring consistency. In evaluating the essay item, the teacher must be open to divergent thinking, unanticipated insights and thought patterns that are appropriate to the question but do not match the answers developed on the scoring key. Due credit must be allowed for such divergent responses.

How Are Recall Items Constructed?

Sometimes, teachers assume that if students can recall the important facts in an area, they will make actual applications when needed. Using an illustration cited earlier, one would assume that a student who could describe the symptoms and appropriate treatment for shock would be able to apply that knowledge. Considerable evidence, however, indicates that a broad gap exists between *verbal* understanding and application of that understanding.

True-false item. The true-false item has lost much of its popularity within recent years. There are many serious limitations associated with its use. Among the most serious is the tendency of the user to emphasize isolated facts that hold slight validity in relation to the course objectives. Contrary to popular belief, the true-false item is so difficult to construct that it has little meaning. This type of question tends to penalize the brighter student since he or she is more likely to think of the exception that can alter the intended meaning. Furthermore, test makers tend to make more items true than false, to use specific determiners (*all, never,* or *entirely,* for example), and to use textbook language.

It is possible, however, to improve the true-false item substantially so that it can serve a useful function. For example, in emphasizing broad concepts and selection of alternatives on an exam, one might also test for specified data. In this context, the true-false test item becomes quite useful. The item can be substantially improved by encouraging students to apply a minor concept or generalization in some way. To illustrate in the field of art:

Concept: Color is derived from light.

Item: A red coat will appear red to the eye <u>because it absorbs red color waves and reflects blue color waves.</u>

One of the most important ways of improving the true-false item is to modify it by asking students to correct all incorrect items. In order to guard against the addition or deletion of something like the word "not" as a means of correcting an item, it usually is necessary for the test maker to underline certain key clauses or phrases. The student is asked to change the underlined portion to make the statement correct. If change is necessary, the student should alter the underlined portion only. Students may be allowed some credit for merely recognizing a true or false statement and additional credit for making appropriate corrections.

Completion test item. The completion test item also has been overemphasized. Like the true-false item, its answer is easy to defend merely by referring the student to a particular page in the textbook. As a consequence, specific details and, all too often, meaningless verbalisms are emphasized. The objectives of the course often are forgotten when tests are being constructed. The inevitable result is a tendency to gear the entire instructional process to memorizations. Students, realizing they will be tested in such a manner, tend to study only specific details and terminology and often cram for tests.

Despite the inherent weaknesses of this measurement, there are occasions when the meaning of a term is important enough to employ a completion test. In fact, most tests will contain a limited number of completion items. As its name implies, the item is answered by the completion of a statement. There is an ever-present danger, however, that a statement will be so contrived that the respondent will be unable to understand the meaning intended. For this reason, some teachers have changed the uncompleted statement to a question. To illustrate:

Subject: Art

Concept: Color is derived from light.

Item: The color purple is a combination of _____
              What colors are combined to produce a purple color?_____

Although both forms elicit the same information, the second one is probably easier to answer because it is worded as a complete thought. Furthermore, the answers can be placed in a column to facilitate marking.

Matching test item. Like the completion item, the matching question is of relatively minor importance. It is used when teachers desire students to relate such things as dates and events, terms and definitions, persons and places, or causes and events. Its chief disadvantage is that it does not adapt very well to the measurement of real understandings. Because the separate items in the exercises should be homogeneous in nature, there is the likelihood that test clues will reduce their validity. Multiple-choice items should be used whenever possible to replace the matching test item.

Appropriate use of the item is facilitated by (1) having at least five and not more than twelve responses, (2) including at least three extra choices from which responses must be chosen, and (3) using only homogeneous items or related materials in any one exercise.

How Are Rating Scales Employed?

Although rating scales have been developed and used as effective *measuring* instruments, they are usually most effective as *general guides to evaluation.* Rating scales are used for evaluating situations or characteristics that are present in varying degrees. The word *"scale"* indicates a graduated measurement. Rating scales seem to work best for judging behavior or products that are easily observable. Due to their subjective nature, they are usually used to supplement evaluations or in areas in which more objective instruments are not available.

As in the case of other instruments used for evaluative purposes, the teacher first must decide what is to be judged. If goals have been stated in behavioral terms, the task is relatively easy. The instructional objectives form the main points on the scale. Each trait or dimension to be evaluated is broken down into three or more descriptions, representing qualitites of performance. These are usually arranged systematically below a horizontal line. The evaluator checks each category at the point on the scale that represents the student's level of performance. By writing out somewhat detailed descriptions, greater validity may be assured. The illustration that follows was one teacher's attempt to devise a scale for evaluating the *approach* or *beginning* of an oral presentation. (A complete rating scale is provided in Table 10-1.)

Attention-getting, indicative of general content.	Beginning apparently planned, but effectiveness somewhat lacking.	Beginning poorly given; rambling statements; apologies.

The number of categories for each trait or dimension being scaled has been a subject of some discussion. Generally, the greater the number of categories, the greater the accuracy of the observation will be. Because of the difficulty of constructing and using several categories, many teachers prefer scales with three to five categories.

The reliability of a rating scale can be improved if the rater is permitted to disregard any dimension(s) that does not seem to be present in sufficient quantity for an evaluation. Somewhat related to this is the problem of agreement between observations or observers. For many purposes, at least three observations should be obtained. By pooling the judgment of a number of persons, greater reliability can be achieved.

Another technique for increasing validity is use of an *anchor item,* thus enabling the observer to make a general appraisal of the effectiveness displayed. An anchor item may be necessary for several reasons. In the first place, construction of a rating scale makes it necessary for the user to predict all dimensions of importance in the performance. Seldom is this possible, especially when one considers the wide variability of student personalities in a heterogeneous group of youngsters. Furthermore, there is some evidence that a general impression dimension, although inadequate as the *only* criterion, may effectively serve as *one* criterion.

The fallacy of using a rating scale as a *measuring* instrument becomes evident when one realizes that, based on normal variability, the units or categories are arbitrary and the comparative interval sizes are not equal at all points along the continuum. For example, small differences at the extreme "desirable" or "undesirable" end of the scale indicate a greater variation than an equal difference at the middle of the scale. Thus one person may earn an "average" score on the basis of an "average" rating on all dimensions. On a similar scale, another student may receive a better-than-average score even though one or two dimensions are extremely weak. The scores may not be indicative of the relative worth of the performances, as indicated by the following illustrations.

> Mary was awarded a numerical score near the average category on the basis of the following dimensions deemed important in an oral report: lesson beginning, audience contact, enthusiasm, content, audience reaction, objectivity, use of communication skills (voice, posture, articulation, etc.). She was rated near average on *all* dimensions.

> Susie was awarded an above-average score on the basis of the same dimensions. Although she was especially strong in most traits, she received very low ratings on content and communication skills. These low ratings, however, still enabled Susie to earn more points than Mary.

It should be obvious, therefore, that extremely low (or high) ratings on one or more dimensions can, in effect, render all other dimensions valueless. A *numerical score* sometimes fails to reveal special weaknesses or strengths.

Many teachers, instead of attempting to use the rating scale to *measure* dimensions of a performance, use the ratings as *guidelines* in *evaluating* the performance. The need for some systematic scheme or measure is, however, a real one. Students frequently have difficulty understanding the limitations of the rating scale, and teachers themselves often want an instrument that can be somewhat more standardized. This has led to interesting modifications. One is to group the traits or dimensions being evaluated into three or four broad categories. When using such a scheme one must understand that a very low rating on any one dimension within a given group or category will render the entire category ineffective. Three such categories as bases for evaluating oral presentations might be delivery, content, and audience reaction. In some cases, however, the teacher-made rating scale is used as a *measuring* instrument if the likelihood of extremely low ratings appears remote.

Table 10-1 represents a rating scale for evaluating oral presentations. The instrument is illustrative of four broad categories or dimensions, suggested to minimize the effect of extremely low (or high) ratings on certain dimensions.

In addition to the preceding problems associated with the use of rating scales, the user should be aware of certain other factors that can limit their usefulness.

1. *"Halo" effect.* This factor seems to be associated with a response set of the person or object being rated. While there is some basis for the belief that it

helps to reverse some of the dimensions being evaluated, some teachers find the practice a bit confusing.

2. Tendency to avoid extremes.
3. *Personal bias.* This factor can cause a rater to exaggerate certain dimensions and to minimize others in terms of his or her preconceived ideas.

Despite the many errors commonly associated with rating scales, they do serve a useful purpose and should be included in every instructional program. There are numerous characteristics that can be assessed only through observational procedures. A number of personality traits, however, can be evaluated by using rating scales. These include efficiency, originality, perserverance, quickness, judgment, energy, scholarship, and leadership. As more precise definitions are developed, other personality traits may soon receive a fair evaluation from rating scales.

When Are Checklists Used?

A checklist differs from a rating scale in that no effort is made to evaluate the dimensions. Its chief function is to call attention to the items themselves rather than to their relative importance. The instrument has many uses. It often is used when some standardized sequence of operation is involved, such as in a laboratory experiment. Sometimes, it is used to note certain characteristics, such as the qualities of some finished product, or to record the completion points of some class project in art, industrial arts, or home economics. The dramatics teacher frequently employs a checklist when preparing for stage productions as does the physical education instructor in teaching the skills associated with baseball, for example.

What Is the Role of Feedback in Testing Procedures?

All tests (with the possible exception of a final exam) can be used as learning devices. Each test should be graded and then discussed with students not later than the following class period. (Behaviorists, such as B.F. Skinner, recommend breaking a test into parts small enough to facilitate feedback the very same class period.) The teacher should begin the discussion by first calling attention to the concept involved *and then* identifying those items that call for application of the identified concept. *Then,* new concept applications should be introduced in order to extend the processes of reflection.

Students who had extreme difficulty with the test are often too preoccupied with their low scores to profit substantially from the follow-up discussion. Yet these are the individuals who most need this type of feedback. One technique for coping with this problem is to divide the class into three subgroups: high, average, and low achievers. Usually the high achiever group can clarify misconceptions with little or no direct help from the teacher. The middle group should be helped by a teaching assistant or by one or two of the high achievers. The low achiever group needs direct assistance from the instructor. The realization that others also experienced difficulty may help relieve the anxieties and frustrations of these pupils. By taking the time to meet with these students, the teacher communicates the very important message "I do care"; "I sincerely desire to help you learn."

Low achievers are further encouraged when given an opportunity to "try again." (This is a basic essential of all criterion-referenced evaluation, treated in Chapter 15). Although students may not be able to earn extra credit by taking a follow-up norm-referenced test, such an exam can do much to enhance learning and give low achievers renewed confidence in their abilities. Normally, one class period can be profitably devoted to a follow-up of a test. This discussion, of course, should be followed with individual assistance as needed.

Frequent quizzes are also useful for providing feedback and increasing learning. Based on a review of several recent instructional innovations, Kulik and Jaksa have concluded that formative quizzes, especially when immediate feedback is provided, can have a substantial impact on final examination performance.[7] They note that performance is higher when students repeat quizzes until mastery is demonstrated.

How Are Test Results Used?

Any test worth giving is worthy of review. This, of course, entails much more than merely clarifying those items that were missed. The concept (on which each item is based) must be clearly identified and other illustrations provided to enable the learner to perceive the necessary applications. Some teachers systematically review all major tests with students, item by item. Generally, such a practice is to be discouraged, especially when the tests are objective in nature, since the lesson can easily deteriorate into a bickering session with students who see an opportunity for talking the teacher into "additional credit." A better procedure is to analyze general areas of difficulty and to use them as a basis for reviewing items selectively.

A student who incorrectly responds to a given test item is admitting a learning deficiency. By examining all items devoted to each concept, the teacher may obtain a reasonably sound basis for remedial instruction. If all or most class members display similar problems, special group activities may be provided. Many, if not most, deficiencies, however, will be individual in nature. This necessitates individualized remedial instructional. Generally, each individual should be given additional opportunities to make conceptual applications in the areas of deficiency evidenced on his or her test paper. These may take the form of a subsequent test, or they may merely involve informal written statements pertaining to areas of deficiency. When the instructor is satisfied that deficiencies have been corrected, partial credit may be allowed for the effort made.

---

[7] James A. Kulik and Peter Jaksa, "PSI and Other Educational Technologies in College Teaching," *Educational Technology* 56 (September 1977): 12-19.

The author has found that students often appreciate brief explanations of why certain responses were considered incorrect. This, however, can easily deteriorate into clashes between student and teacher. One technique of minimizing this problem is to ask students to request a rereading of certain items (on the top of the first page of the test). This enables the instructor to reconsider answers without undue pressure. Changes that affect a student's stanine (or other standard score) can be brought to their attention. Those students who still have questions should be able to confer with the instructor privately. In particular, students who experienced considerable difficulty on the examination should be encouraged to confer privately with the instructor.

The Value of Tests

When used appropriately, test items offer a sound measure of the learner's ability to apply what has been learned.

Diagnostic tests help both the learner and the teacher identify areas in which relearning and reteaching are needed.

The quantitative nature of test results accommodates group evaluation. Thus test results are often more valid than results obtained through other measures.

Test items are extremely flexible. By using various types, the teacher can assess almost any level of goal attainment. This applies especially to the cognitive domain.

Tests, when used appropriately, can motivate the learner to greater effort. Students must be assured a reasonable chance of success, however. Competition with bright, or even average, students for class marks is self-defeating for less able students.

Limitations of, and Problems with, Tests

A student's achievement on teacher-made tests is often *inappropriately* assessed in terms of all other students in class. Mastery testing must be made independent of class standing.

Tests that demand mere recall of information tend to relegate learning to memorization. While some items appropriately should test recall of facts, more items should test the achievement of important class goals through instructional techniques and problem-solving techniques. Accordingly, testing devices should seek to determine progress in these areas.

Passing tests has often become the end of education, at least in the minds of many students. While appropriate tests themselves should measure progress toward more basic goals, the *intent to remember and to apply beyond the confines of a test* is an extremely important psychological principle.

Tests, as often used in today's schools, tend to encourage cheating and other forms of dishonesty. Also involved may be the development of some form of status order that is often closely related to community social class lines.

Evaluation, when overemphasized, tends to be made at the expense of other, more effective instructional procedures. Furthermore, the difficulty of evaluating certain basic educational goals (affective goals, for example) tends to limit the extent to which they will be taught and achieved.

Whenever possible, situational items are emphasized in the selected illustrations.

MULTIPLE-CHOICE ITEMS

I. Useful in biology classes

Unit: Similarities and Variations

Concept: Mendelian ratios explain the basic principles of heredity.

Item

  A. You purchased certified hollyhock seeds two years ago and their quality was exceptionally high, producing double white flowers. Those seeds that germinated the following year, however, produced many unsightly, single-petaled flowers. Which of the following probably accounts for your inferior flowers?
   1. Double whites were pollinated by red recessive singles.
   2. Dominant red singles pollinated the double whites.
   3. A mutation accounted for the changes.
   4. The multiple whites were incompletely dominant for color and petal.
   5. All hybrid flowers in the second generation reverted back to the original characteristics.

  B. Defend your answer.

II. Useful in chemistry classes

Unit: The Gas Laws

Concept: The volume of a gas is directly proportional to temperature.

Item

  A. The main function of baking powder is to furnish CO_2 gas in order that the cake will be light. Which of the following would you do to make a cake in an area where the altitude is 20,000 feet above sea level?
   1. Increase the measure of baking powder.
   2. Decrease the measure of baking powder.
   3. Leave it out altogether.
   4. Use the amount you would use at sea level.

  B. Explain your answer.

III. Useful in mathematics classes

Unit: Financial Matters

Concept: Taxes are an essential part of the American economy.

Item

A. If the tax on your property is 3 per cent of the assessed valuation, which one of the following would be representative of this assessment?
    1. .30 per $1.00 assessed valuation.
    2. $10.00 per $1,000 assessed valuation.
    3. 30 mills per $1.00 assessed valuation.
    4. $30.00 per $100 assessed valuation.
B. Support your answer by computing a 3 percent property tax for assessed values of $1.00, $100, and $1,000.

IV. Useful in home economics classes

Unit: Marriage

Concept: Each marriage partner must be flexible for a satisfying marriage relationship.

Item

A. Because of financial difficulties, Pam has decided to take a job, even though both she and her husband would prefer that she not work. Which of the following adjustments is probably most basic?
    1. Changed role patterns for each partner.
    2. Changed decision-making pattern relative to financial matters.
    3. Changed attitude toward each other's work.
    4. A flexible scheduling of meals.
    5. All of these of equal importance.
B. Defend your answer.

ESSAY ITEMS

I. Useful in biology classes

Unit: Similarities and Variations

Concept: Mendelian ratios explain the basic principles of heredity.

Item

The offspring of a cross between a white snapdragon and a red snapdragon yields a plant with pink flowers. A cross of two of the pinks yields white and red offspring. Explain the Mendelian law implied here, illustrating the expected ratios of the second filial generation.

II. Useful in English literature classes

Unit: The Aspiring Mind of the Elizabethan Period

Concept: Fusion of Greco-Roman dramatic principles with English content and exuberance brought about a mature, artistic drama.

Item

A drama, to be popular, has to contain an appeal. Discuss features of *Macbeth* that have such an appeal. Treat the following aspects: atmosphere, movement, poetry, and character development.

III. Useful in American literature classes

Unit: The Beginnings of the American Tradition

Concept: Political writers influenced the development of democratic ideals.

Item

Select three of Thomas Jefferson's political ideals, contained in the Declaration of Independence, and tell what they mean today.

IV. Useful in industrial arts classes

Unit: Precision Measurement and Systems Used

Concept: Proper care and use of precision measuring instruments are essential to their accuracy.

Item

In cutting a block of steel to 1.500" square on a milling machine, give the sequence to follow, including precautionary steps to take before and during the squaring operation.

V. Useful in physical education classes

Unit: Teamwork in Sports and Society

Concept: Teamwork is an excellent method for attaining goals.

Item

John and five of his classmates have been assigned the problem of reporting the life of Babe Ruth. John feels the other members are not putting forth a very effective team effort. Discuss the steps that John should take to make the team more effective.

TRUE-FALSE ITEMS

I. Useful in home economics classes

    Unit: Marriage

    Concept: Many factors influence marriage success.

    Item

        In the film *Are You Ready for Marriage?* the marriage of Bill and Mary was threatened because Mary was career minded.

    Concept: Marriage customs vary from one culture to another.

    Item

        In the child-rearing customs of Japan, the male was highly favored because someday he would be the authority of the household.

II. Useful in English literature classes

    Unit: The Aspiring Mind of the Elizabethan period

    Concept: Ambition can work to the benefit or detriment of the individual.

    Item

        An individual told to accomplish something must do everything he or she is told to do in order to accomplish the goal.

    Concept: Emancipation of restricted classes provides new opportunities for individuals in all aspects of life.

    Item

        The lower social classes accomplished more during the Elizabethan period than in the Middle Ages because the European governments paid them extra for overtime.

EVALUATION PROCEDURES

Key Concepts

1. The attainment of minimum-essentials objectives, to be achieved by *all* students, is judged by absolute measures rather than by the relative scores of individuals in class.
2. Developmental objectives, to be achieved in varying degrees by different students, may be assessed in terms of the class norm.
3. Evaluational experiences, when interpreted in terms of group performance, are recorded as *standard* (as opposed to *raw*) scores.
4. Standard scores (letter or stanine marks) are based on the normal probability curve and thus can be weighted directly and combined for marking purposes. (Raw scores cannot be so combined.)
5. A good test item (when used to measure developmental objectives) has a difficulty value of between 50 and 60 percent.
6. Validity of class marks is increased when many different dimensions of performance are assessed.
7. Grading on the basis of the normal probability curve is based on the assumption that every individual has a reasonably equal chance of success.

New Terms

1. Normal Probability Curve   The expected frequency distribution (bell-shaped) in any unselected group. Scores characteristically cluster near the middle and taper off uniformly toward each extreme.
2. Standard Score   Derived from a raw score, a standard score is based on a uniform standard scale (*normal probability curve*). Its use simplifies comparisons and interpretations of scores on different tests.
4. Minimum Passing Score   The lowest score that can satisfy a particular requirement. It essentially separates students into "pass" or "fail" groups. Determination usually involves a number of somewhat arbitrary decisions.

5. Formative Evaluation Tests and other techniques used during the instructional process as teaching tools. Examples include pretests, self-assessment items, diagnostic measures, and posttests.

6. Summative Evaluation Tests and other techniques used to assess achievement of overall objectives. This type of evaluation is not instructional in nature, if no feedback is possible.

Questions to Guide Your Study

1. In theory, what would be the lowest acceptable score on a minimum-essentials test? Why would acceptable standards vary in practical class situations?

2. What basic assumptions are associated with the normal probability curve? How valid are such assumptions in today's secondary school?

3. Why is marking on the basis of the normal probability curve more appropriate in homogeneously grouped classes than in nonselected groups?

4. What is the relationship between traditional percentage marks and the normal probability curve? Which of the two is more realistic today?

5. What advantages do standard scores have over the mere accumulation of raw score points?

6. Less emphasis should be devoted to tests and grading in today's colleges and universities. Defend or refute.

Although certain measuring instruments can be scored objectively, evaluation and reporting techniques are highly subjective. In the final analysis, the instructor *and* students must judge the worth of basic learning experiences. The process, however, need not be haphazard or unscientific. Some traditional practices are based on faulty assumptions; others are used for purposes of expediency. Therefore, the problems treated in this chapter were selected in order to disclose certain misconceptions (as in the case of combining test scores) and to offer sound techniques economical in time and effort (for example, stanine distribution techniques).

Fundamental Properties

Evaluation, perhaps more than any other aspect of teaching, reflects a teacher's value system, something that must be thoroughly examined and re-examined as time and local conditions change. It is hoped that this section will enable the practitioner to develop an evaluational procedure consistent with current instructional technology.

What Is the Difference between Formative and Summative Evaluation Tests?

It is a well-known fact that considerable student anxiety is associated with college and university testing practices. All too often, one or two tests become the major factors in determining a student's grade for a course. It is not unusual for some students to stay up all night prior to an important test, "cramming" for the big event. Such a state of affairs has resulted recently in a de-emphasis on grades and grading at a time when the public is demanding a "return to the basics."

Evaluation done at the end of a course is called *summative* evaluation. The purpose of the test, according to Bloom and others,[1] is to determine the degree to which the more comprehensive outcomes have been reached. Usually, the only feedback to the student is a final grade for the course. Since grades in most courses reflect (at least in part) a student's standing relative to other students in class, summative tests usually are norm-referenced exams. It is not possible or perhaps wise to abolish summative evaluation. Rather than do this, the professor should emphasize *formative* evaluation throughout a course as an aid to learning.

Formative evaluation is done during instruction when the primary aim is to improve learning. Formative tests may take many forms. First, *pretests* may be used to determine what students already know about the material to be taught. Thus repetition can be avoided and new material can be linked with prior learning. As Hartley and Davies point out,[2] pretests can also increase students' sensitivity to the learning situation, alert them to unnoticed issues and problems, and help them perceive the basic structure of the learning task. From examination of considerable research evidence, Hartley and Davies suggest that detailed knowledge of results has a positive effect on subsequent learning. In fact, many current self-instructional learning modules and programs include feedback. For example, the author's book, *Secondary/Middle School Teaching: A Handbook for Beginning Teachers and Teacher Self-Renewal* includes answers to all pretest items and explanations for each answer.[3] Moreover, on the basis of field testing, pretests have been relabeled "preassessment items" at the suggestions of students. Pretests should be comprehensive, including all the important elements of a unit. They should be identical or similar to posttests.

Another type of formative test is the *self-assessment exam.* These tests are conceptual in nature and given at intervals, usually following each major class activity.

---

[1] Benjamin S. Bloom et al, *Handbook on Formative and Summative Evaluation of Learning* (New York: McGraw-Hill Book Company, 1971) ch. 4.

[2] James Hartley and Ivor K. Davies, "Preinstructional Strategies: The Role of Pretests, Behavioral Objectives, Overviews and Advance Organizers," *Review of Educational Research* 46, no. 2 (Spring 1976): 241-42.

[3] Kenneth H. Hoover, *Secondary/Middle School Teaching: A Handbook for Beginning Teachers and Teacher Self-Renewal* (Boston: Allyn and Bacon, Inc., 1977).

They may be an oral or written exercise. Whatever their form, feedback must be provided. To illustrate in the area of measurement and evaluation:

> Many beginners find that the stems of multiple-choice items become rather complex, opening the door for more than one interpretation or frame of reference. How can this problem be minimized?[4]

Still another type of formative test is the *diagnostic test.* Diagnostic tests are used at the beginning of instruction to place students according to ability and throughout the instruction, to identify learning deficiencies. The pretest may serve this first function, and all other types of tests may be useful in detecting deficiencies. Once an area of deficiency has been identified, the diagnostic test examines the area thoroughly to identify the major source(s) of difficulty blocking progress.

A final type of formative evaluation test is the *posttest,* a paper or project required near the end of the instructional unit or module. If mastery has not been achieved, some review or optional activities are provided. For example, the learner may be given help in revising or reworking a written assignment. Enough time must be allowed in the instructional schedule for the learner to complete the additional tasks. *A posttest is not a summative test,* however, since it is given during the course. Upon satisfactory completion of all posttests over a given period of time (the first half of the course, for example), the learner should be well prepared for a summative (midterm or final) test.

The anxieties associated with traditional summative testing can be substantially minimized if formative testing is used often and judiciously to provide needed feedback as learning progresses. *The traditional midterm and final test (summative in nature) are today as desirable and useful as they were in the past.* Their function, however, is relatively minor in comparison with the many types of formative tests.

What Is the Difference between Criterion-referenced and Norm-referenced Evaluation?

Traditionally, performance has been assessed on the basis of a student's relative position within the class. Although norm-referenced assessment procedures may reveal where each student stands on a random collection of test items, they do not provide an adequate sample of learning outcomes sought *or indicate the overall achievement of the group.* Perhaps, the best way of improving assessment procedures is to develop test items and devices consistent with the behavioral outcomes developed during preplanned instructional experiences and to devise at least some criterion-referenced measures for assessing mastery.

---

[4] Ibid., p. 324.

Recall from Chapter 2 that there are two kinds of behavioral outcomes: minimum essentials and developmental. Minimum-essentials assessment is limited to fairly short units (modules) of work in the skills area. Mastery in the skills area is a prerequisite for further learning. A spread of scores is not sought. Each student is expected to demonstrate mastery before being permitted to proceed to the next related experience. (It is assumed that all students if given enough time can reach mastery level.) This involves criterion-referenced assessment.

Developmental assessment involves the more complex realms of learning. Since *varying degrees of goal achievement* are expected, a spread of scores is sought. Degree of mastery is probably best determined by an individual's relative position in the total class group. This involves norm-referenced assessment.

Some combination of criterion-referenced and norm-referenced assessment is recommended for the purpose of assigning grades. Indeed both types of items may be included on the same test. The tests must be scored separately, however. Students who fail to reach mastery level on the criterion-referenced items can be given incomplete grades until mastery has been achieved, or else they must be failed. Different grades then may be awarded on the basis of relative mastery on norm-referenced items.

Many professors evaluate term papers and projects on the basis of criterion-referenced scales. Thus achievement is based on individual performance as an absolute standard. *When evaluated by criterion-referenced measures, papers and projects must be rejected until they meet each of the established criteria.* Thus some students must rewrite papers one or more times. This means more work for both instructor and student at a time when end-of-term pressures are high. As indicated in Chapter 4, the liberal use of incomplete grades usually becomes necessary. The author has found that thoroughly explaining term-paper criteria to students near the time when they are preparing for these projects can be most effective in improving the quality of work submitted. Providing illustrated samples of areas where other students have had difficulty meeting the criteria is also most helpful.

All too often, teachers assess term papers and projects by using criterion-referenced measures. Later, however, when they grade the papers, the teacher passes some as long as they meet some of the established criteria. Thus a student might be awarded a C for meeting some of the criteria reasonably well. This represents a violation of adequate criterion-referenced assessment. As Popham points out, "... users of criterion-referenced tests [or other measures] unthinkingly rely on normative data as a determiner of performance standards."[5] Instead, a careful analysis of how well each of the established criteria has been met is essential in deciding proficiency standards. Since mastery is essential in *some areas of most courses,* some tests or parts of tests must be evaluated using criterion-referenced measures.

---

[5]W. James Popham, "Normative Data for Criterion-Referenced Tests," *Phi Delta Kappan* 57 (May 1976): 593-94.

What Are the Relative Merits of Maximum, Minimum, and Multiple Standards?

Maximum standards usually are set above the ability level of all but the most capable students in class. Under a satisfactory standard of 60 or 70 percent of the maximum, most students have an opportunity for success. Such a system works fairly well in relatively select groups. Most college classes today, however, are heterogeneous. Often as many as one-half of the class members may be *unable* to achieve acceptable maximum standards. Realizing the state of affairs, many individuals cease to try for maximum achievement. Thus both teacher and student often become extremely frustrated.

Some teachers have attempted to modify the procedure by lowering the level of maximum standards to enable most students to succeed. Although rewarding to the mediocre student, this practice tends to create problems for more able students. They find it possible to succeed with a minimum of effort. High standards of achievement cease to hold meaning for them.

Other instructors have attempted to resolve the difficulty by applying the normal distribution curve to the various degrees of achievement. (The normal distribution curve is discussed more fully later in this chapter.) A rigid interpretation of the normal curve guarantees a fixed number of top marks and an equal number of low marks. Too frequently, this results in marks based on *ability* rather than on *achievement.* In effect, this solution may result in a complete lack of standards since students come to realize the futility of competing with others of different abilities.

A teacher expects every student to demonstrate certain *minimum standards* within the capacity range of all students. Those with greater ability and interest will be able to advance well beyond these standards and are encouraged to do additional assignments on the basis of their own or the teacher's suggestions. Scores on a *minimum-essentials test* should be almost perfect—allowing for errors of reliability and validity. Deficiencies are corrected through repeated teaching and testing.

Work beyond the minimum is evaluated *in terms of the individual involved.* Since all students are expected to progress beyond the minimum, even the smallest achievement will warrant credit for some pupils. Evaluation of work beyond the minimum is based on a number of factors, such as effort, achievement, thoroughness, neatness, and time involved. Due recognition can be given for special reports, for example. Whenever possible, the student is given an opportunity to pursue special interests *after* minimum standards have been satisfied. Some teachers construct tests with two kinds of questions: Those that measure achievement of minimum essentials and those that determine *degree of progress* toward developmental instructional goals. Near perfect scores are expected on the minimum-essentials questions. Answers to questions that determine progress toward developmental goals are evaluated in terms of the relative scores of all comparable class members.

By establishing *multiple standards* to operate in parallel, a teacher allows students to pursue special interests and at the same time, to meet basic course requirements. Vocational courses have been set up in this manner. Sometimes multiple standards are applied to project work of all kinds. There is no necessity for lowering standards to reduce failures since pupils can find success in numerous ways. Each pupil is judged on his or her own merits. Although multiple standards have been used effectively in small classes, the method soon becomes unwieldy in large classes. With thirty-five to forty students in any given class, there may be little chance for making the procedure operational.

The reader will note that little attempt has been made to recommend one type of standard over another. As indicated, much of the decision must be based on the particular circumstances in which teachers find themselves. Some teachers have solved the problem by applying a combination of minimum and multiple standards. Others have developed a system of flexible subgrouping within the classroom to facilitate the establishment of maximum standards. Teachers will undoubtedly want to develop their own set of standards subject to modification as circumstances permit. What *does* seem important, however, is that every student must be given an opportunity to succeed relative to his or her own capacities, according to some defensible standard of performance.

What Are the Relative Merits of Growth versus Status Marking?

Recognizing extreme differences in ability, some teachers prefer to assess achievement in terms of individual growth rather than in terms of one's status among peers. Such a practice is defensible when *one assesses mastery of minimum essentials.* As indicated in Chapter 14, however, minimum-essentials marking is most effective in the skills area and at the lower levels of cognition. Logically, it might seem reasonable to carry the procedure one step further by establishing initial base performance on the basis of pretest and other preliminary observations. Differences between these and subsequent test scores and other measures would thus provide a reasonable estimate of growth.

Unfortunately, there are a number of serious problems associated with this procedure. Among the most serious is the inability to assess a student's standing in class. A weak student, for example, may make remarkable progress in an area such as mathematics but still be well below the competence level of the class. A "high" mark on a test in terms of growth does little to encourage students when they realize that their progress is poor in comparison with the rest of the class. Students realize that competence is what counts, that rate of growth is important only to the extent that it contributes to class standing.

In addition, each test contains errors of measurement.[6] For most teacher-made

---

[6] An error of measurement is the difference between an obtained score and the corresponding true score. If it were possible to administer a test several times, then one's average score could be said to represent one's true score. Usually, however, a test is administered only once. Thus allowances must be made for expected differences between the actual score and one's theoretically true score.

tests of forty-nine items or less, the estimated error of measurement is approximately three score points. Thus differences between individual pretest and posttest scores frequently will result from errors of measurement. Still another difficulty is the ceiling level for better students. An individual who already knows the answers to a considerable number of pretest items, for example, may find it extremely difficult to demonstrate actual rate of growth. In actual practice, or course, students soon get testwise, making sure that their pretest scores will be low enough to allow for reasonable improvement.

Assessment based on growth rate obviously creates a dilemma for the teacher. On the one hand, the weak student is encouraged when he or she is rewarded for mediocre work that may indeed represent superior progress for the individual involved. On the other hand, the student soon realizes that such achievement does not really measure up to the rest of the class. If status marking is employed, however, such an individual experiences continual frustration and discouragement if he or she happens to be in a class with students of much higher ability.

In resolving the dilemma, the teacher should first expect all students to master the minimum essentials. Individuals who do not should be required to repeat the course until they do achieve this minimum level. (If the existing school program does not permit this type of recycling, such persons should be failed.) It is unrealistic to "pass" an individual who cannot cope with the minimum essentials of a course. (Such criterion-referenced measures are assessed independently of the achievement of other students in class.) Progress beyond the minimum essentials (achievement of developmental objectives) should be made on the basis of standing in the class. As Ebel suggests,[7] the alert teacher provides opportunities for various kinds of achievement. Thus status or norm-referenced marking need not mean that some students will always "win" while others will always "lose." Success is important to each person, but none of us should expect to succeed all the time. By the same token, none of us should be placed in a position of failing all the time.

How Is the Minimum Passing Score Determined?

In theory, the minimum passing score on a minimum-essentials (criterion-referenced) test is a perfect score. Since test perfection and flawless performance are ideals seldom reached, a minimum passing score of 80 to 90 percent is usually recommended. At the present time, this figure is more or less arbitrarily established.

In norm-referenced tests, a minimum passing score is perhaps more arbitrary than in minimum-essentials tests. The actual scores are influenced by many factors such as type of item, whether the test is "hard" or "easy," the ability level of the student, and

---

[7]Robert L. Ebel, *Essentials of Educational Measurement* (Englewood Cliffs, N.J., Prentice-Hall, Inc., 1972) p. 331.

how well the concepts have been taught, for example. With true-false items, for example, there is an expected chance score of 50 percent. Similarly, the multiple-choice item (with four alternatives) produces an expected chance score of 25 percent. Ebel has described several ways of ascertaining an appropriate minimum passing score. Unfortunately, some of the techniques are somewhat laborious or difficult in design. As a general rule of thumb, the passing score may be defined as the midpoint between the mean or average score and the lowest score. Since this is a rather arbitrary determination, considerable flexibility and good judgment must be exercised.

What Are Some Problems in Combining Test Scores?

Professor Martin has developed a point system to assist in evaluational procedures. Although he gives students some indication of mark equivalents on each test or exercise, he enters raw scores in his record book, reasoning that the raw scores on each test can be added, with perhaps some additional weight given to the final test. He considers the individual tests as constituting parts of one big test on the entire course.

While Martin's system of evaluation can be defended on logical grounds, it has at least two serious disadvantages.

1. Mark equivalents on each test are not likely to correspond to the final letter-grade standing at the end of the course. Although it is not always necessary to indicate mark equivalents on separate tests, most students like to know where they stand. Furthermore, knowledge of progress is a sound psychological principle that seems to enhance learning.
2. When several tests are combined, those with greater variability have greater weights. The point is illustrated by the following examples.

Timothy made the top score (80 points) on a unit test covering three weeks of material. At the end of the next unit (also covering three weeks of material), he made a top C, with a score of 50 points. When the two numerical scores were combined, he had a total of 130 points.

Nadine, on the other hand, made a top C on the first test, but because of less variability in the scores, she earned 60 raw score points. On the next test, however, she made the top score, which was 80 points. When the two test scores were combined, she had a total of 140 points.

If the tests were supposed to be of equal importance, they were not. The discrepancy tends to become even more pronounced when a unit test is compared to a final examination. Let us suppose that the range for one unit test is 30 points, whereas the range in the longer final test is 90 points. If the raw scores are added, the final test actually counts three times as much as the unit test because it has three times the variability of the unit test. A teacher (unaware of the influence of variability) may decide to double the weight of the final test by multiplying the scores by two. Actually, however, the final test now receives a weight of six, instead of two.

Although it is true that a test of greater variability *may* be more reliable, the difference in variability is more likely attributable to the arbitrary nature of different units of measurement in the two tests. In a practical classroom situation, it is extremely unlikely that variability of tests of equal importance can be kept equal. The range difference between the two tests will be as much as 30 points for no apparent reason. It is possible to correct for this difference by adding a constant to the test with least variability, but most students are unlikely to understand the real reason for such a practice.[8]

The most reliable procedure is to convert scores on each test to some type of standard score. Teachers traditionally have used a five-point system of letter marks for this purpose. It should be pointed out, however, that through such a procedure, information is lost unless a plus-and-minus system is added. This, of course, takes considerable time and effort. A preferable system involves the use of stanine scores, described later in this chapter. Stanine scores can be readily added and then averaged for the purpose of deriving grades. Furthermore, under the Stanine system of measurement, point scores are grouped into more divisions (nine instead of five), thereby making the standard score more accurate. In other words, there are likely to be fewer objections from those who miss a mark by one or two score points. For example, a C is automatically divided into three categories, with stanines of 4, 5, and 6. By converting each set of scores into standard scores, the teacher can quite easily assign different weights to them when they are combined at the end of the course.

There is one occurrence, however, that should be taken into account when standard scores are averaged. That is the tendency for marks *to regress toward the mean or average.* Thus progress of weaker students will tend to be less than indicated. Similarly, actual progress of better students will tend to be more than indicated. To illustrate:

> Jack made a top mark on one test, but could not do better than a B on the next one. Even if he made A's on every subsequent test, it would be difficult to bring his final mark up to an A, simply because it represents the highest mark possible.

> Tommy, however, made a D on one test. With a reasonable amount of effort, he can earn a B on the next one. Thus, it will not be too difficult for him to maintain a C average.

The problem may be corrected at the end of the course by subjecting the final average stanine (or letter mark) to a frequency distribution. Thus a stanine average of 7.3 *may* be sufficient for a mark of A. Such an evaluation would depend on the percent of A's deemed appropriate by the instructor.

---

[8] For a thorough description of the technique, the reader is referred to Robert L. Ebel, *Essentials of Educational Management*, pp. 348-51.

There has been a great deal of controversy concerning the relative percentages of marks. Much depends on the *quality* of student performance, which is also a reflection of the individual teacher's effort. As indicated earlier, marking on the basis of the normal curve is dependent on each student's having a *fairly equal chance* and on the teacher's having a *representative sampling* of students. When these two conditions are met, the percentages developed for the use of stanines seem to be reasonable. Teachers must bear in mind, however, that normal achievement is expected under normal conditions only. They may have helped their group make a greater achievement than was expected, however. If so, they would be fully justified in assigning a higher percentage of high marks than low marks. In the final analysis, the teacher is responsible for determining the number (if any) who should fail, the number who should make A's, and the like. The normal curve concept can serve as a guide only.

Techniques of Evaluation

The measuring instruments discussed in Chapter 14 are merely tools to facilitate evaluation. A superior test has minimal value in the hands of an incompetent evaluator. Unfortunately, cases of incompetence do exist. At least some of the difficulties can be attributed to the rapidly changing nature of colleges and universities.

Today's college instructor, in attempting to accommodate the needs of a diverse range of students, finds many conventional evaluational techniques partially or wholly invalid. The time-honored practice of evaluating each individual in terms of his or her relative class standing, for example, is highly questionable in classes where the ability range is great. It is equally inappropriate when the ethnic or cultural backgrounds of various class members are different.

What Statistical Concepts Are Essential?

Time after time classroom instructors must find a way of making raw scores meaningful. The scores, in and of themselves, have very little meaning until they are compared to some sort of previously developed criterion or standard. *Ideally,* this standard would be a comparison of a student's performance with his or her own capacities. In courses that rely heavily on performance, it is relatively easy to evaluate a student on this basis, as the following demonstrates:

Mary was delivering her fourth prepared speech. Mr. Brody noted definite and consistent progress in several areas. He had before him a rating scale of each of Mary's previous performances. Although Mary's speech was below that of many of the other students in class, *for her* it represented satisfactory and consistent improvement.

Tom's performance was at least as good as Mary's, but for *him* it represented unsatisfactory progress. Tom had started the year off with a superior performance, but his work has declined ever since then. Mr. Brody noted that he had to repeat suggestions for improvement on each succeeding speech critique. He guessed that Tom had only devoted a few minutes before the class to preparing his speech.

Evaluating performance on the basis of individual progress can be applied to courses in speech, home economics, industrial arts, vocational agriculture, music, art, and typing, for example. For the more academic courses, however, a teacher will find it extremely difficult to assess progress on the basis of one's capacity for progress. Although pretests often reveal useful data, they are usually insufficient basis for later comparisons of individual progress. While some teachers have been able to develop techniques for assessing individual progress on the basis of one's capacity for progress in very small classes, such an assessment is difficult to make in large classes, and the trend is toward even larger classes. Consequently, this discussion focuses on measurements useful in large academic classes.

Normal probability curve.   Lacking adequate means of evaluating progress on the basis of one's capacity for progress, one must turn to techniques for assessing an individual's progress in terms of that of the group (norm-referenced evaluation). An extremely useful device widely used in secondary school and college classes is the *normal probability curve*. Almost any characteristic, trait, or dimension is present in varying degrees in any *representative* population. The *pattern* of variation expected will *always* approach a bell-shaped curve. For example, the weights of a large number of randomly selected twenty-year-old coeds would vary from extremely light to extremely heavy; most of them would fall some place between the two extremes. Most coeds would weigh fairly close to *average weight*. A graphic picture of this dimension is reproduced in Figure 15-1.

Another investigation, as long as it were *representative* of all twenty-year-old coeds, would tend to show the same pattern. Similarly, with any such group and with *any* dimension, measurements tend to distribute in the form of a bell-shaped curve. This concept is often identified as the *normal distribution* or *probability curve*. One

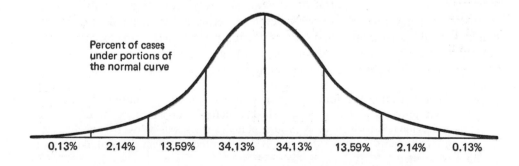

Percent of cases under portions of the normal curve

0.13%   2.14%   13.59%   34.13%   34.13%   13.59%   2.14%   0.13%

FIGURE 15-1 *Normal Probability Curve*

important assumption must be emphasized, however: the group must be *representative* of the entire population. Small groups (fewer than thirty) usually distribute unevenly along the curve. In some cases, chance factors will influence the distribution toward the right or left. A perfect bell-shaped curve exists in theory only. The curve concept can be applied to normal-sized class groups as long as the user employs it as a rough guide only and as long as he or she has reason to believe that the group is representative of the entire population of the trait being measured.

One of the more important developments of the twentieth century in education was the scholastic aptitude test—commonly referred to as the *IQ test.* Through the use of IQ tests, a teacher sometimes can predict a child's *capacity* to do school work. It has been established that one's capacity for school work remains relatively constant throughout life. Thus it becomes quite possible for a teacher to predict, within reasonable limits, a student's potential for academic achievement. Assuming a group is representative in terms of academic aptitude, we can expect about two-thirds (68.13 percent) of its members to fall within the *average category* of aptitude, but the remaining third would be evenly distributed between the below-average and the above-average range of aptitude. Now that we have a *representative amount* of progress, we can apply the normal curve, which would give those students with lowest ability failing marks, and those with highest ability the highest marks. *In effect, we are awarding a class mark on the basis of one's ability rather than on the basis of actual achievement. In other words, when a teacher uses the normal probability curve as a basis for the distribution of test marks, it is assumed that all students have a fairly equal chance.* Yet, through a similar process, it has already been discovered that all students do *not* have an equal chance.

In many of our four-year colleges and universities, the assumption that all students have a fairly equal chance is still reasonably valid. (The slow student may not even be admitted.) This may not be so in our junior colleges, however, where ability levels vary more since the admissions standards are very liberal. In certain classes, open only to those with average or above average ability, the use of a curve may still be quite appropriate. But in classes open to *all* students, the practice is indefensible as long as scholastic aptitude is not taken into account.

At this point, the reader may be surprised to learn that most judgements based on student progress are either directly or indirectly based on the normal distribution curve, as the following illustrates.

Dr. Burton boasted that he had no use for the normal curve. He proudly announced that he was sticking with the "tried and tested" percentage system of marking (that is, 93-100 points equal A; 86-92 points equal B, 78-85 points equal C, 66-77 points equal D and 0-65 points equal F). In this manner all students could theoretically earn A's, or they could all fail.

Dr. Knox based marks on acceptable standards of performance identified by key students. If her brighter students found the test difficult, she made the passing score lower than usual and adjusted the other scores accordingly.

Both of these teachers used the concept of the normal curve. The percentage distribution employed by Burton is derived from a normal distribution. His assertion that all could theoretically make A or F was truly *just* theory. Unless the test was extremely hard or easy or unless all his students were below or above average in ability, this could not possibly happen. By utilizing such a technique, Burton was assuming that all of his test items were reliable and valid. This is highly unlikely. Similarly Knox's reasoning was fallacious. She was using the concept of a normal distribution, but instead of basing the distribution on what might be reasonably expected, she was bringing in personal judgment. Although personal judgments are frequently necessary, when one relies on them alone, personal favoritism is almost certain to become an important factor.

What basis should a teacher use to evaluate test marks? The following combination of methods may be useful:

1. *Minimum, combined with multiple, standards.* Minimum standards can be used effectively as long as every student can attain them.
2. *Subgrouping within the classroom.* If below-average, average, above-average students are arranged in subgroups for the purposes of evaluation, the normal curve can be appropriately applied to each group; each student thus will have an approximately equal opportunity for success.
3. *Use of the normal distribution curve.* In classes limited to average and above-average students, the inaccuracies of this method will be minor; each student will have a fairly equal opportunity for success. Similarly, a class of below-average students can be evaluated on the basis of a normal curve. Quite understandably, a comparison of marks between these classes will not be accurate. It must be remembered, however, that marks supposedly represent *achievement* rather than ability. Ability can best be measured from other types of measures.
4. *Performance ratings.* In some skills areas, a direct observation of performance is possible. Marks can then be based on observable progress in terms of one's ability.

Stanine distribution. The stanine distribution, a simple nine-point scale of standard scores, represents the simplest, yet most accurate, application of the normal curve that a busy teacher can make. The word stanine is derived from the words STAndard NINE. Raw scores are converted to standard scores, ranging from 1 (low) to 9 (high). Just as the traditional A, B, C, D, and F scale represents five divisions of a normal distribution curve, so does the stanine represent nine divisions of a normal distribution. The stanine system has at least two practical advantages over the five-letter scale distribution system.

First, it enables a teacher to divide class scores directly into nine intervals or classes of whole numbers. This whole process takes about ten minutes. The traditional five-letter procedure takes more time. Letter marks, when combined, must be transposed into numbers and then back again into letter marks for student interpretation. Furthermore, if greater accuracy is sought through the use of plus and minus signs, the use of decimals becomes necessary.

Second, stanine scores for one test or project are easily weighted for the purpose of combining them with other stanine scores. For example, if a teacher decides that a given test should count twice as much as another test, he or she merely multiplies the stanine scores of the more important test by two and adds the product to the stanine score of the other test.

Stanine scores will conform to the proportions of the *normal curve*. Percentages of the class group(s) that fall within each of the nine stanine classifications for a normal population are shown in Figure 15-2. A useful characteristic of stanines is the equal distance between steps.

Stanines can be just as readily applied to written papers, drawings, products, or other exercises as they can to test scores. The only requirement is that the papers or products be ranked from high to low. For example, individual class projects in industrial arts can be assigned ranks of *excellent, very good, good, fair,* and *poor.* Then each project *within each rank* can be ranked from high to low. After ranking all the projects in this manner, one can easily determine the number of cases at each stanine level.

For convenience, a list of percentages for stanine scores is given in Table 15-1. The reader will note that percentages have been computed for 100 cases. If the group is larger than 100, the appropriate number of actual cases for each stanine score can be readily determined by multiplying the number by the percentage of cases at each stanine level.

In referring to Table 15-1, the teacher merely reads across to determine the theoretical number of students who should receive a given stanine score. In a class of forty students, for example, the stanine distribution would be as follows: 1–1; 2–3;

Meaning of Stanines
STA = Standard Score; NINE = Nine-Step Scale

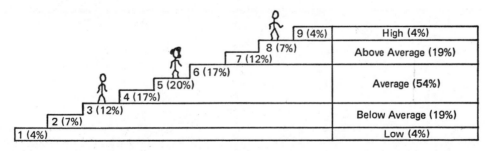

FIGURE 15-2 *Percentage of Cases at Each Stanine Level* (From Test Service Notebook, no. 23, New York: Harcourt Brace & World, Inc., 1961. Used by permission of The Psychological Corporation.)

TABLE 15-1 *Stanine table, showing number of cases falling at each level of a*
9-point normalized standard score scale when the mean equals 5
and the standard deviation equals 2

Directions. Under N, find the number corresponding to number of cases in the group. Entries in columns 1 to 9 give the number of cases that should receive the stanine score indicated at the top of the column. These figures are computed by multiplying the total number of cases in the group by the percentage of cases at each level. The figures are rounded-off values to give a symmetrical distribution of cases for any value of N given in the table.

				Percentage of Cases at Each Level				
Number of Cases	4%	7%	12%	17%	20%	17%	12%	7%	4%
					Stanines				
N	1	2	3	4	5	6	7	8	9
20	1	1	2	4	4	4	2	1	1
21	1	1	2	4	5	4	2	1	1
22	1	2	2	4	4	4	2	2	1
23	1	2	2	4	5	4	2	2	1
24	1	2	3	4	4	4	3	2	1
25	1	2	3	4	5	4	3	2	1
26	1	2	3	4	6	4	3	2	1
27	1	2	3	5	5	5	3	2	1
28	1	2	3	5	6	5	3	2	1
29	1	2	4	5	5	5	4	2	1
30	1	2	4	5	6	5	4	2	1
31	1	2	4	5	7	5	4	2	1
32	1	2	4	6	6	6	4	2	1
33	1	2	4	6	7	6	4	2	1
34	1	3	4	6	6	6	4	3	1
35	1	3	4	6	7	6	4	3	1
36	1	3	4	6	8	6	4	3	1
37	2	3	4	6	7	6	4	3	2
38	1	3	5	6	8	6	5	3	1
39	1	3	5	7	7	7	5	3	1
40	1	3	5	7	8	7	5	3	1
41	1	3	5	7	9	7	5	3	1
42	2	3	5	7	8	7	5	3	2
43	2	3	5	7	9	7	5	3	2
44	2	3	5	8	8	8	5	3	2
45	2	3	5	8	9	8	5	3	2
46	2	3	5	8	10	8	5	3	2
47	2	3	6	8	9	8	6	3	2
48	2	3	6	8	10	8	6	3	2
49	2	4	6	8	9	8	6	4	2
50	2	3	6	9	10	9	6	3	2
51	2	3	6	9	11	9	6	3	2
52	2	4	6	9	10	9	6	4	2
53	2	4	6	9	11	9	6	4	2
54	2	4	7	9	10	9	7	4	2

55	2	4	7	9	11	9	7	4	2
56	2	4	7	9	12	9	7	4	2
57	2	4	7	10	11	10	7	4	2
58	2	4	7	10	12	10	7	4	2
59	3	4	7	10	11	10	7	4	3
60	3	4	7	10	12	10	7	4	3
61	3	4	7	10	13	10	7	4	3
62	3	4	7	11	12	11	7	4	3
63	3	4	7	11	13	11	7	4	3
64	3	4	8	11	12	11	8	4	3
65	3	4	8	11	13	11	8	4	3
66	3	4	8	11	14	11	8	4	3
67	3	5	8	11	13	11	8	5	3
68	3	5	8	11	14	11	8	5	3
69	3	5	8	12	13	12	8	5	3
70	3	5	8	12	14	12	8	5	3
71	3	5	8	12	15	12	8	5	3
72	3	5	9	12	14	12	9	5	3
73	3	5	9	12	15	12	9	5	3
74	3	5	9	13	14	13	9	5	3
75	3	5	9	13	15	13	9	5	3
76	3	5	9	13	16	13	9	5	3
77	3	6	9	13	15	13	9	6	3
78	3	6	9	13	16	13	9	6	3
79	3	6	10	13	15	13	10	6	3
80	3	6	9	14	16	14	9	6	3
81	3	6	9	14	17	14	9	6	3
82	3	6	10	14	16	14	10	6	3
83	3	6	10	14	17	14	10	6	3
84	4	6	10	14	16	14	10	6	4
85	3	6	10	15	17	15	10	6	3
86	3	6	10	15	18	15	10	6	3
87	4	6	10	15	17	15	10	6	4
88	3	6	11	15	18	15	11	6	3
89	4	6	11	15	17	15	11	6	4
90	4	6	11	15	18	15	11	6	4
91	4	6	11	15	19	15	11	6	4
92	4	6	11	16	18	16	11	6	4
93	4	6	11	16	19	16	11	6	4
94	4	7	11	16	18	16	11	7	4
95	4	7	11	16	19	16	11	7	4
96	4	7	11	16	20	16	11	7	4
97	4	7	12	16	19	16	12	7	4
98	4	7	12	16	20	16	12	7	4
99	4	7	12	17	19	17	12	7	4
100	4	7	12	17	20	17	12	7	4

Reproduced from *Test Service Notebook,* no. 23 (New York: Harcourt Brace & World, Inc., 1961). Used by permission of The Psychological Corporation.

3–5; 4–7; 5–8; 6–7; 7–5; 8–3; 9–1. This is only a theoretical grouping, however, based on a normal distribution. In relatively small groups, the distribution usually is skewed to the right or left. As in any evaluation scheme, the teacher must use his or her best judgment as to desirable adjustments. In any event, however, *all students with identical raw scores or identical ranks receive the same stanine score.*

Use of the stanine distribution has been effectively illustrated by Durost in his list of directions for Table 15-2.

1. Arrange test papers on answer sheets in rank order from high to low. On a separate piece of paper, list every score in a column from the highest obtained score to the lowest (column A.) Opposite each score, write the number of individuals who obtained that score. This may be done by counting the papers or answer sheets having the same score, or it may be done by tallying the scores in the manner shown in column B.

2. Add the frequencies (C) and write the total at the bottom of the column (D). This is shown to be 90.

3. Beginning at the bottom, count up (cumulate) to one-half the total number of scores, in this case 45(one-half) of 90. This falls opposite the score of 34 (E), which is the median to the nearest whole number.

4. In the column at the extreme left of the Stanine Table [15-2], look up the total number of cases (90). In this row are the theoretical frequencies of cases at each stanine level for 90 cases (18) to which a stanine of 5 should be assigned. Starting with the median, lay off as nearly this number (18) of scores as you can. Here it is 20.

5. Working upward and downward from scores falling in stanine 5, assign scores to stanine levels so as to give the closest approximation possible to the theoretical values. It is helpful to bracket these scores in the manner shown in column A.

6. After having made a tentative assignment, make any adjustments necessary to bring the actual frequencies at each level into the closest possible agreement with the theoretical values. Remember, however, that all equal scores *must* be assigned the same stanines.[9]

How Should Class Marks Be Derived?

By this time, the reader has probably reached the conclusion that class marks should be abolished. Despite the problems associated with them, marks are essential. The major task is to reduce their unwholesome influence on the educational endeavor.

The following guidelines are not ideal, or would all educational authorities agree with them. They do appear to be consistent with the analysis presented in this book. Furthermore, they go at least one step beyond most current practices. The task would

---

[9] Walter N. Durost, "The Characteristics, Use, and Computation of Stanines," *Test Service Notebook,* no. 23 (New York: Harcourt Brace & World, Inc., 1961), p.6.

TABLE 15-2 *Distribution of Raw Test Scores in a Stanine Distribution*

Stanine	Score Interval (A)	Tallies (B)	Frequencies (C)	Grouping Actual	Grouping Theoretical
9	58	/	1	4	4
	57		—		
	56	/	1		
	55	//	2		
8	54		—	7	6
	53		—		
	52		—		
	51	/	1		
	50	/	1		
	49	//	2		
	48		—		
	47	///	3		
7	46	/	1	12	11
	45	///	3		
	44	//	2		
	43		—		
	42	₩ /	6		
6	41	//	2	12	15
	40	//	2		
	39	//	2		
	38	/	1		
	37	₩	5		
5	36	₩	5	20	18
	35	//	2		
	34 (E)	₩ //	7		
	33	///	3		
	32	///	3		
4	31	₩	5	14	15
	30	/	1		
	29	///	3		
	28	///	3		
	27	//	2		
3	26	////	4	13	11
	25	₩ /	6		
	24	///	3		
2	23	/	1	4	6
	22	/	1		
	21	//	2		
1	20	/	1	4	4
	19		—		
	18	/	1		
	17	//	2		

90 (D)

Reproduced from *Test Service Notebook*, no. 23 (New York: Harcourt Brace & World, Inc., 1961). Used by permission of The Psychological Corporation.

essentially involve establishing one or more continuums from zero to one hundred for each class subject. Degree of proficiency along this continuum would provide a basis for class marks. Instruction would be adapted to the person's beginning position on the continuum. (Some students would be farther along than others, so subgroups might be essential.) An advanced typing student, for example, who could type sixty words per minute would be marked on the basis of *his or her own progress* on a scale of proficiency set for such a course. A proficiency level of eighty words per minute, for example, might be worth a mark of A. Indeed, such a procedure *is already being used* in such skills areas as typing and shorthand. *It could be applied to all areas!*

In those areas where more than one continuum is necessary, a composite score might be employed. For example, social studies outcomes have been evaluated on the basis of critical-thinking skills. These have been defined as (1) identifying critical issues, (2) recognizing underlying assumptions, (3) evaluating evidence or authority, and (4) making warranted conclusions. Each is necessary for the entire process of critical thinking. Thus proficiency levels along the four continuums could be averaged for marking purposes.

Another guideline for the derivation of class marks could be based on some procedure involving the use of the normal curve of probability. For example, for those students who start at a given level, there may be times when none would reach the predetermined level of proficiency set for an A mark. If the predetermined proficiency level were realistically determined (based on the attained proficiency levels of other students), generally low achievement levels would suggest the presence of a class problem, possibly beyond the control of the students. Thus adjustments could be made on the basis of group progress.

Introduction of the criterion-referenced system can begin in a small way with those skills that are most easily identified. During the transition period, at least, both criterion-referenced and normative scores would be essential in the derivation of marks.

How Are Several Class Marks Combined for Grading Purposes?

In most classes today, students are graded on many different items, for example, short quizzes, reports, discussions, debates, tests, and many other activities. How can scores on these disparate elements be combined into one class mark?

First, the teacher records the results of *each* measure as a standard score. (The stanine has been offered as a useful device for this purpose.) It is worth repeating that raw scores are not comparable. *Thus they are not usually recorded at all* unless the teacher is able to develop an elaborate weighting system.

Second, the teacher determines the major dimensions that appropriately enter into derivation of a class grade. For example, ten quizzes, four class papers, two oral presentations, and a midterm test might be judged of equal importance. The final test might be considered equal to *two* of the preceding activities.

Third, the *standard* scores for each dimension are averaged. For example, the ten quizzes would be averaged, then the four class papers, followed by the two oral presentations.

Fourth, each of the *averaged* marks, in turn, are averaged in order to develop an average standard score. Since averaging of averages tends to produce a regression effect toward the mean, the final average standard scores can be evaluated on the basis of a normal curve. From this, one grade can be determined.

Such a procedure is inappropriate if it is possible to evaluate an individual on his or her own performance, as in the skills areas. Until such time as teachers have developed adequate criterion-referenced scales in the academic areas (as described in the preceding problem), some such approach can be used. In the final analysis, however, marks must be adjusted in terms of the particular class group (as well as the individual.) In short, the normal curve is merely a tool to be used as a starting point in determining grades.

If criterion-referenced assessment is used, all students who meet the minimum standards (usually about 90 percent) for each assignment should be passed. (Note that optional activities merely provide additional experiences for those who cannot meet minimum standard; they in no way suggest exceptional performance quality.) Those who do not meet minimum requirements should repeat the course until they do pass or they should be given a failing grade. If, as in many cases, criterion-referenced measures are combined with norm-referenced measures, a standard C, or average mark, may be used for those who meet the minimum essentials only. A's and B's might also be used for those who achieve highly on norm-referenced measures only. Relatively few classes today employ only criterion-referenced measures.

The Value of Evaluation

Evaluation is a valuable communication link between teacher and student as well as between teacher and parent. It may be the *only* major communication link between teacher and parent.

Evaluation enables learners to ascertain how well they compare with the rest of the class. Although evaluation can precipitate numerous psychological traumas, most individuals need such information in coping with the realities of the school environment.

The best form of evaluation enables learners to assess progress and to improve their record.

Evaluation can be systematized to include both norm-referenced and criterion-referenced measures.

Evaluation of students may necessitate teachers' examining their own teaching efforts in an effort to create a better learning situation.

Limitations of, and Problems with, Evaluation

Evaluation at best is somewhat subjective. Unfortunately evaluative judgments, reflected in marks and letter grades, have an important bearing on the learner's future.

Norm-referenced evaluation may be self-defeating to poor students if assessment is made solely on the basis of class performance.

Criterion-referenced evaluation is still rather arbitrary in many respects. How well criteria have been achieved ultimately rests with the evaluator.

A poor student may interpret inadequate achievement as indicative of personal inadequacy.

In classes where norm-referenced evaluation predominates, able students may not be sufficiently challenged to do their best work.

Evaluation, to a marked degree, depends on the values of the teacher involved. Thus grades in different classes are not fully comparable. This may create considerable misunderstanding between student and teacher.

Illustrated Evaluational Applications

I. Deriving stanine marks and letter grades from a written test.

Theoretical	Actual	Raw Scores	Frequency	Stanine (N = 40)
1	2	122		9
		120		
		115		
3	3	114		8
		112		
		108	−2	
5	5	106		
		104		7
		103		
		101		
7	6	99	−3	6
		96		
		93		
		90	−2	
8	8	89		5
		88	−3	
		85		
		79		
		76		
7	8	75	−2	
		74		4
		73	−2	
		69		

		$\underline{68}$		
5	4	66	·	3
		63		
		$\underline{60}$	−2	
		52		
3	3	50		2
		$\underline{46}$		
1	1	38		1

Note that slight variations from the theoretical stanine are sometimes advisable (as in stanine 9 of the illustration). Certainly, all students receiving the same test score will be awarded the same stanine grade. Normally stanines only are recorded.

If the user prefers to record letter grades (instead of stanines) the following guide is recommended.

$$9-8 = A \qquad 3 = D$$
$$7 = B \qquad 2-1 = E$$
$$6-5-4 = C$$

Note that the preceding stanine and letter grade assessment are based on a normal curve of probability. Although adjustments (to fit a unique class group) can be made for each set of data, many teachers prefer to make adjustments at the end **of** the course after all data have been averaged.

II. Deriving an average-term stanine for each student from a variety of data

The teacher's first task is to develop a series of stanine units that can be averaged. For example, in the illustration, the teacher decides that seven class quizzes will equal one stanine dimension (unit). This is derived by adding all seven quiz stanine marks and finding an average stanine. Since it is advisable (in the illustration) to let the final test count more than one-sixth, an additional stanine is added. (This makes the test count two-sevenths of the total assessment [except for those who completed optional assignments]).

N=30

Name	Seven Quizzes	15 Periods of Class Participation	Four Reading Analysis Reports	Midterm Exam	Term Project	Opt. Work	Final Exam	Term Average
George	2.4	5	6.3	7	8	7.6	2 2	5.0
Grace	3.7	3	7.3	5	7		5 5	5.1
Mary	3.9	9	7.7	4	9	9.0	7 7	6.8
Jo	3.7	6	5.7	4	7		7 7	5.5
Bill	5.4	9	8.0	3	6		4 4	5.6
Tom	6.3	7	8.0	9	4		8 8	7.2
Wilson	2.3	6	8.3	7	4		4 4	5.1

Debra	5.1	6	7.7	2	8		6 6	5.8
Sue	5.0	5	1.0	5	8		6 6	5.1
Glenda	2.7	5	5.7	3	6		5 5	4.6
Mike	2.1	6	5.7	3	1		5 5	4.0
Rhonda	2.7	6	5.0	2	6	5.0	5 5	4.5
Debbie	1.7	2	7.7	8	9		5 5	5.5
Wanda	1.9	6	8.0	6	6	8.0	2 2	5.0
Allan	5.3	7	8.0	2	8		9 9	6.9
June	4.2	7	3.0	7	8		5 5	5.6
Virgie	6.1	6	4.7	4	6		4 4	5.0
Gary	4.9	6	7.7	9	7	8.9	3 3	6.2
Fred	4.0	6	2.0	5	7		7 7	5.4
Cathy	5.7	5	3.7	5	7		4 4	4.9
Billy	2.3	2	7.3	6	5		4 4	4.4
Greg	3.0	4	5.0	4	7		4 4	4.4
Meg	7.0	7	5.0	4	6		1 1	4.4
Ruth	3.4	7	7.0	7	5	8.6	3 3	5.5
Linda	1.4	7	8.7	8	7	8.0	6 6	6.6
Hank	7.2	5	7.0	4	6		8 8	6.5
Bob	7.4	5	6.7	9	5		7 7	6.7
Larry	6.6	5	7.0	5	7	7.3	7 7	7.4
Yvonne	4.9	4	6.7	5	7		8 8	6.2
Judy	4.1	8	8.0	5	9		6 6	6.6

III. Deriving a course average from an average stanine using data from problem II.

Theoretical	Actual	Average	Frequency	Stanine (N = 30)
1	1	7.4		9
		7.2		
2	2	6.9		8
		6.8		
4	4	6.7		7
		6.6	−2	
		6.5		
5	4	6.2	−2	6
		5.8		
		5.6	−2	
6	6	5.5	−3	5
		5.4		
		5.1	−3	
5	6	5.0	−3	4
		4.9		
4	3	4.6		3
		4.5		
2	3	4.4	−3	2
1	1	4.0		1

Recall that when averages are averaged, there is a regression toward the mean. In effect, this eliminates extremes. In assessing letter grades the teacher decides (somewhat subjectively) whether or not any E's or A's will be awarded. Students who receive the same stanine, however, must be awarded the same letter grade.

IV. Assessing criterion-referenced data

11 Students completed all required activities and all optional requirements with a 90 percent accuracy level.

6 Students completed all required activities with a 90 percent accuracy level.

9 Students originally completed all required activities with a 75 percent accuracy level. After reworking the assignments, all achieved a 90 percent accuracy level.

4 Students completed all required activities with a 50 percent accuracy level and did not bother to rework their assignments.

Since optional work is a choice of the student, its completion should not play a part in this type of assessment.

The teacher *may* want to award A's to these nine students. However, reworked assignments may be reviewed as warranting a lower grade than those which were satisfactorily completed the first time.

Students who fail to meet the minimum standards (90 percent in the illustration) should not pass.

V. Combining norm-referenced and criterion-referenced assessments

Student	Average Norm-referenced	Mark Criterion-referenced	Letter Grade
George	5.0	A	B
Grace	5.1	A	B
Mary	6.8	A	A
Jo	5.5	B	C
Bill	5.6	B	C
Tom	7.2	A	A
Wilson	5.1	B	C
Debra	5.8	A	B
Sue	5.1	A	B
Glenda	4.6	E	E
Mike	4.0	B	D
Rhonda	4.5	A	C
Debbie	5.5	A	B
Wanda	5.0	B	C
Allan	6.9	A	A
June	5.6	A	B
Virgie	5.0	A	B
Gary	6.2	E	E
Fred	5.4	B	C
Cathy	4.9	E	E

Billy	4.4	B	D
Greg	4.4	A	C
Meg	4.4	A	C
Ruth	5.5	A	B
Linda	6.6	A	A
Hank	6.5	E	E
Bob	6.7	A	A
Larry	7.4	A	A
Yvonne	6.2	B	B
Judy	6.6	B	B

In this illustrated grade assessment, norm-referenced and criterion-referenced measures should be counted equally. The relative weight assessment will vary from one class situation to another. In academic courses, for example, most marks are likely to be norm referenced and thus will receive the most weight in evaluation. In some skills subjects, most marks are likely to be criterion referenced and thus will carry the most weight in assessment procedures.

Evaluating Professional Performance

Most college and university professors, as well as educational directors of business enterprises, are employed basically to instruct others. The previous five units of this book suggest the tremendous reponsibility placed on these professionals. All teachers must be accountable to the employing institution or agency and to the public for their performance. This accountability aspect of the teaching profession is the subject of Unit VI.

The specialized body of knowledge that characterizes a profession, in effect, frees the professional from control by management. Although management can control the resources connected with work and even the terms and conditions of work, the professional controls the work itself and that work is the key to production. The very nature of professional work, however, is such that the individual must make many spontaneous, often unique, decisions. Should any questions arise about these decisions, the individual is answerable only to other professionals. Only one's colleagues are qualified to determine if the decisions made were appropriate to the conditions existing at the time. Thus the professional is the ultimate authority in his or her field. Who, other than similarly qualified specialists, can challenge professional decisions and activities?

The quality of educational instruction has been a controversial issue with the U.S. public for many years. Not fully understanding the nature of teaching, individuals and groups sometimes have made unreasonable demands on teachers. To complicate the issue even more, college and business administrators are seldom, if ever, permitted to observe instructional activities directly. Thus the issue of competence is left almost entirely for professors and their students to decide.

Chapter 16 deals with this critical issue of teacher competence, pointing out that students can be a valuable resource in evaluating instructor performance. In addition to being competent instructors, professionals are expected to keep up with, and add to, their specialized knowledge. Traditionally, professionals have demonstrated their constant growth and acquisition of knowledge by publishing. For this reason, most leading universities and some business enterprises have adopted a "publish or perish" policy. Essentially, this means that stability of employment, promotion, and often merit salary increases are based on a professional's publication record. There are many kinds of writing and levels of research open to professionals. At the very least, they should explore problems directly associated with their subject area. Chapter 17 offers many useful techniques for teachers who need help in publishing their research efforts.

EVALUATION
OF TEACHING COMPETENCE

Overview

Key Concepts

1. Mastery of subject matter does not automatically qualify one for effective teaching.
2. The basic function of any instructional evaluation program is faculty self-renewal.
3. An effective instructional evaluation program must be developed and monitored by the faculty.
4. Paper-and-pencil tests designed to measure instructional effectiveness are generally poor. "General effectiveness" items are somewhat related to learning; the specifics of instructional competence are not so related.
5. The best *single indicator* of instructional competence is student evaluation. Several evaluations should be obtained, however.
6. Student evaluation is not valid unless complete anonymity is assured.

New Terms

1. Self-renewal Development and expansion of a teacher's knowledge of instructional methods and techniques.
2. Halo Effect The tendency of raters to let their overall impression of an experience influence evaluation of specific aspect of that experience.
3. Leniency Effect The tendency of evaluators (especially students) to be generous in their ratings, thus giving an instructor the benefit of the doubt.
4. Closed-Form Items Items answered by checking "the best answer" or a point on a scale. These items are generally multiple-choice questions.
5. Open-Form Items Items answered with a written explanation.

Questions to Guide Your Study

1. The overwhelming majority of university professors and instructional leaders of business enterprises have had little or no training in instructional methods. Why is this?
2. Student evaluation of instruction can be the most useful single indicator of teaching competence, but often it is not. Explain.
3. Student evaluation, when handled completely by the individual teacher involved, negates teaching competence as a criterion for instructional advancement. Explain why.
4. An effective instructional improvement program usually includes an evaluator from outside the faculty or business community. Why is this?

Professor Peter Thomas Jennings was stunned. As he read the dean's announcement of a plan for evaluating teaching, he vaguely remembered some discussion of the matter earlier in the year. The idea of instructional evaluation in itself was not so shocking; rather it was what was being evaluated that was upsetting to him. In his two years of college teaching, Professor Jennings had been concerned solely with developing and improving lecture notes. He noted that such items as concept teaching, behavioral objectives, lessons plans, and instructional variety were listed as the primary criteria for evaluation in the dean's plan.

Professor Jennings's frustrations were soon replaced with deep feelings of despair when he realized for the first time that not one course in his doctoral program had been concerned specifically with procedures and techniques of teaching. To be sure, he had been given the rare opportunity of teaching under the tutelage of a leading historian from a major university. But, again, instructional emphasis had been placed on subject-matter content almost exclusively. Everyone had seemed to assume that subject-matter mastery was analogous to good teaching.

Professor Jennings's dilemma is common among college and university professors everywhere. Indeed most teachers have had no real training in teaching; they have been expected to teach as *their* teachers taught; thus often their only real training has been in the lecture method. Scholarly productivity has been emphasized at the expense of teaching excellence, although from time to time, there have been public outcries about the quality of teaching.

Student discontent, expressed forcibly in the early 1970s, coupled with the high cost of education, has increased pressures on faculties to find effective ways of documenting instructional effectiveness. Indeed today's college administrators and business employers alike are likely to make teacher evaluation a condition of stable employment, promotion, and merit salary increases.

Because of traditional neglect of this vital aspect of education, professionals themselves must often assume leadership in developing self-renewal programs. This chapter focuses first on some fundamental properties of an effective evaluation program and then on effective techniques for implementing such a program.

Fundamental Properties

A program for improving the quality of faculty instruction is based on several basic assumptions and conditions. Prominent among these are the evaluational devices to be employed. As Doyle points out,[1] most educational practices merely involve an individual and a task. Evaluation, however, involves a third variable, *the ratee.* The presence of this person immediately raises the question of what constitutes appropriate criteria.

What Purposes Are Served by Evaluating Teachers

Teaching effectiveness is evaluated for many purposes. The most basic of these is to improve the instructional program. As Miller points out, "Improvement in instruction means using the results to assist those who are uncertain."[2] Such a program may include minicourses, conferences and workshops, internships with master teachers, and special study programs, for example. In the final analysis, the basic responsibility of professionals is to teach effectively those who enroll in their classes or who work under their tutelage. Although scholarly productivity may substantially increase a professional's *potential* contribution as a teacher, translating such growth into an effective instructional program requires skills independent of those needed for scholarship.

Teaching effectiveness is also used as a basis for making various administrative decisions concerned with faculty placement, tenure, promotions, and salary increments. The tenure decision is the most important one made about a professional and influences the long-range developmental patterns of an institution. In the past, effective teaching was all too often simply assumed. Today, however, teaching technology has developed sufficiently to invalidate such an assumption. Still another function of instructional evaluation is its use in providing criterion measures for research on the adequacy of various teaching techniques. Research in the area of teaching can be no more valid than the measures developed for its assessment.

What Are the Principal Requirements for Setting Up Such a Program?

The most important requirement of any faculty evaluation program is participation. Every teacher should play a part in the program's development, utilization, and

---

[1] Kenneth O. Doyle, Jr., *Student Evaluation of Instruction* (Lexington, Mass.: D.C. Heath and Co., 1975), p. xv.

[2] Richard I. Miller, *Developing Programs for Faculty Evaluation* (San Francisco: Jossey-Bass Publishers, 1974), p. 8.

refinement. Faculty members must concern themselves with such questions as: What specific instructional goals are being sought? What specific needs are paramount with this particular group of students? What specific innovations are being (or have been) attempted?

The principal role of higher administrative officials is to encourage and fund the program. Once results have been obtained, these officials must see that they are implemented and in the manner intended. Sometimes, all that may be required to start such a program is the organization of workshops—especially true in smaller institutions. In other cases, however, a center for instructional development or self-renewal may be needed. Actual monetary and other types of rewards should also be provided. A weak but promising instructor should be rewarded for substantial improvement just as a superior instructor should be rewarded for continued instructional excellence.

Who Should Evaluate and Who Should Be Evaluated?

One basic aspect of instruction is evaluation of students. Teachers are expected to assess the quality of student work and to administer grades. The ultimate end of evaluation, however, is student self-evaluation. Thus as they grow and develop, students learn to assess realistically their own strengths and shortcomings.

Similarly, faculty and administrators should be evaluated. The group of evaluators should be as broad and diversified as possible and should include students, one's peers, an individual's superiors, and finally the individual himself. If used effectively, each evaluation source, taken from a slightly different perspective can add validity to the overall assessment.

The best single source of instructional effectiveness is student evaluation. Students have the unique opportunity of observing the instructor daily. Obviously, students should not be asked to assess certain aspects of instruction for which they are not qualified to judge. If given proper guidance, however, students can be most helpful in any faculty improvement program. Hammond and others pinpoint the dilemma of faculty evaluation by stating, "Administrators ask for evidence of scholarly competence but assume teaching competence. And students ask for evidence of teaching competence but assume scholarly competence."[3]

What Should Be Evaluated?

Recently the term "Product Accountability" has received considerable attention as an evaluation criterion. Product accountability means responsibility for the development of various learning programs. In some cases, elementary and secondary school students have been evaluated on the basis of overall performance in such

---

[3] P. E. Hammond et al, "Teaching Versus Research: Sources of Misconceptions," *The Journal of Higher Education* 40 (1971): 682-89.

programs. Teachers generally have opposed such a system of assessment, however, on the grounds that there are too many uncontrolled variables present. Teachers generally prefer a system of assessment that might be called *process accountability*. It essentially entails responsibility for those *processes* involved during the instructional experience.

What Characteristics of Teaching Do Students Relate to Classroom Effectiveness?

Of the many studies that have been made, most generally agree with that of Crawford and Bradshaw who identified four criteria: (1) thorough knowledge of subject matter, (2) well-planned and organized lectures, (3) enthusiastic, energetic, lively interest in teaching, and (4) student orientation, expressed by a friendly attitude and willingness to help.[4]

Another approach to determining the criteria students use to evaluate teachers involves a statistical procedure for identifying which of a number of specific variables rates the highest. Of the several studies available, the one by Doyle and Whitely seems especially appropriate since it is limited *to items descriptive* of instructor traits and behaviors.[5] Five factors emerged from this study: (1) clear presentation of subject matter, (2) attitudes toward students, (3) interest in the subject, (4) stimulation of ideas and thinking, and (5) application of course material to related areas of knowledge. Other factors such as age of the instructor, class size, nature of the course, and anticipated course grade seem to have little or no bearing on student evaluation. However, many of these factors have not been thoroughly examined yet.

From the evidence available, it appears that general ratings of overall effectiveness are most defensible as a basis for making decisions about faculty tenure and promotion and ratings on specific aspects of performance are most valuable in helping instructors improve what they are doing. As Contra states,[6] however, some instructional practices work well for some but not all teachers. It is quite likely, for example, that not all teachers must develop close relationships with students in order to facilitate learning.

What Are Some Sources of Evaluation Errors?

Rating methods, at best, produce approximations of reality and often produce a distorted view because of the rater's personal feelings about the individual being

---

[4]P. L. Crawford and H. L. Bradshaw, "Perception of Characteristics of Effective University Teaching: A Scaling Analysis," *Educational and Psychological Measurement* 28 (1974): 259-74.

[5]K.O. Doyle and S.E. Whitely, "Student Ratings as Criteria for Effective Teaching," *American Educational Research Journal* 11 (1974): 259-74.

[6]J.A. Contra, "Student Ratings of Instruction and Their Relationship to Student Learning," *American Educational Research Journal* 14 (1977): 17-24.

evaluated or about the criteria themselves. If the evaluation is to be effective, the rater must be as objective as possible.

The *halo effect* is the tendency of a rater to be influenced by his or her overall impression of the experience. For example, a general feeling of course satisfaction is likely to diminish the ratee's ability to identify specific weaknesses.

Student raters especially tend to be influenced by the *leniency effect,* that is, they tend to be generous in their evaluations, giving the teacher the benefit of the doubt. This need not be a serious problem if one merely identifies those specifics that receive the lowest ratings even though all may appear relatively high.

Other, less serious, misrepresentations result from *central tendency, proximity,* and *logical errors.* A central tendency error results when the rater marks near the midpoint, especially on bipolar scales. A proximity error results when adjacent items are rated the same. A logical error results when traits are rated similarly because the rater (logically) feels they just naturally "go together." These sources of error can be overcome by using a carefully constructed instrument. For this reason a faculty might well consider adapting an existing instrument rather than developing its own.

What Practical (Political) Considerations Should Be Observed?

All evaluations must be kept confidential. Sometimes, students want faculty evaluations published to help them in choosing courses. However, since faculty consent is required, usually only high ratings are published. Often too, professors object to this practice on philosophical grounds.

A second point to be emphasized is that evaluation does exist at all levels. Such procedures then merely represent attempts to objectify and streamline evaluation processes already at work. Sometimes they may be seen as merely the addition of another dimension of the evaluative process.

Often, it is also desirable to emphasize the experimental nature of faculty evaluation procedures. This encourages needed feedback and provides a basis for useful adjustments. As previously indicated, the specifics of instructional evaluation may vary somewhat from one instructional area to another.

Finally, open hearings on the proposed procedures are in order. This gives individual faculty members an opportunity for hearing the attitudes of their colleagues concerning the evaluation procedures. (Some instructors will "go along" if certain key colleagues agree to the proceedings.) In addition, each faculty member should be given a chance for offering suggested improvements, both in the hearings and on the basis of actual practice in the classroom.

Evaluation Techniques

In any comprehensive program, several types of evaluation will be employed. Some of these are discussed in the following section.

How Is Student Evaluation of Instruction Used Most Effectively?

Student evaluation of instruction *can be effective* if certain precautions are taken. Students quite naturally are reluctant to reveal basic criticisms unless complete anonymity is assured. For most accurate results, *evaluations must not be signed; students should not be asked to enter written comments on them; and the instructor should not be present when the evaluations are being completed.* It is also important to tell students that their evaluations will be analyzed and that any suggestions will be taken seriously.

The nature of evaluation varies tremendously, as discussed in the last section of this chapter. A part of this diversity relates to the need for evaluation forms that require specific kinds of responses. Generally, the constructed type of response is superior to the closed-form type (where answers are merely checked off), *in providing specific information.* Constructed (open-ended) responses, however, may cause some students to become overly cautious since they fear that the teacher will identify their writing or manner of expression.

The dilemma can be resolved by first using closed-form items and then employing open-ended questions in a separate session. Use of the Hoover Course Evaluation Form (see Appendix C), for example, may suggest to the instructor that item four, Teacher's Encouragement to Thinking, needs improvement. In a later session, an informal discussion (or written evaluation) may be used to pinpoint *how* this might be accomplished.

The author has found that the closed-form item is most useful in suggesting specific areas that need improvement. One must be especially mindful of the *leniency effect,* however. For example, all scale items may receive a favorable evaluation from at least 80 percent of the students. However, two or three items are nearly always rated at least slightly lower than the other items. Rather than feeling satisfied, the instructor should seek to improve these areas of instruction *even though they already show a generally positive rating.* A "good" beginning teacher can always improve instructional competence.

After teaching five or six years, an instructor may find it impossible to improve further specific aspects of instruction. Because of this impossibility, the closed form used to evaluate the instructor should be replaced by an informal discussion session in which specific instructional techniques are examined for the purpose of streamlining and adding clarity. At this stage in time, the closed form may be used only every two or three years as a guide for improvement. (It may be needed every year, however, as a basis for certain administrative decisions such as merit salary increases.)

The new professor who sincerely desires to improve instructional competence might well consider making use of student evaluation early in the course and again toward the end of the session. Such a practice will enable him or her to make needed adjustments with the group directly involved in the evaluation. It may also demonstrate to higher administrative officials that improvement has been accomplished.

How Is Colleague Assessment Used in Evaluation?

Students are in a poor position to judge the *course content* and *subject* competence of the teacher. These must be the responsibility of professional colleagues. How often and by whom assessments should be made is still an unresolved issue. Miller suggests that the colleague visiting team might consist of two individuals, one in the instructor's discipline and one outside of it.[7] The date of the initial visit is usually set by the teacher, and copies of the day's lesson plan should be distributed to the visiting team in advance of the visit. The evaluators will attempt to answer such questions as the following:

1. Is the material sound?
2. Is it up to date?
3. Does the instructor bring in various scholarly points of view?
4. Are controversial issues offered in an unbiased manner?

Each assessment is followed by a conference as soon as possible after the event. In the conference, the teacher is given an opportunity for responding to any suggestions and judgments entered into the proposed final report and for offering a self-evaluation. At least three such visits should be made during the instructor's tenure year. Perhaps the first might serve as an orientation, the second for evaluation, and the third for summarization and confirmation of previous judgments.

Faculty visits are time-consuming but necessary if valid decisions are to be made involving faculty development and related personnel matters. Usually, the department head or an assistant assumes this visitation responsibility. In some schools, however, visitation is the responsibility of a graduate assistant especially trained for the task. The University of Massachusetts, for example, has developed a teaching improvement clinic. Improved through experience and testing over a five-year period, the clinic's program consists of the following procedures.[8]

> The program begins with an initial interview between the Teaching Improvement Specialist (TIS) (usually a graduate student) and the individual faculty member. During this interview the specialist explains the clinic process in a step-by-step fashion. Thus the teacher knows exactly what will happen and the purpose of each phase of the program. In addition, the TIS gathers information relative to teaching styles and preferences, instructional goals, problem areas or concerns, and the general nature of the professor's current students. A date is then set for the first observation.

---

[7] Richard I. Miller, *Developing Programs for Faculty Evaluation*, p. 21.

[8] Michael A. Melnik and Dwight W. Allen, "Clinic Teaching Improvement Process," in *Institutionalization: Clinic to Improve University Teaching, 4th Annual Report*, 1975-76. Unpublished report. (Amherst; University of Mass., 1977). Used by permission.

During the initial observation, data are collected relative to the professor's general teaching skills and behaviors. The purpose of this visit is to gather baseline data on the teacher.

In the next step, the faculty member is videotaped in his or her class, often with a focus on teacher-student interaction. Again, advance arrangements are made with full approval of the instructor.

Next, students provide an assessment of the instructor based upon data obtained from the Teacher Analysis by Students (TABS) instrument. [See Appendix C.] This is a diagnostic questionnaire of twenty teaching skills and behaviors.

While the students are working on the TABS questionnaire the professor also completes the instrument *in terms of how he or she thinks students will respond* and engages in a self-assessment of relative strengths and weaknesses. This enables one to more fully understand and assess his or her teaching effectiveness.

After the TABS data have been subjected to a correlational analysis (computer derived), they are made available to both TIS and the professor for independent study and analysis. This is followed with a data review session where the teacher's strengths and weaknesses are discussed. Data collected during the first observation and the videotaped session are used to illustrate and support the TABS data and to discover teaching patterns.

At this point the graduate assistant (TIS) and the instructor begin working on identified problems and teaching strategies needed for improvements. Further consultations with the TIS or other educational specialists, micro-teaching, simulations, repeated videotaping, etc. may be in order. In any event the TIS works with the professor as long as his or her services are needed.

Although some may view this program as "overkill," it seems to hold considerable merit when instructional improvement is the primary goal. Use of an especially trained graduate assistant helps minimize a potential psychologically threatening situation for teachers. Note that the program also includes colleague assessment in addition to both student and self-evaluation.

How Can Self-Evaluation Be Used Effectively?

In some institutions of higher education and in businesses, faculty evaluation is totally dependent on self-evaluation. This procedure usually results in glowing reports, often based on student evaluation. Each instructor can easily obtain the kind of student evaluation that is desired by merely requiring students to sign their name to the evaluation reports. Such a procedure eliminates instructional excellence as a basis for faculty advancement since *everyone* (in this way) "becomes" an excellent teacher.

Evidence clearly indicates that systematic self-evaluation is extremely difficult. Superior teachers may be too modest. They tend to underrate their instructional qualitites. Conversely, weak instructors tend to overestimate their instructional qualities.

Perhaps, the best strategy is to assume that all instructors can improve their instructional competence. Each teacher should be asked to list his or her three greatest weaknesses as a basis for an instructional improvement program and then to confirm them against student judgments. Under such circumstances, serious attempts at objective student evaluation are likely.

Once each teacher has identified two or three aspects of instruction that might be improved, adequate resources for accomplishing this task must be made available. Somebody must be responsible for helping the teacher alter instructional behavior accordingly. As indicated earlier, the University of Massachusetts trains a graduate student as a teacher improvement specialist. Certain courses and workshop experiences must also be made available. Such a program is expensive and time-consuming but well worth the effort if instructional excellence is to be the fundamental goal of the college or university faculty.

How Is Administrative Evaluation Performed?

It is no less important to evaluate administrative officials at all levels than it is to evaluate the teaching staff. This especially applies to the instructor's immediate supervisor, often the department or division head. Essentially, evaluation is effected by two distinct groups of people: the staff whom the administrator supervises and the superior closest to the individual involved.

There is a definite trend among major universities for administrators to be appointed one year at a time for a specified number of years. Reappointment is usually based on positive ratings from a majority of the faculty. Then after four to six years the individual is replaced, thus effecting a continuous system of faculty rotation. Often faculty members become administrators; sometimes, however, these positions are filled by someone from outside the institution.

It may be difficult for the faculty to rate administrators, especially in large universities. Some teachers, for example, may not be fully aware of the various activities of an administrator. Nevertheless, an administrative official's basic responsibility is to serve the faculty. When this is not being done, the official should be replaced. The same holds true for deans, vice-presidents, and presidents.

What Instructional Improvement Programs Are Needed?

Because the majority of today's college and university professors have had little or no specific preparation in the art of teaching, any serious instructional improvement program must start from the beginning and will usually entail four or five basic steps.

First, there must be a basic understanding of the method or technique that needs development. This handbook is designed to fulfill this basic need.

Second, the specific techniques and procedures must be demonstrated, enabling the professor to see how the technique is applied. For example, if a professor has difficulty in constructing review lessons, he or she should have an opportunity to observe a more experienced teacher. (Videotaped experiences can be substituted for live experiences.) The demonstrated experience(s) should parallel as closely as possible the basic cognitive map of the learner (gained through preliminary reading, etc.). This experience is usually made meaningful if followed by a small-group discussion noting the specific techniques involved and any problems that need resolving. The teacher improvement specialist must make every effort to clarify misconceptions.

Third, the teacher should practice the methods and techniques learned in his or her own classes. Some observation of these attempts should be made so that any deficiences can be corrected.

Fourth, the teacher should visit other classes in which the given methods or techniques are employed. It is here that various departures and innovations become apparent. Efforts should be made to help the teacher distinguish between those practices that are equally effective (with the model) and those that tend to undermine the entire process. Finally, a concluding review lesson should be conducted. The recall of facts, for example, cannot be effective. At the same time, a review may completely bypass any reference to the various unit activities employed and still be effective (see chapter 9).

The preceding represents a systematic program for teaching faculty how to use certain methods and techniques. Sometimes, however, the basic structure of the method or technique may be clearly understood, but effectiveness still may be lacking. In this case, an entirely different approach may be utilized, for example, workshops, conferences, or merely a few expository presentations. Often, however, class visitations are needed for diagnostic purposes. Change can be effected only after the instructor clearly perceives the element blocking effective use of the technique.

The Value of Instructional Evaluation

Systematic evaluation of instruction is necessary if teaching is to be improved.

Teachers are often unable to assess their instructional competence without the assistance of others.

Most university professors and business executives have instructional deficiencies because of their inadequate background in instructional techniques. Thus systematic evaluation serves to pinpoint such deficiencies.

Use of student evaluation increases the teacher's credibility with students and with administrators.

Instructional effectiveness as one criterion of professional advancement is invalid in the absence of a systematic evaluation program.

Limitations of, and Problems with, Instructional Evaluation

If no controls are enforced, instructors can influence students to give them a high rating.

Effective evaluation of instruction involves a number of parties; thus it is both expensive and time-consuming.

Development of an effective faculty development program demands employment of especially trained personnel.

Public pronouncements about improvement of teaching effectiveness are generally ignored in the absence of a systematic faculty improvement program.

Instructional evaluation poses a threat to the individual teacher and will be resisted unless developed objectively and systematically.

Crowded classrooms and large lecture classes tend to discourage methodological variety.

Illustrated Evaluations

I. Student evaluation of teachers (see Appendix C)

II. Evaluation of teacher-student interaction

The ratio of teacher to pupil interaction seems to offer a valid clue to successful teaching. Evidence indicates that the effective teacher relies heavily on pupil input. By checking classroom behavior every ten seconds for a period of ten minutes, the observer can gain a rather clear indication of the degree of teacher-student interaction and of teacher dominance.

The rater should complete a series of observations and compare the data with those obtained from observing another professor who is distinguished as an outstanding teacher. (This will provide a frame of reference for discussion.) The following is one type of form that can be used for the observation.

Teacher being observed _____ Date _____

Observer _____ Observation time (in minutes) _____

	Presents information	
	Asks questions	
Teacher Talk	Answers questions	
	Corrects students	
	Reinforces students	
	Asks questions	
Pupil Talk	Answers teacher questions	
	Answers pupil questions	

Silence
or confusion
(unclassifiable)

By analyzing the categories that are most heavily marked, the professor will be able to shift instructional emphasis if necessary. For example, if it is discovered that much of the time is spent in presenting information, the teacher may want to consider a different instructional method or technique.

chapter 17

RESPONSIBILITIES FOR PROFESSIONAL GROWTH: WRITING TECHNIQUES

Overview

Key Concepts

1. Professional writing consists of many skills that can be learned.
2. The basic requirements for effective professional writing are disciplined use of time and a quiet environment.
3. Financial reward for professional writing is often minimal or nonexistent. The real payoff is the enhanced prestige and recognition afforded the professional and the institution.
4. Professional writing is a time-consuming activity. Thus competing activities must be curtailed if the writing effort is to be productive.
5. Preparation of materials for publication demands considerable rewriting.
6. Professional journals represent the "cutting edge" of knowledge. Thus through journal writing, the professional keeps abreast of latest developments in his or her areas of special interest.

New Terms

1. Journal Articles   Usually short contributions (three to six pages) designed to advance knowledge. Their purpose may be to explain theory, to clarify principles or issues, or to describe teaching techniques, for example.
2. Monographs   Contributions of a "book" nature, designed for a single printing and directed at a specialized or limited audience. In length the monograph is intermediate between an article and a book.
3. Referred Publications   The practice (used by editors) of submitting manuscripts to individuals in the field for critical evaluation and recommendation concerning the potential for publication. Professional journal editors usually use two field editors; book editors may use three or four or even more.
4. Humanistic Approach   A personalized writing style in which a problem is developed in terms of individuals, personalities, or groups. This style is highly recommended for introductions to professional articles.

5. Deductive versus Inductive Writing In deductive writing, the conclusion is given in the introduction, followed by supporting facts and logic. In inductive writing, facts or points of logic are presented first and followed by concluding comments. Although both approaches are used, the deductive approach is usually preferred by professional writers.
6. Topic Sentence A key sentence in a paragraph (usually the first or second) that provides the substance of the paragraph.

Questions to Guide Your Study

1. What is the basic argument for a "publish or perish" policy?
2. What are some fallacies associated with this argument?
3. What rewards from professional writing may be anticipated?
4. What basic personality components are associated with effective professional writing?
5. What basic skills are necessary?
6. Some college and university professors should not be expected to write. Defend or refute.

Last November, Thomas Cannon thought his immediate future was pretty much assured.

The literature department of American University had endorsed his "tenure-track" reappointment, and he had received an even heartier endorsement from his dean.

Mr. Cannon knew he was widely regarded as an able and creative teacher. (Later in the year, he would be the nominee of the college of arts and sciences for American University's outstanding teaching award.) Moreover, the assistant professor was in his fifth year of teaching—which left another year before the crucial "up-or-out" tenure review.

So when the provost's letter came, just before Christmas, Mr. Cannon was not prepared for its message: his sixth year of teaching at American University would be his last. The university had decided to give him a "terminal contract."

Mr. Cannon was astonished. The problem, however, was quite clear. Mr. Cannon's record, the letter said, did not indicate "satisfactory improvement in the area of scholarship."

In other words, Mr. Cannon had not published. And the university, he realized, was not "taking the risk."[1]

---

[1] Margaret L. Weeks, "The Teacher Learns What Really Counts." Appeared originally in *The Chronicle of Higher Education.* Copyright 1977 by Editorial Projects for Education.

Thomas Cannon's dilemma is representative of those of thousands of college professors throughout the nation. Indeed, most leading universities (along with some that are not as eminent) have or are in the process of establishing a "publish or perish" policy. Why? What makes publishing so important to most university administrators?

Traditionally, it was assumed that college professors represented the "elite of intelligentsia," that the basic frontiers of knowledge existed in universities (the citadels of learning), and that professors were continually making original contributions to knowledge.

Such lofty ideals are not (perhaps never have been) fully valid. In today's society, a college education theoretically is available to all. A professor's *expertise as a teacher* is assumed his or her most basic responsibility to students. Although some studies have revealed a (low) relationship between expertise in teaching and scholastic productivity, most recent studies have found no correlation at all. With the publication of the Social Sciences Citation Index (SSCI) in 1973, a new measure of the relationship between effective teaching and published research efforts has become available.[2] Using several SSCI variables of research quality and student evaluation scores in multivariate analysis, Dent and Lewis found no significant correlations among any of the variables.[3]

This does not fully resolve the dilemma, however. In making a plea for writing, Simpson cites an actual case.[4] One professor who conducts three classes per week and who teaches about 180 students in one year has sold over 75,000 copies of two textbooks over the past two years. Assuming (quite conservatively) there is one reader for each copy sold, this teacher has taught by print in two years over 200 times as many individuals as he has taught in his classes. Although this particular professor may be an exception, Simpson suggests that if teaching can be defined as informing, enlightening, or educating, it follows that many college professors do their best teaching through their writings. He points out that usually writings are better screened and edited than lectures.

Although the "publish or perish" policy is highly contested, the fact remains that most college professors (and some business leaders) must demonstrate their scholarship by publishing. Both effective teaching *and writing* are expected! Thus this chapter explains basic fundamentals of writing for publication and also introduces several useful writing techniques. As Ewing contends,[5] professionals write for limited audiences; thus, unlike journalists, they use a specific strategy *that can be mastered by*

---

[2] The SSCI lists social scientists alphabetically and their publications by year and publisher.

[3] P.L. Dent and D.J. Lewis, "Relationship between Teaching Effectiveness and Measures of Research Quality," *Educational Research Quarterly 1* (Fall 1976): 3-16.

[4] R.H. Simpson, "Teaching by Personal Appearance or by Print?" *Improving College University Teaching* 23 (Summer 1975): 184-85.

[5] David W. Ewing, *Writing for Results* (New York: John Wiley & Sons, Inc., 1974), pp. 10-12.

most. For convenience, professional writing and research reporting are discussed separately.

Fundamental Properties

The topics treated in this section set the stage for productive effort. Unfortunately, few professional writers may be aware of those preconditions that perhaps more than anything else, separate writers from nonwriters.

Why Must Professors Publish?

In stressing the need for professors to publish, most administrators are quick to point out that traditionally the majority of research efforts and instructional innovations have originated at the university level and that most college textbooks, in part, are written by college professors. Further support to the publishing argument is offered by the logic that professional writing forces one to keep abreast of developments in specialized areas. Few would deny the validity of such logic *provided that the quality of professional contributions is carefully assessed.* Even so, not all publishing professionals are among the most competent teachers.

In fact, inadequate background preparation for teaching, coupled with an overemphasis on publishing productivity, sometimes has resulted in a serious neglect of teaching responsibilities.

Whatever position the reader takes, many professionals are expected to become productive professional writers. While some may become more productive than others, it is assumed that *all* can reach at least a minimum degree of competence.

What Rewards Are Forthcoming?

The major financial rewards for the professional writer are stability of employment, promotion, and sometimes merit pay increases. Rarely are there any substantial royalties.

For short contributions of a nonresearch nature (for example, articles, monographs, and chapters to books), writers usually are given two or three extra copies of the work. They may even be expected to pay part of the cost of publishing a research report since such a work serves limited audiences. Although book publishing companies do offer royalties (ranging from 5 to 15 percent of gross sales), the odds against any substantial financial rewards are about twenty-five to one.

The nonfinancial rewards from professional writing can be substantial. There can be considerable ego satisfaction in the knowledge that other professionals and teachers throughout the nation and the world are able to profit professionally from one's contributions. (The "cutting edge of knowledge" is to be found in journal articles.) Further support is often forthcoming through worldwide requests for reprints. Many professionals fail to realize that many other countries look to the United States as a leader in objective reporting of professional activities and developments.

How Should One Approach the Writing Task?

Fear of writing, like the fear of math and statistics, may develop early in life. All too frequently, teachers allow the trauma they experienced in developing their doctoral dissertation to make them fearful of undertaking any further writing. This is indeed unfortunate. A "trying" thesis experience is not a valid barometer of one's potential as a professional writer. (After all, the truly incompetent writers are never able to complete their dissertations.) As opposed to a doctoral dissertation, professional writing is more specific in nature and aimed at a particular audience. Dissertations, however, do include material suitable for articles.

An appropriate attitude for a professional to adopt is "I have something to share with my professional colleagues that is worthwhile. I can—I must—share my knowledge with them!" This kind of attitude encourages one to write a first draft, always the most difficult task. This "I'll try" attitude, coupled with perseverance, represents more than half the battle. Usually an individual who persists eventually succeeds, and each success in turn contributes to future successes.

Should Professors Solicit the Help of Colleagues?

Most professional writers have found it desirable to use someone as a "sounding board" for their ideas. This person may be a professional colleague or merely a friend or spouse. The opportunity of discussing an idea with someone who is willing to be a patient listener often produces a fresh look at a problem. Oddly enough, however, too much discussion may destroy the original enthusiasm for an idea. Sometimes too, prolonged discussions become an excuse for delaying the writing effort.

The charge has been made, with some justification, that every college professor is a prima donna. Indeed it is true that each professor is (or should be) a specialist in his or her own field. This fact, however, should not interfere with other aspects of professional interaction. An individual who aspires to become a professional writer should seek the help of a colleague who is already an accomplished writer. By viewing such a relationship from a teacher-learner framework, the aspiring writer can learn many things. Occasionally, it may be desirable to seek a co-author whose function is to edit the manuscript and to write some portions of the book or article.

Often the writer is his or her own best critic. The ego involvement and enthusiasm that enters into a written document, however, tends to block critical analysis for a time. Consequently, most successful writers put aside their completed manuscripts for a couple of weeks so that they will have a more objective viewpoint when reviewing them. Sometimes a close colleague may review the manuscript. All too often, however, a colleague who wants to be supportive may be fearful of expressing his or her true sentiments.

What Special Precautions and Ethical Considerations Are Important?

The written word is much more permanent than the spoken word. A writer, in effect, puts his or her reputation on the line each time a manuscript is published. Sometimes an ill-advised or even ill-chosen statement can haunt the writer for some time to come. Especially in sensitive areas, it is wise to mitigate arguments that might create resentment. Most writers learn to avoid making absolute statements (characterized by such words as "always," "never," "good," "bad," "right," and "wrong"). Qualified statements (characterized by such words as "apparently," "tend," "sometimes," and "occasionally") convey just as much meaning and are less offensive.

Because professors work with students constantly, they may wish to include some student papers in their professional writings. Such a practice is ethically acceptable only if the student agrees to such a plan and if the student is listed as one of the authors. In fact, any time a student source is used in any identifiable way in a written document, written permission should be secured. The Privacy Act of 1974 assures this sort of protection from potential threats of the federal government. According to Weinberger,[6] there is considerable sentiment for extending the law's provisions in modified form to private and public sectors alike.

Once a manuscript has been submitted to a journal for consideration, the writer should not submit it to another journal until the first journal has formally rejected the article. With a time lag of three to four months from submission to acceptance or rejection, the writer quite naturally becomes impatient. In addition, most journal editors have no use for revised versions of previously published articles.

In the case of lengthy book manuscripts, it may be expeditious to send them to more than one publisher at a time. (The time lag for book manuscripts is normally at least six months.) In such instances, however, the writer is responsible for clearly informing the publisher that the manuscript has been submitted to competitors.

When a co-author is involved, there must be clear agreement between the two authors about division of labor and the nature of the written report. Each of the authors is equally responsible (both legally and ethically) for the substance of the report, even though one of the parties may have been responsible for preparation of the manuscript.

What Publishing Resources Are Available?

There are many available resources for professional writings. There is considerable competition, however, in most areas. Professional journals generally are "refereed" publications, meaning that the journal editor usually sends the manuscript to at least two field editors (referees) for evaluation. Favorable reviews usually result in publication of the manuscript.

---

[6] Jo Ann Weinberger, "Federal Restrictions on Educational Research: A Status Report on the Privacy Act," *Educational Researcher* 6 (February 1977): 5-8.

Professional journals represent the major resource for publication of new knowledge. They exist in all major fields. While most national journals are refereed, many nonrefereed state and local journals do exist. These are likely resources for beginners. Writing for journals generally takes relatively little time and thus probably offers the greatest potential reward for the effort made.

Monographs are another resource for professional writings. As Fisher and Smith point out,[7] monographs are subject to only one press run. Many professional organizations that publish journals also publish a limited number of monographs each year. Monographs, like articles, are usually refereed publications. Often, however, they are solicited.

Books represent the greatest investment of an author's time and effort. Generally, it takes about three years from submission of the manuscript for a book to be published. As Fisher and Smith suggest,[8] a book must set a trend and make its own market. (Magazine articles concern contemporary issues for which a market is already established.) Most book publishers ask for a preface, a table of contents, and three or four chapters before considering a manuscript for publication. Although the investment is considerable, a book has the longest life of any professional work and offers the greatest potential financial reward. It is usually wise to send out a letter of inquiry before submitting a manuscript.

Book publishers, of course, vary considerably. A few companies will publish almost anything so long as they can be assured of the original cost of publication. At the extreme end of the continuum are the so-called "vanity presses," where the writer assumes most or all the cost of publication. Professional writers generally are wise to avoid vanity presses as the total impact of their book on their profession is usually limited. The university presses offer still another publication resource. Little financial reward can be expected from university presses, however, since they primarily publish valuable works that otherwise may be overlooked and for which there is a limited audience.

Professional Writing Techniques

Any attempt to provide a prescription for professional writing is doomed to failure. Writing, like teaching, is a creative endeavor and thus varies widely among individuals. As with teaching, however, there are certain essentials common to all written communication. This section describes some of these.

---

[7] Margaret B. Fisher and Margaret Ruth Smith, *Writing as a Professional Activity* (Washington, D.C.: National Association for Women Deans, Administrators and Counselors, 1976), p. 40.

[8] Ibid., p. 29.

How Does One Generate Ideas for Writing?

Every professional has an "inspiration" from time to time as he or she goes about daily professional activities. The thrill and excitement of trying something new generates an enthusiasm that is quickly caught by students. This is the sort of experience that may be written up in an article. While the idea is still fresh, while the inspiration is still exciting, the professor or business executive should write out the experience as if intended for another colleague. Later, of course, he or she should research the subject area to assess existing knowledge. Although the original draft may change substantially after research is completed, at least the original inspiration has been recorded and has become a starting point for the article.

Systematic curiosity, according to Fisher and Smith, can uncover a variety of questions or experiences that people usually take for granted. They list several ways of cultivating this curiosity. These include thinking about:

What interests you most in your daily routine.
What you would most like to change, preserve, or invent.
What you hope a conference, planning session, or workshop will produce.
What you admire in a colleague or colleagues.
What you are curious about.
What you find irritating, frightening or unbearable.
What you have tried six different ways to do, and one of them worked.
What everybody said couldn't be done, and you did it.
What commonplace ideas or ways of work you have found to be outworn, oversold, wasteful, or absurd.
What shortcuts and lazy man's ways you have invented to make things easier.[9]

Since all professionals are asked to make speeches or to consult from time to time, these activities can also become the bases for articles. In addition, through their scholarly research on their specialized area of knowledge, professors may find suggestions for articles or bookwriting.

How Is the Outline Developed?

Any important, written communication demands some planning. Preparing an outline enables one to sort ideas according to their sequence and importance. Once the writing experience has begun, the outline reminds the writer of the intended organization of the subject matter. Without it, the writer may forget important subpoints and illustrations. The writer, of course, will want to add ideas, especially illustrations, that are prompted during the writing process.

---

[9] Ibid., p. 3.

The nature and extent of the outline will vary in terms of the complexity of the task. Outline notes for a journal article may be no more than a few key words and phrases. Those for a chapter of a book may consist of several major and minor points. Table 17-1 presents the actual outline prepared for this chapter.

TABLE 17-1   *An Outline of Chapter 17*

Fundamental Properties

	1.	Basic assumptions (leadership; keeping up)
(below)	1.	Sources of ideas (lit.; your work; speeches)
	2.	Rewards (nonfinancial)
	5.	Ethical considerations (faculty, students' co-authoring; one journal at a time)
	4.	Being teachable (help from colleagues)
	6.	Outlets
(below)	8.	Time & place
	9.	Using critiques
	3.	Predisposed attitudes

Writing Techniques

	6.	Style (short; direct; no repetition; qualifiers)
	4.	Introd. & purpose ("catch" the reader)
	9.	Tailoring to journal
	10.	Timeliness
(above)	7.	Rewriting (put away; outside help)
	3.	The message (documentation; say something; examples)
	5.	Closing (sum; implications; abstract)
	11.	Plagiarism (use of ideas)
	12.	Ref. to sex
	2.	Outline

Note that the outline includes only two of the five major chapter divisions. The overview, values, limitations, and illustrations sections are not present since these divisions are included in each chapter of this book and have the same format. (The writer, however, did jot down key words to be defined in the Overview.) Also note the scrambled numbering system in the outline. This occurred as a result of jotting down subpoints as they occurred. Later, a sequence of presentation was developed. To save time, the writer did not bother to make a second (corrected) copy. Two subpoints (sources of ideas, and time and place) were originally considered for the Fundamental Properties section. After sorting the points, the writer decided that these items might more appropriately be discussed in the Writing Techniques section. Thus the notation "below" appears in the left margin. Similarly, the writer decided to put the subtopic on rewriting in the Fundamental Properties section. One item, the title, was unintentionally omitted from the outline but noted as the logical sequence of writing was considered.

An outline is a working paper. It will vary according to the needs of each writer. As Table 17-1 clearly demonstrates, an outline need not be a "prefect" finished document to guide the writer in his or her work. The outline will also vary in terms of the presentation pattern followed. Ewing describes a number of presentation patterns.[10] Two of the most common ones are presented below.

PROBLEM ANALYSIS

Topics to Cover

Precise description of the problem
Cause or causes of the problem
Alternative solutions
Steps to get started

HOW-TO DIRECTIONS

Topics to Cover

Purpose, nature of the activity
Materials necessary
Steps necessary to complete the activity
Problems

Note the close parallel between the Techniques section of this chapter and the How-to Directions outline.

How Is the Title Developed?

The title (and subtitle, if any) creates the first impression of an article. As Bird suggests,[11] most publishers in their initial review of a manuscript pay particular attention to the title and subtitle (if any), the illustrations, the general appearance of the manuscript, the writer's name and affiliation, and the introduction. If these elements are considered inadequate, the manuscript is usually rejected outright. (Usually the first reading of a manuscript is done by an assistant staff member.)

Length and style of the title must be slanted to the particular publication. Some editors prefer a striking or provocative statement; others favor the use of a label or a

---

[10] David W. Ewing, *Writing for Results*, pp. 183, 197.

[11] George L. Bird, *Modern Article Writing* (Dubuque, Iowa: William C. Brown Publishers, 1967), p. 112.

cliché; a few like a question, a quotation, an exclamation, or a statement. By scanning a few recent issues of the journal, one can easily determine editorial preferences. Although many editors reserve the right to change or alter titles, the original title can do much to "sell" the manuscript.

For most professional publications, the title should be short, usually not exceeding five or six words. Generally a title should be a conservative one, avoiding anything that might offend the reader's moral, racial, or religious preferences.

Sometimes, a subtitle should be included to expand the idea of the title and to prepare the reader further for the subject matter. It can be twice as long as the title.

The article subheads (if any) can be used to extend this process still further. Subheads should be no more than three or four words long, occurring about every 200 words. A subhead on the first page should be avoided.

Many times the writer may not select the title until the manuscript has been completed. It may be useful to jot down ideas for a title (and subtitle) as they occur during the preparation of the manuscript. One way of developing ideas for a title is to list the outstanding features of the article. Title selection is a creative process of utmost importance.

How Is the Introduction Developed?

The beginning of an article in large measure determines the saleability of the potential publication. Few readers (including editors) will read an article if the beginning is uninteresting. In fact, editors judge the beginning as an indication of what the writer can do. Its purpose is to arouse interest and to entice the reader to continue with the article. Frequently a single short sentence will accomplish this purpose. At other times, a short paragraph is needed.

In the introductory paragraph(s), the writer specifies his or her purpose, clarifies the major issues or questions to be considered, and provides the reader with at least a general idea of the major conclusion to be reached. Fife and Carstons describe this as a *deductive* as opposed to an *inductive* approach.[12] In deductive writing, the conclusion is provided at the outset, followed by supporting facts and logic. In inductive writing, on the other hand, the writer leads his or her readers to the conclusion by providing facts one at a time. The *deductive* approach is preferred since it enables the reader to evaluate each supporting detail against the conclusion.

The best way to generate reader interest in the introduction is to relate the subject matter to some concrete, human experience. This can be done by providing a short anecdote or vignette. The following might be used to open a lengthy article or book on teaching reading.

---

[12]Jim Fife and William F. Carstons, *A Practical Approach to Writing* (Glenview, Ill: Scott, Foresman and Co., 1967), p. 8.

Benjamin Harrison Smith was a troubled high school senior. Now that graduation day was only a few months away, he realized that he had no chance of succeeding in college simply because he could not cope with the written language. "It's too late now," Ben thought, "to go back to learn what I should have learned in my early years of school."

Reflecting back, Ben knew that his problems began early in his elementary school experiences and had become progressively worse as he advanced through junior and senior high. From an early reading indifference, he had developed an intense dislike for the written word, avoiding written assignments whenever possible. Fortunately, he was capable enough to make average grades in most classes on the strength of his verbal ability and "practical intelligence." He suspected that some of his teachers had been totally unaware of his reading problem.

When the guidance counselor asked Mr. Tompkins if Ben had experienced reading difficulty in senior science class, Ben's teacher replied, "No more than many of my students. Many students either cannot or will not read directions. They read science assignments only if forced to do so." When asked what action had been taken to help students cope with the language of science, Mr. Tompkins retorted, "Look, my job is to teach science. Students are supposed to learn to read in elementary school. I realize that the job is often not very well done, but I simply do not have time to teach reading *and* science." Literally thousands of high school students, like Ben, are academically crippled as a result of . . . .

These introductory paragraphs "capture" the reader immediately and almost compel him or her to finish the article. The writer's purpose can be easily defeated, however, if the approach is excessively long or complex. Moreover, it must be directly related to the problem or purpose of the article.

Another way to generate reader interest is to open with a provocative statement. Readers like to be startled or surprised. To illustrate, "Article writing can be fun." The next sentence, of course, must somehow suggest why. Still another alternative is to ask a question. If, for example, one asks "Would you like to be a successful writer?" the reader subconsciously will attempt to formulate an answer (in the affirmative, if the writer is successful). A quote or cliché can also be used. To illustrate, "The words 'publish or perish' send cold chills up and down the spines of literally hundreds of young professors. Yet, this need not be so if . . . ."

How Is a Publication Concluded?

The conclusion of a publication varies with the nature of the writing. A chapter to a book or monograph often demands a summary that pulls together major ideas of the publication. No new ideas or terms should be presented in the summary. If the summary includes the major points of the book or article, they should be listed in the same order as originally presented.

Recently, the summary has been adapted to serve as a type of advance organizer (see Chapter 10). When used as an advance organizer to each chapter and when it includes all the essential ideas in the chapter, the summary helps the reader comprehend more readily the material in the chapter. Sometimes (especially in research reporting) a summary is treated as an abstract and appears in front of the publication. In this chapter, the Overview section serves such a function.

Complex journal articles usually have summaries; other articles end with a paragraph that suggests how the textual material can be applied in real-life situations. This type of closure can be especially useful in the how-to type of article.

Research reports often end with a conclusions section offering the results or findings and explaining their relevance to the existing body of knowledge. Another type of conclusion, according to Mills and Walter,[13] is the decision reached following the discussion of a practical problem for which a solution must be offered. For example, "This leads the writer to conclude that the wisest course of action must be . . . ."

Sometimes, a publication closes with a short paragraph concerning the general message of the contribution. There is a tendency here either to introduce new information, or to rehash old material. Neither is acceptable.

What Writing Style Should Be Observed?

Professionals sometimes unknowingly use abstractions that the average person cannot comprehend. Thus they may speak and write in a dry fashion that can best be described as "bloodless." Making simple acts seem impersonal and detached is one of the most widespread faults of professional writers. For example, rather than say that an individual indulged in an act of generosity, come to the point and say that he or she gave a dollar to a tramp.[14]

The effective professional writer should vary the structure and length of sentences, but keep them simple as opposed to complex. The active voice is preferred over the passive voice. Simple, everyday adjectives are preferable to long, little used ones.

Oddly enough, most professional writings are written in third person. For some reason the pronoun "I" does tend to become offensive when overworked.

Especially in long publications, qualified terms are preferable to absolute terms. Use of qualifiers minimizes the chances of the communication sounding too direct and final. Indeed, accuracy is usually increased by making allowances for exceptions in this manner.

Unlike writers for trade journals, professional writers usually avoid vulgarisms and euphemisms. The prevalent use of four-letter words that were once uttered only

---

[13]Gordon H. Mills and John A. Walter, *Technical Writing,* 4th ed. (New York: Holt, Rinehart and Winston, 1978), p. 242.

[14]David Lambuth et al, *The Golden Book on Writing* (New York: The Viking Press, 1964), pp. 32-33.

behind closed doors is still offensive to some people. In a sense such expressions merely suggest a limited vocabulary. In addition, writers should avoid euphemisms. Instead of saying that Professor Jones was "sacked" or fired, one might more appropriately state that Jones received a terminal contract or, preferably, that Jones was not rehired. Instead of saying that Tom and Mary are "shacking up", it is preferable to suggest that Tom and Mary are living together.

What Rewriting Techniques Are Needed?

The writer's cliché "There is no writing; just rewriting" makes a lot of sense to anyone who has ever completed a worthy manuscript. Most writers will readily admit that the first draft (and the most important) is "talked" through. Often this involves writing just as rapidly as possible until the flow of ideas is exhausted. Sentence structure and grammar are totally disregarded. The objective is to get major ideas down on paper so that the "writing process" can begin.

After putting the manuscript aside for a day or two, the writer reads through the first draft without stopping, making marginal notes concerning those areas that need revision or deletion. It is at this point that the writing process begins in earnest. Some troublesome sections will need considerable attention. At all times, the intended audience is kept in mind. After the second revision, the beginning writer may want to ask an interested colleague for his or her criticisms. Again, the writer might gain greater objectivity by putting the manuscript aside for a time. Some writers prefer to type the second draft, triple-spacing it and leaving wide margins. Others prefer to merely patch up the original.

In developing the final draft (usually the third revision) the writer polishes and tightens sentence structure and grammar. When this process is completed, the writer should read the manuscript through again and "call it quits." A manuscript is never completed; it is merely abandoned!

As previously indicated, most national publishers employ field editors (referees) to evaluate manuscripts received. Field editors then submit their critiques to the managing editor. Some managing editors share these critiques with the writer (usually true in textbook and often in journal publishing). There is probably nothing more deflating to the ego than a thorough critique of one's manuscript. Nevertheless, the critique can be an invaluable guide for revision. Another aspect of revision involves adapting the manuscript to each different journal solicited—the subject of the next section.

How Is a Manuscript Tailored to a Particular Journal?

Usually the inside back cover of a journal includes a statement of publishing policy, indicating the general format the article should take and the number of manuscript copies required. Sometimes, there is a request to submit the title and author's name separately. (This preserves the anonymity of the writer during the process of evaluation.)

By examining recent editions of a journal, one can readily discern the type of article preferred. Some journals are philosophical in nature; others feature how-to articles. Still others cater to controversial issues; a few are dedicated to the advancement of theory. Occasionally, no preference is evident.[15]

After the kind of material desired, length is probably the most important criterion to a journal publisher. If a manuscript is twice as long as the average length of articles in a recent issue, for example, it is likely to be rejected. Similarly, a short manuscript may be rejected if the editor prefers lengthy ones. Closely associated with length is the matter of subheadings. Some editors like them; others do not. Other considerations involve bibliographies, sources cited, and footnotes. Even articles about techniques, for example, need documentation in some journals.

Obviously, a manuscript must be tailored to each prospective journal. A rejection from one certainly should not discourage the writer. It merely means that another journal must be selected and the manuscript rewritten to conform with the policies and preferences of a different editor. This author has sent manuscripts to at least six different publishers before giving up. Strangely enough, this sort of persistence usually pays off.

What Are the Essentials of a Book Review?

A book review is the surest and quickest way of breaking into print. At the same time, it offers a much needed service to the consumer. All professional journals maintain selected books for review, usually listed on the back pages of each journal issue. Although book reviews do not usually qualify officially as professional publications, writing them provides much needed experience for the beginner.

The book review should be short, about twelve short paragraphs. Its function is to evaluate the author's contribution fairly and clearly. To some extent, the fate of the author rests with the reviewer. Complete publication data are given first in the book review. Give the author's full name, the complete title of the book (including subtitle, if any), the place, publisher, and date of publication. (If the book is a revised edition, also note this.)

The first paragraph should capture the interest of the reader and describe briefly the purpose and scope of the book. (The author establishes purpose in the preface or in the first chapter of the book.) The first sentence, as with any beginning, should make the reader want to read further. For example, the introduction "A new theory of social change" is preferable to the common beginning "This book is. . . ."

The major thesis (original idea or new contribution) of the book is discussed in the

---

[15]The *Directory of Scholarly and Research Publishing Opportunities* provides a complete list of periodicals by subject and describes topics of interest to each journal. Also specified are preferred format and procedures for submitting articles.

second paragraph. In the next two paragraphs, the reviewer analyses the author's main contentions and supporting evidence.

In paragraphs six and seven, the reviewer should discuss how the author's contribution relates to other books on the same subject in order to provide the reader with a needed frame of reference. In the next two paragraphs the reviewer should point out the major flaws of the book (if any). Does the author discuss the opposing views of other writers? What evidence is offered in support of the author's own point of view? If the author provides outstanding supporting arguments, the reviewer should say so.

In paragraphs ten and eleven, the reviewer should analyze how and whether the book has contributed to its field of interest. What further work, if any, is needed to clear up doubtful points? For every generalization, the reviewer should offer one or two specific examples of what is meant. All specific quotes must be referenced by page (in parentheses following the quote or in a footnote). Each quotation, according to Hammett,[16] should be clearly related to the idea being discussed. Material should be quoted only when the author has said something more eloquently or precisely than the reviewer can explain it.

Finally, in the last paragraph, the reviewer should attempt to strike a balance between the merits and faults of the contribution, ending with a few words about the author. The book review represents one of the few places where the writer is expected to offer his or her opinion. However, reasons for the opinion must also be given. At all times the reviewer's opinion must be clearly distinguishable from that of the author. What is said in the review, rightly or wrongly, will be accepted as truth. Do not mention what the author has omitted if these omissions are cited in the preface. Biographical data on the author usually can be found in major reference books, such as the *Who's Who* series. If the author has published other books in the area, this fact might be noted. Lastly, the reviewer should acknowledge the amount of time and effort required to write such a book.

How Does One Find a Time and Place for Writing?

One does not find time to write; one makes time. Weekends and holidays are prime times. Some professors (as a matter of university policy) are able to set aside one morning, one afternoon, or perhaps a whole day each week for this sort of professional activity. Some write during the early morning hours; a few are able to write in the evening.

Professional writing demands considerable discipline. Generally, uninterrupted blocks of time are needed. For example, this author needs at least three hours of uninterrupted time. After about five hours of writing, mental exhaustion occurs. Sleep

---

[16]Hugh B. Hammitt, "How to Do a Book Review," *Social Studies* 65 (November 1974): 263-65.

or a change of activity becomes essential. Other writers report different needs. Fisher and Smith, for example, say, "It is best to write in short, regular periods of something less than an hour to keep from getting jaded, so plan to work in 'spells and breaks.' "[17]

Most writers report that ideas do not flow evenly. They come in sudden flashes of insight—in spurts. It takes considerable discipline to persist in the writing effort when ideas are not forthcoming. There is a strong tendency to escape from this "mental torture." It is easy to say "Today is just not my day" and give up. If such a luxury is permitted, the next session is likely to become even more difficult. Finally, all attempts at professional writing may be avoided. Rather than letting the mind find an "out," the writer should persevere for the full time allotted. Eventually ideas will flow, sometimes to the point of having difficulty writing them down fast enough. This is the ultimate payoff!

The place for writing should be selected carefully and used consistently. If possible, one might seek complete isolation in a library. Interruptions must be kept to an absolute minimum. Taking a "coffee break" and visiting with students and colleagues, for example, tend to interfere with productive effort. If one must have his or her coffee every few minutes, it is probably advisable to take a full mug along each day. Drink in private; it is the social affair that is the most devastating to the professional writer.

Another way of cultivating the flow of ideas is by researching periodical literature in one's field. Thus the pun "While other people are enjoying life, the professional writer is living in the library" is extremely appropriate. One should take some breaks, however, as long as they do not interfere with the regular writing schedule. Indeed, there is no better way of encouraging the flow of ideas than by taking a break, such as working in the garden.

How Can the Professional Writer Minimize the Danger of Plagiarism?

One hazard of professional writing (especially textbook writing) is the unfair use of another's work. A writer should even research those literary sources with which he or she is familiar to ensure that no ideas are being taken from someone else. Sometimes, one may gain ideas and wish to quote from as many as a dozen sources in a single chapter. Copyright law (under its fair use provision) permits a person to quote without permission up to 250 words from a book, or not more than 5 percent of the total work (whichever is greater).[18] Acknowledgment is expected.

Most copyright infringements, however, result from failure to obtain permission for using another's *idea*. Writers often have difficulty separating their own ideas from those of other writers. Probably the best precaution one can take is to put aside reference materials when beginning to write. Thus all major points will be stated in

---

[17] Fisher and Smith, *Writing as a Professional Activity*, pp. 5-6.

[18] Public Law 94-553, Section 107 94th Congress (October 19, 1976).

one's own words. If an idea is expressed in different ways in a variety of sources, unfair use is unlikely. On the other hand, if a given idea can be traceable to a single course, permission is needed. Permission to quote is the responsibility of the writer, not the publisher. A copyright extends for fifty years beyond the death of the writer.

Textbook writers often desire to "field test" their materials prior to publication. In such instances, it is a good idea to personally obtain copyright, for one's own protection. This can be done by sending two copies of the completed manuscript and ten dollars to the Register of Copyrights, Copyright Office, Library of Congress, Washington, D.C. (Copyright notice must appear on the first page of every copy of the manuscript used.) When the materials are published, the copyright automatically belongs to the publisher.

How Does the Professional Writer Avoid a Sexist Style?

Most professional writers were educated in a time when the pronoun "he" was used in all written communication unless the reference specifically concerned a female. The 1970s, however, brought about a consciousness of sex discrimination, characterized by many customs and practices that perpetuate the idea that females are the "weaker sex". Included in many "sexist" practices, it seems, is current grammar usage. In a world of men and women, so the argument goes, both must be included in written communication. Thus such words as "he," "his," or "himself" should be preceded or followed by the word "her," "hers," or "herself." In this book, for example, such expressions as "he or she," "his or hers," and "himself or herself" are used.

Another change involves the use of "Ms." as opposed to "Miss" or "Mrs." Many women even prefer the salutation "Dear Ms." over the more traditional "Dear Madam."

A rather subtle, but nevertheless objectionable, form of discrimination is the practice of pointing out a woman's physical characteristics in situations where they are irrelevant and in which one would not do the same in describing a man. Thus if one is unlikely to describe Tom Jones as handsome, one should not refer to Susie Smith as beautiful. In addition, occasionally a writer, almost subconsciously, refers to a woman by her first name in a bibliographical reference, but refers to a male by his surname. Surnames, should be used to refer to both men and women.

Still another discriminatory practice is refering to a woman as a "girl". This is parallel to the outmoded derogatory custom of referring to a black man as "boy".

In any such movement, of course, there is the lunatic fringe element. Some have even suggested that the word "woman" itself is discriminating since "man" is part of the word. In college and university communication, the expression "chairperson" is gaining acceptance as a replacement for "chairman." At present, the extent of this movement is not clear. Most professional writers, however, will find that most of the previous suggestions can be easily employed. Since they are less offensive to the contemporary female, why not use them!

Currently, it is still appropriate to refer to all men and women by using such expressions as the following:

All men are created equal.
All mankind is a creature of habit.
Man is by nature neither good nor bad.

The professional writer must be alert to other forms of sexist writing as they emerge. It is an established fact that discrimination of all kinds is imbedded in both the spoken and the written word.

The Value of Professional Writing

Professional writing in a growing number of leading universities and businesses is an avenue to employment stability, promotion, and merit salary increases. Professional writing affords one a visible leadership role among colleagues.

Writing is one way of forcing a professional to keep up with latest developments in his or her field.

Professional writing can increase one's competence as a teacher.

In some instances, (for example, textbook publishing), professional writing offers considerable financial reward.

Limitations of, and Problems with, Professional Writing

Some professionals, because of their personalities and limits on their time, are unable to become competent writers.

Professional writing is one of several indications of professional competence. Since professional writing is the most visible one, there is a tendency to use it almost exclusively for evaluational purposes.

Considerable amount of time and effort are necessary for effective results. Writing demands often interfere with other, equally important, professional activities.

Excessive attention to professional writing activities may reduce a professional's instructional effectiveness.

Professional writing sometimes is used as an avenue to professional advancement with little consideration for the quality of the work published.

Professional writing, as a prerequisite for stability of employment in a growing number of institutions, is sharply increasing competition for jobs. Even though they improve the overall quality of the literature in the field, professional contributions may become outdated by the time they are published. Since more professors are submitting journal articles, the time lag between submission and publication has increased from twelve to eighteen months.

**Illustrated
Aspects of
Professional
Writing**

Introductions

There are many ways of beginning an article, from plunging directly into the topic to offering a short attention-getting statement. Complex or lengthy articles often call for a preliminary paragraph or two, designed to catch the reader's immediate attention. The author prefers the personalized approach, illustrated earlier in the chapter. By checking the opening paragraphs of each chapter in this book, the reader will find other illustrations of introductions. Other types of introductions are offered in the following sections.

Analogy. After the personalized introduction, the analogy is probably the most widely used method for beginning complex or lengthy articles. (Chapter 13 of this book opens with an analogy.) For example:

> Just as the salesperson must first get a foot in the door to be effective, so must the reading specialist have the ability to get a foot in the classroom door to improve the teaching of reading. This means not just the classroom doors which may be already ajar—those of the language arts and reading teachers—but the doors of teachers in content areas where resistance to the teaching readings skills is often met.
>
> It is with this latter group, content area teachers, that the effectiveness of the reading specialist is truly tested. The problem is really one of salesmanship.
>
> This article refers to. . . .[19]

> A good theatre person worth his or her salt knows that the script, the playright's words, is only the starting point for the total theatrical experience. Devoid of the appropriate sets, costumes and lighting, the result is a boring evening (or matinee), and a great deal of wasted money. The best intentions and the best script may die an untimely death on stage, for all to see.
> And our classrooms are no different. . .[20]

Anecdote. Sometimes a short anecdote or vignette is used to capture the attention of the reader. This approach is often used when the article is short. For example:

---

[19] Russel E. Burgett, "Increasing the Effectiveness of the Reading Specialist," *Journal of Reading* 20 (October 1976): 6-8.

[20] Lawrence B. Rosenfield, "Setting the Stage for Learning," *Theory into Practice* 16: (June 1977): 167-73.

In her novel, *The Nine Tailors,* Dorothy Sayers shows a young Anglican clergyman leaning forward in his pulpit, stabbing an accusing finger at his congregation and saying, "Now *you* think that Belshazzar was Artaxerxes the First. But he wasn't; he was Artaxerxes the Second!" This story illustrates nicely a favorite theme of mine. . . . [21]

Rare is the principal who has not heard teachers make comments similar to the following:

"Kids have changed since you taught."
"I think administrators should teach classes so that they can keep in touch."
"You should see what a burden the administration's regulations have on a classroom teacher."
"Once you become an administrator, you forget what it is like in the classroom."

While these comments are widespread, one wonders whether they are valid. . . . The procedure I used to get back into the classroom was. . . . [22]

Closings

Sometimes, the last paragraph of a book or article may bring the communication to its logical conclusion. Often, however, an additional short paragraph is needed or a special section labeled "summary", "summary and conclusions," or "implications."

Short concluding paragraph.   This type of closing is frequently found in articles of a philosophical nature and in those that tend to be rather lengthy. For example:

The inequalities discussed in this article contribute to a kind of servitude of the mind in the Third World. The struggle to build independent sources of intellectual power, to make sure that educational systems serve indigenous needs, and to engender intellectual originality and self-respect is a long and difficult one. Impressive gains have been made in recent decades in raising literacy rates, building schools, and establishing universities, scientific institutions, and publishing firms. But much remains to be done. This analysis is dedicated to the ideal that greater understanding of the nature of relationships between the industrialized nations and the Third World will lessen dependency and diminish the partial servitude that now exists. [23]

---

[21] Daniel L. Morris, "Be Rigorous? . . . or Teach!" *The Science Teacher* 44 (December 1977): 21.

[22] John L. Robinson, "The Principal in the Classroom," NASSP Bulletin 61 (December 1977): 30-33.

[23] Philip G. Altbach, "Servitude of the Mind? Education, Dependency, and Neocolonialism," *Teachers College Record* 79 (December 1977): 187-204.

I have tried to suggest that out of the last decade with personalized instruction have come two tools—a more substantial technology and a new mechanism for teaching. Both provide.... Both go beyond.... a systematic analysis of education and systematic improvements in teaching and learning now seem possible.[24]

Summary or abstract. Almost without exception, a research report contains either a summary or an abstract. Each presents in a "nutshell" the essentials of the study and is most helpful to the reader who may not be interested in, or have time to, digest the entire article. The only difference between the two is that the abstract appears in front of, rather than at the end of, the article. More and more, summaries or abstracts are being used in nonresearch writings, especially when the writing concerns a complex design or model or contains extensive explanations. For example:

> This paper seeks to place the phenomenon of child maltreatment in the perspective of family development. While it is concerned with the problem of neglect, it addresses child abuse most directly. The paper focuses on necessary and sufficient conditions and the research implications of an ecological perspective. Maltreatment as consequence of stressful role transition is the major theme explored in this paper.... The problem of child maltreatment is thus best understood as an issue in the study of the ecology of family life, the development of the caregiver role and the provision of effective feedback for parents.[25]

---

[24]Sherman J. Gilmour, "Individualizing Instruction Is Not Enough," *Educational Technology* 17 (September 1977): 56-60.

[25]James Garbarino, "The Human Ecology of Child Maltreatment: A Conceptual Model for Research," *Journal of Marriage and the Family* 39 (November 1977) 721-35.

appendix
A

AN ILLUSTRATED TEACHING UNIT

The Yearly Plan

Introduction

Perhaps most of us are wondering how a study of general business methods will benefit us. What is meant by distribution of goods? As consumers, what effect does distribution of goods have on our lives? How is distribution related to production? To business policies? What effect does distribution have on our economy?

To answer these and many more questions that might arise, let us make a quick overview of the development of distribution, or marketing—the words can be used interchangeably.

Early man eked out a bare existence. He picked berries, caught fish, and in general lived off the land. He was barely able to provide for his own needs. This can be described as subsistence living.

As the population expanded and people began to live in communities, they began to divide up the work—men doing the hunting and fishing and the women taking care of the children and preparing the food and clothing. This type of arrangement was better than one in which one person did everything, but living conditions were still at a subsistence level. What countries in the world today still live under this type of existence? (India and Africa are examples; 85 percent of the people there still live in such circumstances.)

As these communities began to rise above the subsistence level, they began to specialize and develop special talents. One community of people living along the river would specialize in pottery and fishing; another nearby community would specialize in hunting. As these communities developed surpluses, they naturally began to exchange commodities. Thus marketing began.

As specialization and surpluses increased, marketplaces developed. They were usually about two to fifteen miles apart, depending on the density of the population in the area. Slowly towns grew around these market areas, and often a town hall would be built to protect customers and wares. What countries of the world today have common marketplaces? (Mexico is one; show slides of Mexico's marketplace.) Many of the countries of the world today have this kind of marketplace development.

Starting about 1700, many nations became involved in what we call the industrial revolution. The development of new and better machinery increased productivity and allowed the production of new and established commodities at lower prices. With more products available for sale, trade increased and markets expanded.

Here in the United States, trade developed along the seacoast and then spread inland. Local markets were established and grew into permanent establishments. Many of the early colonies were settlements established by traders who wanted an outlet for their products in the new world and a source for raw materials needed by the factories in the mother country.

However, as this nation's people moved west, away from the seacoast, they began to develop manufacturing centers of their own. Coastal towns became wholesale and manufacturing centers for the inland towns. This development gave rise to one of the innovations in marketing—the Yankee peddler. This individual would visit the eastern port cities and fill up a wagon with wares and then make regular circuits to the inland farm areas. The peddler had pots and pans, cloth, herbs, and almost anything that farmers could not produce themselves. Peddlers who became known in a certain locality would sometimes settle there and establish general stores. These stores carried about the same variety of goods as the traveling peddlers but in a little larger supply. The local people came to the store rather than wait for the store to go to them.

As populations shifted, many general stores became wholesale houses, supplying goods to other retailers, and others became specialized shops. Many internal developments in the history of the United States led to this expansion. Wars, railroads, and capital investments all made a contribution.

By the late 1800s, many manufacturers became dissatisfied with the distribution system and thus began to send out their salespeople to advertise their products. As the economy moved from one of subsistence to production of luxury items, interest in the needs of the consumer increased, eventually resulting in the establishment of chain stores, supermarkets, and discount houses common to today's market.

From our brief discussion on the development of retailing, let us make a list of the processes involved in distribution or marketing. This list should include (1) buying (2) selling (3) transporting (4) storing (5) grading (6) financing (7) taking risks, and (8) obtaining market information.

In this course, we will study consumer wants and demands as they relate to our personal situations. We will also explore how advertising and sales promotion help producers introduce their goods to the consuming public.

Course Concepts

1. Production standards in the United States make this nation the distribution center of the world.
2. Retail markets in the United States are consumer-oriented.
3. Selling is a joint process of communication between buyer and seller.

4. Because the customer market is constantly changing, it must be studied continuously if one is to stay abreast of current developments in it.
5. Differences in the structure and style of a product can be stated as sales appeals.
6. A sound business enterprise is based on adequate financing.
7. Business decisions are based on market trends.

Major Unit Titles

The United States: Distribution Center of the World (four weeks)
The Consumer Determines the Market (six weeks)
Sales Promotion and Advertising (four weeks)
The Consumer: A Constantly Changing Variable (four weeks)
Sales Appeal (five weeks)
Financing a Business Enterprise (six weeks)
Market Trends (three weeks)

The Unit Plan

Introduction to Unit in Sales Promotion and Advertising

The marketer must understand the needs, attitudes, and expectations of the consumer in order to succeed. He or she must be sensitive to the human factors that combine to motivate behavior. Consumers are motivated by primary and secondary needs.

Basic, or primary, needs are physiological and safety and security needs. What type of items might be included under physiological needs? This list might include food, clothing, and shelter—the basics of existence. Safety and security needs include such things as insurance, fringe benefits, and safety guarantees.

Secondary needs are psychological ones. They include recognition and social and self-actualizing needs. An example of a recognition need is being the first in a neighborhood to own a new product or some distinctive piece of furniture or style of golf clubs. An example of a social need is belonging to a group made up of individuals who all own similar merchandise. In other words, it involves the bandwagon philosophy. Self-actualization is involved when an individual can make creative use of his or her natural ability by engaging in do-it-yourself projects or by acquiring information and education. Basic needs must be satisfied before an individual has a desire to satisfy higher needs. For example, people living under subsistence conditions are not interested in an education, do-it-yourself projects, or being the first to own a new product. They are primarily interested in where their next meal is coming from.

Needs seem to follow a circular pattern. A need will become a drive that will result in a behavior pattern that, in turn, will serve either to satisfy or frustrate the need. Once there are new needs, the pattern starts all over again.

Different socioeconomic groups in the United States tend to be motivated by different need levels. The lower classes tend to be motivated by the first three need groups: physiological, safety and security, and recognition needs. The middle and upper classes are motivated more by social and self-actualization needs.

Behavioral psychologists have established that rewards are better motivators than threats. We remember pleasant experiences and tend to forget unpleasant ones. Since people forget rapidly, repetition in a sales promotion campaign is necessary for driving the point home.

How can these factors affect our response to customers as they enter the store? What stores do you like to shop in? Why do you like to shop in them? (Develop through informal class discussion.)

We mentioned that an advertising message should be repeated. This is necessary in order to presell an individual on a product and to make him or her respond positively to the five basic buying decisions: (1) the need, (2) the source, (3) the product, (4) the price, and (5) the time. By preselling the product through advertising, the amount of personal salesmanship is minimized. To help the potential customer make the decision to buy, the marketer follows the AIDA formula (A—Attention, I—Interest, D—Desire, and A—Action).

As we know, not all people want the same products, and thus each manufacturer must decide which people the product will appeal to. This process is known as finding the target market. The target market is determined through an analysis of the current and anticipated market situation. Because the consumer market is constantly changing, it must be constantly evaluated. One must assess people's buying habits, what products they want, their knowledge of existing similar products, and what they can afford. There are many sources of market information available, both public and private.

Once the consumers for a new product have been determined, the advertisements that will appeal to their wants and desires can be written. The advertiser's job is to organize the pictures and written materials in such a way that preselling of the product can take place.

Unit Content

In discussing this unit, we will place major emphasis on how the customer's needs influence the development of new products and on how producers develop appeals to encourage consumers to buy their products.

1. Markets as people
   a. The roots of human behavior.
   b. Psychological guidelines.
   c. The advertising appeal.
2. Marketing strategy
   a. Steps in the marketing process.
   b. Marketing as a continuous process.

3. Consumer demand
   a. Market trends.
   b. Market information.
4. Consumer buying decisions
   a. Kinds of advertising copy.
   b. The sales message.

Unit Concepts

1. Customer satisfaction is the most important product.
2. Customer needs are the prompters for purchasing decisions.
3. Advertising can be an effective means of preselling products.
4. Advertisements use customer motives that can be restated through a personal selling approach.
5. Because the customer market is in a state of constant change, it must be studied continuously if one is to stay abreast of current developments in it.
6. Sales appeals must be consistent with ethical standards of advertising.

Instructional Goal and Outcomes

Unit concept I: Customer satisfaction is the most important product.

Unit goal I: After this unit, the student should have furthered his or her understanding of the importance of customer satisfaction in sales promotion and advertising, as evidenced by:

1. The ability to synthesize various aspects of customer satisfaction from a case study.
2. The ability to analyze the merits of a debate on customer satisfaction.

Learning activities

1. Case analysis

   Problem: What psychological factors should be considered in selling?

   Case: "The Factors That Count!"

2. Debate

   Proposition: Resolved, that a dissatisfied customer should have the privilege of returning goods.

Instructional Goal and Outcomes

Unit concept II: Customer needs are the prompters of purchasing decisions.

Unit goal II: After this unit, the student should have furthered his or her understanding of the role of basic human motives and wants in selling, as evidenced by:

1. The ability to apply appropriate psychological principles in a simulation game.
2. The ability to interpret sales resistance in a sociodrama.

Learning Activities

1. Simulation

   Game: "People U.S.A."

2. Sociodrama

   Problem: How might a customer feel when pressured into buying a product?

   Broad situation: Mary wants to buy a gift for her husband's birthday. Jim is a salesman in a department store.

Instructional Goal and Outcomes

Unit concept III: Advertising can be an effective means of preselling products.

Unit goal III: After this unit, the student should have furthered his or her understanding of the relationship between impulse buying and advertising, as evidenced by:

1. The ability to test hypotheses of impulse buying in a class discussion.
2. The ability to apply appropriate advertising principles in role-playing situations.

Learning activities

1. Class discussion

   Problem: What can we as marketers do to stimulate buying?

2. Role playing in buzz groups

    Problem: What are the essentials of good advertisement?

Instructional Goal and Outcomes

Unit concept IV: Advertisements use customer motives that can be restated through a personal selling approach.

Unit goal IV: After this unit, the student should further appreciate the role that basic motives play in advertising, as evidenced by:

1. The ability to evaluate selected advertisements on the basis of their basic motive appeal.
2. The ability to develop an acceptable advertisement, using basic motive as a basis.

Learning activities

1. Analysis of advertisements

    Problem: Evaluate the basic motives employed in the selected advertisements.

2. Development of advertisements

    Assignment: Develop an advertisement utilizing the basic motives provided.

Instructional Goal and Outcomes

Unit concept V: Since the customer market is constantly changing, continuous study is essential if one wants to stay abreast of current developments.

Unit goal V: After this unit the student should have furthered his or her understanding of factors determining the products market, as evidenced by:

1. The ability to predict the market value of selected new products.
2. The ability to analyze consumer demands as reflected in selected advertisement.

Learning activities

1. Written analysis

    Problem: What is the market value of the products before you?

2. Class discussion

Problem: Predict the elements of consumer demand reflected in advertisements given you.

Instructional Goal and Outcomes

Unit concept VI: Sales appeal must be consistent with advertising ethics.

Unit goal VI: After this unit the student should have furthered his or her appreciation of the ethics of motivational appeals in advertisements, as evidenced by:

1. The ability to evaluate selected sales campaigns in terms of basic civil liberties.
2. The ability to develop an advertising slogan that is consistent with advertising ethics.

Learning activities

1. Case analysis of sales campaign

Problem: What are the appropriate ethical limits of selling?

Case: "The Quick Buck Auto Sales Company Sells a Car"

2. Written assignment

Problem: What are the prudent limits of advertising?

Assignment: Develop an advertising slogan for a new home.

The preceding illustration represents the extent of preplanning experiences for teaching. As one teaches, he or she will develop lesson plans for many learning activities and test items and evaluational devices for assessing concept attainment.

appendix B

ILLUSTRATED ASPECTS OF A LEARNING ACTIVITY PACKAGE

Formulating Instructional Objectives

Rationale

Here the purpose of the Learning Activity Package (LAP) is clarified *for the user*.

Overview

This section, although not essential, is a feature of the LAPs developed by the writer. It consists of key concepts to be gained from the experience. To illustrate, "Instructional objectives, with their projected behavioral outcomes, provide a sound basis for subsequent instructional and evaluational experiences."

Concepts are followed with new terms, defined for the learner.

Objectives

Objectives of the experience are expressed in behavioral terms. Since they are written as minimum-essentials objectives, the *specific conditions* and the *minimum level of acceptability* are clarified fully. To illustrate

After this experience you should be able to develop instructional objectives and behavioral outcomes for teaching, as evidenced by your ability to select eight out of nine appropriately stated behavioral outcomes (minimum essentials and developmental) from a provided list of twenty.

Objectives usually ranged from simple to complex levels of cognition, for example, from "listing" to "constructing."

Portions of this learning activity package were taken from the author's *Secondary/Middle School Teaching: A Handbook for Beginning Teachers and Teacher Self-Renewal* (Boston: Allyn and Bacon, Inc., 1977).

Preliminary Reading

If a LAP is to be self-instructional, adequate preparation for the experience is essential. Background reading is usually involved. In some subject areas, however, there may be considerable ambiguity among the literature read. Thus key excerpts were provided in the illustrated LAP to help develop a common frame of reference for the experience. Preliminary reading must be kept brief.

Preassessment Items

The student usually rates this aspect of the LAP experience the most valuable. It enables one to gain an overall perspective of the LAP experience and to pinpoint learning deficiencies in the area. Indeed the writer has found that preassessment items are very effective learning tools. In this LAP this is accomplished by providing supporting reasons for both correct and incorrect responses at the end of the unit. Preassessment items must be consistent with objectives. The illustrated items demand a relatively low level of cognition. By providing supporting reasons, however, mere recognition is brought to the levels of application and analysis.

From the list of "outcomes" place a check by nine of those that meet the criteria for either developmental or minimum-essentials outcomes.

1. Understands the prejudicial structure of the English language.
2. Shows interest in the variety of art forms in the special school display.
3. Checked out at least ten books from the library voluntarily over the past month.
4. Selects an appropriate color combination in eight of ten instances from twenty-five assorted ensembles.
5. Displays appropriate speech behavior and voice quality during a fifteen-minute presentation.
6. Identifies logical contradictions in the senator's speech on honesty in politics.
7. Lists the grammatical errors in a theme on our national forests.
8. Selects the most appropriate workshop tool in eight of ten instances from twenty-five woodworking tasks.
9. Appreciates home safety rules.
10. Responds during a class discussion on the impact of mass transit systems on large cities.
11. Defends art media used in connection with the assigned project.
12. Demonstrates the ability to employ analysis-level questions during a discussion.
13. Employs an appropriate genetic cross in eight of ten instances from provided problems.
14. Comprehends fallacies in the speaker's argument.
15. Types a perfect copy of a typing drill.
16. Interacts with committee members on the need for political reform.
17. Explains the merits of using pickets during a labor dispute.

18. Understands the basic essentials of first aid.
19. Displays interest in the merits of the extended family.
20. Is aware of grammatical errors in a three-page document on our national debt.

Answers to preassessment items. 3, 4, 6, 8, 10, 11, 13, 15, 17. (Each of these describes some specific behavior.)

Reasons for rejected outcomes

(1) Understanding is internal; no behavior indicative of understanding is offered.
(2) Does not call attention to any specific behavior that would suggest interest.
(5) Includes two distinct aspects of delivery; a behavioral outcome should be restricted to one specific behavior.
(7) In an area involving a definite skill, a minimum-essentials objective should be used. No minimum level of acceptability is offered.
(9) Appreciation is internal; an identified behavior is needed before this appreciation can be assessed.
(12) This is vague; a number of specific behaviors might suggest this ability.
(14) Comprehension is internal; it is necessary to specify evidence of this.
(16) This is vague; the nature of this interaction should be specified.
(18) Understanding is internal; a specific behavior indicative of this understanding is needed.
(19) Interest is internal. What behavior would suggest this?
(20) What would be evidence of this awareness?

Following the preassessment experience, the learner checks his or her level of understanding and proceeds to the next LAP if the accuracy levels prescribed in the objectives were reached. At this point, considerable reinforcement is offered. To illustrate from the LAP, "Even if you 'struck out' on the preassessment items (as expected), do not be discouraged. The writer has provided . . . a series of practical learning experiences to help you quickly attain mastery in the area. Good luck!"

Learning Activities

(Since the learning experiences are the heart of the LAP, this section has been reproduced completely.)
Work through each learning activity, complete the self-assessment items, and check your answers before moving to the next one. Note that the last learning activity is optional, depending upon your needs and circumstances at that point. You should be able to complete this LAP in about four hours.

A: Read. Re-examine the overview and the preliminary reading sections for this LAP and for the preceding one (Formulating Concepts). You will broaden your understanding substantially by studying Chapter 2 in *The Professional Teacher's Handbook,* 2nd ed., and by studying the selected references listed at the end of this LAP. Note specifically the following points:

1. The overlap between the three domains.
2. Those levels of the affective and the psychomotor domains that are ordinarily beyond the scope of the individual classroom teacher.
3. How the unit concepts, instructional goals, and behavioral outcomes are integrated.
4. The rationale for beginning each goal with the introductory clause "After this unit (lesson) the student should. . . ." and culminating the goal with the phrase "As evidenced by. . . ."

Self-assessment items

1. Why is the evaluational level of the cognitive domain seen as overlapping with the affective domain?
2. Identify the levels of the affective and the psychomotor domains that are generally beyond the scope of the *individual* classroom teacher.
3. How are concepts tied in with instructional objectives?
4. Why is it recommended that each goal begin with the clause "After this unit (lesson) the student should . . . ." and culminate with the phrase "As evidenced by . . . ."

At this point, you may select either Option B_1 or Option B_2, depending on your particular situation. Those who are presently teaching should select Option B_1. Those who are not teaching or who do not have immediate access to students should select Option B_2.

Option B_1: Examination of objectives models. This experience can be acquired in several ways. First, a number of useful films and filmstrips have been developed for this purpose. Most of these, however, feature the writing of *minimum-essentials* behavioral outcomes only. Such aids are readily accessible from a number of commercial suppliers.*

The illustrations section of Chapter 2 of the Hoover texts and a number of other books provide a variety of objectives and outcomes in various fields. Some especially useful sources are Bloom, Krathwohl, and Harrow's books on the cognitive, the affective, and the psychomotor domains. In addition, Gronlund's book on behavioral objectives provides some useful developmental outcomes.

Another approach might include an analysis of goals and outcomes prepared by selected teachers in your school.

Whatever means are utilized, it is imperative that the examined materials be modeled as closely as possible after the approach offered in this LAP. Any existing discrepancies should be thoroughly understood by the user.

Working in a committee of three, if possible, direct your attention to the following:

---

*One filmstrip series, entitled *Developing and Writing Performance Objectives*, is available from Multi-Media Associates, 4901 E. 5th St., Tucson, Ariz. 85732.

1. The nature and role of action verbs in behavioral outcomes.
2. Identify the cognitive level of each outcome.
3. Note the differences between minimum-essentials and developmental out-
    comes.
4. Identify possible learning activities that are foreshadowed in the behavioral
    outcomes.
5. Identify those outcomes that could be considered en route and those that
    could be considered terminal in nature.

Self-assessment items

1. Illustrate the role of action verbs in determining cognitive level of outcomes.
2. Why are minimum-essentials outcomes deemed more appropriate for the skills
    area, whereas developmental outcomes often are preferred in academic areas?
3. In what way do behavioral outcomes foreshadow learning activities?
4. What is the difference between en route and terminal outcomes?

Option B₂: Preliminary objectives application and comparison. Develop one
cognitive, one affective, and one psychomotor instructional objective with two
accompanying outcomes for each. Make sure that both minimum-essentials and
developmental outcomes are represented. Use the area of Woodworking (industrial arts
area) for this experience.

Cognitive domain

1.
2.

Affective domain

1.
2.

Psychomotor domain

1.
2.

Using objectives and outcomes from selected books as models (noting especially
the illustrations in the Hoover texts), compare them with your own efforts. If you are
working with other students, the formation of small groups is recommended. Proceed
as follows:

1. Differences in specificity of instructional goals when a concept is and is not
    embodied in the statement.
2. Levels of specificity of the various behavioral outcomes.

3. Degree to which the higher levels were represented in the various behavioral outcomes.
4. Problems which were (or might be) evident when the phrase "as evidenced by" was omitted.
5. Basic differences between minimum-essentials and developmental outcomes.

Self-assessment items

1. Cognitive, affective, and psychomotor outcomes may appear under instructional goals that feature only one of the three objective domains. Defend or refute.
2. Some authorities recommend emphasis on minimum-essentials outcomes in the cognitive domain (as well as in the psychomotor domain). What is likely to be the effect of such a practice on learning?
3. Why are some action verbs, such as "interest," "understand," and "know," deemed inappropriate for use in behavioral outcomes?

C: Instructional application. Using three of your unit concepts as a basis (developed in connection with the LAP on gaining the concept), prepare an instructional objective (goal) and several behavioral outcomes for each of the selected unit concepts. Focus on one instructional objective in the cognitive domain (understands), another in the affective domain (appreciates, interests, or values), and the third in the psychomotor domain (skills and habits). Proceed as follows:

1. Prepare at least eight behavioral outcomes for *each* instructional objective. Then combine and delete until about half of the original outcomes remain.
2. Make sure that both higher and lower levels of the taxonomies are represented.
3. Be sure to construct minimum-essentials outcomes for the psychomotor objectives and developmental outcomes for the cognitive and affective objectives.
4. Now attempt to change your developmental outcomes into minimum-essentials outcomes, noting difficulties.

After completing these tasks, discuss your experience with other new teachers, if possible. Focus on both the rationale and the difficulties encountered in each of the above.

Self-assessment items

1. Why is it desirable to initially construct several behavioral outcomes for each instructional objective?
2. Why is the valuing level of the affective domain so difficult to assess within the classroom setting?
3. Why are the words "understand," "appreciate," "value," and "skills," considered appropriate in instructional goals but inappropriate in behavioral outcomes?

4. Why does a minimum-essentials outcome in the cognitive domain tend to be at a relatively low level of cognition?
5. Why is a minimum-essentials outcome at the valuing level of the affective domain meaningless?

If, after reviewing your learning activities for this LAP, you feel that you can meet the stated objectives, proceed to the posttest. If not, you should complete the optional activity. Note that it provides for a number of optional situations, depending upon your own individual circumstances.

D: Visit with experienced teachers. (This activity is optional.) Working in a committee of three, if possible, arrange to visit experienced teachers who work in areas that emphasize the different domains of instructional objectives. (You may elect to invite such individuals to visit with your committee.) Proceed as follows:

1. Have one member of your committee visit a *social science* teacher for the purpose of obtaining the following information:
   a. A list of the objectives for the *unit* being studied.
   b. A list of the objectives for the *lesson* being studied.
   c. If the teacher's objectives are not written out, determine, if you can, how the teacher would phrase objectives. (Be sure to ascertain key verbs preferred.)
   d. Obtain the teacher's views about the importance of goals and behavioral outcomes as a basis for developing unit and lesson plans.
2. Have a second member of your committee visit a *literature* teacher. Obtain the same information as in the above.
3. Have a third member of your committee visit a teacher who deals with a *skills class* (e.g., physical education, home economics, industrial arts, foreign language, mathematics, speech, certain business courses). Obtain the same information as in the above.*
4. Following the visits, compare notes and discuss the following questions:
   a. What action verbs predominated ("understand," "learn," "name," "list," "apply," etc.)?
   b. What level of behavioral outcomes predominated? What influence might this have on instructional activities?
   c. Logically, the social science teacher might be expected to emphasize cognitive, the literature teacher to emphasize affective, and the skills area teacher to emphasize psychomotor objectives. Did this pattern seem to apply? Speculate on any wide deviations from the foregoing emphasis.
   d. Discuss the probable impact of ill-defined (or inappropriate) goal domain emphasis on instruction in the subjects represented.
   e. What were the teachers' overall assessments of the role of objectives and outcomes in teaching?

---

*If working alone, you may be able to reduce the number of visits by visiting a teacher(s) who is emphasizing more than one type of instructional objective at the time of your visit.

Self-assessment items

1. Why do ill-defined goals and behavioral outcomes increase the tendency for "textbook teaching"?
2. You will recall that unit concepts deal with current applications. This necessitates a two-step process for the history teacher. First, the teacher must identify several major content ideas and then translate these into concepts (with current applications). What influence might a breakdown in this two-step process have on the history teacher's goals and behavioral outcomes?
3. Most professional educators consider goals and outcomes the "hub around which all other instructional activities evolve." Explain.
4. Distinguish between unit and lesson outcomes.

Note that after each learning experience, the student is provided several key self-assessment items (with answers in back). This serves to expand learning and to enable the student to check level of progress. Again, the reader will notice that learning experiences advance from low to high levels of cognition.

Posttest

The posttest will be very similar or even identical to the preassessment items.
Finally, reinforcement and directions for the next LAP experience are provided.
To illustrate:

Your successful completion of this LAP represents a significant step on your way to becoming an outstanding teacher. Indeed, instructional goals and behavioral outcomes set the stage for effective planning activities. Even if you failed to fully satisfy the recommended mastery level for this LAP, proceed to the next one on planning for teaching. Concept formation, instructional objectives, and planning are so closely related that clarification of one tends to contribute to understanding of the others.

appendix C

STUDENT EVALUATION OF TEACHERS

Hoover Course Evaluation Form

You can help your instructor improve this course by giving thoughtful responses to the questions below. Blacken the appropriate space on your answer sheet.

1. Organization of course
   (1) Well organized.
   (2) Adequate; could be better.
   (3) Inadequate organization detracts from course.
   (4) Confused and unsystematic.
2. Teacher's speaking ability
   (1) Skilled in presenting material; voice and presence excellent.
   (2) Adequate; does not detract from course.
   (3) Poor speaker; detracts from course.
   (4) Poor speaking techniques; a serious handicap in course.
3. Teacher's ability to explain
   (1) Explanations clear and to point.
   (2) Explanations usually adequate.
   (3) Explanations often inadequate.
   (4) Explanations seldom given or usually inadequate.
4. Teacher's encouragement to thinking
   (1) Great ability to make you think for yourself.
   (2) Considerable stimulation to thinking.
   (3) Not much stimulation to thinking.
   (4) Discouragement to thinking.
5. Teacher's attitude toward students
   (1) Sympathetic, helpful, actively concerned.
   (2) Moderately sympathetic.
   (3) Routine in attitude; avoids individual contact.
   (4) Distant, aloof, cold.
6. Teacher's attitude toward subject
   (1) Enthusiastic; enjoys teaching.
   (2) Rather interested.
   (3) Rather bored; routine interest.
   (4) Not interested; disillusioned with subject.

7. Sense of proportion and humor
   (1) Sure of oneself; not overly critical or sensitive.
   (2) Usually well balanced.
   (3) Sometimes well balanced.
   (4) Overly serious; no sense of relative values.
8. Personal characteristics
   (1) Free from annoying mannerisms.
   (2) Usually free from annoying mannerisms.
   (3) Moderately free from objectionable mannerisms.
   (4) Often exhibits irritating mannerisms.
9. Tolerance to disagreement
   (1) Encourages and values reasonable disagreement.
   (2) Accepts disagreement fairly well.
   (3) Discourages disagreement.
   (4) Dogmatic; intolerant of disagreement.
10. How course is fulfilling your needs (immediate as well as ultimate goals)
    (1) Course extremely valuable; now and later.
    (2) Much of course is or probably will be useful.
    (3) Have difficulty in seeing much value in this course.
    (4) Course is a waste of time.
11. Suitability of amount and value of assigned work
    (1) Amount and value of outside work well balanced.
    (2) Amount and value of outside work reasonable.
    (3) Too much work for the benefits received.
    (4) No outside work or no value to it.
12. Weight given tests in determining class marks
    (1) A variety of measures gave balance to different dimensions of this course.
    (2) Some variety in measuring instruments utilized.
    (3) Too much reliance on one or two tests.
    (4) Evaluation depended on one or two tests.
13. Coordination of tests with major goals of course
    (1) Tests demanded application of principles consistent with class goals.
    (2) Tests somewhat consistent with major goals of class.
    (3) Frequently had some difficulty in seeing relationship of tests to class goals.
    (4) Relationship of tests to class goals was purely coincidental.
14. Teaching methods employed
    (1) Variety gave me new insights into problems.
    (2) Variety helped to maintain interest.
    (3) Variety seemed to impede class progress.
    (4) Variety tended to confuse.
15. Overall course evaluation (as compared with all other courses taken in college)
    (1) One of the best courses I have taken.
    (2) Above average.
    (3) Average.
    (4) Poor.
16. Overall instructor evaluation (as compared with all other college instructors)

        (1) One of the best instructors I have had.
        (2) Above average.
        (3) Average.
        (4) Poor.

Teaching Analysis by Students [TABS]*

The Clinic to Improve University Teaching is working with instructors to improve the quality of teaching which they offer to their students. The Clinic is designed to help instructors identify and effectively use their particular teaching strengths, to isolate their specific teaching problems, and to develop improvement strategies directed at these problems.

In order to identify these strengths and problems, we are collecting information about teaching in this course by discussing course objectives and teaching patterns with your instructor, by observing and video-taping some classes, and by asking for student opinions about performance on some specific teaching skills and behaviors. The information will be used to obtain a clearer understanding of specific teaching strengths and weaknesses so that your instructor can work toward improvement. Thus, your responses will be of most value to your instructor if they are thoughtful and honest. Your cooperation will be very much appreciated.

Section 1—Teaching Skills and Behaviors

In this questionnaire, there are some statements concerning a variety of specific teaching skills and behaviors. Please read each statement carefully and then indicate the extent to which you feel your instructor needs improvement. Respond to each statement by selecting one of the following:

1. No improvement is needed (very good or excellent performance).
2. Little improvement is needed (generally good performance).
3. Improvement is needed (generally mediocre performance).
4. Considerable improvement is needed (generally poor performance).
5. Not a necessary skill or behavior for this course.

Please make your decisions about the degree of improvement needed on the basis of what you think would be best for this particular course and your learning style. Try to consider each statement separately, rather than let your overall feelings about the instructor determine all the responses.

———————————

*Clinic to Improve University Teaching, School of Education, University of Massachusetts at Amherst. © Clinic to Improve University Teaching 1974. Used by permission.

1. The instructor's explanation of *course* objectives.
2. The instructor's explanation of the objectives for each class session and learning activity.
3. The instructor's ability to arouse my interest when introducing an instructional activity.
4. The instructor's explanation of the work expected from each student.
5. The instructor's ability to maintain a clear relationship between the course content and the course objectives.
6. The instructor's skill in clarifying the relationships among the various topics treated in the course.
7. The instructor's skill in making clear the distinction between major and minor topics.
8. The instructor's skill in adjusting the rate at which new ideas are covered so that the material can be followed and understood.
9. The instructor's ability to clarify material which needs elaboration.
10. The instructor's speaking skills.
11. The instructor's ability to ask easily understood questions.
12. The instructor's ability to ask thought-provoking questions.
13. The instructor's ability to answer questions clearly and concisely.
14. The instructor's overall effectiveness as a discussion leader.
15. The instructor's ability to get students to participate in class discussions.
16. The instructor's skill in facilitating discussions *among students* as opposed to discussions only between the instructor and students.
17. The instructor's ability to wrap things up before moving on to a new topic.
18. The instructor's ability to tie things together at the end of a class.
19. The instructor's explanation of precisely how my performance is to be evaluated.
20. The instructor's ability to design evaluation procedures which are consistent with course objectives.
21. The instructor's performance in periodically informing me of my progress.
22. The instructor's selection of materials and activities which are thought-provoking.
23. The instructor's ability to select materials and activities which are not too difficult.
24. The instructor's provision of *variety* in materials and activities.
25. The instructor's ability to use a variety of teaching techniques.
26. The instructor's demonstration of creativity in teaching methods.
27. The instructor's management of day-to-day administrative details.
28. The instructor's flexibility in offering options for individual students.
29. The instructor's ability to take appropriate action when students appear to be bored.
30. The instructor's availability for personal consultation.
31. The instructor's ability to relate to people in ways which promote mutual respect.

32. The instructor's maintenance of an atmosphere which actively encourages learning.
33. The instructor's ability to inspire excitement or interest in the content of the course.
34. The instructor's ability to relate the subject matter to other academic disciplines and real-world situations.
35. The instructor's willingness to explore a variety of points of view.
36. The instructor's ability to get students to challenge points of view raised in the course.
37. The instructor's performance in helping me to explore the relationship between my personal values and the course content.
38. The instructor's performance in making me aware of value issues within the subject matter.

Section II—Other Information

Please mark the appropriate response for each of the following items beside the correct statement number on the answer sheet.

39. Class:
    (1) Freshman.
    (2) Sophomore.
    (3) Junior.
    (4) Senior.
    (5) Graduate student.
40. Sex:
    (1) Male.
    (2) Female.
41. Grade point average:
    (1) Less than 1.50 (lowest).
    (2) 1.50-2.49.
    (3) 2.50-2.99.
    (4) 3.00-3.49.
    (5) 3.50-4.00 (highest).
42. In terms of the directions my life is taking, this course is:
    (1) Relevant.
    (2) Somewhat relevant.
    (3) Irrelevant.
    (4) I am unsure.
43. In this course I am learning:
    (1) A great deal.
    (2) A fair amount.
    (3) Very little.
    (4) I am unsure.

44. As a result of this course, my attitude toward the instructor is:
    (1) Becoming more positive.
    (2) Becoming more negative.
    (3) Unchanged.
45. As a consequence of participating in this course, my attitude toward the subject matter is:
    (1) Becoming more positive.
    (2) Becoming more negative.
    (3) Unchanged.
46. I would prefer that this course:
    (1) Become more structured or organized.
    (2) Become less structured or organized.
    (3) Maintain about the present level of structure.
47. Which of the following descriptions of student learning styles most nearly approximates your own? (Choose only one.)
    (1) I like to think for myself, work alone, and focus on learning personally relevant content.
    (2) I prefer highly structured courses and will focus on learning what is required.
    (3) I try to get the "most out of classes," and like sharing my ideas with others and getting involved in class activities.
    (4) I am competitive, concerned about getting good grades, and try to learn material so that I can perform better than others.
    (5) I am generally turned off as a student, uninterested in class activities, and don't care to work with teachers or other students.
48. About how much time and effort have you put into this course compared to other courses of equal credit?
    (1) Much more.
    (2) Somewhat more.
    (3) About the same amount.
    (4) Somewhat less.
    (5) Much less.
49. Generally, how valuable have you found the assigned readings in terms of their contribution to your learning in this course?
    (1) Very valuable.
    (2) Fairly valuable.
    (3) Not very valuable.
    (4) There have been no assigned readings.
50. Overall, I would rate this course as:
    (1) Excellent.
    (2) Good.
    (3) Mediocre.
    (4) Poor.

How to Discriminate Evaluation Items**

Item validity was sought via a jury of experts composed of teachers, administrators, and school board members from a large midwestern school district. Reliability and discriminatory power were analyzed using the Menne and Tolsma (1971) adaptation of the F test. Students, peer teachers, administrators, and the subjects themselves were used to obtain 1,277 appraisals of 69 elementary and secondary teachers. Ninety-four items proved to be sufficiently powerful to separate high teacher performance from mediocre performance after examining a total of 360 performance descriptors.

The 30 items in the table are illustrative of the pool of 94 valid, reliable, and discriminating items. Each of the items in the pool appears to fall into one of five rubrics descriptive of teacher behavior—productive teaching techniques, positive interpersonal relations, organized/structured class management, intellectual stimulation, and desirable out-of-class behavior. The performance rating items are placed in order of discriminatory power under each rubric.

Discriminating Evaluation Items

Productive teaching techniques

1. The teacher uses probing questions for understanding of concepts and relationships, and for feedback to the teacher.
2. The teacher uses student ideas in instruction.
3. The teacher uses structuring comments, such as examples, to serve as advance organizers.
4. The teacher uses varied teaching strategies and materials that stimulate student learning.
5. The teacher explains things well, puts ideas across logically and in an orderly way.
6. The teacher provides opportunities for pupils to learn material on which they will later be tested.

Positive interpersonal relations

1. The teacher shows respect for his pupils.
2. The teacher is tolerant of students whose ideas differ from his.
3. The teacher uses supportive criticism rather than blame, shame, or sarcasm.
4. The teacher is readily available to students.

**Richard P. Manatt, Kenneth L. Palmer, and Everett Hidlebaugh, "Evaluating Teacher Performance with Improved Rating Scales, "*NASSP Bulletin* 60 (September 1976): 21-24. Used by permission of the authors and the publisher. Richard P. Manatt is professor of education at Iowa State University, Ames, Iowa. Kenneth L. Palmer is assistant professor of educational administration at California State University, Los Angeles, California. Everett Hidlebaugh is superintendent of schools in Dyke, Iowa.

5. The teacher is fair, impartial, and objective in treatment of pupils.
6. The teacher provides opportunities for all pupils to explain success.

Organized/structural class management

1. The teacher constantly monitors pupil progress and adjusts the pace accordingly.
2. The teacher presents material in a well-organized fashion in order to use class time efficiently.
3. The teacher has well-defined objectives for his pupils, and works toward them.
4. The teacher uses pupil assignments that are relevant and sufficient for in-depth learning.
5. The teacher is businesslike and task-oriented in behavior.
6. The teacher keeps the "difficulty level of instruction" appropriate for each individual.

Intellectual stimulation

1. The teacher inspires students to seek more knowledge.
2. The teacher is an exciting, vibrant person.
3. The teacher is enthusiastic.
4. The teacher sustains pupil attention and response with activities appropriate to the various pupil levels.
5. The teacher makes classwork interesting.
6. The teacher and pupils share in the enjoyment of humorous situations.

Desirable out-of-class behavior

1. The teacher is a good team worker.
2. The teacher strives for improvement through positive participation in professional growth activities.
3. The teacher assumes responsibilities outside the classroom as they relate to school.
4. The teacher is committed to the primary goal of assisting pupil growth.
5. The teacher utilizes community resources in instruction.
6. The teacher effectively reports pupil progress to parents.

The 30 items produced by this research have been used repeatedly in five-point Likert-type responses. Preliminary norming experience with the scale indicates that these 30 items are adequate to discriminate between teachers of high, medium, and low performance. Indeed, the six items relating to out-of-class behavior could be dropped with little loss in efficiency.

The process of the performance evaluation cycle will vary depending upon the ratio of appraisers to appraisees, state laws, the skill of the appraiser, and school district policies. Nonetheless, procedural due process and sound supervisory practice suggest at the very least:

1. Self-appraisal for familiarization and preparation for the post-conference.
2. Pre-observation conferences to discuss instructional objectives, methods, and the learners.
3. Classroom observations—two or three periods per cycle.
4. Post-observation conferences to discuss critical classroom incidents, progress, and to exchange questions.
5. Agreement on a plan of action.
6. Time to improve, help to improve, and mutual (appraiser-appraisee) monitoring of change.
7. Report of the summary evaluation to appraisee and to superiors.

References

Blumberg, Arthur. *Supervisors and Teachers; A Private Cold War*. Berkeley: McCutcheon Publishing Corp. 1974.

Boyan, Norman J. "The Emergent Role of the Teacher in the Authority Structure of the School." In *Collective Negotiations and Educational Administration*, edited by R. Allen and J. Schmid. Fayetteville, Arkansas: The University of Arkansas Press, 1967.

Menne, John W. and Tolsma, Robert J. "A Discrimination Index for Items in Instruments Using Group Responses." *Journal of Educational Measurement*, 1971.

INDEX